Conversations with Lincoln

*Lincoln talks wth General McClellan at field headquarters
shortly after the Battle of Antietam.*

Conversations

with
Lincoln

Compiled, Edited and Annotated by
Charles M. Segal

with a new preface by the editor
and an introduction by
David Donald

Transaction Publishers
New Brunswick (U.S.A.) and London (U.K.)

Second printing 2013
New material this edition copyright © 2002 by Transaction Publishers,
New Brunswick, New Jersey. Originally published in 1961 by G. P. Putnam's
Sons.

This book is printed on acid-free paper that meets the American National
Standard for Permanence of Paper for Printed Library Materials.

Library of Congress Catalog Number: 2001057011
ISBN: 978-0-7658-0933-9
Printed in the United States of America

Library of Congress Cataloging-in-Publication Data

Lincoln, Abraham, 1809-1865.
    Conversations with Lincoln / [compiled, edited, and annotated by] Charles
    M. Segal ; with a new preface by the editor and an introduction by
    David Donald.
       p. cm.
    Includes bibliographical references and index.
    ISBN 0-7658-0933-8 (pbk. : alk. paper)
    1. Lincoln, Abraham, 1809-1865—Interviews. 2. Presidents—United
    States—Interviews. 3. United States—History—Civil War, 1861-1865.
    4. United States—Politics and government—1861-1865. I. Segal,
    Charles M. II. Title.

E457.15 .L5 2002
973.7'092—dc21   2001057011

For Ninel

Contents

Chapter One

"MISCELLANEOUS AND INCONGRUOUS ELEMENTS"

Chapter Two

"FORTUNATE FOR THE PEACE"

Contents 5

Chapter Six

"THE GASES OF PUBLIC EXASPERATION"

Chapter Seven

"LIKE A CHINAMAN BEATING HIS SWORDS"

Chapter Eight

"ANYTHING BUT A BED OF ROSES"

Chapter Nine

"A LEADER TO SPEAK THE BOLD WORD"

Chapter Ten

"IT IS NOT BEST TO SWAP HORSES"

Contents

Chapter Eleven

"IT MADE MY HEART JUMP"

Preface to the Transaction Edition

W HEN Abraham Lincoln was elected President of the United States, he was still not yet well known in the country. Born in the backwoods of Kentucky and raised in the wilds of Indiana, he had less than one year of formal schooling. Nevertheless, he pulled himself up by his bootstraps. Lincoln began to educate himself—he taught himself grammar, and developed a love for reading, especially Shakespeare, Byron, and Oliver Wendall Holmes. He studied law on his own and became a well-known lawyer. He developed an abiding interest in politics, served in the Illinois State Assembly and one two-year term in the U.S. Congress, and ran unsuccessfully for the U.S. Senate against Stephen A. Douglas. In 1860, he was elected President—the first successful candidate of the relatively new Republican Party for the highest office in the land.

As President, Lincoln faced overwhelming problems. He was a Commander-in-Chief who confessed to having no knowledge of military affairs. The Union was divided and had to be restored. The people craved military victories that too often seemed to be too few and far between—until Ulysses S. Grant took command. President Lincoln also faced political problems with anti-slavery Republicans and abolitionists who sought to make slavery the fundamental issue of the southern states' rebellion. There was danger that the border states might defect to the Confederacy. Finally, there were diplomatic problems as well. The Union had a Chief Executive who was unschooled in international affairs and yet, he had to keep the British and the French from recognizing the Confederacy—at the very least influence them to be neutral in the conflict.

9

Attacks on the President were vociferous. He was ridiculed by—among others—Congressional antagonists, abolitionist leaders such as Wendell Phillips and William Lloyd Garrison, newspapers, and the people. He was maligned as an uneducated person devoid of social graces, a "baboon," a "Simple Susan" who was "unfit," a "political coward," a "dictator," "timid and ignorant," "pitiable," "too slow," and "shattered, dazed, and utterly foolish." While Lincoln was en route to Washington in February 1861, the younger Charles Francis Adams characterized the President-elect as "perambulating the country, kissing little girls and growing whiskers." It was fashionable to attack him with such comments as: "A respectable mule would have done better" and "You cannot fill his . . . empty skull with brains."[1] There were calls for him to resign. So great was the Republican Party's opposition to Lincoln's policies that they refused to nominate him as their candidate for re-election in 1864; the President, nevertheless, was victorious on the National Union Party ticket.

Lincoln told the artist Francis B. Carpenter: "If I were to read, much less answer, all the attacks on me, this shop might as well be closed for any other business. I do the very best I know how—the very best I can; and I mean to keep doing so until the end. If the end brings me out all right, what's said against me won't amount to anything. If the end brings me out wrong, ten angels swearing I was right would make no difference."[2]

Throughout his Presidency, and in spite of all the ridicule he was enduring, Lincoln remained a "man of the people." And the people— from all walks of life—kept streaming into the White House on "public days," laying before him their own personal problems and concerns, and he always had time to listen with compassion and understanding.

In April 1865, things changed. The rebellion ended with a Union victory, and slavery was now abolished in all the states. The focus was now on binding up the nation's wounds "with malice towards none." On April 15, 1865, Abraham Lincoln lay dead in the Peterson House across the street from Ford's Theatre.

So great was the outpouring of national bereavement that Radical Republicans, who had so maligned Abraham Lincoln, began to join "the people" in mourning their fallen President.

In each generation in our country and abroad, people have sought— and seek—to take the "full measure" of President Lincoln. Each generation sees him from its own unique perspectives. Indeed, the Congressional Research Service has reported that more than 17,340 books on Abraham Lincoln have been published up to 2001. In 1999 alone, 7,098 articles on Lincoln appeared in various publications. Lincoln manuscripts, artifacts, and other memorabilia are in great demand. The quest for information about him continues and is expected to continue indefinitely.

My purpose in producing *Conversations with Lincoln* was to help bring the reader closer to the Civil War-era Abraham Lincoln from a different vantage point. I hope I have succeeded. I am deeply indebted to Dr. Sacvan Bercovitch, Cabot Professor of American Literature at Harvard University, for facilitating the publication of this edition. I am also most grateful to Dr. Irving Louis Horowitz, Chairman of the Board and Editorial Director of Transaction Publishers, for his many courtesies, and to Alfred Christensen, Head of the Research Section of the Congressional Research Service, Library of Congress. My dear wife, Ninel, shall always have my gratitude for her sage counsel and many suggestions.

I would be amiss if I concluded this preface without again expressing my thanks to Dr. David Herbert Donald, Professor Emeritus of American History and American Civilization at Harvard University, who was "in at the creation" of *Conversations with Lincoln.*

C.M.S.

Notes

1. See J.G. Randall, "The Unpopular Mr. Lincoln," *Abraham Lincoln Quarterly*, Vol. II, No. 6 (June 1943), pp. 255-280. Permission to use quotations by courtesy of The Abraham Lincoln Association.
2. Francis B. Carpenter, *Six Months at the White House with Abraham Lincoln* (New York: Hurd and Houghton, 1855), pp. 258-259.

Acknowledgments

The editor acknowledges with thanks the permission graciously granted him to quote material from published works, periodicals and manuscripts, as follows:

The Abraham Lincoln Association, for permission to quote excerpts from *The Collected Works of Abraham Lincoln*, edited by Roy P. Basler *et al.* (Copyright 1953, by the Abraham Lincoln Association), and *Concerning Mr. Lincoln . . .* , edited by Harry E. Pratt (Copyright 1944, by the Abraham Lincoln Association).

Harper & Brothers, for permission to quote excerpts from *Mary, Wife of Lincoln*, by Katherine Helm (Copyright 1928, by Katherine Helm).

Dodd, Mead & Company, for permission to quote excerpts from *Lincoln and the Civil War in the Diaries and Letters of John Hay*, edited by Tyler Dennett (Copyright 1939, by Dodd, Mead & Company, Inc.).

Houghton Mifflin Company, for permission to reprint excerpts from *Journals of Ralph Waldo Emerson*, IX, edited by Edward Waldo Emerson and Waldo Emerson Forbes (Copyright 1913, 1941 by Houghton Mifflin Company); *A Cycle of Adams Letters*, I, edited by Worthington C. Ford (Copyright 1920, 1948 by Worthington C. Ford); and *The Real Lincoln: A Portrait*, by Jesse W. Weik (Copyright 1922, by Jesse W. Weik, 1950 by Houghton Mifflin Company).

Little, Brown & Company, for permission to quote excerpts from *Lincoln's War Cabinet*, by Burton J. Hendrick (Copyright 1946, by Burton J. Hendrick), and *The Negro in the Civil War*, by Benjamin Quarles (Copyright 1953, by Benjamin Quarles).

Illinois State Historical Library, for permission to reprint excerpts from *Diary of Orville Hickman Browning*, I (Illinois State Historical Library Collections, Vol. XX), edited by T. C. Pease and James G. Randall (Copyright 1927, 1955 by the Illinois State Historical Library).
12

Coward-McCann, Inc., for permission to quote excerpts from *Lincoln the Politician* . . . , by Don C. Seitz (Copyright © 1931, 1958, by Don C. Seitz).

G. P. Putnam's Sons, for permission to reprint excerpts from *The Pinkerton Story*, by James D. Horan and Howard Swiggett (Copyright 1951, by James D. Horan and Howard Swiggett).

The Macmillan Company, for permission to reprint excerpts from *The Diary of George Templeton Strong*, III, edited by Allan Nevins and Milton Halsey Thomas (Copyright 1952, by The Macmillan Company).

Henry E. Huntington Library, San Marino, Calif., for permission to reprint excerpts from *Lincoln and the Baltimore Plot 1861: From Pinkerton Records and Related Papers*, edited by Norma B. Cuthbert (Copyright 1949, by the Henry E. Huntington Library & Art Gallery), and from the letter, HM 21996, Charles Sumner to W. W. Story, December 16, 1866.

American Historical Association, for permission to reprint excerpts from *The Diary of Edward Bates 1859-1866* (Vol. IV of the Annual Report of the American Historical Association for the Year 1930), edited by Howard K. Beale; Montgomery C. Meigs, "General M. C. Meigs on the Conduct of the Civil War," in *American Historical Review* (January 1921); and *Southern Editorials on Secession*, edited by Dwight L. Dumond (Copyright © 1931, 1959 by the American Historical Association).

Ralph Newman, for permission to quote excerpts from *The Civil War: The American Iliad* . . . , I, edited by Otto Eisenschiml and Ralph Newman (Copyright 1956, by Ralph Newman), and *Diary of a Public Man: An Intimate View of the National Administration, Dec. 28, 1860 to March 15, 1861* (Copyright 1945, by the Abraham Lincoln Book Shop; 1946 by the Trustees of Rutgers College in New Jersey).

Doubleday & Company, for permission to quote excerpts from *Retrospections of an Active Life*, I, by John Bigelow (Copyright 1909, by Baker & Taylor Co.; 1937 by Doubleday & Company).

Mississippi Valley Historical Association, for permission to reprint portions of the *Liverpool Mercury*, Oct. 9, 1862, in "Fort Sumter Again," edited by D. R. Barbee and M. L. Bonham, Jr., in *Mississippi Valley Historical Review* (June, 1941), 63-73.

Brown University, for permission to publish excerpts from the Manuscript Diary of John Hay.

The State Historical Society of Wisconsin, for permission to reprint excerpts from the Manuscript Diary of Joseph T. Mills.

The Bancroft Library, University of California, for permission to reprint excerpts from the Unpublished Memoir of Mrs. Jessie Benton Frémont and her undated Memorandum on her visit to President Lincoln.

Massachusetts Historical Society, for permission to quote excerpts from the *Proceedings of the Massachusetts Historical Society*, and material in the John A. Andrew MSS., and Henry W. Bellows MSS.

Virginia Historical Society, for permission to reprint the Memorandum by G. A. Myers in "Abraham Lincoln in Richmond," edited by C. G. Chamberlayne, in *The Virginia Magazine of History and Biography* (October 1953).

Cosmopolitan Magazine, for permission to quote excerpts from "Lincoln's Last Day Described in the Letters of His Wife," by Honoré Willsie Morrow, first published in *Hearst's International-Cosmopolitan* (February 1930).

The New York Times, for permission to reprint quotations from Samuel R. Weed's interview with Lincoln, published in *The New York Times*, February 14, 1932.

Introduction

BY DAVID DONALD

A LINCOLN book which says something new is a rarity. *Conversations With Lincoln* is just such a book. In it Charles M. Segal has collected and presented more than one hundred interviews with Lincoln as President-elect and as President. This is a composite portrait of the Civil War executive as he was seen by "office-seekers, wire-pullers, artists, poets, prosers (including editors, army correspondents, attachés of foreign journals, and long-winded talkers), clerks, diplomatists, mail contractors, railway directors." Compiled in large measure from manuscript letters, newspaper accounts, contemporary diaries, and rare recollections, Mr. Segal's scholarly and skillfully edited anthology will be a treasured source for historians. As a revelation of the intimate, human side of Abraham Lincoln, it will provide endless fascination to every reader interested in the Civil War era.

The conversations Mr. Segal has collected range from brief remarks to extended discussions. They concern matters as petty as the selection of a postmaster and as great as the issuing of the Emancipation Proclamation. Naturally as historical records they vary widely in quality. Some were recorded almost contemporaneously; others were written long after the event. Some of the interviewers caught Lincoln at his happiest and best, but others—notably Ralph Waldo Emerson—seem to have heard nothing but commonplaces from him. Most of Mr. Segal's listeners had an acute ear for the rhythms of

15

Lincoln's own language but some—like the insufferable Lucius Chittenden—attributed to him pompous phraseology that was wholly out of character. Virtually all the interviewers had the unforgivable fault of more clearly remembering their own less than memorable questions than of recalling Lincoln's replies.

But, taken as a whole, these conversations provide a vivid and authentic mosaic of Lincoln. The first impression Mr. Segal's book gives is of the infinite variety of the President's moods. Here is Lincoln angry, denouncing some New England petitioners as "a set of liars and knaves"—yet here, too, is Lincoln quietly submitting to impertinent threats from Galusha Grow. Toward the wife of a Pennsylvania deserter the President behaved with chivalrous tenderness, but he failed even to offer a chair to the wife of John C. Frémont. Some interviewers thought the President solemn and serious, oppressed by the responsibilities of his position, which "prevented him from using anecdotes"; others heard him lightheartedly punning or making jokes, such as the stale one about breaking the camera when his picture was taken at Brady's studio. Often in these conversations Lincoln revealed himself as proudly humble, calling himself "a boy brought up in the woods," admitting to no knowledge of Latin, and declaring, "I don't know anything about the law of nations." But on other occasions he showed that he was a careful student of the Bible and of Shakespeare, rendering Hamlet's soliloquy "with a feeling and appreciation unsurpassed by anything . . . witnessed upon the stage."

Behind these surface diversities, however, one can, through Mr. Segal's selections, get glimpses of the consistent inner core of the man. Lincoln's conversations show that his philosophical fatalism and his political experience combined to give him a realistic view of his powers as President. He knew that in a democracy like the United States public opinion "was a reality and should be taken into the account" in making political and military decisions. He recognized, too, that he was "but one horse in the team" of government; "if the others pulled in a different direction," he told an interviewer late in the war, "it would be a hard matter for him to out-pull them." Accordingly, early in the secession crisis, he set the pragmatic tone of his Administration by telling an alarmist: "Well, we won't jump that ditch until we come to it."

Mr. Segal's book contains much revealing material upon Lincoln's political dexterity. Though harassed almost beyond endurance by radical criticism, he recognized what we would now call the psychological basis of his opponents' carping; since most of them had spent their "political lives working in minorities," he said, they had "got into the habit of being dissatisfied." Accordingly, he realized that they must be handled with special care, and the skill with which he managed the radicals in the cabinet crisis of December, 1862, is the supreme example of the President's political adroitness.

Lincoln was only able to succeed, as Mr. Segal's conversations show, by rigorously separating his personal wishes from his Presidential responsibilities. On the vexed question of slavery, for example, he "did not pretend to disguise his Anti-Slavery feeling," even when addressing sensitive Border State congressmen; he told them bluntly that he thought the peculiar institution "was wrong and [that] he should continue to think so." But, as he explained in others of these conversations, he did not allow his own wishes to confuse him as to his executive duties. Not until public opinion was ready and military necessity demanded it did he act against slavery. Indeed, he declared, late in the war, "If the people over the river [pointing across the Potomac] had behaved themselves, I could not have done what I have; but they did not, and I was compelled to do these things."

That note of compulsion from outside force is a recurrent theme in *Conversations With Lincoln.* "I claim not to have controlled events," the President himself declared in one of his letters, "but confess plainly that events have controlled me." By this he meant not a spineless yielding to circumstances but a recognition that a higher power had the ultimate control over the nation's destinies. Repeatedly in these interviews he expressed his desire to "be an instrument in God's hands of accomplishing a great work." "Whatever shall appear to be God's will," he assured a group of abolitionists, "I will do."

For those who think of Lincoln as vulgar, aimless, or unsophisticated, Mr. Segal's book will provide wholesome instruction. For those who admire and revere the great wartime President, it will be a fresh recreation of Lincoln's very thought and voice.

Preface to Conversations with Lincoln

THIS volume does not pretend to be the complete story of Abraham Lincoln from his nomination in May 1860 until his assassination in April 1865, although it is concerned with this period of his life. Nor is it a full narrative of the Civil War. What I have attempted to do, I hope with success, has been to present a composite portrait of Lincoln—in a mosaic of moods and attitudes—as he was conceived through his conversations as politician, President, statesman, humorist, military strategist, peace negotiator, husband, father and friend.

Conversations with Lincoln is, obviously, based on memory—the memories of the different people who were with Lincoln when he talked on matters large and small, by day or night, in a multitude of circumstances and under a variety of conditions. These interviews were not recorded by stenographers or stenotypists. There were no tape-recording devices to reproduce the exact words and voices of the participants. Many of the conversations were committed to paper within a few hours of their occurrence; others were put down in writing at various points ranging from a few days to many years later.

What has come down to us—through diaries, journals, letters, newspapers, memoirs, reminiscences and autobiographies—as accounts of conversations with Lincoln, in every instance has been influenced by the vicissitudes of memory and the complex processes of remembering.

19

Salmon P. Chase, Lincoln's Secretary of the Treasury, put his finger on the perplexing problem of remembering when, trying to recall some aspects of his own life, he wrote: "It is curious how men best acquainted with each other mistake as to matters of personal history." [1] He amplified this observation somewhat in another statement: "It is strange to me how dim every thing is in that distant time [his earlier years]. I see just one little part of things—glimpses of transactions— the (reality-totality?) hid behind clouds with little fissures revealing a part of an affair or person, and that little with mist clinging round and obscuring it. I dare not vouch for the entire authenticity even of what I seem to remember best." [2]

We do not remember or communicate everything about an actuality in our personal past. The actuality having occurred only once, vanishes, never to be repeated or recaptured. All we retain in memory are our impressions of what was once brute reality and, as time goes on, new impressions keep crowding out the old ones. When we record a past incident or experience, it is from our very latest impressions of it that we create our oral or written account. We cannot eliminate the personal equation. We sift, select and arrange our mental images or ideas of that event in terms of what they mean to us now.

It is within this framework that we must consider *Conversations with Lincoln,* where some accounts attempt to reproduce dialogue *verbatim,* others to present discussion essentially in paraphrase, and still others to report only what Lincoln presumably said. Some accounts are written out in great detail, while others are distinguished by brevity.

Whether the words placed in quotation marks—attributed to Lincoln or others—were actually spoken as reported is something we shall never know. Conceivably, some of Lincoln's remarks were correctly retained by his listeners. But conceivably, too, some have been distorted by the vagaries of memory and recollection. Only one thing is certain: All are interpretations by Lincoln's contemporaries of their conversations with him or of those of his conversations to which they simply listened.

The fact that we cannot proclaim these accounts as literal reproductions of every syllable uttered by every participant in a conversation with Lincoln does not negate their value as historical evidence. For the historian has no truer records of conversations with which to work. This is his only means—by utilizing the written traces, the vestiges of vanished realities—of dealing with the thoughts, emotions, actions and events that once influenced the course of human affairs.

It is, of course, desirable to have records which were produced as soon as possible after an actual conversation. Every effort has been made to secure such material for this volume. I have used no second-hand or hearsay evidence. I have made use, to the best of my ability, of the earliest authentic sources and have included nothing but what I know or feel to be reliable reports of conversations with Lincoln. Where I have used the *only available* reports of conversations and their accuracy has been questioned, I have noted this in my comments on the particular conversations.

However, where a later account of a discussion not only contains the information in an earlier one but adds verifiable details, I have— where it was deemed necessary—given it precedence over the former account. This was done on the psychologist's premise that the purpose for remembering a past actuality on one occasion can enable a witness to recall certain aspects of it that he had no reason to recollect previously. But such material has been used as sparingly as possible and only after the competence of the witnesses—and their motivations in making the later records—have been established.

Where more than one account of a particular conversation was obtainable, I have used the most detailed portions of each to cover the various aspects of the discussion.

I have given particular credence to conversations recorded in diaries, journals, contemporary letters and newspapers. Letters, of course, are in a somewhat special category; they have the advantage of having been written close to the actual conversation. On the other hand, they may or may not have been written by a trained observer. Materials derived from diaries, journals and contemporary newspapers, naturally, have been considered as most important sources. For such materials come to us from the pens of individuals who, by the very nature of their compulsion to chronicle human affairs, have been able to develop an above-average acuity of observation. Still, the newspaper source presents its problems. While a journalist usually is permitted to take notes in the course of a discussion he is covering, his task is to get a news story, to select from the discussion information of greatest interest to his reading public. Thus he must invariably sacrifice the sequence of dialogue in ordering his material on the basis of first things first, as he evaluates its importance. In addition, the newspaperman is affected by his newspaper's policy as well as by the editorial blue pencil. There is also the make-up editor, who may—where there is a shortage of space—arbitrarily cut sentences or entire paragraphs from the report. Nevertheless, the competent newspaperman is, theoretically, the best-trained observer we have— the one most likely to provide accurate accounts of the happenings he covers. But when we read his report of a conversation, we must assume that only its substance ultimately gets into print and that it is by no means a stenographic report.

In some instances, I have included recollections of interviews with Lincoln which have been given as sworn testimony before Congressional committees. I feel that these are much better than written accounts since sworn testimony given in a spontaneous report and in answer to questions framed in a nonsuggestive manner makes it possible for a witness to render a truer deposition.

Finally, I have utilized published memoirs or reminiscences of conversations. Here I have gathered—with very few exceptions—only those accounts I know to have been based on diaries, journals or letters written soon after the discussions. But here, too, we must assume that the final products—as originally printed—did not escape the fine point of the editorial pencil or the influences upon the authors that derive from consciousness that the subject matter must be confined to a specific number of pages.

Conversations with Lincoln is arranged chronologically. In cases of partially dated accounts, I have placed them in what appeared to me to be their proper sequence in time. I have maintained original punctuation and capitalization. Major errors in spelling are indicated by *sic*. I have shown omissions—regardless of their lengths—only in the body of the material by three points—as in the ellipsis (. . .). I have indicated in the annotations any other liberties I have taken with the texts.

This, then, has been my approach in selecting and arranging the different accounts that make up *Conversations with Lincoln*—a compilation of known and little-known materials which are the stuff of history, integral to an understanding of Lincoln the Man and Lincoln the President.

In the preparation of this volume, I have come to owe much to many people. My greatest debt is to Dr. David Donald, Professor of

History at Princeton University, whose great scholarship and wise counsel have been always at my disposal. Dr. Donald read this volume in manuscript at various stages, made numerous suggestions and pointed the way to materials of value to this undertaking. For his vital role in helping to transform the idea for this book into a reality, I am deeply grateful.

I also wish to thank Miss Lois Dwight Cole, Editor, G. P. Putnam's Sons, for her patience, encouragement and advice as I labored on this project.

Among others to whom I am heavily indebted are Miss Margaret A. Flint, Assistant State Historian of Illinois, for constant assistance over the years in my research for this volume; to Dr. David C. Mearns, Chief, Manuscript Division, Library of Congress, for many courtesies; to Dr. C. Percy Powell, Head, Reader Service, Manuscript Division, Library of Congress, for providing important manuscript leads and for his helpfulness and hospitality during my visits to Washington; and to Paul L. Berry, Chief, Serial Division, Library of Congress, for going out of his way in checking Civil War newspapers and making available reproductions of many important items.

To my dear friend, the late Paul Tobenkin, a reporter *extraordinaire* of the *New York Herald Tribune,* I must record my special gratitude. His constant interest in this project and his generous advice continued until his final illness in June 1958.

Valuable assistance was rendered by the New York Public Library and for this I thank R. H. Carruthers, Chief, Photographic Division; G. Fielstra, Assistant Chief, Photographic Service; Mrs. Carol M. Cronkhite, Head, Microfilm Section, Photographic Service; Harold Merklen, Research Librarian; and Robert W. Hill, Keeper of Manuscripts. My thanks, too, go to John A. Gault, former First Assistant, Photographic Service, for many kindnesses.

I also wish to extend my thanks to Dr. Clyde C. Walton, State Historian of Illinois; George W. Bunn, Jr., President of the Abraham Lincoln Association; Dr. Wm. Kaye Lamb, Dominion Archivist, Public Archives of Canada; Matthew Redding, Librarian, *The New York World Telegram & The Sun*; John Barr Tompkins, Head, Public Services, Bancroft Library of the University of California; Donald C. Holmes, Chief, Photoduplication Service, Library of Congress; R. N. Williams, 2nd, Director, and Miss Sarah A. G. Smith, of the Historical Society of Pennsylvania; Stephen T. Riley, Director, Massa-

24   *CONVERSATIONS WITH LINCOLN*

chusetts Historical Society; John R. Turner Ettlinger, in charge of Special Collections, and his assistant, Mrs. Alex Kacen, John Hay Library of Brown University; Kenneth A. Lohf, Assistant Librarian, Butler Library of Columbia University; Mrs. Elizabeth R. Martin, Librarian, Ohio Historical Society; Miss Josephine L. Harper, Manuscript Librarian, The State Historical Society of Wisconsin; Miss Blanche Jantzen, Manuscript Librarian, Chicago Historical Society; Miss Geraldine Beard, Chief of the Reading Room, New York Historical Society; Dr. Wayne C. Temple, Director of Lincolniana, Lincoln Memorial University; and Miss Geneva Warner, Curator of Special Collections, The University Libraries, Indiana University.

I have received important research assistance at the Library of Congress from Dr. James E. Hewes, Jr., of Farmington, Conn., who is engaged on a study of Senator Henry Cabot Lodge and the League of Nations.

I have received aid also from the late Miss Loula D. Lasker of New York City; Dr. James J. Talman, Chief Librarian, Lawson Memorial Library of the University of Western Ontario; Professor Fred Landon of London, Ontario; L. N. Bronson, Librarian, *The London Free Press;* Sol Moss of Montreal, Quebec; D. A. Bulen of Meadville, Pa.; Reuben Rabb and Mrs. Berton Braley of The Eton Shop in New York City; Dr. Benjamin A. Brozen of Brooklyn, N. Y.; Miss Selma Kalman of New York City; Mrs. Jerome Spector of St. Louis, Mo.; Mrs. Carl Spector of Brookline, Mass.; and Miss Harriet Cohen of Brooklyn, N. Y.

CHARLES M. SEGAL

Chapter One

"MISCELLANEOUS AND INCONGRUOUS ELEMENTS"

THE Presidential year of 1860 was crucial to the preservation of the United States as a federal union. The political party as well as the man to win the Presidency would influence the course of history for the Union, then composed of only thirty-three—eighteen free and fifteen slaveholding—states.

The American scene had been tense for many years. Southern extremists fancied themselves different from the people in the rest of the Union. They believed that they needed to protect their particular kind of civilization from the threat of disintegration by Northern radicals. The Southerners had no use for Northern customs and mannerisms. They held that the mass of Europeans with their strange tongues and thoughts had transformed the Northerners into an unrecognizable race. The Southerner thought of himself as a cavalier; he believed in "rational liberty and the support of authority" in opposition to what he termed the Northerner's "licentiousness and morbid impulse of unregulated passion and unenlightened sentiment." [1] To the Southerner, Northern cities reeked with filth, crime and poverty, where labor and capital were always at each other's throats; where, according to William H. Russell, the distinguished correspondent of the London *Times,* "wisdom is paltry cunning" and "valor and manhood have been swallowed up in corruption, howling demagoguery, and in the marts of dishonest commerce." [2] Southern civilization, extremists in that section maintained, could thrive only under a government that protected slavery not only where it already existed but wherever the Constitution prevailed.

On the other hand, Northern agitators regarded the clash with the South on the slavery issue as a test between slavocracy and democracy. They accused the Southerners of being "disunionists," of trying to abrogate the Constitution in a desperate attempt to rule or destroy the Union in an effort to perpetuate slavery in the states and in the territories. Northerners attacked the Dred Scott decision; they refused to accept a Supreme Court decree that defined human beings as "lawful property" to be treated as inanimate objects. They abhorred the Fugitive Slave Act, the kidnaping of freed Negroes, the smuggling of slaves into America and the legalizing of the foreign slave trade. Northern vituperation contained such epithets as "slavocrats," "fire eaters," "nigger drivers," who were pictured as engaging in a "slaveholders' conspiracy" to foster "slave breeding." They looked down upon their Southern neighbors as "shiftless" and "unenlightened" illiberals, who sought Biblical justification for human bondage.

These agitators, North and South, were becoming increasingly vocal, underscoring the differences between the two sections of the country. Tempers rose to fever pitch as dry-throated Americans shouted loud the great issue of slavery. Appeals to reason were ineffective in calming agitators on either side of the Mason-Dixon line.

In the midst of such crosscurrents of antagonism, the political parties of the country held their national conventions to adopt platforms and nominate Presidential and Vice-Presidential candidates for the November elections.

On April 23rd, the Democratic Party convened its national convention at Charleston, South Carolina. But critical division manifested itself almost immediately in Democratic ranks on the question of platform. Southern delegates, aided by those from California and Oregon, demanded a platform that would guarantee the rights of citizens to settle in the territories with their slaves and to this end the protection of the Federal Government "in the Territories, and wherever else its constitutional authority extends." [8] Northern Democrats, pressing for the nomination of Senator Stephen A. Douglas of Illinois, argued that their candidate could never stand on a platform that would be unacceptable in the North. In an attempt to compromise, the followers of the "Little Giant"—as Douglas was called—

contrived a temporizing resolution that "inasmuch as differences of opinion exist in the Democratic party as to the nature and extent of the powers of a Territorial Legislature, and as to the powers and duties of Congress under the Constitution of the United States over the institution of slavery within the Territories, the Democratic party will abide by the decision of the Supreme Court of the United States upon questions of Constitutional law." [4]

However, seven cotton states refused to be conciliated and withdrew from the convention. In their own assembly, they later nominated John C. Breckinridge of Kentucky for President, and Joseph Lane of Oregon for Vice-President.

Ultimately, on June 18th, the Douglas Democrats reconvened at Baltimore, where their leader was finally nominated for the Presidency, and Herschel V. Johnson of Georgia for the Vice-Presidency.

Earlier, between the adjournment of the Charleston convention and the reassembling of the Democrats at Baltimore, a new party came into being calling itself the Constitution-Union Party. Composed of old-line Whigs and former Know-Nothings (an anti-foreigner element), the Constitution-Union Party had also met in Baltimore and had nominated a slaveholder, John Bell of Tennessee, for President, and Edward Everett of Massachusetts for Vice-President. The Constitution-Unionists were strong in the South, where they formed the major opposition to the Democrats. A conservative party, it defended the rights of slaveholders.

The Republican National Convention, held in the newly constructed Wigwam at the corner of Lake and Market Streets in Chicago, from May 16th through May 18th, presented an entirely different picture. Republican delegates approached their task with boisterous enthusiasm. The Republican Party was made up of many political elements, and while they may have had disagreements on other questions, they were united in their determination to stop the extension of slavery.

Democrat George Lunt, in his book *The Origins of the Late War,* had this to say about the Republican Convention of 1860:

"Probably no deliberative body ever came together, even in France, during the old revolutionary period, composed of such miscellaneous and incongruous elements. There were Free Soil Whigs in the largest proportion, and with them Free Soil Democrats, Native Americans, and foreign adventurers; abolitionists and their life-long opponents; those for saving the Union, and those for dividing it; professed conservatives and the most thorough-going radicals; sentimentalists and ideologists; 'economists and calculators'; a sprinkling of delegates pretending to represent some sort of constituency in two or three of the border slave states; and to crown all, Mr. Horace Greeley of the New York *Tribune* as an accredited deputy from the somewhat distant regions of Oregon." [5]

Leading contender for the Republican nomination was Senator William H. Seward, former Governor of New York. For twelve months preceding the convention, he had been thought the man certain to be nominated by the Republicans. However, by the time the delegates assembled at Chicago, Seward's position—though still strong—was fraught with many weaknesses. Seward had labored strenuously for the nomination and in the process had incurred the wrath of many political leaders. The Know-Nothing element of the Republican Party was vehemently opposed to him. In addition, there was his stand on the slavery issue; Seward's "higher law" doctrine, enunciated at Rochester, New York, in October 1858, was more extreme than the position Lincoln took in his "House Divided" speech a few months earlier at Springfield, Illinois. For these and many personal reasons harbored against him, Seward's "availability" was found deficient when the convention got down to the business of selecting a standard-bearer.

There were other Republican candidates in the field besides Abraham Lincoln of Illinois. Men like Edward Bates of Missouri, William L. Dayton of New Jersey, Simon Cameron of Pennsylvania, Salmon P. Chase of Ohio, and Nathaniel P. Banks of Massachusetts were all considered—by many Republican delegates—more worthy than the honorable gentleman from Illinois.

Lincoln wanted the nomination, although originally he had been reluctant to consider himself a candidate. He had first achieved national prominence in his debates with Douglas in 1858. He followed up that eventful canvass for the Illinois Senatorship with speeches in the East and in states adjoining his own. In all he said he made clear his moderate position on slavery. Lincoln's candidacy was also helped considerably when the convention site chosen was in his home state of Illinois. This enabled his friends and supporters to turn out in full force to champion his cause.

On the third convention day, the delegates were gripped with suspense as Lincoln showed steadily increasing strength during the first two ballots. On the third ballot, it was 231½ for Lincoln and 180 for Seward. Needed to nominate: 233. At this point, a spectator recalled, "a profound stillness . . . fell upon the Wigwam; the men ceased to talk and the ladies to flutter their fans; one could distinctly hear the scratching of pencils and the ticking of telegraph instruments on the reporters' tables." [6] Then, Judge David K. Cartter of Ohio leaped to his feet to announce a switch of four votes from Chase to Lincoln. And it was all over. Shortly thereafter, Senator Hannibal Hamlin of Maine was nominated for Vice-President.

Back in Springfield, amid the wild jubilation of the townsfolk, was Abraham Lincoln. Almost entirely self-educated, he had been rail-splitter, storekeeper, postmaster, mill hand, surveyor, soldier, circuit lawyer, member of the Illinois Legislature, and Congressman. Now he stood a good chance to be President of the United States.

"Pennsylvania Bows to Illinois"

SATURDAY, MAY 19, 1860

¶ *The day after the adjournment of the Republican National Convention in Chicago, an official committee of party leaders was on its way to Springfield to notify Abraham Lincoln of his nomination for the Presidency. According to a report in the May 25th issue of the* New York Daily Tribune, *a great crowd waited at the Springfield depot to welcome the committee, which was headed by George Ashmun of Massachusetts, formerly a bosom friend of Daniel Webster and a leading Whig in the Old Bay State, who had presided over the Wigwam convention. With him were chairmen of different state delegations.*

The Republican officials were greeted with shouts of enthusiasm and were accompanied to the hotel by the crowd "and two or three bands, discoursing music." The newspaper reporter noted that "the appearance and names of the more distinguished Delegates were received with vociferous applause, especially the venerable and famous Francis P. Blair of Maryland, and his sons, Frank and Montgomery; the Hon. E. D. Morgan, Governor of New-York; and Gov. [George S.] Boutwell of Massachusetts."

Among the other delegates composing the committee were William

M. Evarts of New York, accomplished and eloquent spokesman of the Empire State delegation and friend of William H. Seward, who had been Lincoln's leading contender for the nomination; Judge William D. Kelley of Pennsylvania, a tall, veteran member of Congress; John A. Andrew of Massachusetts, a round-faced, handsome man, who had seconded the motion to make Lincoln's selection unanimous in convention; James F. Simmons, gray-headed United States Senator from Rhode Island; brave old George D. Blakey of Kentucky; and loud-voiced David K. Cartter of Ohio, who, in the balloting, had announced his delegation's switch of four votes to assure Lincoln's candidacy.

After the delegation had "partaken of a bountiful supper," it proceeded quietly "by such streets as would escape the crowd" to Lincoln's home on Eighth Street. Quite a few "outsiders" came along, among whom were a dozen editors, including Henry J. Raymond of The New York Times.

Lincoln's house was "an elegant two-story dwelling, fronting west, of pleasant exterior, with a neat and roomy appearance, situated in the quiet part of town, surrounded with shrubbery." After being greeted by Lincoln's young sons—Tad and Willie—the delegates entered the residence. The report of the New York Daily Tribune[1] *continues:*

Having all collected in the large north parlor, Mr. Ashmun addressed Mr. Lincoln, who stood at the east end of the room, as follows:

"I have, Sir, the honor, in behalf of the gentlemen who are present, a Committee appointed by the Republican Convention, recently assembled at Chicago, to discharge a most pleasant duty. We have come, Sir, under a vote of instructions to that Committee, to notify you that you have been selected by the Convention of the Republicans at Chicago, for President of the United States. They instruct us, Sir, to notify you of that selection, and that Committee deem it not only respectful to yourself, but appropriate to the important matter which they have in hand, that they should come in person, and present to you the authentic evidence . . . of that Convention; and, Sir, without any phrase which shall either be considered personally plauditory [laudatory?] to yourself, or which shall have any reference to the principles involved in the questions which are connected with your nomination, I desire to present to you the letter which has been prepared, and which informs you of the nomination, and with it the platform, resolutions and sentiments which the Convention adopted. Sir, at your convenience we shall be glad to receive from you such a response as it may be your pleasure to give us."

Mr. Lincoln listened with a countenance grave and earnest, . . . regarding Mr. Ashmun with the profoundest attention, and at the conclusion of that gentleman's remarks, after an impressive pause, he replied in a clear but subdued voice, with that perfect enunciation which always marks his utterance, and a dignified sincerity of manner suited to the man and the occasion, in the following words:

"MR. CHAIRMAN, AND GENTLEMAN OF THE COMMITTEE: I tender to you, and through you to the Republican National Convention, and all the people represented in it, my profoundest thanks for the high honor done me, which you now formally announce. Deeply, and even painfully sensible of the great responsibility which is inseparable from this high honor—a responsibility which I could almost wish had fallen upon some one of the far more eminent men and experienced statesmen whose distinguished names were before the Convention, I shall, by your leave, consider more fully the resolutions of the Convention, denominated the platform, and without unnecessary or unreasonable delay, respond to you, Mr. Chairman, in writing, not doubting that the platform will be found satisfactory, and the nomination gratefully accepted.[2]

"And now I will no longer defer the pleasure of taking you, and each of you, by the hand."

Mr. Ashmun then introduced the delegates personally to Mr. Lincoln, who shook them heartily by the hand. Gov. Morgan, Mr. Blair [the father], Senator Simmons, Mr. [Gideon] Welles [bearded newspaper publisher from Connecticut, who had left the Democratic Party to join the Republicans], and Mr. [George G.] Fogg of Connecticut [of New Hampshire, publisher of the *Independent Democrat* at Concord], were first introduced; then came hearty old Mr. Blakey[8] of Kentucky, Lincoln's native State, and of course they had to compare notes, inquire up old neighborhoods, and if time had allowed they would soon have started to tracing out the old pioneer families. Major Ben Eggleston of Cincinnati was next, and his greeting and reception were equally hearty. Tall Judge Kell[e]y of Pennsylvania was then presented by Mr. Ashmun to Mr. Lincoln. As they shook hands, each eyed the other's ample proportions with genuine admiration—Lincoln, for once, standing straight as an Indian during this evening, and showing his tall form in its full dignity.

"What's your height?" inquired Lincoln.

"Six feet three; what is yours, Mr. Lincoln?" said Judge Kell[e]y, in his round, deliberate tone.

"Six feet four," replied Lincoln.

"Then, said Judge Kell[e]y, "Pennsylvania bows to Illinois. My dear man, for years my heart has been aching for a President that I could *look up to,* and I've found him at last in the land where we thought there were none but *little giants* [an obvious allusion to Senator Douglas]."

Mr. Evarts of New-York expressed very gracefully his gratification at meeting Mr. Lincoln, whom he had heard at the Cooper Institute, but where, on account of the pressure and crowd, he had to go away without an introduction.

Mr. Andrew of Massachusetts said, "We claim you, Mr. Lincoln, as coming from Massachusetts, because all the old Lincoln names are from Plymouth Colony."

"We'll consider it so this evening," said Lincoln.

Various others were presented when Mr. Ashmun asked them to come up and introduce themselves. "Come up, gentlemen," said Mr. [Norman B.] Judd [Lincoln's friend who nominated the Rail-splitter at Chicago], "it's nobody but Old Abe Lincoln." The greatest good feeling prevailed. As the delegates fell back, each congratulated the other that they had got just the sort of man. A neatly-dressed New Englander remarked to us, "I was afraid I should meet a gigantic rail-splitter, with the manners of a flat-boatman, and the ugliest face in creation; and he's a complete gentleman."

"He Liked to See His Friends"

THURSDAY, JUNE 21, 1860

¶ *Fortunate newspapermen from various Northern states drew the choice assignment of covering the activities of Abraham Lincoln. In describing the scene at Springfield, one correspondent for the* New York Herald *wrote: "This handsome little prairie town, with its quiet look of a New England village, its unpromising hotels near the railroad station, its half dozen churches sending their white spires high up into the clear blue sky, and its snug homes half hidden from view in the thick foliage with which they are surrounded, appears to possess at this time a special interest in the eyes of the politicians. Every day some one or more . . . who are perambulating the country, from the banks of the Penobscot to the banks of the Kansas, find that they have some little business requiring their attention here. That business invariably brings them into personal communication with the great celebrity of the place—the ex-rail splitter—who, to his own and the country's astonishment, suddenly found himself famous by the action of the Chicago Convention. . . . If these gentlemen do not get an opportunity of serving their country for the next four years, in positions where there is little work and much pay, you may depend upon it that it will not be for want of blowing their own trumpets nor from any modesty in magnifying their own achievements. . . ."* [1]

Lincoln unpretentiously went about his business, meeting the people and letting them meet him without formality. He kept his finger on the progress of the campaign; played a behind-the-scenes role in dispensing advice on strategy to Republican leaders. He set up an office in the Governor's Room on the second floor of the State House. John G. Nicolay, a former Pike County editor and lately a clerk in the office of Ozias M. Hatch, Illinois' Secretary of State, was appointed Lincoln's private secretary to handle a voluminous correspondence. Later, John Hay, nephew of Lincoln's good friend Milton Hay, was to be hired to assist Nicolay.

Lincoln's visitors came in floods—townsmen, country folk, relatives, artists, photographers, journalists, politicians, and those who wished merely to stare out of sheer curiosity at a live Presidential candidate. Most of them visited him at the State House; only a few were privileged to see him at home.

A newspaperman—probably Ellis Henry Roberts—reported on an evening at home with Lincoln. In an article which appeared in the June 27, 1860, issue of the Utica (N. Y.) Morning Herald, *the reporter remarked that "after you have been five minutes in his company you cease to think that he is either homely or awkward. You recognize in him a high-toned, unassuming, chivalrous-minded gentleman, well posted in all of the essential amenities of social life, and sustained by the infallible monitor of common sense."* [2] *Of his conversation with Lincoln, the newsman relates:*

He approached, extended his hand, and gave mine a grasp such as only a warm-hearted man knows how to give. He sat down before me on the sofa, and commenced talking about political affairs in my own State with a knowledge of details that surprised me. I found that he was more conversant with some of our party performances in Oneida County than I could have desired, and made some pointed allusions to the great Congressional struggle which resulted in the election of Mr. [Roscoe] Conkling in 1858. I asked him if he was not very much bored with calls and correspondence. He replied that he liked to see his friends, and as to the letters, he took care not to answer them. He referred playfully to the various "attempts upon his life," and the poor success that attended some of them. His greatest grievance[s] were with the artists; he tried in vain to recognize himself in some of the "Abraham Lincolns" of the pictorials.

I asked him if he continued his professional business since his nomination. He said he had attempted it but pitied his clients. He had been arguing a case the day before [Lincoln represented the plaintiff in the patent case Dawson vs. Ennis and Ennis], but said that the demands of his position made him an indifferent lawyer. He spoke with great freedom of corruption in high places. He regarded it as the bane of our American politics; and said he could not respect, either as a man or a politician, one who bribed or was bribed. He said he was glad to know that the people of Illinois had not yet learned the art of being venal. The whole expense of his campaign with Douglas did not exceed a few hundred dollars. I wish the thousands of people in my own State who loathe corrupt practices could have heard and seen Mr. Lincoln's indignant denunciation of venality in high places. I can now understand how the epithet of "Honest Abraham Lincoln" has come to be so universally applied to him by the Great West.

He related many pleasant incidents connected with his contest with Douglas. He told me that he spoke, in all, sixty-four times—nine or ten times face to face with his antagonist. His estimate of the "Little Giant" is generous. He concedes to him great hardihood, pertinacity and magnetic power. Of all men he has ever seen, says Mr. Lincoln, he has the most audacity in maintaining an untenable position. Thus, in endeavoring to reconcile Popular Sovereignty and the Dred Scott decision, his argument, stripped of sophistry, is: "It is legal to expel slavery from a Territory where it legally exists!" And yet he has bamboozled thousands into believing him.

I asked Mr. Lincoln if he saw much of the Democratic papers. He said some of his friends were kind enough to let him see the most abusive of them. He should judge the line of tactics which they intended to pursue was that of personal ridicule. The Chicago *Times* tried that in '58, and helped him (Lincoln) amazingly. He was inclined to believe that the present efforts of his enemies would be attended with like happy results.

"If They Hear Not Moses . . ."
MONDAY, NOVEMBER 5, 1860

¶ *Almost from the moment of his nomination, requests for public utterances on the slavery issue were repeatedly pressed upon Lincoln. Business interests in the East were especially persistent in their appeals. Horace Greeley observed that "the mercantile fears of convulsion and civil war, as results of Mr. Lincoln's election, were so vivid and earnest that the contest at the North was . . . prosecuted by his combined adversaries with the energy of desperation." Greeley saw "Big Business" as possessed of "painful apprehensions of Southern revolt" in the event of a Republican victory, the thought of which "rendered the 'merchant princes,' whose wealth was largely, if not wholly, locked up in the shape of Southern indebtedness, ready to bleed freely for even a hope of preventing a result they so dreaded as fatal to their business, their prosperity, and their affluence."* [1]

However, Lincoln believed that no assurance he might give "disclaiming all intention to interfere with slaves or slavery in the States" would suffice. For, he reasoned, "if they hear not Moses and the prophets, neither will they be persuaded though one rose from the dead." [2]

The day before the election, a New England political leader— probably Henry S. Sanford of Derby, Connecticut—made a personal plea for a statement that would allay the fears of businessmen in the East. In Abraham Lincoln: A History,[3] *Nicolay and Hay— using Nicolay's notes made at the time—chronicle the interview:*

On November 5, the day before the Presidential election, there arrived at Springfield, and called upon him [Lincoln], a gentleman from New England, of prominence in political and official life, who brought and presented letters . . . from a considerable number of citizens representing commercial and manufacturing industries in that region. He was one of those keen, incisive talkers who go direct to the heart of a mission.

"I have called to see," he said, "if the alarm of many persons in New England engaged in commerce and manufactures cannot by some means be relieved. I am myself largely interested in manufactures. Our trade has fallen off, our workmen are idle, we get no orders from the South, and with the increasing chances of civil war, bankruptcy and ruin stare us in the face."

Something in the persistence and manner of his interlocutor, something in the tone of the letters presented, and still more in the character of the signers, irritated Lincoln to a warmth of retort he seldom reached. He divined at once the mercenary nature of the appeal, and it roused him to repel the pressure. His visitor closed by asking some conservative promise "to reassure the men honestly alarmed."

"There are no such men," bluntly replied Lincoln. "This is the same old trick by which the South breaks down every Northern victory. Even if I were personally willing to barter away the moral principle involved in this contest, for the commercial gain of a new submission to the South, I would go to Washington without the countenance of the men who supported me and were my friends before the election; I would be as powerless as a block of buckeye wood."

The man still insisted, and Lincoln continued:

"The honest men (you are talking of honest men) will look at our platform and what I have said. There they will find everything I could now say, or which they would ask me to say. All I could add would be but repetition. Having told them all these things ten times already, would they believe the eleventh declaration? Let us be practical. There are many general terms afloat, such as 'conservatism,' 'enforcement of the irrepressible conflict at the point of the bayonet,' 'hostility to the South,' etc., all of which mean nothing without definition. What then could I say to allay their fears, if they will not define what particular act or acts they fear from me or my friends?"

At this stage of the conversation his visitor, who with true military foresight had provided a reserve, handed him an additional letter numerously signed, asking if he did not there recognize names that were a power.

"Yes," retorted Lincoln sharply, glancing at the document, "I recognize them as a set of liars and knaves who signed that statement about Seward last year."

The visitor was taken aback at this familiarity with the local politics of his State, but rallied and insisted that there were also other names on the list. Lincoln now looked through the paper more carefully, his warmth meanwhile cooling down a little.

"Well," answered he, laughing, "after reading it, it is about as I expected to find it. It annoyed me to hear that gang of men called respectable. Their conduct a year ago was a disgrace to any civilized citizen."

Here his visitor suggested that the South was making armed preparations.

"The North," answered Lincoln, "does not fear invasion from the slave States, and we of the North certainly have no desire, and never had, to invade the South. They have talked about what they intend to do, in the event of a Black Republican victory, until they have convinced themselves there is really no courage left in the North."

"Have we backed this time?" interrupted the visitor.

"That is just what I am pressed to do now," replied Lincoln. "If I shall begin to yield to these threats, if I begin dallying with them, the men who have elected me (if I shall be elected) would give me up before my election, and the South, seeing it, would deliberately kick me out. If my friends should desire me to repeat anything I have before said, I should have no objection to do so. If they required me to say something I had not yet said, I would either do so or get out of the way. If I should be elected, the first duty to the country would be to stand by the men who elected me."

"Pronounced Not Guilty . . ."

WEDNESDAY, NOVEMBER 7, 1860

¶ *On election day, November 6th, Lincoln was in "one of his most amiable moods." While displaying a lively interest in the election, "it was noticeable that he scarcely ever alluded to himself or his candidacy." When he cast his ballot, he voted for every Republican candidate but himself. That night, accompanied by friends, he received the election returns in the telegraph office opposite the State House. After a New York dispatch assured his victory, Lincoln started homeward only to find himself "almost dragged" by enthusiastic townsfolk to a neighboring restaurant to celebrate his election.*

At ten o'clock the next morning, Lincoln was back in the State House to receive friends and other callers who had come to congratulate him. Samuel R. Weed, a St. Louis newspaperman assigned to cover the election at Springfield, tells us what happened that morning in an article written in 1882—apparently from detailed notes made at the time—which was first published in The New York Times on February 14, 1932:

While he [Lincoln] seemed in good spirits and received these friendly greetings with a sincere pleasure and good nature, there was a sort of sadness in his face which was remarked by more than one of those present. But he kept it under, amid the warm congratulations which poured in upon him, and talked with all who got near enough to him for the purpose with his old-time freedom.

He sat a portion of the time in a big armchair with his feet on the lower edge of a large stove and had a word for everybody. Very early in the day he had said to one group of callers: "Well, boys, your troubles are over now, but mine have just begun." He repeated this remark a half-dozen times in two hours and I have no doubt it came direct from his heart.

After a while the callers became so numerous that he stood up and held a regular levee and took every offered hand. . . . An old gray-haired, grizzled farmer shook hands with him, and as he did so exclaimed: "Uncle Abe, I didn't vote for yer, but I am mighty glad yer elected just the same."

The President-elect quickly replied: "Well, my old friend, when a man has been tried and pronounced not guilty he hasn't any right to find fault with the jury."

Chapter Two

"FORTUNATE FOR THE PEACE"

WHEN the votes cast in the November 6th election were counted, Lincoln had 1,866,452; Douglas 1,376,957; Breckinridge 849,781; and Bell 588,879. In the Electoral College, it was 180 votes for Lincoln; 72 for Breckinridge; 39 for Bell; and 12 for Douglas.[1]

What kind of campaign had it been? It was a hard-fought, hectic drive. But not for Lincoln. Acceding to the custom of the time, Lincoln took no active part in the campaigning. He remained in Springfield, tending to his affairs and bearing his honors "meekly."[2] At the same time, however, Republican committees worked feverishly on the national, state and local levels. Party clubs mushroomed in hundreds of cities and towns. In various communities, Republicans erected headquarters fashioned after the Chicago Wigwam, where Lincoln had been nominated.

Lincoln symbols were to be found aplenty everywhere in the North, especially axes and Lincoln rails. Manufacturing "authentic" Lincoln rails for a ready market had become a lucrative business in Springfield. There was parading, flag waving, booming of cannon. Citizens turned out to watch torchlight processions of the Wide-Awakes, the popular Lincoln supporters with their colorful oilcloth uniforms, marching to martial music. Another group of marchers called themselves "Lincoln Rangers."

There were barbecues, rallies, and special political forays into farming areas. Leading politicians took to the stump. Republican orators drew mammoth crowds as they pressed their attacks against their adversaries, primarily against Douglas and all he stood for. Breaking with tradition—by which Presidential candidates refrained from active campaigning—Douglas threw himself into the canvass in a desperate attempt to stem the Lincoln tide. To add to the bluster of the campaign, newspapers North and South fired political salvos and countersalvos at their respective opponents.

The air was charged with political excesses. The Republicans had exuberance galore. There was a time for marching. There was a time for oratory. There was always a time for propagandizing. They had their own party newspaper, *The Rail-Splitter*. They had all sorts of party literature. They had their own glee clubs and bands and campaign songs. To the tune of "The Old Gray Mare," they would sing "Old Abe Lincoln came out of the wilderness," or they would join lustily in rendering "Ain't I glad I joined the Republicans." They were going to make an impact upon the country, no holds barred. And they did.

Lincoln derived great strength from the division among his opponents. In New York, New Jersey and Rhode Island, Lincoln's adversaries presented a single electoral slate in a joint attempt to defeat him. In New Jersey, Douglas, Bell and Breckinridge representatives formed a "Fusion" ticket. But when Douglasites balked at voting for Breckinridge and Bell, Lincoln won four electoral votes in the state although the popular vote was against him. California and Oregon gave Lincoln pluralities, as did every other free state. All except four slave states went to Breckinridge. Maryland lumbered into the Bell column, while Douglas captured Missouri. In summarizing the election results, the veteran Congressman, James G. Blaine, observed: "For the first time in the history of the government, the South was defeated in a Presidential election where an issue affecting the slavery question was involved."

Now that the election was over, Lincoln faced the trying period of waiting for the inauguration. The formation of his Cabinet brought him many a perplexing problem. In addition, he became the focus of patronage-hungry supporters and a mounting flood of applications for offices. On this subject, he wrote Seward on December 8, 1860: "In regard to the patronage, sought with so much eagerness and jealousy, I have prescribed for myself the maxim 'Justice to all.' "[3]

Apart from this, he continued to withstand the increasing demands that he issue a public policy statement. Since his nomination, Lincoln had steadfastly refused to make any declaration in the belief that even a repetition of his already well-known position would only tend to antagonize political factions within his own party and be subject to distortion by his enemies. He made only one concession, on November 20th, when he wrote some paragraphs for inclusion in a speech Senator Lyman Trumbull was to make that evening, which read:

I have labored in, and for, the Republican organization with entire confidence that whenever it shall be in power, each and all of the States will be left in as complete control of their own affairs respectively, and at as perfect liberty to choose, and employ, their own means of protecting property, and preserving peace and order within their respective limits, as they have ever been under any administration. Those who have voted for Mr. Lincoln, have expected, and still expect this; and they would not have voted for him had they expected otherwise. I regard it as extremely fortunate for the peace of the whole country, that this point, upon which the Republicans have been so long, and so persistently misrepresented, is now to be brought to a practical test, and placed beyond the possibility of doubt. Disunionists *per se,* are now in hot haste to get out of the Union, precisely because they perceive they can not, much longer, maintain apprehension among the Southern people that their homes, and firesides, and lives, are to be endangered by the action of the Federal Government. With such *"Now, or never"* is the maxim.

I am rather glad of this military preparation in the South. It will enable the people the more easily to suppress any uprisings there, which their misrepresentations of purposes may have encouraged.[4]

Reaction to Trumbull's speech proved Lincoln right in refusing to issue any public declaration on the policy he planned to pursue as President.

The lines of battle were being drawn in the national arena. In the White House, James Buchanan, old and weary, struggled to maintain Federal authority in a country gripped by the tension and anxiety inherent in a growing awareness of impending crisis. Early in December, President Buchanan sent a message to the opening session of the new Congress, condemning secession and advocating "peaceful constitutional remedies"[5] to conciliate the nation's sectional differences. Subsequently, the House Committee of Thirty-three and the Senate Committee of Thirteen met to devise means for forestalling a Southern revolution. But their deliberations came to nought. Before the close of 1860—on December 20th—South Carolina became the first state to adopt an ordinance of secession, and by February 1, 1861, six more slave states followed suit. A peace conference initiated by the Virginia Legislature assembled in Washington in January and remained in session through most of February. It, too, failed to resolve the national crisis.

Against these events, Lincoln shaped his Administration and took the oath of office as President.

"My Declarations Have Been Made"

TUESDAY, NOVEMBER 13, 1860

¶ *An interesting interview with Lincoln reflects his attitude toward some of the problems that faced him as President-elect. The meeting was with a correspondent of the* New York Evening Post [1] *who signed himself "Albany," and whose report was copied in the* New York Daily Tribune *on November 20, 1860. In his story, "Albany" states that "the timid gentlemen who are expecting Mr. Lincoln to issue a* pronunciamento *after the manner of successful Mexican chiefs, wherein his policy will be declared for the conciliation of the madmen who are threatening the secession of a few of the States of the South, do not know the President elect." The correspondent then goes on to narrate what was said at the interview with Mr. Lincoln:*

It was my good fortune to talk with him an hour yesterday [November 13th] in relation to the secession movement, and though he makes no concealment of the uneasiness which the contemplated treason gives him, he is not a bit alarmed by the aspects of affairs, nor is he at all inclined to yield an inch to the well-intended but mistaken solicitations of his friends. He believes that his success is only a public pretext for what has been long preparing [the movement toward secession]; that his position on all questions of public concern—all which affect the Slavery question nearly or remotely—is so well known that no declaration of his would change treasonable purposes already announced, and that a reiteration of views which are patent to all men who have sought to know them, would be an evidence of timidity which he does not feel, and of which he would have no man suspect him. He is cautious, discreet and wise in his replies to questions as to what may or will be done. But those who know the steadfastness of purpose and the conscientious firmness which are his distinguishing characteristics, have no doubt that he will adopt that policy, when President, which a proper regard for the *whole country* dictates, and that he will pursue it firmly, persistently, and, if necessary, obdurately, to the end. "I know," said he, "the justness of my intentions and the utter groundlessness of the pretended fears of the men who are filling the country with their clamor. If I go into the Presidency, they will find me as I am on record—nothing less, nothing more. My declarations have been made to the world without reservation. They have been often repeated; and now, self-respect demands of me and of the party that has elected me that when threatened I should be silent." While he holds this language in relation to a public letter, he does not hesitate in his private letters to the South (he has already a large correspondence in that section) and in conversation with his visitors, in answer to proper inquiries, to give any assurances which are consistent with his views heretofore expressed and the party platform on which he stands.

I found Mr. Lincoln, when I called upon him, engaged in reading up anew the history of the attempted nullification of 1832, including the discussions on the celebrated "Force bills," and Gen. [Andrew] Jackson's more celebrated proclamation. I am debarred from saying what comments these documents provoked; but Mr. Lincoln's friends may be assured that, while he has no ambition to be an imitator of that old chief, nature has endowed him with that sagacity, honesty, and firmness which made Old Hickory's the most eminently successful and honorable Administartion known to the republic.

[The reporter noted that Lincoln's letters from the South included "missives which no decent man could write." Most of them were anonymous. Some were signed "Sacred Order" or "Southern Brotherhood," and threatened the President-elect "with a sudden and untimely taking-off." Says "Albany":]

He is not, I am glad to say, annoyed by these. Assured that no man who will write anonymous and threatening letters is worthy of being feared, he tosses all such aside, as he says, to illustrate at some future day, the comical side of his Administration.

The rush for office has already commenced. While I was with Mr. Lincoln he handed me a note from a gentleman from an adjoining State who was exceedingly importunate for the promise of a certain place, as a specimen [*sic*] of many which he is daily receiving. I may be pardoned for relating what thousands ought to know: "I have made up my mind," said he, "not to be badgered about those places. I have promised nothing, high or low, and will not. By-and-by, when I call somebody to me in character of an adviser, we will examine the claims to the most responsible posts, and decide what shall be done. As for the rest, I shall have enough to do without reading recommendations for country postmasterships; these, and all others of the sort, I will turn over to the heads of departments, and make them responsible for the good conduct of their subordinates."

"A Relative of Mrs. L."

FRIDAY, NOVEMBER 16, 1860

¶ *Many people volunteered advice to Lincoln on who should go into his Cabinet. Some of the suggestions came in the mails; others were made in interviews and conferences. Nicolay, in one of his memoranda,[1] records the following:*

Judge [Daniel] Breck[2] of Kentucky, quite an old man, a relative of Mrs. L[incoln], who is on a visit here, had a long talk with Mr. Lincoln this morning. He strongly urged upon him [the President-elect] the duty of saving the country by making up his Cabinet of "conservative men"—one or more of them from the South, and who should not be Republicans, saying that by such a course Kentucky would stay in Union. But that if obnoxious men like Seward, Cassius M. Clay, &c. were put in the Cabinet, and a sectional administration organized, the people of Ky would feel themselves driven to go with S[outh] C[arolina]. Judge B., while he disclaimed any desire to have Mr. L. abate any principle, yet made a very strong appeal to him to make his administration conservative in the way he pointed out.

Mr. Lincoln listened to him attentively and only replied briefly. He asked the Judge to tell him in what speech Mr. Seward had ever spoken menacingly of the South, and said that so far as he knew, not one single prominent public Republican had justly made himself obnoxious to the South by anything he had said or done, and that they had only become so because the Southern politicians had so persistently bespattered every Northern man by their misrepresentations to rob them of what strength they might otherwise have.

He told the Judge that the substance of his [the judge's] plan was that the Republicans should now again surrender the Government into the hands of the men they had just conquered, and that the cause should take to its bosom the enemy who had always fought it, and who would still continue to fight and oppose it.

He told him he should however give his views a serious and respectful consideration.

"Mr. Lincoln Did Not Believe . . ."

THURSDAY, NOVEMBER 22 [?], 1860

¶ *From November 21 to 26, Lincoln was in Chicago to confer with Hannibal Hamlin of Maine, his Vice-President-elect, on Cabinet matters. It was during this visit, and on Hamlin's recommendation, that Lincoln agreed to include Gideon Welles of Hartford, Connecticut, in the Cabinet. As was to be expected, Lincoln's stay in the Windy City was hectic. He saw some of the city's sites, including the Wigwam, where the Republicans had given him the nomination for the Presidency, and met with politicians and well-wishers. At one point, the subject of Southern intentions came under discussion. Donn Piatt, an Ohio newspaperman and Republican politician, gives us a brief—but not too friendly—description of this conversation in his book,* Memories of the Men Who Saved the Union, *which was published in 1887:* [1]

Mr. Lincoln did not believe, could not be made to believe, that the South meant secession and war. When I told him . . . at a dinner-table in Chicago, where the Hon. Hannibal Hamlin, General [Robert E.] Schenck, and others, were guests, that the Southern people were in dead earnest, meant war, and I doubted whether he would be inaugurated at Washington, he laughed and said the fall of pork at Cincinnati had affected me. I became somewhat irritated, and told him that in ninety days the land would be whitened with tents. He said in reply:

"Well, we won't jump that ditch until we come to it," and then, after a pause, added, "I must run the machine as I find it."

I take no credit to myself for this power of prophecy; I only said what every one acquainted with the Southern people knew, and the wonder is that Mr. Lincoln should have been so blind to the coming storm.

The epigrammatic force of his expressions was remarkable, as was also the singular purity of his language. What he said was so original that I reduced much of it to writing at the time. One of these sayings was this on secession:

"If our Southern friends are right in their claim the framers of the Government carefully planned the rot that now threatens their work with destruction. If one State has the right to withdraw at will, certainly a majority have the right, and we have the result given us of the States being able to force out one State. That is logical."

"Friendly Towards the South"

FRIDAY, DECEMBER 7 [?], 1860

> ¶ *Among those to discuss public affairs with Lincoln was a correspondent for the* Philadelphia Evening Bulletin, *whose story was copied in* The New York Times *of December 20, 1860. The journalist, who had been in Chicago on "private business," made a special trip to Springfield to see the President-elect, accompanied by "a couple of personal friends, who were acquainted with Mr.* LINCOLN." *After arriving in the Republican Mecca at 6:00 A.M., they washed up, had "a good breakfast," walked around the city to kill time, and "soon after 9 o'clock" showed up at the State House to see the newly elected Chief Magistrate:*

Mr. HATCH, the Secretary of State, accompanied us, and without any ceremony, we were introduced. Mr. LINCOLN already had a visitor, and his secretary was seated at a desk heaped up with letters and documents. As we entered, we found the President elect seated by a stove, and there was not the least difficulty in recognizing his strongly marked and by no means handsome face. His tall figure, which an Irish friend says "can be cut in two three times, when he is seated," unfolded itself, and he left his chair to shake each visitor cordially by the hand, with pleasant words of greeting and inquiries after the health of his Chicago friends and their families. He at once made every one feel at his ease, and some minutes were passed in lively chat about ordinary subjects, each of which was illustrated by some anecdote, told with the readiness and humor for which Mr. LINCOLN is noted.

At length, one of the party asked him if he had any news from the South. "No," he replied; "I have not yet read the dispatches in the morning papers. But," he added, "I think, from all I can learn, that things have reached their worst point in the South, and they are likely to mend in the future. If it be true, as reported, that the South Carolinians do not intend to resist the collection of the revenue, after they ordain secession, there need be no collision with the Federal Government. The Union may still be maintained. The greatest inconvenience will arise from the want of Federal courts; as with the present feeling, judges, marshals, and other officers could not be obtained." On this point Mr. LINCOLN spoke at some length, regretting its difficulty, but adding that his mind was made up as to how it should be overcome. His tone and language were moderate, good-humored and friendly towards the South.

He then went on to speak of the charges made by the South against the North, remarking that they were so indefinite that they could not be regarded as sound. If they were well defined they could be fairly and successfully met. But they are so vague that they cannot be long maintained by reasoning men even in the Southern States. Afterwards he spoke of the course pursued by certain Republican newspapers at the North, which I need not name, in replying to threats of secession from Southern States, by saying, "Let them secede; we do not want them." This tone, he remarked, was having a bad effect in some of the border States, especially in Missouri, where there was danger that it might alienate some of the best friends of the cause, if it were persisted in. In Missouri and some other States, where Republicanism has just begun to grow, and where there is still a strong Pro-Slavery party to contend with, there can be no advantage in taunting and bantering the South. Leading Republicans from those States had urged him to use his influence with the journals referred to, and induce them to alter their present tone towards the South. He did not say he had promised to do this, and I only gathered from his manner and language that he would prefer to see the bantering tone abandoned.

There was no caution given in regard to keeping his remarks private, and as he knew my professional position and yet gave no such caution, there can be no violation of confidence in publishing this very brief sketch of his remarks, omitting, of course, many things, but giving their general tone with fidelity. The only reservation he made was when he was expressing his views of affairs in the South. He said he had arrived at them after much study and thought; they were his views at the present time but of course liable to be modified by his more mature judgment after further information and further study of the progress of events.

Having thus discussed public affairs for some time, Mr. LINCOLN then changed the conversation, making pleasant allusions to incidents of his recent visit to Chicago. The inquiry was then made whether he expected to leave Springfield again before his departure for Washington. "I think not," was his reply; "I shall have a good deal to do here between this and the middle of February, when I expect to start for Washington. I don't want to go before the middle of February, because I expect they will drive me insane after I get there, and I want to keep tolerably sane, at least until after the inauguration." In answer to a question as to which route he would take to the East, he said he had not thought on the subject. I ventured to recommend the route by Pittsburgh and Philadelphia, but he said there would be time enough to decide when he was ready to depart.

Other visitors coming in, we rose and left, Mr. LINCOLN cordially shaking each of our party by the hand, and expressing the pleasure he had had in seeing us.

"I Accepted His Invitation"

SATURDAY, DECEMBER 15, 1860

¶ *Considering the temper of the country—particularly Maryland, Kentucky and Missouri, who were leaning toward secession—*

Lincoln felt it important that the Border States should be represented in his Cabinet. In this connection, he planned a visit to St. Louis to confer with Edward Bates, who was characterized by Carl Schurz as "a lawyer of high standing and a very worthy gentleman," [1] *despite his Know-Nothing inclinations, "but an old Whig [never a Republican] who was supposed to be against slavery in a mild, unaggressive way." Hearing of Lincoln's intention, Bates confided to his Diary: "I thought I saw an unfitness in his coming to me, and that I ought to go to him, as soon as his wish to see me was known."* [2]

On Friday night, December 14th, Bates showed up in Springfield. A Virginian by birth, whom Joseph Medill of the Chicago Tribune called "a fossil of the Silurian era," [3] *Bates—a former slaveowner—in his late sixties possessed a white shrubby beard although his hair had remained reddish. Lincoln once gave a reason for this: "Bates uses his chin more than his head."* [4] *Nicolay, who studied Bates' appearance the following morning, noted that "he is not of impressive exterior . . . his face shows all the marks of age quite strongly."* [5]

Like Lincoln, Bates did not believe the Union would be disrupted by a few Southern extremists. Even after South Carolina had announced secession, he was to maintain: "I think that (except for a few demented fanatics) it is all brag and bluster." [6] *He was opposed to the repeal of the Missouri Compromise. But his personal attitude toward slavery was influenced by his Virginia background.*

Himself a Presidential hopeful during the Chicago Convention, Bates—on account of his age, he claimed—did not take the stump for Lincoln. Instead, he wrote an effective letter endorsing the Illinois "Rail Splitter" and the Republicans were grateful.

The interview with Lincoln that Saturday is reconstructed from a memorandum by Nicolay[7] *and a Diary*[8] *entry by Bates. We begin with Nicolay's account:*

Their meeting (they had an acquaintanceship of eight year's [*sic*] standing) was very cordial; and the ordinary salutations being over, Mr L.[incoln] entered at once upon the important subject matter of the interview.

Without further prelude Mr L.[incoln] went on to tell him [Bates] that he had desired this interview to say to him, that since the day of the Chicago nomination it had been his purpose, in case of success, unless something should meantime make it necessary to change his decision, to tender him (B.) one of the places in his cabinet.

Nothing having occurred to make a change of purpose necessary, (he had waited thus long to be enabled to act with caution, and in view of all the circumstances of the case) he now offered him the appointment.

He [Lincoln] said in doing this, he did not desire to burden him with one of the drudgery offices. Some of his (B's) friends had asked for him the State Department. He could not now offer him this, which was usually considered the first place in the Cabinet, for the reason that he should offer that place to Mr Seward—in view of his ability, his integrity, and his commanding influence, and fitness for the place. He did this as a matter of duty to the party, and to Mr Seward's many and strong friends, while at the same time it accorded perfectly with his own personal inclinations—notwithstanding some opposition on the part of sincere and warm friends. He had not yet communicated with Mr Seward, and did not know whether he would accept the appointment—as there had been some doubt expressed about his [Seward's] doing so. He [Lincoln] would probably know in a few days. He therefore could not now offer him (B.) the State Department, but would offer him what he [Lincoln] supposed would be most congenial, and for which he [Bates] was certainly in every way qualified, viz: the Attorney Generalship.

[Bates picks up the story here:]

He did not state, and I did not choose to press him to state, who would probably fill the other Departments, or any of them. Inde[e]d, I suppose he does not yet know—so much depends on Mr. Seward's position, and upon the daily-changing phases of political affairs.

He assured me however, that I am the only man that he desired in the Cabinet, to whom he has yet spoken . . . [or] written a word, about their own appointments[.]

I told Mr. L.[incoln] [9] with all frankness, that if peace and order prevailed in the country, and the Government could now be carried on quietly, I would decline a place in the Cabinet, as I did in 1850 [when a Cabinet post had been tendered him by President Millard Fillmore]—and for the same reasons. But now, I am not at liberty to consult my own interests and wishes, and must subordinate them to my convictions of public duty, and to the necessity in which I find myself, to sustain my own personal character, by acting out, in good faith, the principles to which I stand pledged. And that, therefore, and as a matter of duty, I accepted his invitation, and in that view, would take either office in which he might think I would be most useful. That as a matter personal to myself, and in regard to my private affairs, the Att.y. Genl.'s place is most desirable. . . .

I suggested that my visit to Springfield could hardly escape the vigilance of the press and probably the truth would leak out—He said he didn't care if it did, for his mind . . . was fully made up as to me. And further, if I thought, after consultation with friends, that it would be best to let his offer be known, and would write him so, he would stop conjectures, by letting it be known as a fact—but not the particular office. . . .

Feeling under necessity to offer the *State* Dept. to Mr. S.[eward] and having some reason (hope at least) to beli[e]ve that he w[oul]d. decline it, he is anxious to *know* the fact; and I must try the best methods I can to ascertain it for him, without committing him.[10]

[Nicolay continues the narration:]

Mr Lincoln expressed himself highly gratified at his [Bates'] determination. By way of preparing himself for the question which the new administration were likely to encounter, he [Lincoln] desired him between this time and the inauguration, to examine very thoroughly, and make himself familiar with the Constitution and the laws relating to the question of secession, so as to be prepared to give a definite opinion upon the various aspects of the question.

On one other point he [Lincoln] desired him also to make some examination. Under the present administration the mails in the South had been violated with impunity, and with the sanction of the Government. Under the new government, he feared some trouble from this question. It was well understood by intelligent men that the perfect and unrestrained freedom of speech and the press which exists at the north was practically incompatible with the existing institutions at the South, and he feared that Radical Republicans at the North might claim at the hands of the new administration the enforcement of the right, and endeavor to make the mail the means of thrusting upon the South matter which even their conservative and well-meaning men might deem inimical and dangerous.

Mr Bates said he would carefully look into both these questions. On the latter he had without special investigation always easily arrived at the opinion that the U.S. mails ought by right to be sacred and inviolable. Certainly the present practice, which permitted petty postmasters to examine and burn everything they pleased, would not be tolerated or countenanced by the most despotic governments. At the same time he foresaw the practical difficulty of enforcing the law at every crossroad.

Much further conversation was had both durin.[g] the morning, and in the afternoon when Mr L.[incoln] called on him again at the hotel. Their views were very frankly and fully exchanged.

Mr Bates' conversation shows him to be inflexibly opposed to secession, and strongly in favor of maintain.[ing] the government by force if necessary. He forcibly illustrates his temper by saying that he is a man of peace, and will defer fighting as long as possible; but that if forced to do so against his will, he has made it a rule never to fire blank cartridges.

[In a Note appended to his *Diary* entry on the interview, Bates states:]

Mr. L.[incoln] read me a letter that he had just recd. from Mr. [John A.[11]] Gilmer M.[ember of] C.[ongress] of N[orth] Carolina,[12] urging him to make some declarations &c and a draft of his ans[we]r., which ought to be satisfactory, declining to publish any thing, but referring to his speeches—to particular passages—the pages of the printed debates[.]

"The 'Black Republican' Lion"

WEDNESDAY, DECEMBER 19, 1860

¶ *Lincoln imposed no restrictions upon his visitors at the State House and the crowd, according to one newspaperman, was "always of motely* [sic] *description." Everyone living in the vicinity of Springfield or passing through the city came to take a look at the President-elect—or so it seemed. "Offensively democratic exhibitions of free manners occur once in a while," the journalist wrote. "Churlish fellows will obtrude themselves with their hats on, lighted segars and their pantaloons tucked into their boots. Dropping into chairs, they will sit puffing away and trying to gorgonize the President with their silent stares until their boorish curiosity is fully satisfied."* [1]

On December 19th, a Mississippian, sporting the "Blue Cockade" —symbol of secession—loomed up in Springfield, where "the fellow received some rather severe rebuffs in his cruisings around town, and retired to his hotel in consequence." That afternoon, "doubtless braced up by divers doses of whisky, for the daring feat of facing the 'Black Republican' lion 'in his den,'" the Southerner went to see Lincoln.[2] *A correspondent for the* Cincinnati Commercial *did a story on this incident, which was copied in* The New York Times *on December 27, 1860:* [3]

Introducing himself as Mr. D. E. RAY, of YAZOO, Miss., he took his seat with all the meekness of a lamb, and "sat in silent expectation" for about twenty minutes—holding, however, his hat so that the object of his terror could not fail to observe the cockade. Insulting as the sight must have proved to the President elect, he perceived at once of what stuff the man was made, and hence hardly appeared to notice him, but quietly continued his conversation with some other visitors. A Missourian, who happened to be present and seated near the Mississippian, at last directed his attention to the latter. He asked him a number of questions in relation to the proposed secession of Mississippi. The sullen answers of the Southerner struck the ear of a radical Republican Yankee, likewise in attendance on the same occasion. Waxing angry at the Mississippian's disunion sentiments, he inquired tauntingly of him: "Isn't that all gas?" Whereupon the President elect, evidently uneasy at the prospect of a violent altercation, interposed by joining in the conversation. In its course the Southron asserted that the people of his State were not afraid of Mr. LINCOLN, but the party that elected him. This latter apprehension was at once pronounced groundless by some of the visitors. One of them inquired of the cockade man "whether he had ever read Mr. LINCOLN's debates with Senator DOUGLAS." Being answered in the negative, he requested the former to furnish a copy to the fire-eater; the latter also expressing a desire for the book, the President elect procured one, and having appropriately inscribed it on the title page, handed it to him [the Mississippian], remarking: *"You will find that the only difference between you and me is, that I think Slavery wrong, and you think it right; that I am opposed to its extension, while you advocate it; and that as to the security of the institution and the protection of slave property in the States where it has a lawful existence, you will find it as great under my Administration as it ever was under that of Mr. Buchanan."*

Mr. LINCOLN also found occasion to state, "that if the Southern States concluded upon a contingent secession, that is, upon awaiting aggressive acts on the part of his Administration, they would never go out of the Union." All of this the southerner received in unbroken silence. He was obviously at a perplexing loss what to say. His embarrassment finally made him so uncomfortable, that he got up and tried to make his way out. Mr. LINCOLN saw him to the door, shook hands with him, and told him playfully that he hoped the Southern people were not afraid of getting hurt by him. "No we aint," was the reply.

"Never a Boss Cabinet-Maker"

THURSDAY, DECEMBER 20, 1860

¶ *Seward's failure to secure the Presidential nomination was a heartbreaking blow to Thurlow Weed, who had devoted more than two decades to advancing the Senator's career. Nevertheless, after overcoming the initial impact of the defeat at Chicago, Weed—powerfully wealthy New York political boss and publisher of the* Albany Evening Journal—*wrote Seward "that a prompt and cheerful aciquiescence [sic] in the Nomination, and an early return to Washington is not only wise but a duty."* [1]

During the campaign, Weed co-operated with Lincoln's managers —Judge David Davis and Leonard Swett, who had worked feverishly for Lincoln's nomination—in raising funds and mapping strategy. Davis and Swett had become deeply impressed with this big-time politician, whose unsavory reputation for masterminding "schemes of plunder" [2] *and "corruption at Albany"* [3] *was well-known.*

Except for one term in the New York Legislature, Weed had sought no elective office. His prime interests lay in acquiring power, patronage and spoils.

Even before Lincoln's election, Weed was in conference at Saratoga with Davis and Swett and possibly Simon Cameron of Pennsylvania, another crooked political boss, whom the New York Herald *had labeled a "Democratic Know Nothing Republican Conservative."* [4] *Their object: to join forces to control the Lincoln Administration. For although the next President was not to be Seward, "the Dictator"—as Weed was called—refused to abandon an attempt to dominate the new regime.*

In the matter of Cabinet appointments, this combine was arrayed against another bloc composed of Salmon P. Chase of Ohio, William Cullen Bryant, George Opdyke, David Dudley Field and other New York anti-Weed Republicans. Knowing that Chase figured prominently in Lincoln's Cabinet plans, the Weed men "vehemently opposed" the Ohio leader. Without Chase in the Cabinet, the Weedites believed they would have "little difficulty in shaping the policies of the Administration," Gideon Welles was to state in later years.[5]

Feuding over who was to go into the Cabinet was becoming increasingly intense and bitter. Lincoln had to act. With some reluctance, he summoned Weed to a conference in Springfield, which was also attended by Davis and Swett. According to Lincoln, it lasted nearly one day.[6] Weed, in his Autobiography—apparently influenced by the passage of time and events—said it was two days.[7]

Weed was with Lincoln on the day South Carolina seceded from the Union. A report of the discussion is given by Weed in the Autobiography, which was published in 1883: [8]

Mr. Lincoln remarked, smiling, "that he supposed I had had some experience in cabinet-making; that he had a job on hand, and as he had never learned that trade, he was disposed to avail himself of the suggestions of friends." Taking up his figure, I replied, "that though never a boss cabinet-maker, I had as a journeyman been occasionally consulted about State cabinets, and that although President [Zachary] Taylor once talked with me about reforming his cabinet, I had never been concerned in or presumed to meddle with the formation of an original Federal cabinet, and that he was the first President elect I had ever seen." . . .

Mr. Lincoln observed that "the making of a cabinet, now that he had it to do, was by no means as easy as he had supposed; that he had, even before the result of the election was known, assuming the probability of success, fixed upon the two leading members of his cabinet, but that in looking about for suitable men to fill the other departments, he had been much embarrassed, partly from his want of acquaintance with the prominent men of the day, and partly, he believed, that while the population of the country had immensely increased, really great men were scarcer than they used to be." He then inquired whether I had any suggestions of a general character affecting the selection of a cabinet to make. I replied that, along with the question of ability, integrity, and experience, he ought, in the selection of his cabinet, to find men whose firmness and courage fitted them for the revolutionary ordeal which was about to test the strength of our government; and that in my judgment it was desirable that at least two members of his cabinet should be selected from slave-holding States. He inquired whether, in the emergency which I so much feared, they could be trusted, adding that he did not quite like to hear Southern journals and Southern speakers insisting that there must be no "coercion;" that while he had no disposition to coerce anybody, yet after he had taken an oath to execute the laws, he should not care to see them violated. I remarked that there were Union men in Maryland, Virginia, North Carolina, and Tennessee, for whose loyalty, under the most trying circumstances and in any event, I would vouch. "Would you rely on such men if their States should secede?" "Yes, sir; the men I have in my mind can always be relied on." "Well," said Mr. Lincoln, "let us have the names of your white crows, such ones as you think fit for the cabinet." I then named Henry Winter Davis of Maryland, John M. Botts of Virginia, John A. Gilmer of North Carolina, and Bailey Peyton of Tennessee. As the conversation progressed, Mr. Lincoln remarked that he intended to invite Governor Seward [unknown to Weed, Lincoln had already extended that invitation on December 8th⁹] to take the State, and Governor Chase the Treasury Department, remarking that, aside from their long experience in public affairs, and their eminent fitness, they were prominently before the people and the convention as competitors for the presidency, each having higher claims than his own for the place which he was to occupy. On naming Gideon Welles as the gentleman he thought of as the representative of New England in the cabinet, I remarked that I thought he could find several New England gentlemen whose selection for a place in his cabinet would be more acceptable to the people of New England. "But," said Mr. Lincoln, "we must remember that the Republican party is constituted of two elements, and that we must have men of Democratic as well as of Whig antecedents in the cabinet."

Acquiescing in this view the subject was passed over. And then Mr. Lincoln remarked that Judge Blair had been suggested. I inquired, "What Judge Blair?" and was answered, "Judge Montgomery Blair." "Has he been suggested by any one except his father, Francis

P. Blair, Sr.?" "Your question," said Mr. Lincoln, "reminds me of a story," and he proceeded with infinite humor to tell a story, which I would repeat if I did not fear that its spirit and effect would be lost. I finally remarked that if we were legislating on the question, I should move to strike out the name of Montgomery Blair and insert that of Henry Winter Davis. Mr. Lincoln laughingly replied, "Davis [Judge Davis, uncle of Henry Winter Davis] has been posting you up on this question. He came from Maryland and has got Davis on the brain. Maryland must, I think, be like New Hampshire, a good State to move from." . . . It was very evident that the selection of Montgomery Blair was a fixed fact. . . .

General Cameron's name was next introduced, and in reference to him and upon the peculiarities and characteristics of Pennsylvania statesmen we had a long conversation. In reply to a question of Mr. Lincoln's, I said that I had personally known General Cameron for twenty-five years; that for the last ten years I had seen a good deal of him; that whenever I had met him at Washington or elsewhere he had treated me with much kindness, inspiring me with friendly feeling. "But you do not," said Mr. Lincoln, "say what you think about him for the cabinet." On that subject I replied that I was embarrassed; that Mr. Cameron during a long and stirring political life had made warm friends and bitter enemies; that while his appointment would gratify his personal friends, it would offend his opponents, among whom were many of the leading and influential Republicans of that State; that I was, as I had already stated, in view of an impending rebellion, anxious that Mr. Lincoln should have the support of not only a strong cabinet, but one which would command the confidence of the people. We continued to canvass General Cameron. . . . I told him that if it were a personal question I should not hesitate to do so, for that I liked General Cameron, and entertained no doubt of his regard for me, but that as I was not sure that his appointment would give strength to the administration I must leave the matter with himself. "But," said Mr. Lincoln, "Pennsylvania, any more than New York or Ohio, cannot be overlooked. Her strong Republican vote, not less than her numerical importance, entitles her to a representative in the cabinet. Who is stronger or better than General Cameron?" To this question I was unprepared for a reply, for among General Cameron's friends there was no one eminently qualified, and it would have been equally unjust and unwise to take an opponent, and finally General Cameron's case was passed over, but neither decided nor dismissed.

I now renewed my suggestion about having the slave States represented in the cabinet. "But," said Mr. Lincoln, "you object to Judge Blair, who resides in a slave State." "I object to Judge Blair because he represents nobody, he has no following, and because his appointment would be obnoxious to the Union men of Maryland; and that, as I believe, while he can look into Maryland, he actually resides in the District of Columbia." "Very well," said Mr. Lincoln, "I will now give you the name of a gentleman who not only resides in a slave State, but who is emphatically a representative man. What objection have you to Edward Bates of Missouri?" "None, not a shadow or a shade of objection. That is a selection, as Mr. [Daniel] Webster might have said, 'eminently fit to be made.' The political record of Mr. Bates is proverbially consistent. He was a reliable Whig member of Congress from the State of Missouri thirty years ago; he was the able and popular president of the great River and Harbor Improvement Convention at Chicago twenty years ago; his high personal and professional character, his habits of industry, his equable temper, and his inalienable devotion to the government and Union, fit and qualify him in my judgment admirably for a cabinet minister." . . .

It was now settled that Governor Seward was to be Secretary of State, Governor Chase, Secretary of the Treasury, and Mr. Bates the Attorney General. I was satisfied that Mr. Lincoln intended to give Mr. Welles one of the other places in the cabinet; that he was strongly inclined to give another place to Mr. Blair, and that his mind was not quite clear in regard to General Cameron. Only one place, therefore, remained open, and that, it was understood, was to be given to Indiana; but whether it was to be Caleb B. Smith or Colonel [Henry S.] Lane was undetermined. I inquired whether, in the shape which the question was taking, it was just or wise to concede so many seats in the cabinet to the Democratic element in the Republican party. He replied that as a Whig he thought he could afford to be liberal to a section of the Republican party without whose votes he could not have been elected. I admitted the justice and wisdom of this, adding that in arranging and adjusting questions of place and patronage in our State we had acted in that spirit, but that I doubted both the justice and the wisdom, in inaugurating his administration, of giving to a minority of the Republican party a majority of his cabinet. I added that the national convention indicated unmistakably the sentiment of its constituency by nominating for president a candidate with Whig antecedents, while its nominee for vice-president had been for many years a Democratic representative in Congress. "But," said Mr. Lincoln, "why do you assume that we are giving that section of our party a majority in the cabinet?" I replied that if Messrs. Chase, Cameron, Welles, and Blair should be designated, the cabinet would stand four to three. "You seem to forget that *I* expect to be there; and counting me as one, you see how nicely the cabinet would be balanced and ballasted. Besides," said Mr. L., "in talking of General Cameron you admitted that his political status was unexceptionable. I suppose we could say of General Cameron, without offence, that he is 'not Democrat enough to hurt him.' I remember that people used to say, without disturbing my self-respect, that I was not lawyer enough to hurt me." I admitted that I had no political objection to General Cameron, who, I was quite sure, would forget whether applicants for appointment had been Whig or Democrat. I then renewed the suggestion relating to North Carolina or Tennessee, earnestly pressing its importance. Messrs. Davis and Swett united with me in these views. Mr. Lincoln met us with strong counter views, the force of which we were constrained to admit. "If," said Mr. L., "contrary to our hopes, North Carolina and Tennessee should secede, could their men remain in the cabinet? Or, if they remained, of what use would they be to the government?" We, however, continued to press our point, until Mr. Lincoln yielded so far as to say that he would write a letter to the Hon. John A. Gilmer, then a member of Congress from North Carolina, briefly stating his views of the duty of the government in reference to important questions then pending, and inviting him, if those views met his approval, to accept a seat in the cabinet.

"Now," said Mr. Lincoln, "if Mr. Gilmer should come in, somebody must stay out, and that other somebody must be either Judge Blair or Mr. Bates." Messrs. Davis, Swett, and myself exclaimed against dropping Mr. Bates; and so Mr. Lincoln left us to infer that if Mr. Gilmer came in Mr. Blair would be excluded. . . .

In the course of our conversations Mr. Lincoln remarked that it was particularly pleasant to him to reflect that he was coming into office unembarrassed by promises. . . . "I have not," said he, "promised an office to any man, nor have I, but in a single instance, mentally committed myself to an appointment; and as that relates to an important office in you State, I have concluded to mention it to you,—under strict injunctions of secrecy, however. If I am not induced by public considerations to change my purpose, Hiram Barney will be collecter of the port of New York." . . . I remarked that until I met him at the Chicago convention my acquaintance with Mr. Barney was very slight; but that after the convention adjourned Mr. Barney joined us (my daughter and a lady friend) in an excursion down the Mississippi and through Iowa, and that my impressions of him personally and politically were favorable, and that I believed he would make an acceptable collector. . . .

And now, as I was preparing to depart, Mr. Lincoln said: "Some gentlemen, who have been quite nervous about the object of your visit here, would be surprised, if not incredulous, were I to tell them that during the two days we have passed together you have made no application, suggestion, or allusion to appointments." I replied that nothing of that nature had been upon my mind, and that I was much more concerned about the welfare of the country and the successful working of his administration than about matters which would come to perplex all upon whom responsibilities rested, but which it would be both premature and indelicate to obtrude upon him now. "This," said Mr. Lincoln, "is undoubtedly a proper view of the question, and yet so much were you misunderstood that I have received telegrams from prominent Republicans warning me against your efforts to forestall important appointments in your State. Other gentlemen who have visited me since the election have expressed similar apprehensions; but I have remarked that while our friends were extremely sensitive in relation to your designs, they brought along an axe or two of their own to be ground." I told Mr. Lincoln that I had been a great many years actively engaged in political affairs; . . . but that I entertained too high a sense of the honor which the confidence of distinguished statesmen in high public position conferred, to annoy them or stultify myself by thrusting before them unseasonably . . . questions of office . . . that would unavoidably come in due time to engross their thoughts and perplex their judgment. . . .

It is proper to add, before closing . . . that Mr. Lincoln made me the bearer of his letter to Mr. Gilmer, with which I repaired to Washington.

[Lincoln also gave Weed three suggested resolutions for the consideration of the Senate Committee of Thirteen.[10] Weed brought them to Senator Trumbull, who discussed them with Vice-President-elect Hamlin and Senator Seward, who amended them somewhat. The resolutions were then deliberated upon by the Senate Committee and ultimately rejected.[11]]

"Good Ground to Live and to Die By"

SATURDAY, DECEMBER 22, 1860

¶ *In Washington, the weak Buchanan engaged in confused efforts to save the Union and rumors were set afloat of treachery in the councils of the President. Buchanan was debating day and night to determine what to do with the forts—Sumter and Moultrie—in South Carolina. A plot was forming to seize the capital before or on the day of Lincoln's inauguration. In session were committees of Congress deliberating over the thickening crisis. The substance of Lincoln's resolutions—given to Weed for transmission to Washington—were being considered.*

On December 20th, South Carolina formally seceded from the Union, an action Lincoln received calmly. Two days later, South Carolina named three commissioners to lay the ordnance of secession before President Buchanan and Congress and to treat for the delivery of Federal forts and other property into the hands of the state. That day in Springfield, Nicolay scribbled this memorandum: [1]

When Mr. Lincoln came to the office this morning, after the usual salutations, he asked me what the news was. I asked him if he had seen the morning dispatches. He replied "no." "Then," said I, "there is an important rumor you have not seen. The *Times* correspondent telegraphs that Buchanan has sent instructions to Maj. [Robert] Anderson to surrender Fort Moultrie if it is attacked."

"If that is true they ought to hang him [Buchanan]!" said he with warmth.

After some further conversation he remarked—

"Among the letters you saw me mail yesterday was one to [E. B.] Washburne, (of Ill.) who had written me that he had just had a long conversation with Gen. [Winfield] Scott [commander in chief], and that the General felt considerably outraged that the President would not act as he wished him to in reinforcing the forts &c. I wrote to Washburne to tell Gen. Scott confidentially, that I wished him to be prepared, immediately after my inauguration to make arrangements at once to hold the forts, or if they have been taken, to take them back again."

Afterwards he repeated the substance of the above in another conversation with Wm H Herndon; adding at the close with much emphasis: "There can be no doubt that in *any* event that is good ground to live and to die by."

"The Real Question at Issue"
FRIDAY, DECEMBER 28, 1860

¶ *General Duff Green, a Southern political leader related by marriage to Lincoln, arrived in Springfield for a meeting with the President-elect. Once a confidential adviser to Andrew Jackson, he had sided with John C. Calhoun when the Vice-President broke with "Old Hickory." Green supported Henry Clay for President in 1832 and four years later he backed Calhoun. As he faced Lincoln in his home, Green was an envoy of President James Buchanan, assigned to discuss the state of the Union.*

On December 28th—the day he met Lincoln—he wrote of the interview to Buchanan: [1]

I have had a long and interesting conversation with Mr Lincoln. I brought with me a copy of the resolutions submitted by Mr. [John J.] Crittenden which he read over several times and said that he believed that the adoption of the line proposed would quiet *for the present* the agitation of the Slavery question, but believed it would be renewed by the seizure and attempted annexation of Mexico.— He said that the real question at issue between the North & the South, was Slavery "propagandism" and that upon that issue the republican party was opposed to the South and that he was with his own party; that he had been elected by that party and intended to sustain his party in good faith, but added that the question of the Amendments to the Constitution and the questions submitted by Mr. Crittenden, belonged to the people & States in legislatures or Conventions & that he would be inclined not only to acquiesce, but to give full force and effect to their will thus expressed—Seeing that he was embarrassed by his sense of duty to his party; I suggested that he might so frame a letter to me, as to refer the measure for the preservation of the Union to the action of the people in the Several States, and he promised to prepare a letter giving me his views, by 9 A.M. tomorrow—

[Lincoln did not hand the promised letter to Green the next morning. Instead, he sent it to Senator Trumbull in Washington. The letter Lincoln wrote was one "which I believe could not be used to our disadvantage." However, said the President-elect, "if on consultation with our discreet friends you conclude that it may do us harm, do not deliver it." [2] The letter, which was never made public, was apparently delivered to General Green in January. Later, Green sent a report of his interview with Lincoln to Jefferson Davis, stating: ". . . I went to Springfield to see Mr. Lincoln and urge him to go to Washington and exert his influence in aid of the adjustment of the questions then pending between the North and the South. I was authorized by Mr. Buchanan to say to him that if he came he would be received and treated with the courtesy due to the President-elect. I saw Mr. Lincoln . . . and did urge the necessity of his going to Washington and uniting his efforts in behalf of peace, telling him that in my opinion he alone could prevent a civil war, and that if he did not go, upon his conscience must rest the blood that would be shed." [3]]

"Cameron Cannot Be Trusted"

SUNDAY, JANUARY 6, 1861

¶ *At December's end, Lincoln had conferred with Simon Cameron of Pennsylvania. He had said Cameron would be either Secretary of the Treasury or Secretary of War. Cameron—characterized by Senator Charles Sumner as a "political Judas" who reeked "with the* stench of a thousand political battles" [1]—wanted the Treasury port-folio. The furore created by Lincoln's invitation impelled the President-elect to withdraw the offer a few days later.

The Cameron matter was Lincoln's most thorny Cabinet problem. He considered Cameron the most influential man in Pennsylvania. But he was not oblivious to Cameron's record.[2] Known as the "Winnebago Chief," Cameron could not live down the charge that he had swindled the Winnebago Indians out of their claims. Three Presidents had condemned him as an odious character. They used to say that Cameron held that an honest politician was one who "when bought stays bought." [3] A Philadelphian wrote Lincoln about Cameron: "There exists throughout the state an almost universal belief that his fortune has been acquired by means that are forbidden to the man of honor. . . . His appointment would be a signal to all the vultures of the Union to flock around the Treasury." [4] Trumbull believed: "Another serious objection to Cameron is his connection with Gov. Seward. The latter . . . acts through others, and men believe that Cameron would be his instrument in the Cabinet." [5] And Herndon, Lincoln's law partner, summed it all up by saying: "Cameron's appointment to an office in his cabinet bothers him. If Lincoln do appoint Cameron, he gets a fight on his hands, and if he do not, he gets a quarrel deep abiding and lasting. Poor Lincoln! God help him." [6]

Early Sunday morning, January 6, 1861, Lincoln, harassed by the whole affair, called on his friends Gustave Koerner, a German Republican leader, and Norman B. Judd at their hotel in Springfield. Koerner, in his Memoirs, published in 1909, provides a brief account of the interview: [7]

I unbolted the door and in came Mr. Lincoln. "I want to see you and Judd. Where is his room?" I gave him the number, and presently he returned with Judd while I was dressing. "I am in a quandary," he said; "Pennsylvania is entitled to a Cabinet office. But whom shall I appoint?" "Not Cameron," Judd and myself spoke up simultaneously. "But whom else?" We suggested [Ex-Governor A. H.] Reeder or [David] Wilmot [of "Wilmot Proviso" fame]. "Oh," said he, "they have no show. There have been delegation after delegation from Pennsylvania, hundreds of letters and the cry is Cameron, Cameron. Besides, you know I have already fixed on Cameron, Seward, and Bates, my competitors at the convention. The Pennsylvania people say if you leave out Cameron you disgrace him. Is there not something in that?" I said, "Cameron cannot be trusted. He has the reputation of being a tricky and corrupt politician." "I know, I know," said Lincoln; "but can I get along if that State should oppose my administration?" He was very much distressed. We told him he would greatly regret his appointment. Our interview ended in a protest on the part of Judd and myself against the appointment.

"The Conditions of the Peons"

SATURDAY, JANUARY 19, 1861

¶ *Lincoln had an unusual visitor on January 19th. He was Señor Matias Romero, representative of the Mexican Republic in the United States—the first and only foreign dignitary to have visited the President-elect at Springfield. President Benito Juarez was naturally concerned over Lincoln's attitude toward Mexico at the time. Undoubtedly he had heard of the talk that a compromise between North and South might be achieved by conquering Mexico and annexing it to the Union as a slave state. To determine Lincoln's feelings toward the Latin American republic was, therefore, of great importance.*

On December 22, 1860, the Mexican Minister of Foreign Relations, acting on orders from President Juarez, wrote Romero: "It is the wish of the President that you proceed to the place of residence of President-elect Lincoln and in the name of this government, and to make clear to him in an open manner, if opportunity offers, the desire which animates President Juarez, of entering into the most cordial relations with that government [of the United States]." [1] *Upon receipt of these instructions, Romero left Washington for Springfield.*

The Lincoln-Romero conversation was reported by the envoy to the Mexican Minister of Foreign Relations—with the request that it be made known to President Juarez—on January 23, 1861: [2]

I explained the purpose of my visit and read to him [Lincoln] the previously mentioned Note from Y.[our] E.[xcellency] and left him, at his request, a copy of the note in English which I had taken with me for such purpose. Touching on the substance of Mexican affairs, I told him that the only reason for the constant revolutions that have ravaged the Republic since its independence, can be found in the intrigues carried out by the clergy and the army, which in an effort to retain their privileges and impose their yoke on the nation have done away with all the constitutions and kept the country in a state of constant upheaval; but that now that both classes have been subdued and stripped of all privileges, according to official news which I had received that same day, they have been left powerless to arise again in rebellion which gives us ground to not only hope but be sure that Mexico will be able to enjoy peace and prosperity. I indicated to him that the constitutional Government desired to maintain the closest and friendliest relations with the United States and that it intends to provide full protection to its citizens and to facilitate in every way the development of trade and other activities of mutual interest to both countries; that Mexico wants to adopt the same principles of freedom and progress followed here, that have guided his country to achieve such development and prosperity that is without parallel today. I also told him that the Constitutional Government had viewed with great satisfaction the recent victory scored in this country by the republican ideals because such ideals are more in harmony with the principles most deeply rooted in the hearts of the Mexican people and because Mexico hopes that the policy to be followed by the republican administration, under his direction, will be one of true friendship and not guided by narrow, selfish and anti-human principles which the democratic administrations have followed regarding Mexico and which have been directed to strip the Republic of its land with the purpose of extending slavery.

Mr. Lincoln expressed satisfaction in listening to my oral presentation and, when I concluded, he told me in an explicit and vehement manner that he was keenly interested in the peace and prosperity of Mexico; that during his administration, his government would not think of creating any obstacle that might hinder the attainment of these objectives but on the contrary would do everything possible to help achieve them; that Mexico can be sure that as long as he (Mr. Lincoln) remains in power, justice will be done in all questions pending and whatever new questions arise in the future between the two countries and that all matters will be handled in a spirit of complete and friendly understanding. During the course of the conversation, as it was drawing to a close, he told me that he could not foresee any reason which could prove strong enough to make him change his mind on this subject.

He then told me that he would study Mexico's affairs and that, as soon as time allowed, he would send me a letter touching on matters which I have just mentioned above and whatever views he might develop later on the basis of my oral presentation and after studying some booklets which I left him on the situation of the Republic. . . .

Among the questions he raised regarding Mexico, he asked me to explain to him the conditions of the peons in the Republic as people here have exaggerated concepts as to the conditions of the Indian laborers who work in the "haciendas." It is said that they live under conditions of slavery worse than those found among the negroes on the plantations in the South of this country and it is believed that the abuses which unfortunately are committed against workers in some parts [of Mexico] are general and widespread in the Republic and authorized by law. I explained in detail how these abuses have been committed and he expressed great satisfaction when he found out that such practices are contrary to the laws of the Republic and that a stable Government, when it is established, will try to correct them.

[Romero then gave this impression of Lincoln: "Mr. Lincoln did not appear to be well-informed on Mexican affairs . . . [however] I feel sure that the policy of his administration will be guided by the warm feeling he expressed to me as he is a simple and honest man and his words carry the trademark of sincerity and are not the pompous and empty phrases used by persons educated in the school of false pretenses who have the habit of promising much but doing nothing." [3]]

"No Good Results Would Follow"

SATURDAY, FEBRUARY 9, 1861

¶ *The Cameron imbroglio was a motivating factor in Lincoln's decision to make no further Cabinet appointments until he reached Washington. But there were other questions he kept turning over in his mind, the most vital of which was the fate of the Union. On Saturday, Febrauray 9, 1861, Orville H. Browning, prominent Quincy, Illinois, lawyer and Republican leader, visited his friend Lincoln, who by then had left the house on Eighth Street and moved into the Chenery House, preparatory to his departure for Washington. Browning—with his customary brevity—made an entry on this interview in his Diary:* [1]

At night I called at the Chenery House, and had an interview of an hour with Mr. Lincoln[.] We discussed the state of the Country expressing our opinions fully and freely. He agreed entirely with me in believing that no good results would follow the border State Convention now in session in Washington, but evil rather, as increased excitement would follow when it broke up without having accomplished any thing. He agreed with me no concession by the free States short of a surrender of every thing worth preserving, and contending for would satisfy the South, and that Crittendens proposed amendment to the Constitution in the form proposed ought not to be made, and he agreed with me that far less evil & bloodshed would result from an effort to maintain the Union and the Constitution, than from disruption and the formation of two confederacies[.]

I expressed my views very freely, and there was no point upon which we differed. This is the first interview I have had with him since the election, and though brief it was satisfactory. I found him firmer than I had expected[.]

"No Change in the Firm"

SUNDAY, FEBRUARY 10, 1861

¶ *His last day in Springfield saw Lincoln in his old law office talking with his partner, William Henry Herndon. Herndon, nine years Lincoln's junior, first saw the Rail Splitter in 1832 piloting a flatboat down the Sangamon River, and took an immediate liking to him. As years went by, their acquaintance ripened into warm friendship. Herndon had spent three years reading law in the office of Logan & Lincoln. It was a great opportunity for Herndon and he spent many hours zealously poring over cases, attending court, studying legal procedures, listening to his two masters. Shortly after he had been admitted to the bar in 1844, Herndon received an invitation to become Lincoln's law partner. Stunned by the proposition, Herndon said: "Mr. Lincoln this is something unexpected by me— it is an undeserved honor; and yet I say I will gladly & thankfully accept the kind and generous offer." Said Lincoln: "Billy, I can trust you, if you can trust me."* [1] *The deal was made.*

Lincoln was genuinely fond of Herndon and the latter became more than just a business associate. He became a confidential friend as well. In later years, Herndon was to claim that he knew Lincoln better than Lincoln knew himself. In politics, Herndon was Lincoln's "Man Friday" and ardent campaigner in political battles. Herndon was a fiery abolitionist and his radicalism was at times embarrassing to Lincoln. Nevertheless, the two got along famously notwithstanding even Herndon's affinity for liquor and the fact that Mary Lincoln disliked him. Only after Lincoln's election did the friendship cool, primarily because the President-elect adopted close-mouthed tactics in preparing for his new position. But the Lincoln-Herndon relationship remained cordial.

Lincoln's last visit to the law office is described by Herndon—who was to become his partner's controversial biographer—in Herndon's Lincoln: The True Story of a Great Life, *written in collaboration with Jesse W. Weik and published in 1889:* [2]

In the afternoon of his last day in Springfield he came down to our office to examine some papers and confer with me about certain legal matters in which he still felt some interest. On several previous occasions he had told me he was coming over to the office "to have a long talk with me," as he expressed it. We ran over the books and arranged for the completion of all unsettled and unfinished matters. In some cases he had certain requests to make—certain lines of procedure he wished me to observe. After these things were all disposed of he crossed to the opposite side of the room and threw himself down on the old office sofa, which, after many years of service, had been moved against the wall for support. He lay there for some moments, his face towards the ceiling, without either of us speaking. Presently he inquired, "Billy,"—he always called me by that name,— "how long have we been together?" "Over sixteen years," I answered. "We've never had a cross word during all that time, have we?" to which I returned a vehement, "No, indeed we have not." He then recalled some incidents of his early practice and took great pleasure in delineating the ludicrous features of many a lawsuit on the circuit. It was at this last interview in Springfield that he told me of the efforts that had been made by other lawyers to supplant me in the partnership with him. He insisted that such men were weak creatures, who, to use his own language, "hoped to secure a law practice by hanging to his coat-tail." I never saw him in a more cheerful mood. He gathered a bundle of books and papers he wished to take with him and started to go; but before leaving he made the strange request that the sign-board which swung on its rusty hinges at the foot of the stairway should remain. "Let it hang there undisturbed," he said, with a significant lowering of his voice. "Give our clients to understand that the election of a President makes no change in the firm of Lincoln and Herndon. If I live I'm coming back some time, and then we'll go right on practising law as if nothing had ever happened." He lingered for a moment as if to take a last look at the old quarters, and then passed through the door into the narrow hallway. I accompanied him downstairs. On the way he spoke of the unpleasant features surrounding the Presidential office. "I am sick of office-holding already," he complained, "and I shudder when I think of the tasks that are still ahead." He said the sorrow of parting from his old associations was deeper than most persons would imagine, but it was more marked in his case because of the feeling which had become irrepressible that he would never return alive. I argued against the thought, characterizing it as an illusory notion not in harmony or keeping with the popular ideal of a President. "But it is in keeping with my philosophy," was his quick retort. Our conversation was frequently broken in upon by interruptions of passers-by, who, each in succession, seemed desirous of claiming his attention. At length he broke away from them all. Grasping my hand warmly and with a fervent "Good-bye," he disappeared down the street, and never came back to the office again.

[Another aspect of this meeting—revealed by Herndon—was published by Weik in *The Real Lincoln* in 1922. Here Herndon states: "We had finished the details of our business and for a while were engaged in the exchange of reminiscences when suddenly, . . . he blurted out: 'Billy, there's one thing I have, for some time, wanted you to tell me, but I reckon I ought to apologize for my nerve and curiosity in asking it even now.['] 'What is it?' I inquired. 'I want you to tell me,' he said, 'how many times you have been drunk.' It was, of course, a rather blunt inquiry, but unexpected though it was I realized that it came from an honest inquirer, one who had a right to the information, and I therefore answered it as promptly and definitely as the limited sources of knowledge at my command would warrant. Meanwhile I felt sure a lecture or moral admonition would follow and prepared myself accordingly, but much to my surprise nothing more was said by him on that subject." [3]]

"One Term Might Satisfy"
WEDNESDAY, FEBRUARY 20, 1861

¶ *As Lincoln prepared to leave for Washington, according to Henry Villard of the* New York Herald, *the President-elect began "to wear a more sober, solemn expression than heretofore . . ." and "a certain sadness pervades his conversation and restrains the wonted outbursts of humor. . . ."* [1] *On Monday morning, February 11th, he stood on the rear platform of the train before "hundreds of his fellow-citizens, without distinction of party," who had come to bid him farewell.* [2] *He spoke of the sadness of parting from the place where he had lived for a quarter of a century. He did not know whether he would ever return from the task "before me greater than that which rested upon Washington." And he implored the prayers of his townsfolk "that all will yet be well."* [3]

The train moved off to Tolono and Danville, Illinois; across the state line into Indiana, to LaFayette, Indianapolis and Lawrenceburg; into Ohio to Cincinnati, London, Columbus, Newark, Cadiz Junction, Steubenville, Wellsville; thence to Pennsylvania to Rochester, Pittsburg, and again into Ohio to Alliance, Cleveland, Ravenna, Hudson, Painesville, Ashtabula and Conneaut; and again into Pennsylvania to Erie, and into New York to Westfield, Dunkirk, Buffalo, Batavia, Rochester, Clyde, Syracuse, Utica, Little Falls, Fonda, Schenectady, Albany, Troy, Hudson, Poughkeepsie, Fishkill, Peekskill, and New York. At some places Lincoln stopped for only a few minutes; at others much longer. Along the route, the people turned out to see the next President, to listen to him speak a few words or make a short speech.

New York City was filled with excitement at the arrival of the

President-elect. Among the receptions tendered him during his stay here was one at City Hall, the damp day following his arrival. A report of this occasion is given by the New York Herald *in its February 21, 1861, issue:*

At fifteen minutes past eleven o'clock [in the morning, after Lincoln had met the city officials and a few invited guests in the Governor's Room] the door was opened, and the public admitted. . . . The police carried out their instructions . . . to prevent an unusual rush coming upon the President elect. . . . At first they came steadily and regularly, when Mr. Lincoln remarked, "Oh, I could stand it as thick as they come now for six hours!" "You think you could?" interrogated the Mayor [Fernando Wood]. "Oh, yes! easy enough," replied the President elect. . . .

It was agreed that the great rail splitter should shake hands with all who came until twelve o'clock, after which hour he would merely bow to the citizens as they passed. . . . The majority passed without having their names announced, for to go through all that formality would occupy too much time. . . . But as public officials or well known citizens came forward, their names were pronounced by the Mayor, Mr. Cornell [chairman of the Common Council Committee], or some other member of the committee. The Health Officer made his appearance, and the Mayor introduced "Dr. [John C.] Gunn." After he had passed Mr. Lincoln observed, "I suppose he is the author of Gunn's Domestic Medicine;[4] I believe there is such a work." "Yes," was the reply, "he is the same individual."

The shaking of hands [continued] . . . without . . . interruption. . . . The Mayor suggested that he could shut off the stream . . . if he chose. But Mr. Lincoln said, "No; let them come on, and I will shake hands with them till twelve o'clock, and after that hour I will be satisfied if they will pass me without shaking hands.["] . . . One tall fellow with rather short whiskers, as he passed Mr. Lincoln, was heard to say, "Well, he looks like me." "I did not look at him," remarked Old Abe, "but I take it that he is a very handsome man," at which there was inordinate laughter among the immediate spectators.

The work was getting hard enough, the chosen Chief Magistrate was getting warm, so, assisted by the Mayor, he took off his overcoat, and resumed the shaking of hands with additional vigor. Directly behind a fat man waddling along . . . came a tall lank fellow, who said, in a familiar way and a loud tone, "Friend Abraham, how do you do; how is your wife and family?" This fraternal greeting was the signal for great laughter, in which Mr. Lincoln himself heartily joined. The noise of the tumultuous crowd in the corridors, every member of which wanted to be admitted before everybody else, was distinctly heard inside, so that the President elect was constrained to observe, "I suppose there is a great jam outside." "Yes," replied His Honor, "they will keep you here all day if you stay;" to which Mr. Lincoln retorted, with a characteristic smile, "I will stay the two hours out, so as to keep up to the bargain that I made." Every tall man seemed to have a right, on account of his size, to say something as he passed the President elect, while any one who wore a white choker appeared to claim, as a Divine prerogative, that he should quote some appropriate verse of Scripture or offer up a brief but fervent prayer, *en passant,* for the prosperity of Mr. Lincoln and the wisdom of his administration. . . .

A good looking, rotund gentleman from Staten Island stopped to make a little speech:—"As a representative of the inhabitants of Staten Island," he said, "I give you the hearty congratulations of the people of our Island"—at the same time shaking Mr. Lincoln's hand in such a terrific manner that the few policemen close by seemed to be getting ready, expecting that their services might be called into requisition at any moment—"and to assure you," continued the Staten Island gentleman, "that you have the heartfelt prayers [of] our inhabitants, and their earnest hopes that your administration may be instrumental in reuniting the country." Mr. Lincoln listened attentively, smiled, shook the hand of the speaker, who gave another and a final shake, and the Staten Island gentleman passed on with the rest.

This temporary stoppage had blockaded the line somewhat. . . . It was again suggested that as the crowd had become so pressing, Mr. Lincoln had better desist shaking hands before twelve o'clock, and let the people pass with a bow. "No," he said, "I think we had better stand to what we have said," and the shaking was resumed. . . .

A young man, greatly bewildered, his body shaking and his eyes rolling with phrenzy [*sic*], loudly exclaimed as he passed, "Mr. President." Every one in the room burst out into a roar of laughter, which had the effect of bringing back his wits and restoring somewhat his equilibrium.

Another great rush, and on the people came, tumbling over each other as before. . . . A little gentleman, somewhat advanced in years, as he caught the hand of Mr. Lincoln, said, "Thank the Lord, I have seen another President. I hope you will live a good many years, and I hope His counsel will guide you." This pious person was followed by . . . a gentleman from Charleston, who very cordially shook the hand of Mr. Lincoln. Great laughter was caused by this proceeding, and some one, unable to contain himself, roared out, "O, he is a South Carolinian." The Mayor supposed that the President did not consider that out of the pale of his jurisdiction. Mr. Lincoln replied, "I will shake hands with South Carolinians if they will shake hands with me. That is not a very technical question." In the midst of the merriment the Charlestonian had passed, and given place to an indignant individual, who exclaimed, "Please to take care of the Collector of Georgetown, South Carolina: he is in prison awaiting trial for treason." This request, coming directly after the cordial greeting of the South Carolinian, produced increased ebulitions [*sic*] of laughter. . . .

[The] bell in the Park pealed forth the hour of noon. Now the shaking of hands must cease. . . . Some people, not willing to pass with a bow, would manoeuvre with their hands suggestively, but Mr. Lincoln would say, "They won't let me shake hands," and these few words addressed to an individual directly were more pleasing to him than if he had participated in a fraternal shake.

The Veterans of the War of 1812, some in full uniform, and some simply with badges, now made their way up in a body, headed by their commander, Colonel [Henry?] Raymond. The Colonel said, "I must offer to shake hands with you; we are Union men," and Mr. Lincoln replied, "Certainly, I must shake hands with the Veterans." And then the old men, all bearing the marks of age and the signs of service, walked passed [*sic*] him, some of them shaking their heads and saying that it was the last President's hand they expected to shake. Several . . . ladies then made their appearance, and . . . Mr. Lincoln instinctively took hold of their hands. "You make a distinction in favor of the ladies," observed the Mayor, "Yes; their hands don't hurt me," he replied.

. . . One middle aged man was so bold as to promise, "If you satisfy the people this time, Mr. Lincoln, you will receive the unanimous vote of the next electoral college." This tempting offer caused much merriment . . . and Mr. Lincoln aptly remarked, "I think when the clouds look as dark as they do now, one term might satisfy any man." Turning to Mayor Wood, he said, "If you can ever get the city matters so systematized as to hold your present place with any comfort, you will have a good deal to do." The Mayor intimated that it was a difficult matter, and the reply was, "But you have done a good deal to systematize them already."

. . . Now there entered an exceedingly tall, wiry looking individual, who, the moment he entered the door, commenced straightening himself to the full extent of his altitude. When he came alongside of the gigantic proportions of the President elect, he stopped and disputed the question as to which was the taller. Amid a good deal of merriment Mr. Lincoln said, "I will contest it with you;" whereupon they put their backs together, when Lincoln was found to have a slight advantage. Considerably crestfallen the tall man passed on, the crowd laughing at him as he went. "I saw that he was running a tilt with me, and was stretching himself to make the issue with me," said the taller rail splitter, "and I was determined to take him down." Speaking on the question of altitude, he added, "I have always said on that subject that there is considerable 'outcome' in me." Along the stream continued to flow after this slight interruption. . . .

"I wish to shake hands with you—I'm from Canada," said one individual. Mr. Lincoln complied with the request, remarking "They have forbid me shaking hands, but I will shake hands with a person from a foreign nation." This reply provoked considerable laughter. A gentlemen from Illinois shook hands with Mr. Lincoln, who whispered something in his ear, which seemed to please him exceedingly. . . . Somehow, everybody expected that an exception would be made in their case, and that he would shake hands with them. "They won't let me shake hands with you," he said to one young fellow, "but if you had a sister here, then I could shake hands with her," at which there was a good deal of laughter, and an old gentleman coming past remarked, *appropos* [*sic*], "None but the brave deserve the fair."

. . . [Among the] last incident[s] that marked this curious reception was the entrance of a mammoth man, who . . . was . . . at least a couple of inches taller than the President elect. His appearance at once elicited loud laughter, and as he came near the Mayor said to

Mr. Lincoln, "I guess you will have to come down now." The great rail-splitter shrugged his shoulders and acknowledged that he was beaten. This mammoth man . . . a butter dealer, was six feet six inches in height, and weighed 250 pounds. Mr. Lincoln remarked that he himself was a little short of six feet four inches, with his boots off, calculating all the "outcome" that was in him. Soon, a short gentleman came along and said, "Abe, how d'ye do? I hope you will take care of us all." "You take care of me," said he; and "I will do my duty," replied the man. . . .

One o'clock had now arrived, the doors were closed and no more people admitted.

"Hostility . . . to Gen. Cameron"

THURSDAY, FEBRUARY 21, 1861

¶ *Lincoln continued his journey toward Washington. At Philadelphia, he had an important meeting with Pennsylvania Republicans on the Cameron affair. Fearful that division over Cameron's appointment to the Cabinet might prevent Pennsylvania from being represented in the Presidential council, his enemies had joined his supporters and were now urging Lincoln to consider favorably the claims of the "Winnebago Chief." Thus emissaries of Governor Andrew G. Curtin traveled to Philadelphia for a private interview with the President-elect at the Continental Hotel.*

What happened at this conference is reported by James Millikin,[1] Pennsylvania iron and coal magnate and a Curtin man, and Titian J. Coffey,[2] an organizer of the Republican Party in the Keystone State, who was there to promote Cameron's interests. In separate letters to Cameron dated February 22, 1861, both reported on the interview of the previous day, each manifesting some apprehension over the possibility that Lincoln might wish to retain some members of Buchanan's Cabinet. Millikin begins our narrative:

I had in this room, Mr. [Morton] McMichael [owner and editor of the *Philadelphia North American*], Mr. Tithian J. Coffy [*sic*], Mr. [Samuel A.] Purviance [former Congressman and now], Atty Genl. [of Pennsylvania] and Mr. [Henry D.] Moore, the State Treas. [of Pennsylvania.] My presence at the door, on Mr. L's entrance was discovered, and the *howl* of alarm, on the part of these cormorants, of whom I have spoken [i.e., office seekers], *"that Mr. Millikin was closeted with the President"* was disgusting, some of the particulars of which I reserve for your private ear.

I addressed Mr. Lincoln frankly and candidly. I pointed out our political position, and the importance that the state should stand as a unit on all questions relating to his administration and the state administration, and that I was now authorized to speak, for the Governor, Mr. [Alexander K.] McClure [another founder of the Republican Party in Pennsylvania] and the members of the state administration, present and say that all opposition to your appointment had been withdrawn and your appointment desired. That I also represented the Iron and Coal men of Penn., and for that large class and their interests—with very few individual exceptions—I was also authorised to speak and that they too desired your appointment. That for the Press, Mr. McMichael would speak, which he did, and, that with your appointment, his administration should receive our hearty support.

[Coffey takes up the story here:]

Messrs. Purviance & Moore as members of the State Administration bore to Mr. Lincoln the formal request of Gov. Curtin that you should be made Secty of the Treasury. . . . We thus presented your name from Penna. as a unit and on behalf of the State asked the appointment. Each of us urged this matter from such points of view as occurred to us and, I think, effectively. Mr. Lincoln talked to us very frankly and I desire to give you exactly what he said. He expressed great pleasure at the unanimity of the State for you and added, what you know he has said before, that all along the preponderance in Penna. was so largely in your favor that he did not consider the opposition from Penna. to you, sufficient to prevent your appointment, but he added, the kind of hostility expressed to Gen. Cameron by those who opposed him in Penna. has spread to other states and it is from those states that the greatest opposition is made. He said the question would be settled when he reached Washington and he said there were some questions which might have to be considered then, arising out of the state of the Country, for instance, he added, it *may* become expedient to retain in the Cabinet some of those who are now doing well [in Buchanan's Cabinet] and if any of them be retained, some of those whose claims are pressed on me must be kept out. He said I merely suggest this, without saying it will be done. In this connexion he named [Joseph] Holt & [John A.] Dix, [and, according to Millikin, also Edwin M. Stanton] but said he didn't of course know whether they would consent to remain, if it should be expedient to invite them to do so.

"Mr. Lincoln . . . Had No Fears"

FRIDAY, FEBRUARY 22, 1861

¶ *Lincoln's arrival at Philadelphia on February 21st set off a chain of events that were to involve the President-elect in a series of cloak-and-dagger maneuvers as a means of getting him to Washington. The hero of this episode was a short, bearded Scotsman, Allan Pinkerton, a private detective who had been hired by S. M. Felton, president of the Philadelpia, Wilmington & Baltimore Railroad, to investigate rumors that Baltimore secessionists planned to disrupt the railroad along the Lincoln route in an effort to kill the next President. Reports from Pinkerton's operatives convinced him that the plot was real.*

That night, after Pinkerton had reported the details of the plot to Norman B. Judd, the two hastened to the Continental Hotel, where they held a secret meeting with Lincoln. They urged the President-elect "to leave for Washington on the train to-night," thereby outwitting the "plug uglies" by coming through ahead of schedule. But Lincoln refused. He had to carry out commitments which included raising the flag on Independence Hall "to-morrow morning (Washington's birthday)," and going to Harrisburg later in the day. If Judd and Pinkerton felt he was in danger, then, said Lincoln, "I shall endeavor to get away quietly from the people at Harrisburg to-morrow evening and shall place myself in your [hands"].[1]

According to Pinkerton, the plan adopted was that "if Mr. Lincoln could manage to get away unobserved, from . . . Harrisburg by about dusk to-morrow . . . we could get a special Train on the Pennsylvania Rail Road to bring him from Harrisburg to Philadelphia in time for the train going South . . . when we could secure seats in the sleeping Car which goes through to Washington and thus save us from being observed at Baltimore." [2]

The next night—February 22nd—about three minutes after ten o'clock, Pinkerton, at West Philadelphia, met Lincoln, who was accompanied by Ward H. Lamon and two railroad officials. Lincoln wore "a brown Kossuth Hat, and an overcoat thrown loosely over his shoulders." The evening was chilly but not cold. After the railroad officials had left and Pinkerton had been joined by one of his men, the party entered a waiting carriage. The train was not scheduled to depart until 11:50 P.M. Pinkerton ordered his man "to get on the box with the Driver and consume the time by driving Northward in search of some imaginary person, so that we should not arrive at the Depot until about 11.00 p.m."

Pinkerton's Record Book of 1861 *contains an account of the conversation with Lincoln that night:* [3]

Mr. Lincoln said that after I had left him last night at the Continental, and he had gone to bed, that a son of Governor Seward's [Frederick W. Seward] had called him up, and delivered him letters from his Father (Governor Seward) and General Scott, Stating substantially the same as I had, but much stronger: that about Fifteen Thousand men were organized to prevent his passage through Baltimore, and that arrangements were made by these parties to blow up the Rail Road track, fire the Train &c., and urging him (Lincoln) to change his route. Mr. Lincoln said that he had received the letters, but merely told young Mr. Seward that he would give him an answer at Harrisburg: that he (Mr. Lincoln) had in the morning after leaving Philadelphia told Mr. Judd about this, and on Mr. Judd's advice he had finally told young Seward that "He would change his route": that after pledging himself to me to secrecy he did not think he had the right to speak to anyone on the subject, nor would not until Mr. Judd told him he (Judd) would take the responsibility of his (Lincoln's) telling Seward and make it right with me.

Mr. Lincoln also said that upon his telling Mrs. Lincoln of the step he was about to take that she insisted upon Mr. Lamon accompanying him, and that he (Lincoln) found it impossible to get away from the crowd without the aid of Governor Curtin and Col. [Edwin V.] Sumner, whom he was finally obliged to inform of this movement to secure their co-operation in order to cover his absence: that all approved of the step he had taken, but the Military men were anxious to accompany him, expressing doubt but that I might be leading him into a trap and selling him (Lincoln) to the Secessionists —to all of which Mr. Lincoln said that he knew me, and had confidence in me and would trust himself and his life in my hands.

Mr. Lincoln said that from the great interest I had manifested in this matter he had every confidence in me.

Mr. Lamon offered Mr. Lincoln a Revolver and Bowie Knife and I at once protested, saying that I would not for the world have it said that Mr. Lincoln had to enter the National Capitol Armed: that I anticipated no trouble: that if we went through at all we must do so by stratagem, but that if fighting had to be done, it must be done by others than Mr. Lincoln. Mr. Lincoln said that he wanted no arms: that he had no fears and that he felt satisfied that all my plans would work right.

Mr. Lincoln was cool, calm, and self possessed—firm and determined in his bearing. He evinced no sign of fear or distrust, and throughout the entire night was quite self possessed.

On arriving at the vicinity of the Depot we left the carriage, and I walked round the corner to the Depot. Mr. Lincoln and Mr. Lamon followed. I met Mr. [George R.] Dunn [agent for the Harnden's Express Company, who was working with Pinkerton] in the Depot who showed me to the sleeping car. I entered by the rear, followed by Mr. Lincoln—no one appeared to notice us. . . . Mr. Dunn soon left us and in about three minutes from the time we got aboard the train started.

. . . Mr. Lincoln soon laid down in his Berth, and when the Conductor came around for his Tickets, I handed him the Tickets for Mr. Lincoln. He did not look in the Berths at all—left and did not return again during the trip.

None of our party appeared to be sleepy, but we all lay quiet and nothing of importance transpired.

[The Lincoln party arrived in Washington about 6 A.M., on February 23rd.]

"Plain as a Turnpike Road"

SATURDAY, FEBRUARY 23, 1861

¶ *After breakfast Lincoln, accompanied by Seward, made a courtesy call on President Buchanan. This formality done with, the President-elect and Seward went to General Scott's office only to find him absent. Subsequently the general, hearing that Lincoln had come to see him, hastened to Willard's Hotel to meet the incoming Chief Executive. Others also began flocking to Willard's: Vice-President-elect Hamlin, Francis P. Blair, Sr., Montgomery Blair, the entire Illinois Congressional delegation, including Senator Douglas. All wished to pay their respects to Lincoln; some attempted to confer on Cabinet matters. Later in the day, Mrs. Lincoln and her sons arrived.*

Lincoln's unexpected entry into Washington created quite a sensation. Rumor had it that he had come through Baltimore "locked up in an Adams Express car," [2] wearing a Scotch cap and a borrowed shawl; that he had "crept into Washington" [3] like "a thief in the night." [4] Newspapers explained his unusual arrival as having been motivated "solely by an official communication from General Scott, predicated upon sufficient information which he had received of the danger of a riot at Baltimore, and probably of a desperate determination at assault on the route. . . . While Mr. Lincoln entertained no apprehensions for his own safety, he did not feel justified in hazarding the public peace. . . ." [5]

That night in Parlor No. 6 at Willard's Hotel, Lincoln received delegates to the Peace Conference, which had been called by Virginia, and was being attended by representatives from twenty-one states "to bring back the cotton states and thereby restore the Constitution and the Union of the States."

Lucius E. Chittenden, a member of the Vermont delegation, has left an account of this reception in his Recollections of President Lincoln and His Administration, *published in 1891. However, it should be noted that this record, made many years after the event, was obviously embroidered in the recollection. The language attributed to Lincoln has a stilted, non-Lincolnian tone. Nevertheless it is included in this volume because the reception did take place and the Chittenden account is—to the best of our knowledge—the only one available of this occurrence: [6]*

Mr. Lincoln's reception of the delegates was of an entirely informal character. . . . He had some apt observation for each person ready the moment he heard his name. "You are a smaller man than I supposed—I mean in person: every one is acquainted with the greatness of your intellect. It is, indeed, pleasant to meet one who has so honorably represented his country in Congress and abroad." Such was his greeting to William C. Rives, of Virginia, a most cultivated and polished gentleman. "Your name is all the endorsement you require," he said to James B. Clay. "From my boyhood the name of Henry Clay has been an inspiration to me." "You cannot be a disunionist, unless your nature has changed since we met in Congress!" he exclaimed as he recognized the strong face of Geo. W. Summers, of Western Virginia. "Does liberty still thrive in the mountains of Tennessee?" he inquired as Mr. [Felix K.] Zollicoffer's figure, almost as tall as his own, came into view. After so many years, much that he said is forgotten, but it is remembered that he had for every delegation, almost for every man, some appropriate remark, which was forcible, and apparently unstudied.

There was only one occurrence which threatened to disturb the harmony and good humor of the reception. In reply to a complimentary remark by Mr. Lincoln, Mr. Rives had said that, although he had retired from public life, he could not decline the request of the Governor of Virginia that he should unite in this effort to save the Union. "But," he continued, "the clouds that hang over it are very dark. I have no longer the courage of my younger days. I can do little—you can do much. Everything now depends upon you."

"I cannot agree to that," replied Mr. Lincoln. "My course is as plain as a turnpike road. It is marked out by the Constitution. I am in no doubt which way to go. Suppose now we all stop discussing and try the experiment of obedience to the Constitution and the laws. Don't you think it would work?"

"Permit me to answer that suggestion," interposed Mr. Summers. "Yes, it will work. If the Constitution is your light, I will follow it with you, and the people of the South will go with us."

"It is not of your professions we complain," sharply struck in Mr. [James A.] Seddon's sepulchral voice. "It is of your sins of omission —of your failure to enforce the laws—to suppress your John Browns and your Garrisons, who preach insurrection and make war upon our property!"

"I believe John Brown was hung and Mr. Garrison imprisoned," dryly remarked Mr. Lincoln. "You cannot justly charge the North with disobedience to statutes or with failing to enforce them. You have made some which were very offensive, but they have been enforced, notwithstanding."

"You do not enforce the laws," persisted Mr. Seddon. "You refuse to execute the statute for the return of fugitive slaves. Your leading men openly declare that they will not assist the marshals to capture or return slaves."

"You are wrong in your facts again," said Mr. Lincoln. "Your slaves have been returned, yes, from the shadow of Faneuil Hall in the heart of Boston. Our people do not like the work, I know. They will do what the law commands, but they will not volunteer to act as tip-staves or bum-bailiffs. The instinct is natural to the race. Is it not true of the South? Would you join in the pursuit of a fugitive slave if you could avoid it? Is such the work of gentlemen?"

"Your press is incendiary!" said Mr. Seddon, changing his base. "It advocates servile insurrection, and advises our slaves to cut their masters' throats. You do not suppress your newspapers. You encourage their violence."

"I beg your pardon, Mr. Seddon," replied Mr. Lincoln. "I intend no offence, but I will not suffer such a statement to pass unchallenged, because it is not true. No Northern newspaper, not the most ultra, has advocated a slave insurrection or advised the slaves to cut their masters' throats. A gentleman of your intelligence should not make such assertions. We do maintain the freedom of the press— we deem it necessary to a free government. Are we peculiar in that respect? Is not the same doctrine held in the South?"

It was reserved for the delegation from New York to call out from Mr. Lincoln his first expression touching the great controversy of the hour. He exchanged remarks with ex-Governor [John A.] King, Judge [Amaziah B.] James, William Curtis Noyes, and Francis Granger. William E. Dodge had stood, awaiting his turn. As soon as his opportunity came, he raised his voice enough to be heard by all present, and, addressing Mr. Lincoln, declared that the whole country in great anxiety was awaiting his inaugural address, and then added: "It is for you, sir, to say whether the whole nation shall be plunged into bankruptcy; whether the grass shall grow in the streets of our commercial cities."

"Then I say it shall not," he answered, with a merry twinkle of his eye. "If it depends upon me, the grass will not grow anywhere except in the fields and the meadows."

"Then you will yield to the just demands of the South. You will leave her to control her own institutions. You will admit slave states into the Union on the same conditions as free states. You will not go to war on account of slavery!"

A sad but stern expression swept over Mr. Lincoln's face. "I do not know that I understand your meaning, Mr. Dodge," he said, without raising his voice, "nor do I know what my acts or my opinions may be in the future, beyond this. If I shall ever come to the great office of President of the United States, I shall take an oath. I shall swear that I will faithfully execute the office of President of the United States, of all the United States, and that I will, to the best of my ability, preserve, protect, and defend the Constitution of the United States. This is a great and solemn duty. With the support of the people and the assistance of the Almighty I shall undertake to perform it. I have full faith that I shall perform it. It is not the Constitution as I would like to have it, but as it *is,* that is to be defended. The Constitution will not be preserved and defended until it is enforced and obeyed in every part of every one of the United States. It must be so respected, obeyed, enforced, and defended, let the grass grow where it may."

Not a word or a whisper broke the silence . . . Mr. Dodge attempted no reply. . . . Some of the more ardent Southerners silently left the room. . . . For the more conservative Southern delegates, the statesmen, Mr. Lincoln seemed to offer an attraction. They remained until he finally retired.

A delegate from New Jersey asked Mr. Lincoln pointedly if the North should not make further concessions to avoid civil war? For example, consent that the people of a territory should determine its right to authorize slavery when admitted into the Union?

"It will be time to consider that question when it arises," he replied. "Now we have other questions which we must decide. In a choice of evils, war may not always be the worst. Still I would do all in my power to avert it, except to neglect a Constitutional duty. As to slavery, it must be content with what it has. The voice of the civilized world is against it; it is opposed to its growth or extension. Freedom is the natural condition of the human race, in which the Almighty intended men to live. Those who fight the purposes of the Almighty will not succeed. They always have been, they always will be, beaten."

"If . . . Washington Occupied the Seat"

WEDNESDAY, FEBRUARY 27, 1861

¶ *Shortly after Lincoln's arrival in Washington, Judge Stephen T. Logan, who had been his second law partner in Springfield, went to see Charles S. Morehead of Kentucky. Morehead, a former Whig, had been elected Governor of his state in 1855 on the American or Know-Nothing ticket, and was now in Washington as a member of the Peace Conference. Logan told Morehead—who had served in Congress with Lincoln in 1848—that the President-elect desired a private interview with the Kentuckian.*

Morehead, champion of States' Rights even if it meant forsaking the Union, had recently been assured by Seward that "let me once hold the reins of power in my hands" there would be "no collision between the North and the South." [1] *However, Morehead confessed, he had "little confidence" in Seward. Now that Lincoln beckoned him to a meeting, Morehead insisted that "other gentlemen should be with me." This was apparently agreeable to Lincoln and several days later, Morehead, accompanied by W. C. Rives and George W. Summers, both of Virginia, General Alexander W. Doniphan of Missouri, and James Guthrie of Kentucky, arrived at Willard's Hotel for the conference with the President-elect.*

Morehead made detailed notes of this conversation as soon as it ended. Our report is taken from a speech—obviously antagonistic to Lincoln—he made in Liverpool, England, on October 9, 1862, which was published four days later in the Liverpool Mercury: [2]

Mr. Lincoln commenced the conversation, after receiving us very kindly, by stating that he was accidentally elected President of the United States; that he had never aspired to a position of that kind; that it had never entered into his head; but that from the fact of his having made a race for the Senate of the United States with Judge Douglas, in the state of Illinois, his name became prominent, and he was accidentally selected and elected afterwards as President of the United States; that running that race [with Douglas] in a local election his speeches had been published; and that anyone might examine his speeches and they would find that he had said nothing against the interests of the South. He defied them to point out any one sentence in all the various addresses that he had made in that canvass that could be tortured into enmity against the South, except, he remarked, one expression, namely, that "a house divided against itself must fall; they must either be all slaves or all free states," and he said that he explained afterwards that that was an abstract opinion, and never intended to be made the basis of his political action. He remarked at the same time that the clause in the constitution of the United States requiring fugitive slaves to be delivered up was a constitutional provision, was a part of the organic law of the land, and that he would execute that with more fidelity than any Southern man they could possibly find, and he could not imagine what was the cause of the deep and apparently settled enmity that existed towards him throughout the entire South, looking at me at the time as if to invite an answer from me. I replied that he was very much mistaken if he supposed that the deep pervading feeling throughout the South originated in any personal enmity towards himself; that I did not suppose that there was any feeling of that kind on the part of an individual in the South; that he was the representative of a great party, of a merely sectional party, elected on a platform which they considered would, if carried out, be destructive of their dearest and best rights; and that it was on that account and that alone—the attempt to throw a common government, the government for all the states in antagonism to the interests of a portion of the very states whose government it was—which was the cause of the deep and settled feeling which existed throughout the entire South. We appealed to him then to give the guarantees which were demanded by the Southern men in that Peace Conference, representing to him that it was in his power, that he was at that time a power in the state, that he held in the hollow of his hand the destiny of 30 millions of people, that if he said that the guarantee should be made and would make it, there would be no difficulty in carrying out any programme that might be adopted. He said that he was willing to give a constitutional guarantee that slavery should not be molested in any way directly or indirectly in the States; that he was willing to go further, and give a guarantee that it should not be molested in the district of Columbia; that he would go still further, and say that it should not be disturbed in the docks, arsenals, forts, and other places within the slave-holding states;

but as for slavery in the territories, that his whole life was dedicated in opposition to its extension there; that he was elected by a party which had made that a portion of its platform, and he should consider that he was betraying that party if he ever agreed, under any state of the case, to allow slavery to be extended in the territories. We pointed out to him that there was not an acre of territory belonging to the United States where the foot of a slave could ever tread; that there were natural laws which would forbid slavery going into New Mexico, a mountainous region, and the colder regions of the North; and that it was utterly impossible that slavery could ever be extended there; and we denied that a common government had power to make the prohibition, and asked him why, if he was a really true sincere Union man, have an empty prohibition when the laws of nature were a stronger prohibition than any that could be passed by act of Congress. . . . That he waived by saying that he was committed on this subject. Then it was that I replied to him— "Mr. President, you say you were accidentally selected and elected by a party. You were the candidate of the party; but when you were elected, sir, I thought—I have been taught to believe—that you were the President of the Union. I opposed you, sir," I said to him, "with all the zeal and energy of which I was master. I endeavoured to prevent your election, not because I had any personal feelings of enmity towards you, but because I believed it would lead to the very result we now witness. I opposed you, sir, but you are my President; you have been elected according to the forms of the constitution, and you are the President of the people of the United States, and I think that some little deference is due to the opinions of those who constitute the majority, according to the vote that had been polled, of 1,100,000 men in the United States." He at once rather briskly [brusquely?] said, "If he was a minority President he was not the first, and that at all events he had obtained more votes than we could muster for any other man." I think, as near as I can recollect, those are about his identical words. I responded at once to him that I did not intend to recall to him that he was a minority President, but simply to announce the broad fact that he was the President, not of the men who voted for him, but of the whole people of the United States, and that of the wishes and feelings and interests of the whole people of the United States—the party with 1,100,000 majority as well as the minority party by whom he was elected, ought to be consulted by him. General Doniphan here interposed and presented three alternative propositions to him. First, that he might remain perfectly idle and passive and let the disintegration of the States go on as it had gone on; secondly, give guarantees such as were asked and bring the whole power of his administration to bear in obtaining those guarantees; or, thirdly, resort to coercion and attempt to force the seceding States into obedience. He illustrated very distinctly and clearly those three propositions. When the conversation had slackened a little, I ventured to appeal to him [Lincoln], in a manner in which I never appealed to any other man and never expect to do again. I said that as to the last proposition I desired to say one word—that I trusted and prayed to God that he would not resort to coercion; that if he did, the history of his Administration would be written in blood, and all the waters of the Atlantic Ocean could never wash it from his hands. . . . He asked me what I would do, and if I meant by coercion the collecting of the revenue and the taking back of the forts which he said belonged to the United States. I replied that that was the only mode in which it was possible that he could under the constitution resort to coercion—by an attempt to collect the revenue and to take back the forts. He had placed himself in a chair with rounds to it, with his feet upon the highest round —a long, lanky man, with very large side whiskers, with his elbows upon his knees, and his hands upon the sides of his face, in an attitude of listening, and when he would speak he would drop his hands, and raise his head. Dropping his hands and raising his head, he said he would tell me a little anecdote which had happened when he first came to the bar. An old man, he said, had applied to him to bring a suit, and made out a capital case as he thought, but when the evidence was detailed before the jury it was the worst case that he had ever listened to, and whilst the evidence was going on the old man came listening to the evidence himself, and whispered in his ear, "Guv it up." . . . "Now," said he, "governor, wouldn't this be 'guvin it up'?" I assure you, . . . I don't present it in any light different from that in which it actually occurred—none whatever. I said to him, "Mr. President, it may be said that it would be 'guvin it up,' but hadn't you better 'guv it up' without bloodshed than drench this land with blood, and then *have* to 'guv it up?' " . . . He then asked what he was to do with his oath of office. He said he had sworn [would swear] to see the laws faithfully executed, and addressing himself to

me, he said, "I would like to know from you what I am to do with
my oath of office." I said to him that he had taken [would take] a
solemn oath to see the laws faithfully executed, but that Congress was
then in session, and application had been made to Congress to give
to the President of the United States the power to collect the revenue
by armed vessels outside of the ports, and Congress had refused to
give that power. "If," I said, "Congress fails to give the necessary
power, Mr. President, to you to collect the revenue by vessels outside the ports, how are you to collect it? Do you think that you can
send a collector to the port of Charleston, to the port of Savannah,
or of New Orleans to collect the revenue there? Is it not an impossibility, and does your oath bind you to do a thing that is impossible? As to the forts, that is a matter within your discretion, sir.
You can withdraw the troops if you please. You are the commander-
in-chief, and it belongs to you, either to keep them there or withdraw
them totally, and prevent a collision, and a consequent deadly and
ruinous war." "Well," said he, raising himself again, "I will only
answer you by telling you a little anecdote which struck me—excuse
me," says he, "a little anecdote which struck me as you were going
on. It is from Aesop's Fables, and doubtless in your schoolboy days
you have read it. Aesop, you know," says he, "illustrates great
principles often by making mute animals speak and act, and according to him there was a lion once that was desperately in love with
a beautiful lady, and he courted the lady, and the lady became
enamoured of him and agreed to marry him, and the old people
were asked for their consent. They were afraid of the power of the
lion with his long and sharp claws and his tusks, and they said to
him 'We can have no objection to so respectable a personage as you,
but our daughter is frail and delicate, and we hope that you will
submit to have your claws cut off and your tusks drawn, because
they might do very serious injury to her.' The lion submitted, being
very much in love. His claws were cut off and his tusks drawn, and
they took clubs then and knocked him on the head." . . . I replied,
I think, about in substance this—that it was an exceedingly interesting
anecdote, and very *apropos,* but not altogether a satisfactory answer
to me, and then said to him, "Mr. Lincoln, this to me, sir, is the
most serious and all-absorbing subject that has ever engaged my
attention as a public man. I deprecate and look with horror upon a
fratricidal war. I look to the injury that it is to do, not only to

my own section—that I know is to be desolated and drenched in blood—but I look to the injury it is to do to the cause of humanity itself, and I appeal to you, apart from these jests, to lend us your aid and countenance in averting a calamity like that." Before he replied, Mr. Rives of Virginia got up. We had before that conversed sitting in a semi-circle round the President; but Mr. Rives rose from his chair, and, with a dignity and an eloquence I have seldom heard surpassed in the course of my life, he appealed to him. I could not pretend to give even the substance of his speech, but I remember that he told him that he was then a very old man; that there never had been a throb of his heart that was not in favour of the perpetuation of the Union; that he came there with a hope and a wish to perpetuate it, and that all his efforts had been exerted in endeavouring to procure such guarantees as would perpetuate it; but that he desired to say to him—and he said it with a trembling voice—in order that he might know, and not say thereafter that he was not fully warned, that he agreed with every word I had said with regard to the horrors of this anticipated war, and that if he did resort to coercion, Virginia would leave the Union and join the seceding States. "Nay, sir," he said, "old as I am, and dearly as I have loved this Union, in that event I go, with all my heart and soul." . . . Mr. Lincoln jumped up from his chair, as Mr. Rives was standing, advanced one step towards him, and said, "Mr. Rives! Mr. Rives! if Virginia will stay in, I will withdraw the troops from Fort Sumter." [3] Mr. Rives stepped back and said, "Mr. President, I have no authority to speak for Virginia. I am one of the humblest of her sons; but if you do that it will be one of the wisest things you have ever done. Do that, and give us guarantees, and I can only promise you that whatever influence I possess shall be exerted to promote the Union and to restore it to what it was." We then all of us got up and were standing. I was on the outer circle. He [Lincoln] said, "Well, gentlemen, I have been wondering very much whether, if Mr. Douglas or Mr. Bell had been elected President, you would have dared talk to him as freely as you have to me." I did not exactly hear the answer, but I am told that Mr. Guthrie answered about in this way. "Mr. President, if General Washington occupied the seat you will soon fill, and it had been necessary to talk to him as we have to you to save such a Union as this, I for one should talk to him as we have to you." . . . That closed the conversation.

Chapter Three

"THINK CALMLY AND WELL"

SOUTH CAROLINA's secession on December 20th set off a chain reaction that was to take six other states of the Lower South out of the Union before Lincoln's inauguration. It precipitated secessionist demonstrations not only in such cities as New Orleans, Mobile, Norfolk, Wilmington (Delaware), Baltimore and Petersburg, but even in Washington. The Southerners—even the Unionists among them—believed they had a constitutional right to secede from the Union at will. The fire-eating rebels were determined to exercise that right. And Buchanan did nothing to stop them.

Secessionists began seizing post offices, customhouses, navy yards, Federal arsenals and Federal courts. Southern men were appearing openly in Northern cities to purchase arms and munitions. Rebel militiamen were on the alert. Rabble rousers were active. Said Seward: "Mad men North and mad men South, are working together to produce a dissolution of the Union, by civil war." [1]

There were leading Republicans and prominent Southern leaders who urged: Let the Southern states depart in peace! But the *New Orleans Picayune* thundered: "Peaceful secession is a myth. It is a mere phrase to conceal the sad train of events that are inevitably to follow." [2]

In Washington, there was treason in the Cabinet and rumors of thievery and treachery in the government. Buchanan's own actions betrayed a marked sympathy for the South despite his refusal to withdraw Federal troops from Charleston Harbor with its three

91

forts, Moultrie, Castle Pinckney and Sumter. Major Robert Anderson of Kentucky, commander of Federal forces, had been given permission to withdraw from Moultrie to Sumter if he saw fit to do so. When he did, the Palmettos were quick to occupy the other two garrisons. On January 9, 1861, the unarmed merchant vessel *Star of the West,* sent by Buchanan to reinforce Sumter, was fired upon by rebel shore batteries and forced to turn back. And still Buchanan did nothing. The Sumter dilemma remained unchanged. South Carolinians busied themselves strengthening their own positions in Charleston Harbor.

Early in February, thirty-seven representatives of six of the seceded states—Alabama, Florida, Georgia, Louisiana, Mississippi and South Carolina (Texas did not participate)—met at Montgomery, Alabama, to form a provisional government of the Confederate States of America. In Washington, there was mounting tension. There was talk that the South would seize the capital to prevent the official counting of the electoral vote on February 13th, as General Scott warned: "any man who attempted by force . . . to obstruct or interfere with the lawful count of the electoral vote . . . should be lashed to the muzzle of a twelve-pounder gun and fired out of a window of the Capitol." [3] The vote was counted without incident and Lincoln's election was declared official.

On February 18th, as Lincoln reached Albany on his way to Washington, word came that Jefferson Davis of Mississippi had been inaugurated provisional President of the Confederacy with Alexander H. Stephens of Georgia as his Vice-President. Establishment of the new government was the signal for Southern members of the United States Senate and House of Representatives to take their leave from Washington and return to their respective states.

Such was the situation as Lincoln stepped onto the guarded temporary platform above the steps of the East Portico of the Capitol, "his tall, gaunt figure" rising "above those around him," [4] and prepared to deliver his Inaugural Address, defining the conciliatory but firm policy his incoming Administration proposed to follow.

Speaking amid reports of rebel plots to capture the Federal Government and to obstruct his installation as President by assassination, Lincoln told the nation that Southern states had nothing to fear from a Republican Administration; that "their property, and their peace, and personal security" would not be "endangered." The adjourning

Congress had passed the Thirteenth Amendment to the Constitution —which was never to be ratified by the states—barring forever Federal interference with slavery in the states where it existed. Lincoln had "no objection" to the measure being made "irrevocable." The Fugitive Slave Law would be upheld, he declared, but added that there ought to be "all the safeguards . . . so that a free man be not, in any case, surrendered as a slave."

Declaring that "the Union of these States is perpetual," Lincoln maintained that "the Union is unbroken." He pledged himself to uphold faithfully the laws of the Union—"a simple duty on my part; and I shall perform it, so far as practicable, unless my rightful masters, the American people, shall withhold the requisite means, or, in some authoritative manner, direct the contrary." There would be no bloodshed unless the Federal Government was forced into violence.

"The power confided in me," he stated, "will be used to hold, occupy, and possess the property, and places belonging to the government, and to collect the duties and imposts; but beyond what may be necessary for these objects, there will be no invasion—no using of force against, or among the people anywhere. Where hostility to the United States, in any interior locality, shall be so great and so universal, as to prevent competent resident citizens from holding the Federal offices, there will be no attempt to force obnoxious strangers among the people for that object. While the strict legal right may exist in the government to enforce the exercise of these offices, the attempt to do so would be so irritating . . . that I deem it better to forego, for the time, the uses of such offices." As for the mails, they would continue, unless repelled.

Turning to the question of secession, he stressed that "the central idea" of seceding from the Union "is the essence of anarchy." Those who rejected the will of the majority—"the only true sovereign of a free people"—necessarily "fly to anarchy or to despotism." While "unanimity is impossible; the rule of a minority, as a permanent arrangement, is wholly inadmissable."

As soldiers and sharpshooters—posted in trees and on rooftops— surveyed the crowd, ready to quell any attempt to murder the new President, Lincoln appealed to all Americans to "think calmly and *well,* upon this whole subject." He offered assurances that the "government will not assail *you.* You can have no conflict, without being yourselves the aggressors. *You* have no oath registered in Heaven to destroy the government, while *I* shall have the most solemn one to 'preserve, protect and defend' it." [5]

Widespread reaction to Lincoln's Inaugural Address followed party lines. Some considered it "firm and explicit" [6]; others, "weak, rambling and loose-jointed." [7] Denunciation was almost universal in the press of the seceded states. South Carolina's *Charleston Mercury* talked about Lincoln's "insolence" and "brutality" manifested in the address, and attacked the United States as "a mobocratic Empire," amenable to the new President's "war strategy." [8] The *Chicago Tribune* commended Lincoln on his "freedom from diplomatic vagueness and hackneyed political phrases." [9] The *New York Tribune* lauded Lincoln's "ability, directness, candor and purpose," stating the Inaugural was devoid of all misgivings "concerning his success as Chief Magistrate." [10] But there were papers like the *Baltimore Sun,* which maintained that the address "breathes the spirit of mischief" and "intimates the design to exercise . . . authority to any extent of war and bloodshed, qualified only by the *withholding* of the requisite means . . . by the American people." [11] The *St. Louis Republican* had hoped "for a more conservative and more conciliatory expression of sentiments" from Lincoln.[12]

Jubal A. Early, speaking in Virginia, called the Inaugural "a guarantee that he [Lincoln] would perform his duty" which placed the blame for the "perilous condition" of the country upon the seceded states.[13] John A. Gilmer, commenting upon the address, asked "what more does any reasonable Southern man expect or desire?" [14] But these views were expressed privately and never appeared in the Southern press where they might have done the most good.

The day following the inauguration, the Senate confirmed Lincoln's Cabinet appointments: William H. Seward of New York, Secretary of State; Salmon P. Chase of Ohio, Secretary of the Treasury; Simon Cameron of Pennsylvania, Secretary of War; Edward Bates of Missouri, Attorney General; Gideon Welles of Connecticut, Secretary of the Navy; Montgomery Blair of Maryland, Postmaster General; and Caleb B. Smith of Indiana, Secretary of the Interior.

Rivalries among the various Cabinet members were to result in a division into two major factions with Seward, Cameron and Smith in one, and Chase, Welles and Blair in the other. "In weaker hands," Nicolay and Hay commented more than thirty years later, "such a

Cabinet would have been a hot-bed of strife; under him [Lincoln] it became a tower of strength." [15]

Soon after his installation as President, Lincoln was informed of a dispatch from Major Anderson at Fort Sumter stating that unless the fort could be provisioned by April 15th, it would have to be evacuated. Lincoln called for General Scott's advice. The general held that it would take at least 20,000 volunteers and 5,000 regulars to relieve Sumter.[16] The President summoned his Cabinet and requested written opinions on the subject. The consensus: No attempt should be made to provision Sumter at this time. Lincoln himself reserved decision, but began studying the situation carefully.

During his first sixty days in office, he saw the nation head into fratricidal conflict. Things shaped up like this:

Seward, through intermediaries, attempted to negotiate the Sumter question with Confederate commissioners and actually pledged that the fort would be evacuated. Apparently unaware of this, Lincoln sent emissaries to Sumter and Charleston to secure information on the advisability of provisioning the fort and to gauge popular sentiment in the city. Their reports helped influence him to send reinforcements to Pickens, off Pensacola, Florida, to demonstrate the assertion of Federal authority. This was part of a plan to lessen the impact of a contemplated evacuation of Sumter. And he tried to turn this maneuver into another advantage. The Virginia state convention— convened at Richmond on February 13th, with a majority of Union men, to consider secession—refused to adjourn until the Sumter question was settled, preferably without the use of force. By his Pickens-Sumter strategy, Lincoln hoped to retain Virginia in the Union and influence the course of other loyal border slave states.

At the end of Lincoln's first month as President, the country was beginning to lose confidence in his Administration; there were charges that the government had no policy, that it was just drifting. On April 1st, he received a memorandum from Seward, "Some Thoughts for the President's Consideration." Seward, who considered himself Lincoln's "Prime Minister," proposed to assume Presidential functions to change *"the question before the Public from one upon Slavery, or about Slavery* for a question upon *Union* or *Disunion,"* by involving the United States in a foreign war with France or Great Britain over their intervention in Mexico, and/or Spain because of its interference in Santo Domingo.[17] Lincoln had to put Seward in his place and did it with delicate firmness.[18]

As the nation's attention remained fixed upon Charleston Harbor, Lincoln saw one attempt fail before another succeeded in reinforcing Pickens. But by then it was too late to carry out the original Pickens-Sumter strategy. Lincoln explained his subsequent actions as follows:

"To now re-inforce Fort Pickens before a crisis would be reached at Fort Sumter was impossible—rendered so by the near exhaustion of provisions in the latter-named Fort. In precaution against such a conjuncture, the government had, a few days before, commenced preparing an expedition as well adapted as might be to relieve Fort Sumter, which expedition was intended to be ultimately used, or not, according to circumstances. The strongest anticipated case for using it, was now presented; and it was resolved to send it forward." [19]

However, the Sumter expedition failed. On April 12th—the day Pickens was reinforced "without the firing of a gun, or the spilling of one drop of blood" [20]—Sumter was attacked by South Carolinians. After two days of heavy bombardment, the fort surrendered. Lincoln then declared that an "insurrection" by powerful "combinations" existed against Federal authority and called for 75,000 militiamen for three-month service "to suppress said combinations." He also summoned a special session of Congress to convene on July 4th.[21]

The firing on Sumter led to the secession of Virginia and of the other states of the Upper South; to the blockading of Southern ports by Lincoln's own proclamation. For many—with the attack on Sumter—the long waiting was ended; the lines were now drawn. There could be no turning back from what was to be four years of bitter civil war.

And in the midst of all this—during his first months as President —Lincoln was not only concerned with matters of war, but with making the transition from a Democratic to a Republican Adminis-tration involving "a sweeping change of functionaries," [22] a task that kept him "working early and late." [23] This meant a complete reorganization of the government while, at the same time, conducting business with the full knowledge that traitors and Southern sympa-thizers occupied places in various civil and military departments.

"Some Man . . . Who Could Get on a Horse"
FRIDAY, MARCH 29, 1861

¶ *The Sumter dilemma had plagued the President, his Cabinet and his commanding general almost from the moment the new Administration had taken office. In mid-March, a Cabinet majority had voted against provisioning Sumter.[1] On March 28th, General Scott urged that both Sumter and Pickens be given up to the Confederacy.[2] The next day, at a noon session of the Cabinet, the consensus favored supplying Sumter; some members even felt the fort should be reinforced. Only Seward and Smith wished the fort surrendered.[3] Aside from declaring himself on Sumter, Seward proposed: "I would call in Captain M.[ontgomery] C. Meigs forthwith. Aided by his counsel, I would at once, and at every cost, prepare for a war at Pensacola and Texas, to be taken, however, only as a consequence of maintaining the possessions and authority of the United States."[4]*

When the Cabinet adjourned, Lincoln ordered Captain Gustavus V. Fox, later to be his Assistant Secretary of the Navy, to proceed to New York to prepare an expedition for the relief of Sumter. The ships were to be held in readiness "to sail as early as the 6th of April."[5]

Seward, meanwhile, left to summon his friend, Captain Meigs, an army engineer then in charge of the work on the new wings of the Capitol building, who had the previous January accompanied reinforcements to Key West and the Tortugas. On their way to the White House, Seward told the captain "he wished to have the President talk with some man who would speak of what he knew—not of politics in military affairs and one who could get on a horse in the field too." As for Generals Scott and Joseph G. Totten, the Army's Chief Engineer, "no one would think of putting either of these old men on horseback."[6]

Shortly after this meeting with Lincoln, Meigs recorded the proceedings in his Large Diary:[7]

The President talked freely with me. I told him that men enough could be found to volunteer to endeavor to relieve Fort Sumter, but that persons of higher position and rank than myself thought it not to be attempted, that this was not the place to make the war, etc.

He asked me whether Fort Pickens could be held. I told him certainly, if the Navy had done its duty and not lost it already. The President asked whether I could not go down there again and take a general command of these three great fortresses [Pickens at the western end of Santa Rosa Island, off Pensacola; Taylor at Key West; and Jefferson in the Dry Tortugas] and keep them safe. I told him I was only a captain and could not command majors who were there. He must take an officer of higher rank. Mr. Seward broke out with "I can understand too how that is, Captain Meigs, you have got to be promoted." I said, "That cannot be done; I am a captain and there is no vacancy." But Mr. Seward told the President that if he wished to have this thing done the proper way was to put it into my charge and it would be done, that I would give him an estimate of the means by 4 P.M. of the next day. He [Seward] complimented me much. Said that when Pitt wished to take Quebec he did not send for an old general but he sent for a young man whom he had noticed in the society of London, named [James] Wolfe, and told him that he had selected him to take Quebec, to ask for the necessary means and do it and it was done. Would the President do this now? He [Lincoln] replied that he would consider on it and would let me know in a day or two.

[Meigs noted in his *Diary* entry for that day: "I walked home with Mr. Seward, who said he was much gratified at the result of the interview. . . . That I must wait for a day or two and I should hear again from him."]

"What Have I Done Wrong?"

MONDAY, APRIL 1, 1861

¶ *On Monday, April 1st, Captain Meigs, Lieutenant David D. Porter of the U. S. Navy, and Colonel Erasmus D. Keyes, military secretary to General Scott, were busy at the White House drawing up plans and orders for the Pickens expedition, occasionally benefiting from the advice of Seward and the old general. Without consulting the Secretaries of War and the Navy, Lincoln signed these orders.*

Later, between five and six o'clock in the afternoon, Nicolay delivered a large package from the President to Secretary Welles, who was dining at Willard's Hotel. Welles immediately examined its contents *"and found it contained several papers of a singular character . . . and one in reference to the government of the Navy Department more singular than either of the others."* [1] *This document read:*

(Confidential)

EXECUTIVE MANSION, April 1, 1861.

To the Secretary of the Navy.

DEAR SIR: You will issue instructions to Captain [Garrett J.] Pendergast, commanding the home squadron, to remain in observation at Vera Cruz—important complications in our foreign relations rendering the presence of an officer of rank there of great importance.

Captain [Silas H.] Stringham will be directed to proceed to Pensacola with all possible despatch, and assume command of that portion of the home squadron stationed off Pensacola. He will have confidential instructions to coöperate in every way with the commanders of the land forces of the United States in that neighborhood.

The instructions to the army officers, which are strictly confidential, will be communicated to Captain Stringham after he arrives at Pensacola.

Captain Samuel Barron will relieve Captain Stringham in charge of the Bureau of Detail.

ABRAHAM LINCOLN.

P.S. As it is very necessary at this time to have a perfect knowledge of the personal [*sic*] of the navy, and to be able to detail such officers for special purposes as the exigencies of the service may require, I request that you will instruct Captain Barron to proceed and organize the Bureau of Detail in the manner best adapted to meet the wants of the navy, taking cognizance of the discipline of the navy generally, detailing all officers for duty, taking charge of the recruiting of seamen, supervising charges made against officers, and all matters relating to duties which must be best understood by a sea officer. You will please afford Captain Barron any facility for accomplishing this duty, transferring to his department the clerical force heretofore used for the purposes specified. It is to be understood that this officer will act by authority of the Secretary of the Navy, who will exercise such supervision as he may deem necessary.

ABRAHAM LINCOLN.

Without a moment's delay, the astonished Welles hastened to the President, package in hand. What transpired at this interview Welles recorded in a reminiscence several years later: [2]

He was alone in his office and, raising his head from the table at which he was writing, enquired, *"What have I done wrong?"* I informed him I had received with surprise the package containing his instructions respecting the Navy, and the Navy Department, and I desired some explanation. I then called his attention particularly to the foregoing document, which I read to him and which was in the hand writing of Lieutenant David D. Porter, since made Vice Admiral.[8] The President expressed as much surprise, as I felt, that he had sent me such a document. He said Mr. Seward with two or three young men had been there through the day on a subject which he [Seward] had in hand, and had been some time maturing—that it was Seward's speciality to which he [the President] had yielded, but as it involved considerable details, and he, the President, had his hands full and more too, he had left it with Mr. Seward to prepare the necessary papers which he [the President] had signed, without reading—for he had not time, and if he could not trust Seward he knew not whom he could trust. I asked who were associated with Mr. Seward—["]no one[,"] said the President, ["]but he had these young men here as clerks to write down his plans and orders.["] Most of the work was done, he said, in the other room. I then asked if he knew the young men, [and] he said one was Capt Meigs, the other a companion with whom he [Meigs] seemed intimate, was a naval officer named Porter.

I then informed the President in regard to Barron who was to be forced into personal and official intimacy with me, and of whom he [the President] said he knew nothing except [that he had] a general recollection that there was such an officer in the Navy. The detailing officer of the Department ought to have the implicit confidence of the Secretary, and should be selected by him [the Secretary]. This the President assented to most fully. I then told him Barron had not my confidence, and I thought him not entitled to that of the President. His [Barron's] associations, feelings and views, so far as I could ascertain them were with the Secessionists—that he belonged to a clique of exclusives, most of whom were tainted with secession—that while I was not prepared to say he would desert us when the crisis came on, I was apprehensive of it, and while I would treat him kindly, considerately, and hoped he would not prove false like others of his set, I could not give him the trust which the instructions imposed.

The President reiterated they were not his instructions—that the paper was an improper one—that he wished me to give it no more attention than I thought proper—treat it as cancelled, or as if it had never been written. He said he remembered that both Seward and Porter had something to say about Barron, as if he was a superior officer, and perhaps without any superior in the Navy, but he certainly never would have assigned him or any other man to the position without consulting me. . . .

This was the state of the case when the instructions of the 1st of April were made out and sent to me. I was, on learning from the President who were Mr. Seward's associates satisfied that Porter had urged that Barron should be substituted for Stringham as my detailing and confidential officer. I was unwilling to believe that my colleague Seward could connive at, or be party to, an intrigue which was to interfere with the duties of my department, and jeopard[ize] its operations. What then were the contrivances which he was maturing with two young officers, one of the military and the other of the naval service[?] What had he, the Secretary of State to do with these officers any way? I could get no satisfactory solution from the President of the origin of this movement, which he censured and condemned more severely than myself and which he assured me would never occur again. He was very much disturbed by the disclosure, and repeatedly, said to me that I must pay no more attention to the papers sent me than I thought advisable; but he gave no intimation of the scheme which Seward had in view, farther than that it was a specialty, which he [Seward] required should be kept secret. I of course pressed for no disclosures.

"Mr. President, If I Had Control"
THURSDAY, APRIL 4, 1861

¶ *Lincoln was deeply apprehensive of the course Virginia would take as North and South girded themselves for conflict. At Richmond, the Virginia State Convention was still in session. One Union member of the convention seemed—according to Nicolay and Hay—to express the sentiments of most convention delegates when he declared that "he would neither be driven by the North or dragged by the Cotton States."* [1] *Seward, too, believed in the necessity of saving the Old Dominion from secession "as a brand from the burning."* [2] *Perhaps if Lincoln could bring his personal influence to bear upon the convention, Virginia would stay in the Union? To do this, the President sent a special messenger to Richmond to summon his friend, George W. Summers, or some other influential Virginia Unionist, to a secret White House conference. Summers, "pleading important business in the convention, excused himself from coming." Instead of going to Washington himself, he selected John B. Baldwin as his representative. On April 4th, Baldwin and Lincoln were secluded in lengthy conversation. There were no witnesses to the Lincoln-Baldwin meeting. Baldwin's report of the conference forms the major part of his testimony before the Joint Committee on Reconstruction on February 10, 1866. We offer the pertinent portions of Baldwin's testimony given under questioning by Senator Jacob M. Howard of Michigan:* [3]

Mr. Lincoln received me very cordially, and almost immediately arose and said that he desired to have some private conversation with me . . . As I was about sitting down, said he, "Mr. Baldwin . . . I am afraid you have come too late; I wish you could have been here three or four days ago." "Why," said I, "Mr. President, allow me to say I do not understand your remark . . . you sent a special messenger to Richmond, who arrived there yesterday; I returned with him by the shortest and most expeditious mode of travel known; it was physically impossible that I or any one else, answering your summons, could have got here sooner than I have arrived . . . ." Said he, "Why do you not all adjourn the Virginia convention?" Said I, "Adjourn it!—how? do you mean *sine die?"* "Yes," said he, *"sine die;* why do you not adjourn it; it is a standing menace to me, which embarrasses me very much." Of course you will understand that I do not pretend to recollect the language at all, but this is about the substance of it. Said I, "Sir, I am very much surprised to hear you express that opinion; the Virginia convention is in the hands of Union men; we have in it a clear and controlling majority of nearly three to one; we are controlling it for conservative results; we can do it with perfect certainty, if you will uphold our hands by a conservative policy here. I do not understand why you want a body thus in the hands of Union men to be dispersed, or why you should look upon their sessions as in any respect a menace to you; we regard ourselves as co-operating with you in the objects which you express to seek; besides," said I, "I would call your attention to this view: If we were to adjourn that convention *sine die,* leaving these questions unsettled in the midst of all the trouble that is on us, it would place the Union men of Virginia in the attitude of confessing an inability to meet the occasion; the result would be, that another convention would be called as soon as legislation could be put through for the purpose."

. . . Said I, ". . . and the Union men of Virginia could not, with a proper self-respect, offer themselves as members of that convention, having had the full control of one, and having adjourned without having brought about any sort of settlement of the troubles upon us. The result would be that the next convention would be exclusively under the control of secessionists, and that an ordinance of secession would be passed in less than six weeks. Now, ["] said I, ["] sir, it seems to me that our true policy is to hold the position that we have, and for you to uphold our hands by a conservative, conciliatory, national course. We can control the matter, and will control it if you help us. And, sir, it is but right for me to say another thing to you, that the Union men of Virginia, of whom I am one, would not be willing to adjourn that convention until we either effect some settlement of this matter or ascertain that it cannot be done. As an original proposition, the Union men of Virginia did not desire amendments to the Constitution of the United States; we were perfectly satisfied with the constitutional guarantees that we had, and thought our rights and interests perfectly safe. But circumstances have changed: seven States of the south, the cotton States, have withdrawn from us and left us in an extremely altered condition in reference to the safe-guards of the Constitution. As things stand now, we are helpless in the hands of the north. The balance of power which we had before for our protection against constitutional amendment is gone. And we think now that we of the border States who have adhered to you against all the obligations of association and sympathy with the southern States have a claim on the States of the north which is of a high and very peculiar character. You all say that you do not mean to injure us in our peculiar rights. If you are in earnest about it there can be no objection to your saying so in such an authentic form as will give us the force of constitutional protection. And we think you ought to do it, not grudgingly, not reluctantly, but in such a way as that it would be a fitting recognition of our fidelity in standing by you under all circumstances—fully, and generously, and promptly. If you will do it in accordance with what we regard as due to our position, it will give us a stand-point from which we can bring back the seceded States." I cannot follow the conversation through; but he asked me the question. "What is your plan?" Said I, "Mr. President, if I had control of your thumb and forefinger five minutes I could settle the whole question." . . . "Well," said he, "what is your plan?" Said I, "Sir, if I were in your place I would issue a proclamation to the American people, somewhat after this style: I would state the fact that you had become President of the United States as the result of a partisan struggle partaking of more bitterness than had usually marked such struggle; that, in the progress of that struggle, there had naturally arisen a great deal of misunderstanding and misrepresentation of the motives and intentions of both sides; that you had no doubt you had been represented, and to a large extent believed, to be inimical to the institutions and interests and rights of a large portion of the United States, but that, however, you might, in the midst of a partisan struggle, have been more or less (as all men) excited at times, occupying the position of President of the United States, you had determined to take your stand on the broad platform of the general Constitution, and to do equal and exact justice to all, without regard to party or section; and that, recognizing the fact without admitting the right, but protesting against the right, that seven States had undertaken to withdraw themselves from the Union, you had determined to appeal to the American people to settle the question in the spirit in which the Constitution was made—American fashion—by consultation and votes instead of by appeal to arms. And I would call a national convention of the people of the United States and urge upon them to come together and settle this thing. And in order to prevent the possibility of any collision or clash or arms interfering with this effort at a pacific settlement, I would declare the purpose (not in any admission of want of right at all, but with a distinct protest of the right, to place the forces of the United States wherever in her territory you choose) to withdraw the forces from Sumter and Pickens, declaring that it was done for the sake of peace, in effort to settle this thing; and that you were determined, if the seceded States chose to make a collision, that they should come clear out of their way and do it. Sir,["] said I, ["] if you take that position there is national feeling enough in the seceded States themselves and all over the country to rally to your support, and you would gather more friends than any man in the country has ever had." He said something or other, I do not recollect what, but it created the impression upon me that he was looking with some apprehension to the idea that his friends would not be pleased with such a step, and I said to him, "Mr. President, for every one of your friends whom you would lose by such a policy you would gain ten who would rally to you and to the national standard of peace and Union." Said he, rather impatiently, "That is not what I am thinking about. If I could be satisfied that I am right, and that I do what is right, I do not care whether people stand by me or not." Said I, "Sir, I beg your pardon, for I only know of you as a politician, a successful politician; and possibly I have fallen into the error of addressing you by the motives which are generally potent with politicians, the motive of gaining friends. I thank you that you have recalled to me the higher and better motive, the motive of being right; and I assure you that, from now out, I will address you by the motives that ought to influence a gentleman."

Question. You drew a distinction between a politician and a gentleman?

Answer. Yes, sir; he laughed a little at that. He said something about the withdrawal of the troops from Sumter on the ground of military necessity. Said I, "That will never do, under heaven. You have been President a month to-day, and if you intended to hold that position you ought to have strengthened it, so as to make it impregnable. To hold it in the present condition of force there is an invitation to assault. Go upon higher ground than that. The better ground . . . is to make a concession of an asserted right in the interest of peace." "Well," said he, "what about the revenue? What would I do about the collection of duties?" Said I, "Sir, how much do you expect to collect in a year?" Said he, "Fifty or sixty millions." "Why, sir," said I, "four times sixty is two hundred and forty. Say $250,000,000 would be the revenue of your term of the presidency; what is that but a drop in the bucket compared with the cost of such a war as we are threatened with? Let it all go, if necessary; but I do not believe that it will be necessary, because I believe that you can settle it on the basis I suggest." He said something or other about feeding the troops at Sumter. I told him that would not do. Said I, "You know perfectly well that the people of Charleston have been feeding them already. That is not what they are at. They are asserting a right. They will feed the troops, and fight them while they are feeding them. They are after the assertion of a right. Now, the only way that you can manage them is to withdraw from them the means of making a blow until time for reflection, time for influence which can be brought to bear, can be gained, and settle the matter. If you do not take this course, if there is a gun fired at Sumter—I do not care on which side it is fired—the thing is gone." "Oh," said he, "sir, that is impossible." Said I, "Sir, if there is a gun fired at Fort Sumter, as sure as there is a God in heaven the thing is gone. Virginia herself, strong as the Union majority in the convention is now, will be out in forty-eight hours." "Oh," said he, "sir, that is impossible." Said I, "Mr. President, I did not come here to argue with you; I am here as a witness. I know the sentiments of the people of Virginia, and you do not. . . . I wish to know before we go any further . . . whether I am accredited to you in such a way as that what I tell you is worthy of credence." Said he, "You come to me introduced as a gentleman of high standing and talent in your State." Said I, "That is not the point I am on. Do I come to you vouched for as an honest man, who will tell you the truth?" Said he, "You do." "Then," said I, "sir, I tell you, before God and man, that if there is a gun fired at Sumter this thing is gone. And I wish to say to you, Mr. President, with all the solemnity that I can possibly summon, that if you intend to do anything to settle this matter you must do it promptly. I think another fortnight will be too late.["] . . .

Question. You received from Mr. Lincoln no letter or memorandum in writing?

Answer. Nothing whatever.

Question. No pledge? No undertaking?

Answer. No pledge; no undertaking; no offer; no promise of any sort.

[Whether Lincoln had made Baldwin an offer to evacuate Sumter provided Virginia remained in the Union has never satisfactorily been settled. John Minor Botts maintained that such a pledge was made by the President. John Plumer Smith of Philadelphia, who visited Lincoln "a few days after the Convention at Richmond passed the ordinance of secession," reported in 1863: "During the interview . . . Mr Lincoln spoke very freely of the attempt he had made to hold Virginia firm for the Union—and then . . . mentioned, that amongst other influences, he had sent for Mr Baldwin . . . and told, if they would pass resolutions of adherance [*sic*] to the Union, then adjourn and go home—he, the President, would take the responsibility, at the earliest proper time—to withdraw the troops from Fort Sumter⁴—and do all within the line of his duty to ward off collision.

"He then imposed strict silence upon us in regard to what he then had told us." ⁵]

"The Powhatan Must Be Restored"

SATURDAY, APRIL 6, 1861

¶ *On April 5th, Secretary Welles, with Lincoln's approval, issued orders designating the* Powhatan *as the flagship and Captain Samuel Mercer as the naval commander of the Sumter expedition. Gustavus V. Fox, by special Presidential commission, was placed in charge of the entire operation. The next day, Lieutenant Porter boarded the* Powhatan *at the Brooklyn Navy Yard with different orders signed by the President, which stated: "Lieutenant D. D. Porter will take command of the steamer* Powhatan. . . . *All officers are commanded to afford him all such facilities as he may deem necessary for getting to sea as soon as possible." ¹ The officers held a conference about the conflicting orders. Since Lincoln's authority was higher than that of Welles', Mercer yielded the vessel. Porter soon weighed anchor and set sail for Fort Pickens, but before doing so telegraphed a report of the incident to Seward.*

In Washington that night—between 11 and 12 o'clock—Seward, with his son Frederick, hastened to Welles with the telegram in hand. Seward charged that "the movements were retarded and embarrassed by conflicting orders from the Secretary of the Navy." Welles requested an explanation. Seward stated he presumed it related to the Powhatan *and Porter's command. "I assured him he was mistaken, that Porter had no command, and that the Powhatan was the flagship, as he was aware, of the Sumter expedition," Wells related afterwards. Seward said there must be some mistake and after some conversation, it was decided to take the matter to the President. Before leaving, Welles called for Captain String-*

ham, who was also staying at Willard's, and all left for the White House.

In a reminiscence, Welles wrote: [2]

The President had not retired when we reached the Executive Mansion, although it was nearly midnight. On seeing us he was surprised, and his surprise was not diminished on learning our errand. He looked first at one and then the other, and declared there was some mistake, but after again hearing the facts stated, and again looking at the telegram, he asked if I was not mistaken in regard to the Powhatan—if some other vessel was not the flagship of the Sumter expedition. I assured him there was no mistake—reminded him that I had read to him my instructions to Capt Mercer. He said he remembered that fact, and that he approved of them, but he could not remember that the Powhatan was the vessel. Commodore [then Captain] Stringham confirmed my statement, but to make the matter perfectly clear to the President, I went to the Navy Department and brought and read to him the instructions. He [then] remembered all distinctly and turning promptly to Mr. Seward said the Powhatan must be restored to Mercer—that on no account must the Sumter expedition fail. Mr. Seward asked if the other expedition was not quite as important and whether that would not be defeated if the Powhatan was detached. The President said the other had time and could wait, but no time was to be lost as regarded Sumter, and he directed Mr. Seward to telegraph without delay to New York [an order restoring the Powhatan to Mercer]. Mr. Seward suggested the difficulty of getting a despatch through at so late an hour, but the President was imperative that it should be done.

The President then, and subsequently, informed me that Mr. Seward had his heart set on reinforcing fort Pickens, and that between them they had arranged for supplies and reinforcements to be sent out at the same time we were fitting out for Sumter, but with no intention whatever of interfering with the latter. He took upon himself the whole blame—said it was carelessness, heedlessness on his part—he ought to have been more careful and attentive. [The] President never shunned any responsibility and often declared that he, and not his Cabinet, was in fault for errors imputed to them.

Mr. Seward never attempted any explanation. He was not com-

municative on that night, nor afterwards, though there were occasional allusions to that transaction. . . .
[Nicolay and Hay state that the mix-up in orders occurred on April 1st, when Meigs, Keyes and Porter were drawing up plans and instructions for the Pickens expedition. Supposing that these orders were entirely consistent with the Sumter plans, Lincoln "signed them without reading." [3] The *Powhatan,* however, was never restored to Mercer, as ordered by Lincoln.]

"Mr. President, I . . . Concur"

SUNDAY, APRIL 14, 1861

¶ *Before the Sumter expedition sailed, Lincoln had sent a personal messenger to inform Governor Francis W. Pickens of South Carolina that an expedition was being sent merely "to supply Fort Sumter with provisions only"; that if the Confederates would permit provisioning of the fort, "no effort to throw in men, arms, or ammunition" would be made "without further notice." [1] This was Lincoln's way of demonstrating nonaggressive intentions. After receiving this message, the Governor engaged in anxious consultations. On April 11th, Brigadier-General Pierre Gustave Toutant Beauregard sent three rebel officers to Sumter to demand evacuation of the fort. Anderson refused, but observed: "Gentlemen, if you do not batter the fort to pieces about us, we shall be starved out in a few days." [2] The Montgomery Government then ordered the Palmettos not to "reduce the fort" if Anderson promised not to attack and gave a definite date for the evacuation.[3] On April 12th, Confederate officers visited Anderson, who told them he would quit Sumter by noon on April 15th, unless he received "controlling instructions" from Washington "or additional supplies." [4] The rebels replied that Beauregard would open fire on the fort in one hour. At 4:30 P.M. that day, they saw "the red ball [of a signal mortar] scribe a semi-circle and explode immediately above the fort." [5] Some thirty hours later Anderson was forced to surrender. The naval expedition to Sumter—caught up in a gale— never was able to complete its mission.*

At Washington, according to George Ashmun, news of the Sumter attack brought grave concern and apprehension over "the course which the new Administration would take." Ashmun felt the occasion "was one which demanded prompt action and the cordial support of the whole people of the North, and that this would be greatly insured by a public declaration from Mr. [Stephen A.] Douglas." Ashmun hurried to "The Little Giant" and told him "I desired him to go with me at once to the President, and make a declaration of his [Douglas'] determination to sustain him [Lincoln] in the needful measures which the exigency of the hour demanded to put down the rebellion which . . . flamed out in Charleston harbor." Douglas at first demurred, stating "Mr. Lincoln has dealt harshly with me, in removing some of my friends from office, and I don't know as he wants my advice or aid." But Ashmun finally persuaded the Illinois Senator to yield and the two repaired to the White House.

A record of this historic meeting—albeit a short one of the conversation—was published by Ashmun on October 26, 1864, in the Washington Daily Morning Chronicle:

We fortunately found Mr. Lincoln alone, and upon my stating the errand on which we had come, he was most cordial in his welcome, and immediately prepared the way for the conversation which followed, by taking from his drawer and reading to us the draft of the proclamation [calling for 75,000 men to serve three months in the militia and summoning Congress to a special session on July 4th] which he had decided to issue, and which was given to the country the next morning.

As soon as the reading ended, Mr. Douglas rose from his chair and said: "Mr. President, I cordially concur in every word of that document, except that instead of a call for 75,000 men I would make it 200,000. You do not know the dishonest purposes of those men (the rebels) as well as I do." And he then asked us to look with him at the map which hung at one end of the President's room, where, in much detail, he pointed out the principal strategic points which should be at once strengthened for the coming contest. Among the most prominent were Fortress Monroe, Washington, Harper's Ferry, and Cairo. He [Douglas] enlarged at length upon the firm, warlike footing which ought to be pursued, and found in Mr. Lincoln an earnest and gratified listener. It would be impossible to give in detail all the points presented by him and discussed with the President; but I venture to say that no two men in the United States parted that night with a more cordial feeling of a united, friendly, and patriotic purpose than Mr. Lincoln and Mr. Douglas.

[After the meeting with the President, and again at Ashmun's suggestion, Senator Douglas wrote out the following dispatch for the Associated Press:

"Mr. Douglas called on the President this evening and had an interesting conversation on the present condition of the country. The substance of the conversation was that while Mr. Douglas was unalterably opposed to the administration on all its political issues, he was prepared to sustain the President in the exercise of his constitutional functions to preserve the Union, and maintain the government and defend the Federal capital. A firm policy and prompt action was necessary. The capital of our country was in danger and must be defended at all hazards, and at any expense of men and money. He [Douglas] spoke of the present and future without reference to the past."]

"Troops . . . Through Baltimore"

SATURDAY, APRIL 20, 1861

¶ *Lincoln's call for 75,000 militiamen—flashed over the wires throughout the Northern states—"was everywhere received with the beating of drums and the ringing notes of the bugle, calling the defenders of the capital to their colors."* [1] *According to Ben: Perley Poore, "every city and hamlet had its flag-raising, while its enthusiasm was unbounded. Here and there a newspaper ventured to apologize for the South, but the editor would soon be forced by a mob to display the stars and stripes, amid the cheers and the shouts of those assembled."* [2] *Two days following Lincoln's call for troops—on April 17th, the very day Virginia reluctantly seceded from the Union—the Sixth Massachusetts, fully equipped, embarked in railroad cars for the trip from Boston to Washington. But when the New Englanders reached Baltimore, they were attacked by a mob carrying a secession flag; several soldiers were killed or severely wounded. Commented Henry J. Raymond of* The New York Times: *"This inflamed to a still higher point the excitement which already pervaded the country. The whole Northern section of the Union felt outraged that troops should be assailed and murdered on their way to protect the capital of the nation."* [3]

In Maryland, where secession sentiment was strong, Governor Thomas H. Hicks and Mayor George W. Brown of Baltimore urged the Federal Government that no more troops should be brought through the city. Governor Hicks also proposed that the controversy between North and South be referred for arbitration to Lord Lyons, the British Minister at Washington.[4]

On April 20th, Lincoln summoned Hicks and Brown to a Washington conference. In the absence of Hicks from Baltimore, Brown telegraphed he was "coming immediately." [5] *The day after his conference with Lincoln, Brown issued a statement on the White House meeting. This statement, included in Raymond's* History *of the* Administration of President Lincoln, *reads:* [6]

The President, upon his part, recognized the good faith of the city and State authorities, and insisted upon his own. He admitted the excited state of feeling in Baltimore, and his desire and duty to avoid the fatal consequences of a collision with the people. He urged, on the other hand, the absolute, irresistible necessity of having a transit through the State for such troops as might be necessary for the protection of the Federal Capital. *The protection of Washington,* he asseverated with great earnestness, was the sole object of concentrating troops there; and he protested that none of the troops brought through Maryland were intended for any purposes hostile to the State, or *aggressive* as against the Southern States. Being now unable to bring them up the Potomac in security, the Government must either bring them through Maryland or abandon the capital.

He called on General Scott for his opinion, which the General gave at length, to the effect that troops might be brought through Maryland, without going through Baltimore, by either carrying them from Perrysville to Annapolis, and thence by rail to Washington, or by bringing them to the Relay House on the Northern Central Railroad, and marching them to the Relay House on the Washington Railroad, and thence by rail to the Capital. If the people would permit them to go by either of those routes uninterruptedly, the necessity of their passing through Baltimore would be avoided. If the people would not permit them a transit thus remote from the city, they must select their own best route, and, if need be, fight their way through Baltimore—a result which the General earnestly deprecated.

The President expressed his hearty concurrence in the desire to avoid a collision, and said that no more troops should be ordered through Baltimore, if they were permitted to go [un]interruptedly by either of the other routes suggested. In this disposition the Secretary of War [Cameron] expressed his participation.

Mayor Brown assured the President that the city authorities would use all lawful means to prevent their citizens from leaving Baltimore to attack the troops in passing at a distance; but he urged, at the same time, the impossibility of their being able to promise any thing more than their best efforts in that direction. The excitement was great, he told the President; the people of all classes were fully aroused, and it was impossible for any one to answer for the consequences of the presence of Northern troops anywhere within our borders. He reminded the President, also, that the jurisdiction of the city authorities was confined to their own population, and that he could give no promises for the people elsewhere, because he would be unable to keep them if given. The President frankly acknowledged this difficulty, and said that the Government would only ask the city authorities to use their best efforts with respect to those under their jurisdiction.

The interview terminated with the distinct assurance, on the part of the President, that no more troops would be sent through Baltimore unless obstructed in their transit in other directions, and with the understanding that the city authorities should do their best to restrain their own people.

"About the Law of Nations"
AFTER APRIL 19, 1861

¶ *On April 19, 1861, Lincoln issued a proclamation blockading the ports of South Carolina, Georgia, Alabama, Florida, Mississippi, Louisiana, and Texas, and ordered that "a competent force will be posted so as to prevent entrance and exit of vessels from the ports aforesaid."* [1] *Representative Thaddeus Stevens—"Old Thad," as he was called—was at home in Pennsylvania when news of Lincoln's action reached him. Stevens favored treating the North-South conflict as a "rebellion and the participators in it as traitors to the government of the United States, liable to punishment for their treason." Thus, he reasoned: "If the rebel States were still in the Union, and only in treasonable revolt against the government, we were blockading ourselves." Deeply concerned over the proclamation, which he termed "a great blunder and absurdity,"* [2] *the thickset Stevens, with his dark-brown, wavy-haired wig, hurried to Washington for a consultation with the President.*

Sixteen years later, he told a reporter for the New York Herald *what happened during his interview with Lincoln:* [3]

I laid my views before him [Lincoln], and told him that the blockade was a stultification of the former position of the government in relation to the rebel States; that the ports, instead of being blockaded, should have been closed, and a sufficient number of armed revenue vessels sent out on the seas to prevent smuggling. I pointed out to him the fact that by the act of blockade we recognized to conduct the war, not as if we were suppressing a revolt in our own States, but in accordance with the law of nations.

"Well," said Mr. Lincoln, when he had heard my remarks, "that's a fact. I see the point now, but I don't know anything about the law of nations, and I thought it was all right."

"As a lawyer, Mr. Lincoln," I remarked, "I should have supposed you would have seen the difficulty at once."

"Oh, well," replied Mr. Lincoln, "I'm a good enough lawyer in a Western law court, I suppose, but we don't practise the law of nations up there, and I supposed Seward knew all about it, and I left it to him. But it's done now and can't be helped, so we must get along as well as we can."

In this Mr. Lincoln was right. The blunder had been committed and the rebel States were thenceforth an independent belligerent. Not an independent nation, of course, but an independent belligerent, to be dealt with in accordance with the law of nations.

[On April 27, 1861, after his talk with Stevens, the President issued a proclamation blockading other ports in Virginia and North Carolina.[4]]

"To Lose Kentucky . . ."

FRIDAY, APRIL 26, 1861

¶ *Keeping Kentucky from joining the Confederacy was one of the greatest challenges to face Lincoln, who believed that "to lose Kentucky is nearly . . . to lose the whole game." With Kentucky gone, he maintained, "we cannot hold Missouri, nor, as I think, Maryland. These all against us, and the job on our hands is too large for us. We would as well consent to separation at once, including the surrender of this capital."* [1]

Kentucky, in the early days of the war, sought a neutral position; held herself above the controversy between North and South. When Lincoln called for troops, Kentucky refused to send a single man. However, despite the fact that Kentucky considered herself to have "a common interest in the protection of slavery," she asserted on April 17, 1861, that her "present duty" was "to maintain her present independent position, taking sides not with the Government and not with the seceding States, but with the Union against them both, declaring her soil to be sacred from the hostile tread of either, and, if necessary, making the declaration good with her strong right arm." [2]

Against this background, it was imperative for Lincoln to follow a delicate course in respect to Kentucky. He could risk nothing to antagonize her. In April, former Congressman Garrett Davis of Kentucky made a hurried trip to Washington to determine how Lincoln and his Cabinet intended to treat "our national troubles." His statement on the interview with Lincoln, which reports only the President's side of the conversation, was written two days after its occurrence and is quoted in the Appendix *to the* Congressional Globe, *37th Congress, 2nd session:* [3]

I found the President frank and calm, but decided and firm. He expressed deep concern and regret for the existing condition of public affairs, and his hope that there would yet be a restoration of the Union, and peace and amity among all the States. He remarked that neither he, nor any other President, who had been elected by a party, could administer the Government in exact accordance with his own opinions and judgment; but must make some departure to satisfy those who had placed him in power. That before the Carolinians had made their attack on Fort Sumter, he had decided not to reinforce or to attempt to reinforce its garrison, but merely, and only, to supply its handfull of famishing men with food; and that he had distinctly communicated these purposes to the authorities of the southern confederation. That he had also determined that until the meeting of Congress he would make no attempt to retake the forts, &c., belonging to the United States, which had been unlawfully seized and wrested from their possession, but would leave the then existing state of things to be considered and acted upon by Congress, unless he should be constrained to depart from that purpose by the continued military operations of the seceded States.

The President further said, that events had now reached a point when it must be decided whether our system of Federal Government was only a league of sovereign and independent States, from which any States could withdraw at pleasure, or whether the Constitution formed a Government invested with strength and powers sufficient to uphold its own authority, and to enforce the execution of the laws of Congress; that he had no doubt of the truth of the latter proposition, and he intended to make it good in the administration of the Government to the extent that he should be sustained by the people of the United States.

He remarked also, that he had expected all the States upon which he had made a requisition for military aid to enable him to execute the laws, to respond to that call; and particularly the State of Kentucky, which had been so loyal to the Union and faithful in the performance of all her duties. That he greatly regretted she had not acted up to the principle of her great statesmen now no more, and for which she cast her vote in the late Presidential election, "the Union, the Constitution, and the enforcement of the laws."

That he intended to make no attack, direct or indirect, upon the institution or property of any State; but, on the contrary, would defend them to the full extent with which the Constitution and laws of Congress have vested the President with the power. And that he did not intend to invade with any armed force, or make any military or naval movement against any State, unless she or her people should make it necessary by a formidable resistance of the authority and laws of the United States. That if Kentucky or her citizens should seize the post of Newport [Kentucky], it would become his duty, and he might attempt to retake it; but he contemplated no military operations that would make it necessary to move any troops over her territories, though he had the unquestioned right at all times to march the United States troops into and over any and every State. That if Kentucky made no demonstration of force against the United States, he would not molest her. That he regretted the necessity of marching troops across Maryland, but forces to protect the seat of the United States Government could not be concentrated there without doing so; and he intended to keep open a line of communication through that State to Washington city, at any risk, but in a manner least calculated to irritate and inflame her people.

Chapter Four

"THE HEATHER IS ON FIRE"

"**T**HE assault upon Fort Sumter," commented Horace Binney, "started us all to our feet, as one man." [1]

During the last two weeks of April 1861, business in many cities and towns was "substantially suspended" as men, women and children flooded the streets "with Union favors and flags." Money was raised to sustain the war effort and to support soldiers' families. There were public meetings, demonstrations, resolutions and proclamations almost everywhere.[2] Musicians and orators "blew themselves red in the face with their windy efforts"; choirs kept singing "Red, White, and Blue" and "Rallied 'Round the Flag" until they became "too hoarse for further endeavor." [3]

An Ohio man reported: "The West is all one great Eagle-scream!" A New Englander said that "at Concord the bells were rung and the President's call [for 75,000 militiamen was] read aloud on the village common." During the Baltimore riots, a wounded Lowell man was asked: "What brought you here fighting, so far away from your home . . . ?" He replied: "It was the stars and stripes." Hundreds of such stories were in circulation; newspapers published many of them.[4]

Said the *Detroit Free Press:* "The Star Spangled Banner rages most furiously." [5] Said George Ticknor, noted Boston scholar: "The heather is on fire." [6]

As the nation lumbered into war, Lincoln's big job was to whip a citizens' army into shape without delay. When Sumter was attacked, there were only some 16,000 Federal regulars scattered over the land;[7] the Washington Government was completely unprepared for the present emergency. Relatively few Americans knew the meaning of war.

Nevertheless, this was a time when the North shook with the vibrations of patriotism, and the response to Lincoln's April 15th proclamation was overwhelming. Everywhere in the North, recruiting centers were crowded with men—many having trekked to the cities from backwoods areas. "Everybody eagerly asks everybody else if he's going to enlist," one reporter wrote.[8] Another observer remarked: "If a fellow wants to go with a girl now he had better enlist. The girls sing 'I am Bound to be a Soldier's Wife or Die an Old Maid.' "[9]

Governor William Dennison boasted that Ohio would send "the largest number" of men Washington would receive in response to Lincoln's call. Zachariah Chandler of Michigan telegraphed Washington that his state would send regiments in thirty days "and 50,000 men if you need them." Indiana doubled its quota of 5,000 men. And Governor Samuel Kirkwood of Iowa wired Washington: "For God's sake send us arms. We have the men." [10] Horace Greeley maintained Lincoln could have had 500,000 men for the asking.[11] Edward Everett agreed.[12]

That the army pay of $13 a month influenced most enlistments was considered idle talk.[13] According to Britain's Edward Dicey, visiting the North at the time, "the bulk of the native volunteers" were "men who had given up good situations . . . to enlist, and who had families to support." [14] In army life, they saw an opportunity to escape from everyday routine; an invitation to high adventure and to glory. And they were in a hurry to enlist. The Lincoln Government was preparing for a 90-day war and unless they could get into the service quickly, they felt they would miss a chance of a lifetime.

In the first months of the war, there were more men than the War Department could accommodate, primarily because of shortages of clothing, muskets, ammunition and other supplies. Large numbers of volunteers, turned away by recruiting centers, engaged in "a great deal of very wicked swearing." [15]

Those accepted for service considered themselves the fortunate ones and fancied themselves in flashy uniforms, marching through the streets to the acclaim of admiring citizens. In some cases, uniforms were supplied by the states. Mostly, however, they were made by women's sewing groups. Thus, these uniforms were far from uniform and of every conceivable style and color. Recruits were given whatever arms were available, ranging from obsolete muskets to Sharps's rifles; friends and relatives supplemented these with daggers, havelocks, dueling pistols and bulletproof vests.

Officers were elected by their comrades and because they were "green," training problems had to be met as much as possible by Mexican War veterans and immigrants who had served in European armies. Under these circumstances, the German drill sergeant—a "most exasperating and yet most useful institution"—made his appearance, roaring: "Eyes vront!" "Toes oud!" "Leetle finger mit de seam de banteloons!" ". . . you neffer make a soldier!" Yet the recruits took to army life "as natural as a three-months calf to a pail of warm milk." [16]

All Northern governors answered Lincoln's call for troops. But the President could not count on Virginia, North Carolina, Kentucky, Tennessee and Missouri, and Maryland and Delaware gave only conditional responses to the call.

The April riots in Maryland affected Washington. For several days, Maryland "plug-uglies" cut off communications between the Federal capital and Northern cities. Heartened by discontent in Maryland, the *Richmond Examiner* cried: "The capture of Washington City is perfectly within the power of Virginia and Maryland, if Virginia will only make the effort . . . ; nor is there a single moment to be lost." [17] Safeguarding Washington thus became a major undertaking and troops were poured into the capital, where they were billeted in public buildings and grounds.

On May 3rd, Lincoln issued a call for 42,034 volunteers "to serve for a period of three years, unless sooner discharged," directing "that the regular army . . . be increased." [18] One week later, he proclaimed the suspension of the habeas corpus privilege in Florida.[19]

These were serious steps taken without Congressional consent. But Lincoln had to organize the machinery of war. By the time Congress convened on July 4th, Arkansas had seceded (May 6), as had North Carolina (May 21) and Tennessee (June 8). Richmond had become the Confederate capital in June. In his message to the special session of Congress, Lincoln reviewed the developments since the firing upon Fort Sumter and declared that the measures he had taken, "whether strictly legal or not, were ventured upon, under what appeared to be a popular demand, and a public necessity; trusting . . . that Congress would readily ratify them."

"This is essentially a People's contest," Lincoln stated in his message. "On the side of the Union, it is a struggle for maintaining in the world, that form, and substance of government, whose leading object is, to elevate the condition of men—to lift artificial weights from all shoulders—to clear the paths of laudable pursuit for all—to afford all, an unfettered start, and a fair chance, in the race of life. Yielding to partial, and temporary departures, from necessity, this is the leading object of the government for whose existence we contend." [20]

Congress not only approved Lincoln's acts after March 4th,[21] it authorized enlistment of 500,000 volunteers to serve not less than six months and not more than three years. Subsequently, on July 25th, a supplementary act extended the length of service to read "during the war." [22]

Conscious of the importance of preventing the border states— especially Kentucky and Missouri—from going with the Confederacy, Congress approved the Crittenden resolution, declaring that "this war is not waged . . . in any spirit of oppression, or for the purpose of conquest or subjugation, or . . . of overthrowing or interfering with the rights or established institutions of those [Southern] States, but to defend and maintain the *supremacy* of the Constitution, and to preserve the Union. . . ." The resolution was approved by Congress in July 1861, but the House refused to reaffirm it in December.[23]

On the military fronts, this was the situation in the early stages of the war: On May 24th, Federal forces took Alexandria and Virginia Heights and began fortifying a ten-mile area surrounding Washington for the protection of the city. General Benjamin F. Butler, after occupying Fortress Monroe, declared on May 25th that all Negroes who escaped to his lines would be considered contraband of war. On June 3rd, Union forces under General George B. McClellan defeated the rebels at Philippi. "Forward to Richmond!" became the "The Nation's Battle-Cry." Then, on July 21st, came the first battle of Bull Run and disastrous defeat for the Federals. Said James Russell Young: *"We have sent into Virginia the best . . . of our grand army. We have fought the greatest battle ever fought on the continent, and we have been not only beaten, but our army has been routed, and many of its best regiments wholly demoralized."*[24]

Immediately after Bull Run, Lincoln outlined the nation's military policy and called McClellan to Washington.[25] A West Pointer and Mexican War veteran, McClellan was gaining a wide reputation as a military organizer and administrator. The President now gave him the task of turning the Federal volunteer army into a taut, disciplined, military force capable of waging war against the enemies of the Union with precision and swiftness. To deal with the precarious situation in Missouri, Lincoln sent General John C. Frémont to St. Louis. Frémont, celebrated as an explorer of the American West and the first Republican Presidential candidate in 1856, arrived in St. Louis on July 25th, where he established headquarters and ultimately became a great embarrassment to the Lincoln Administration.

As the American Civil War got under way, the world waited for an answer to the question propounded by Lincoln: "Must a government . . . be too strong for the liberties of its . . . people, or too weak to maintain its own existence?" [26]

"That Has to Come Down"

FRIDAY, MAY 24, 1861

¶ *On Thursday night, May 23rd, 10,000 Federals moved across the Potomac as "a full moon looked peacefully down, and perfect quiet reigned on all the neighboring shores."* [1] *Hours later, the North was stunned by the news that Colonel Elmer E. Ellsworth, twenty-four-year-old personal friend of Lincoln, had become one of the early casualties of the war.*

After landing at Alexandria at 4 A.M. Friday, Colonel Ellsworth's New York Fire Zouaves marched into the center of the town, "no resistance whatever to their progress being offered." As Ellsworth was marching a squad of men to take possession of the telegraph office, he noticed a secession flag flying from a nearby building. Immediately he exclaimed: "That has to come down," and entering the building, "made his way to the roof with one of his men, hauled down the rebel emblem, and, wrapping it around his body, descended." [2]

"While on the second floor," an eyewitness reported, "a secessionist came out of a door with a cocked double barrelled shot gun. He took aim at Ellsworth, when the latter attempted to strike the gun out of the way with his feet, as he struck it one of the barrels was

discharged, lodging a whole load of buckshot in Ellsworth's body, killing him instantly. His companion instantly shot the murderer through the head with a revolver." [3]

The news of Ellsworth's death—"the only casualty that is thus far reported"—was not generally known throughout Washington until about ten o'clock on Friday morning. When word of the assassination reached the populace, "the excitement was intense, especially among the military, who express the greatest impatience and desire to be sent over to Virginia." [4]

Ellsworth, who had accompanied Lincoln from Springfield to Washington, had made considerable impact upon the country as a young man of great promise. [5] *His death struck at the heart of Lincoln, who wrote to Ellsworth's parents: "In the untimely loss of your noble son, our affliction here, is scarcely less than your own. So much of promised usefulness to one's country, and of bright hopes for one's self and friends, have rarely been so suddenly dashed, as in his fall. . . . My acquaintance with him began less than two years ago; yet through the latter half of the intervening period, it was as intimate as the disparity of our ages, and my engrossing engagements, would permit."* [6]

Lincoln's more immediate reaction to Ellsworth's death—a few hours after its occurrence—is chronicled by a New York Herald *reporter:* [7]

I called at the White House this morning, with Senator [Henry] Wilson, of Massachusetts, to see the President on a pressing matter of public business, and as we entered the library we remarked the President standing before a window, looking out across the Potomac, running at foot of Presidential grounds. He did not move till we approached very closely, when he turned round abruptly, and advanced towards us, extending his hand: "Excuse me," he said, "but I cannot talk." We supposed that his voice had probably given way from some cause or other, and we were just about to inquire, when to our surprise the President burst into tears, and concealed his face in his handkerchief. He walked up and down the room for some moments, and we stepped aside in silence, not a little moved at such an unusual spectacle, in such a man, in such a place.

After composing himself somewhat the President took his seat, and desired us to approach. "I will make[8] no apology, gentlemen," said the President, "for my weakness; but I knew poor Ellsworth well, and held him in great regard. Just as you entered the room, Captain

Fox left me, after giving me the painful details of Ellsworth's unfortunate death. The event was so unexpected, and the recital so touching, that it quite unmanned me." The President here made a violent effort to restrain his emotions, and after a pause he proceeded, with a tremulous voice, to give us the incidents of the tragedy that had occurred. "Poor fellow," repeated the President, as he closed his relation, "it was undoubtedly an act of rashness, but it only shows the heroic spirit that animates our soldiers, from high to low, in this righteous cause of ours. Yet who can restrain their grief to see them fall in such a way as this, not by the fortunes of war, but by the hand of an assassin?" Towards the close of his remarks he added, "There is one fact that has reached me, which is a great consolation to my heart, and quite a relief after this melancholy affair. I learn from several persons, that when the Stars and Stripes were raised again in Alexandria, many of the people of the town actually wept for joy, and manifested the liveliest gratification at seeing this familiar and loved emblem once more floating above them. This is another proof that all the South is not secessionist; and it is my earnest hope that as we advance we shall find as many friends as foes."

At this moment Senator [Zachariah] Chandler was announced, and he related to the President some interesting details of the capture of the rebel dragoons, which was effected so quickly that they had not time to mount their horses. It appears that the valiant Senator accompanied "his boys," as he called the Michigan regiment, down to Alexandria, and came back quite satisfied with the whole performance. Though we remarked that by this time the President was quite himself again, still we thought it was not a fitting moment to open a discussion of the matter which had brought us to the White House, so we took our leave without referring to it.

[Ellsworth's funeral service was held in the East Room of the White House on May 25th.[9]]

"Mixed Up with Office-Seekers"

THURSDAY, JULY 18, 1861

¶ *Patronage continued to plague Lincoln. Said Edward Bates: "The rush for office is overwhelming." And Nathaniel Hawthorne's description of Willard's Hotel could well have been applied to the White*

House, the Capitol and the government departments, where "you are [also] mixed up with office-seekers, wire-pullers, inventors, artists, poets, prosers (including editors, army correspondents, attachés of foreign journals, and long-winded talkers), clerks, diplomatists, mail contractors, railway directors, until your own identity is lost among them." All sought something from the Lincoln Government. Some went to see the President personally on matters of patronage; others succeeded in having Congressmen or other influential politicians act as intermediaries.[1]

How Lincoln felt about "the extraordinary pressure upon me" imposed by these people is described by his old New Salem friend and former colleague in the Illinois Legislature, Robert L. Wilson, in a letter to William H. Herndon in 1866. Wilson was at the White House when Galusha A. Grow of Pennsylvania was pressing his claim on Lincoln, who feared that unless the requested "place" was granted, "I can scarcely avoid an 'unpleasantness,' not to say a difficulty, or rupture" with the Speaker of the House.[2]

I was with the President one day, when Mr Grow, from Wilmot district Pa. came in, and in an excited manner deman[d]ed of the President why he did not appoint his Brother-in-law [Joseph E. Streeter] as one of the Judges . . . in one of the new Territories. Mr Lincoln excused himself by saying that he had forgotten his Brother-in-law, at the time the appointment was made, but assured him that his friend Should have an appointment at an early day. Mr Grow was very angry, and talked, as it looked to me, impertinently. Mr Seward came in, and took part [in] defending Mr Lincoln. Mr Grow used threats that surprized [sic] me. After Mr Grow and Mr Seward had retired, and we were alone, he was troubled. Said he had then been President five months, and was surprised [sic] any body would want the office. He went on to speak about the duties; he said he was inaugurated, he supposed that although he realized that the labor of administering the affairs of the Nation would be arduous, and severe, and that he had made up his mind, that he could, and would do it, all the duties were rather pleasant, and agreeable except making the appointments. He had Started out with the determination, to make no improper appointments, and to accomplish that result he imposed upon himself the labor of an examination into the qualifications of each applicant. He found to his surprize [sic], that members of his Cabinate [sic], who were equally interested with himself, in the success of his administration had been recommending parties to be appointed to responsible positions who were often physically, morally, and intellectu[a]lly unfit for the place. He said that it did appear that most of the Cabinate [*sic*] officers, and members of Congress, had a list of appointments to make, and many of them were such as ought not to be made, and they knew, and their importunities were angriest [?] in proportion to the unfitness for the appointee. [H]e said he was so badgered with applications for appointments that he thought sometimes that the only way that he [could] escape from them would be to take a rope and hang himself, on one of the trees in the lawn South of the Presidents House, [Lincoln] looking out at the trees through the window at the same time.

"The Greatest Coward"

TUESDAY, JULY 23, 1861

¶ *The Battle of Bull Run—or Manassas—was the first major engagement of the Civil War. Fought on Sunday, July 21st, by public demand, it resulted in a resounding defeat of the Union forces commanded by General Irvin McDowell. Fortunately for the North, lack of "food and transportation" prevented the rebels from pressing an attack upon Washington after their victory.*[1]

William H. Russell, correspondent for the London Times, *noted early in July that "writers of stupendous ignorance on military matters . . . demand that an army, which has neither adequate transport, artillery, nor cavalry, shall be pushed forward to Richmond." And Weed's* Albany Evening Journal *commented: "Exciting appeals to popular feeling were soon followed by open aspersions and denunciations of Gen. Scott." When Congress assembled, "Senators and representatives, with more zeal than knowledge, caught up and reiterated the cry 'On to Richmond.' . . . A movement upon Manassas was . . . demanded." Lincoln had to fight or face Congressional censure for failing to take "measures essential to the prosecution of the war."*[2]

The Union high command had planned Bull Run carefully. But the Yankees—mostly "green" three-month volunteers—"exhausted with fatigue and thirst and confused by firing into each other," were overwhelmed with crushing force and fled from the battlefield. Russell termed the retreat "a cowardly route—a miserable causeless panic," after witnessing the disorganized Federals—some barefooted—pour-

ing into Washington, "many of them . . . without knapsacks, cross-belts, and firelocks." 3

"Who is responsible for this great national disaster?" asked the Albany Evening Journal. "Officials cannot answer." Scott had been opposed to the Federal advance at Bull Run. "See the results of forcing Gen. Scott against his wishes," Russell taunted.4 In Congress, the question of responsibility for the action elicited spirited debate.

Scott's deep frustration over Bull Run—displayed in a conversation with the President on July 23rd—was reported by Illinois Democrat W. A. Richardson in a speech before the House of Representatives the following day: 5

W. A. RICHARDSON. . . . I will tell the gentleman [FRANK BLAIR of Missouri] what occurred yesterday morning in the presence of my friends [JOHN A.] McCLERNAND, [JOHN A.] LOGAN, and [ELIHU B.] WASHBURNE, of Illinois, and also in the presence of the President of the United States and the Secretary of War. I will try to repeat what was said. General Scott said: "Sir, I am the greatest coward in America." I rose from my seat immediately. "Stop, sir," said he, "I will prove it; I have fought this battle, sir, against my judgment; I think the President of the United States ought to remove me to-day for doing it; as God is my judge, after my superiors had determined to fight it, I did all in my power to make the Army efficient. I deserve removal because I did not stand up, when my army was not in condition for fighting, and resist it to the last." If the gentlemen controverts what I say, I furnish the evidence, the proof. Here are the gentlemen present who heard this conversation. There is your Secretary of War and your President. He said that he ought to be removed because he had fought the battle against his judgment. I stand here to vindicate him. . . .

Mr. WASHBURNE. As my colleague has referred to that conversation, I hope he will state to the House what the President said to General Scott.

Mr. RICHARDSON. I will state it. The President said, "Your conversation seems to imply that I forced you to fight this battle." General Scott then said, "I have never served a President who has been kinder to me than you have been." But, sir, he did not relieve the Cabinet from the imputation of having forced him to fight this battle. He paid a compliment to President Lincoln personally; and, Mr. Speaker, standing here in my place, I desire to say of Abraham Lincoln—and I have known him from boyhood's hour till now—if you let him alone, he is an honest man; but I am afraid he has not the will to stand up against the wily politicians who surround him and knead him to their purposes.

"No Curse Could Be Greater"

TUESDAY, JULY 23, 1861

¶ *Bull Run shocked the North into realizing that this was to be a prolonged war; that victories would not be won on parade grounds. For the troops, it was a blow to morale. "No curse could be greater than invasion by a volunteer army," said William T. Sherman, then a colonel in the New York 69th, who believed the debacle was caused by untrained, undisciplined citizen soldiers. According to Sherman, "some of them were so mutinous" after the battle that he had to resort to "threatening, if they dared to leave camp without orders, I would open fire on them."* [1]

Lincoln and Seward went to Fort Corcoran on July 23rd "to see with their own eyes the state of the troops" under Sherman. The then future general reports the Lincoln-Seward visit in his Memoirs, *published in 1875:* [2]

I was near the river-bank, looking at a block-house which had been built for the defense of the aqueduct, when I saw a carriage coming by the road that crossed the Potomac River at Georgetown by a ferry. I thought I recognized in the carriage the person of President Lincoln. I hurried across a bend, so as to stand by the road-side as the carriage passed. I was in uniform, with a sword on, and was recognized by Mr. Lincoln and Mr. Seward, who rode side by side in an open hack. I inquired if they were going to my camps, and Mr. Lincoln said: "Yes; we heard that you had got over the big scare, and we thought we would come over and see the 'boys.' "
. . . I asked if I might give directions to his coachman, he promptly invited me to jump in and to tell the coachman which way to drive. Intending to begin on the right and follow round to the left, I turned the driver into a side-road which led up a very steep hill, and,

seeing a soldier, called to him and sent him up hurriedly to announce to the colonel (Bennett, I think) that the President was coming. As we slowly ascended the hill, I discovered that Mr. Lincoln was full of feeling, and wanted to encourage our men. I asked if he intended to speak to them, and he said he would like to. I asked him then to please discourage all cheering, noise, or any sort of confusion; that we had had enough of it before Bull Run to ruin any set of men, and that what we needed were cool, thoughtful, hard-fighting soldiers—no more hurrahing, no more humbug. He took my remarks in the most perfect good-nature. Before we had reached the first camp, I heard the drum beating the "assembly," saw the men running for their tents, and in a few minutes the regiment was in line, arms presented, and then brought to an order and "parade rest!"

Mr. Lincoln stood up in the carriage, and made one of the neatest, best, and most feeling addresses I ever listened to, referring to our late disaster at Bull Run, the high duties that still devolved on us, and the brighter days yet to come. At one or two points the soldiers began to cheer, but he promptly checked them, saying: "Don't cheer, boys. I confess I rather like it myself, but Colonel Sherman here says it is not military; and I guess we had better defer to his opinion." In winding up, he explained that, as President, he was commander-in-chief; that he was resolved that the soldiers should have every thing that the law allowed; and he called on one and all to appeal to him personally in case they were wronged. The effect of this speech was excellent.

We passed along in the same manner to all the camps of my brigade; and Mr. Lincoln complimented me highly for the order, cleanliness, and discipline, that he observed. Indeed, he and Mr. Seward both assured me that it was the first bright moment they had experienced since the battle.

At last we reached Fort Corcoran. The carriage could not enter, so I ordered the regiment, without arms, to come outside, and gather about Mr. Lincoln, who would speak to them. He made to them the same feeling address, with more personal allusions, because of their special gallantry in the battle under [Colonel Michael] Corcoran, who was still a prisoner in the hands of the enemy [having been captured at Bull Run]; and he concluded with the same general offer of redress in case of grievance. In the crowd I saw the officer with whom I had had . . . [a] passage at reveille that morning.

[Sherman had caught this officer planning to go to New York without leave and had threatened to "shoot you like a dog!"] His [the officer's] face was pale, and lips compressed. I foresaw a scene, but sat on the front seat of the carriage as quiet as a lamb. This officer forced his way through the crowd to the carriage, and said: "Mr. President, I have a cause of grievance. This morning I went to speak to Colonel Sherman, and he threatened to shoot me." Mr. Lincoln, who was still standing, said, "Threatened to shoot you?" "Yes, sir, he threatened to shoot me." Mr. Lincoln looked at him, then at me, and stooping his tall, spare form toward the officer, said to him in a loud stage-whisper, easily heard for some yards around: "Well, if I were you, and he threatened to shoot, I would not trust him, for I believe he would do it." The officer turned about and disappeared, and the men laughed at him. Soon the carriage drove on, and, as we descended the hill, I explained the facts to the President, who answered, "Of course I didn't know any thing about it, but I thought you knew your own business best." I thanked him for his confidence, and assured him that what he had done would go far to enable me to maintain good discipline, and it did.

By this time the day was well spent. I asked to take my leave, and the President and Mr. Seward drove back to Washington.

"That . . . Is . . . Emancipation"
SUNDAY, AUGUST 4, 1861

¶ *On May 25th, General Butler at Fortress Monroe had ruled that slaves fleeing to his lines would be considered "contraband" of war —a position upheld by Secretary of War Cameron. The next important step toward slavery emancipation was taken by Congress on August 6th—before adjourning its special session—with the passage of the first Confiscation Act, which provided that a master would lose his right to a slave if that slave were employed to advance the insurrection against the United States.[1]*

Democrats and Border State Congressmen, leading a fierce attack against the measure, maintained that Congress had no authority to interfere with slavery and that the war was not being fought for abolition purposes. William Kellogg of Illinois argued that while this was true, Congress had a right to punish treason by confiscating rebel property. Exclaimed Kentucky's Breckinridge: "I tell you, sir, that . . . is a general act of emancipation." Thaddeus Stevens, in a heated outburst, declared: "If their [the South's] whole country must be laid waste and made a desert, in order to save this Union from destruction, so let it be." [2]

Lincoln's attitude toward the first Confiscation Act was expressed in a conversation with Kentucky Congressmen on August 4th. Representative Robert Mallory, who participated in that meeting, reported the discussion to the House on June 15, 1864: [3]

On the Sunday preceding the day on which the extra session of Congress was to adjourn in 1861, I called upon the President by appointment in company with two of my colleagues, now dead, the lamented [John J.] Crittenden, and [James S.] Jackson who fell so gallantly at the battle of Perryville, and my colleague from the Maysville district, [Wililam H. Wadsworth]. . . . We thought we saw in . . . [the Confiscation Bill] the commencement of this emancipation policy of the Government which would lead to disastrous results. We visited the President with a view of trying to induce him to forbid that law. We had a long and free conversation with him. He left the impression on my mind and on the minds of my colleagues that he would not give his sanction to that law. He said that he was opposed to this whole system of legislation, and left the impression on us, although he did not say so in express terms, that he would veto that bill. In the course of that conversation he turned to me and, addressing me personally, said: "Mr. Mallory, this war, so far as I have anything to do with it, is carried on on the idea that there is a Union sentiment in these States, which, when set free from the control now held over it by the presence of the confederate or rebel power, will be sufficient to replace those States in the Union. If I am mistaken in this, if there is no such sentiment there, if the people of those States are determined with unanimity, or with a feeling approaching unanimity, that their States shall not be members of this Confederacy, it is beyond the power of the people of the other States to force them to remain in the Union;" and said he, "in that contingency—in the contingency that there is not that sentiment there—this war is not only an error; it is a crime." That was his declaration at the commencement of this war. Since then he has been induced to change his policy by his friends on the other side of the House [the Republicans].

"Quite a Female Politician"
TUESDAY, SEPTEMBER 10, 1861

¶ *General Frémont arrived in Missouri shortly after Bull Run to find the state in chaos. Not only was the population divided in sympathy between North and South, the Unionists themselves were split into pro-slavery and abolitionist elements. Pay for Federal troops was long overdue and some regiments were mutinying. Strong Confederate forces were creating havoc. To meet this situation, Frémont needed money, arms, ammunition and other military necessities; he needed officers and men. When Washington failed to meet all his requirements, he commandeered Federal funds in Missouri, made unauthorized purchases at stupendous prices, commissioned his own officers, and built his own fortifications. Working feverishly, he isolated himself in an ostentatious St. Louis mansion and made himself inaccessible even to important people who sought audiences with him on vital official business.*

Complaints against Frémont soon begun pouring into Washington. He was deemed "unequal to the command of an army," said General Samuel R. Curtis, and Gustave Koerner felt: "Some of his most intimate friends were undoubtedly cheating and circumventing him." Frémont was considered "honest and honorable himself, but too impulsive and too impressionable." [1]

On August 30th, plagued by rebel activity in northern and central Missouri, Frémont issued a proclamation ruling that all traitors within his lines "shall be tried by court-martial, and if found guilty, will be shot." Furthermore, he decreed, their slaves would be "declared freemen," and their other property—real and personal—would be confiscated. [2]

Although the proclamation took Lincoln by surprise, he wrote Frémont "in a spirit of caution and not of censure," pointing out that "should you shoot a man, according to the proclamation, the Confederates would very certainly shoot our best men in their hands in retaliation." Secondly, Lincoln stated: "I think there is great danger that the closing paragraph, in relation to the confiscation of property, and the liberating slaves . . . will alarm our Southern Union friends, and turn them against us—perhaps ruin our rather fair prospect for Kentucky." He requested Frémont to modify the proclamation. Frémont refused. On September 8th, he wrote that if the President desired modification, "I have to ask that you will openly direct me" to make it. [3]

Frémont, sensing that the Administration was losing confidence in him, wrote a second letter to Lincoln on September 8th, outlining his military plans. This he sent to the President by special messenger —his wife, Jessie Benton Frémont, daughter of the late renowned Senator Thomas Hart Benton.

Mrs. Frémont arrived in Washington late on September 10th, after two days of fatiguing travel from St. Louis. Immediately upon checking in at Willard's, she sent a note to the President inquiring when she might have an interview. His curt reply: "Now, at once." Later that night, she was at the White House, accompanied by Judge Edward Coles of New York City. Her report of the meeting, which follows, is made up of material from two sources: Her undated memorandum, believed to have been written soon after its occurrence, and a later, unpublished Memoir.[4] In her Memoir, she states:

We were shown into the red parlor and told, the President would be there presently. It was some time before he came in, though it was an appointment of his own making and the *"now"* had indicated I was to hasten. When he did enter it was from the far door of the dining room which he pushed to, but it was gently set open again from the other side. The President did not speak only bowed slightly, and I introduced Judge Coles as a member of the New York bar, and as the President still said nothing, I gave him the letter telling him General Frémont felt the subject to be of so much importance, that he had sent me to answer any points on which the President might want more information. At this he smiled with an expression that was not agreeable, then moving nearer the chandelier to see better, read the letter standing. Judge Coles had withdrawn to the door way of the blue parlor where he walked up and down like a sentinel. I had not been offered a seat though I was looking as tired as I felt. The President's unusual manner was a reversal of the old order of things. As he remained standing reading the letter, I drew out one of the row of chairs and sat down for I was trembling from fatigue and recent illness and instinct told me the President intended to discourage me, and I did not intend to appear nervous.

—— At length the President drew up a chair and sat down near me with the letter, saying, "I have written to the General and he knows what I want done." I answered the General thought it would be an advantage for him if I came to explain more fully what he wished him [the President] to know, for, I said "the General feels he is at a great disadvantage of being perhaps opposed by people in whom you have every confidence."

"Who do you mean?" he said, "Persons of differing views"? I answered; "the General's conviction is that it will be long and dreadful work to conquer by arms alone, that there must be other considera-tion to get us the support of foreign countries—that he *knew* the English feeling for gradual emancipation and the strong wish to meet it on the part of important men in the South: that as the President knew we were on the eve of England, France and Spain recognizing the South: they were anxious for a pretext to do so; England on account of her cotton interests, and France because the Emperor dislikes us." The President said "You are quite a female politician."

I felt the sneering tone and saw there was a foregone decision against all listening. Then the President spoke more rapidly and unrestrainedly: [Here we quote Lincoln from Mrs. Frémont's un-dated memorandum.] "[that] *it was a war for a great national idea, the Union, and that General Frémont should not have dragged the negro into it—that he never would if he had consulted with Frank Blair. I put Frank Blair there to advise him*[.]"

The words italicized are exactly those of the President. He first mentioned "the Blairs," in this astonishing connection.

[In her *Memoir,* Mrs. Frémont says:]

"Then," I answered, "there is no use to say any more, except that we were not aware that Frank Blair represented you—he did not do so openly."

I asked when I could have the answer [to the letter she had brought]? "Maybe by to-morrow," said the President, "I have a great deal to do—to-morrow if possible, or the next day." To my saying I would come for it—"No, I will send it to you, to-morrow or the day after." He asked me where I was staying, and was answered at Willard's—and we came away.

As we walked through the grounds Judge Coles said, in his calm way, "Mrs. Frémont, the General has no further part in this war. He will be deprived of all his part in the war; it is not the President alone, but there is a faction which plans the affairs of the North and they will triumph, and they are against the General."

[Lincoln did not give the promised reply to Mrs. Frémont. On September 11th, he wrote the letter to the General—sending it by mail—in which he declared: "The particular clause . . . in relation to the confiscation of property and the liberation of slaves, appeared to me to be objectionable, in it's [sic] non-conformity to the Act of Congress passed the 6th. of last August upon the same subjects. . . . Your answer, just received, expresses the preference on your part, that I should make an open order for the modification, which I very cheerfully do." The revocation of the proclamation brought about a storm of protest from abolitionist quarters. In explaining his position to his friend Orville H. Browning, the President wrote on September 22nd: "The proclamation in the point in question, is simply 'dictatorship.' It assumes that the general may do *anything* he pleases—confiscate the lands and free the slaves of *loyal* people, as well as of disloyal ones." He then turned to the question of policy, stating: "No doubt the thing was popular in some quarters, and would have been more so if it had been a general declaration of emancipation. The Kentucky Legislature would not budge till that proclamation was modified; and Gen. [Robert] Anderson telegraphed me that on the news of Gen. Fremont [sic] having actually issued deeds of manumission, a whole company of our Volunteers threw down their arms and disbanded. I was so assured, as to think it probable, that the very arms we had furnished Kentucky would be turned against us. . . . On the contrary, if you will give up your restlessness for new positions, and back me manfully on the grounds upon which you and other kind friends gave me the election, and have approved in my public documents, we shall go through triumphantly."

Frémont was subsequently relieved from command of the Department of the West. The General's order relinquishing the command was dated November 2nd.]

" 'The Little Corporal' of Unfought Fields"

THURSDAY, OCTOBER 10, 1861

¶ *Six days after Bull Run, the North had a new commander in thirty-four-year-old Major General George B. McClellan, hailed as "the Young Napoleon." But McClellan, as he later wrote, "had no army to command—merely a collection of regiments cowering on the banks of the Potomac, some perfectly raw, others dispirited by the recent defeat." The cigar-smoking general—who also indulged in "the more naked beauties of a quid"—set to work furiously fortifying Washington, organizing and training the Union army for an offensive movement upon the South.[1]*

Commented William H. Russell: "Every one . . . is willing to do as he bids: the President confides in him, and 'Georges' him; the press fawn upon him, the people trust him." McClellan insisted: "I am not spoiled by my unexpected new position." He told his wife: "I receive letter after letter, have conversation after conversation, calling on me to save the nation, alluding to the presidency, dictatorship, etc." Nevertheless, observed Russell, "he is 'the little corporal' of unfought fields." [2]

By the end of August, the volunteer army of Bull Run had been replaced "by better and more numerous levies," but in September the force was still considered unprepared for action. McClellan was spending a great deal of time visiting all the army posts, putting in long hours at his desk, when—according to Russell—"he should be out with his army . . . living among his generals, studying the composition of his army, investigating its defects, and, above all, showing himself to the men as soon afterwards as possible, if he cannot be with them at the time, in the small affairs which constantly occur along the front." To the Britisher, McClellan did not appear to be "a man of action, or, at least, a man who intends to act as speedily as the crisis demands." [3]

McClellan soon incurred the wrath of General Scott. He described "Old Fuss and Feathers" as "the most dagnerous antagonist I have. Our ideas are so widely different that it is impossible for us to work together." He had disdain for these "wretched politicians." As for the Cabinet members, he considered them "some of the greatest geese . . . I have even seen—enough to tax the patience of Job." Toward Lincoln the general felt kindly, but considered the President's visits as interruptions.[4]

One of Lincoln's meetings with McClellan is recorded in John Hay's Diary *under date of October 10th:* [5]

Tonight I went over to McClellan's quarters with the Tycoon [as Hay called Lincoln] and Seward. [Colonel Frederick W.] Lander was with us, part of the way. Lander was gasconading a little. He said he would like a good place to die in with a corporal's guard, to set the nation right in the face of the world after the cowardly shame of Bull Run. The President as Lander walked off, said "If he really wanted a job like that I could give it to him—Let him take his squad and go down behind Manassas and break up their [the rebels'] railroad." Seward said he disbelieved in personal courage as a civilized institution. He had always acted on the opposite principle, admitting that you are scared and assuming that the enemy is. If this matter had been managed on his basis it would have been arranged satisfactorily and honorably before now.

We came to McClellan's quarters and met in the telegraph office a long and awkward youth who spoke in a high-pitched and rapid tone to Seward, "We are just in from a ride of all day." Seward introduced him to me as Captain Orleans [Louis Phillipe d'Orléans, Comte de Paris]. He [Orleans] went upstairs to call McClellan and the President said quietly "One doesnt like to make a messenger of the King of France, as that youth, the Count of Paris would be, if his family had kept the throne."

McClellan came hurriedly in and began to talk with the President. They discussed the events of today and yesterday. McClellan was much pleased at the conduct of his men—no rowdyism or plundering today. He *was merely* today finishing *yesterdays work*. The rest of the week will be used in the same way. Says the Tycoon, "We have gained a day on our Sea expedition [to take Port Royal, South Carolina]. The vessels will leave on the 14th it is thought instead of the 15th." [The naval force, commanded by Captain Samuel F. DuPont, finally sailed on October 29th; McClellan had been opposed to this movement. Port Royal was taken by DuPont on November 7th.]

As we left, McClellan said, "I think we shall have our arrangements made for a strong reconnaissance about Monday to feel the strength of the enemy. I intend to be careful, and do as well as possible. Dont let them hurry me, is all I ask." "You shall have your own way in the matter I assure you" said the Tycoon, and went home.

"I Have a Notion . . ."
SATURDAY, OCTOBER 26, 1861

¶ *As the war entered its sixth month, Northern newspapers and radical Congressmen—led by Bluff Ben Wade of Ohio, a master of profanity; "that Xantippe in pants," Zack Chandler of Michigan; and Lincoln's friend Lyman Trumbull, "a gifted hair-splitter" turned administration critic—renewed the clamor for an attack upon the Confederacy.[1] These Jacobins, as the radicals were called, had undertaken a special mission to Washington in October to press for military action. Not only did they remonstrate with McClellan, they took their complaints directly to Lincoln.*

On October 21st, a Federal regiment commanded by Colonel Edward D. Baker, intimate friend of the President, engaged a superior rebel force at Ball's Bluff, near Leesburg, and was cut to shreds "before the destructive fire of the enemy." Baker himself was killed in battle. While in itself a minor engagement, the defeat at Ball's Bluff created a furore in the North. Somebody would have to pay for this disaster. The Jacobins in Congress were after McClellan, a Democrat and a conservative, but they wound up with the scalp of General Charles P. Stone by impugning his loyalty. Wrote one newspaperman: "McClellan has fallen very much in my opinion since the Leesburg disaster. . . . It is whispered that General Stone, who ordered the movement, is guilty of treason—a common crime of unlucky generals—at all events he is to be displaced, and will be put under surveillance." [2]

On October 26th, John Hay wrote in his Diary:[3]

This evening the Jacobin club, represented by Trumbull, Chandler and Wade, came up to worry the administration into a battle. The wild howl of the summer is to be renewed. The President stood up for McClellan's deliberateness. We then went over to the General's Headquarters. We found Col [John J.] Key there. He was talking about the grand necessity of an immediate battle to clean out the enemy, at once. He seemed to think we were ruined if we did not fight. The President asked what McC. tho[ugh]t about it. Key answered, "The General is troubled in his mind. I think he is much embarrassed by the radical difference between his views and those of General Scott."

Here McC. came in—Key went out—the President began to talk about his wonderful new repeating battery of rifled gun, shooting 50 balls a minute. The President is delighted with it and has ordered ten and asks McC. to go down and see it, and if proper, detail a corp of men to work it. He further told the General that Reverdy Johnson wants the Maryland Vol's in Maryl[an]d to vote in November. All right.

They then talked about the Jacobins. McC said that Wade preferred an unsuccessful battle to delay. He [Wade] said a defeat could be easily repaired, by the swarming recruits. McClellan answered "that he would rather have a few recruits before a victory— than a good many after a defeat."

The President deprecated this new manifestation of senseless popular impatience but at the same time said it was a reality and should be taken into the account. ["]At the same time General you must not fight till you are ready."

"I have everything at stake[,]" said the General. "If I fail I will not see you again or anybody."

"I have a notion to go out with *you* and stand or fall with the battle[,]" [said the President.]

"If Old Scott Had Legs"
FRIDAY, NOVEMBER 1, 1861

¶ *Although McClellan had been brought to Washington on General Scott's recommendation, relations between the two men subsequently grew strained. McClellan had direct access to the President and participated in Cabinet meetings; Scott found this difficult to take. He differed with "the Young Napoleon" on army organization and military tactics. In August, when Scott said Washington was safe, McClellan said it was insecure. Apart from this, the generalissimo suspected that McClellan and some Cabinet members were intriguing against him. Scott had been a Mexican War hero, but now he could barely walk let alone lead his army into action. Although weighed down by age and illness, Scott was still popular. Said one officer: "If old Scott had legs," he would be "good for a big thing yet."* [1]

On November 1st, Lincoln honored Scott's request for retirement. "In the afternoon the Prest: and all the heads of D[e]p[artmen]ts. waited upon Genl. Scott at his quarters and had a very touching interview," wrote Attorney General Bates. "The Prest. made a neat and feeling address, and the Genl. briefly replied, from the depths of his heart—" [2]

Scott's imminent retirement had been rumored for some time. There had been talk that Major General Henry W. Halleck, another West Pointer who had published books on military science and was considered "a soldier, and something more," would succeed Scott.[3] The man who did was McClellan.

John Hay gives us a conversation between Lincoln and the new general in chief shortly after the appointment: [4]

The night of the 1st November we went over to McClellan's. The General was there and read us his general order in regard to Scott's resignation & his own assumption of command. The President thanked him for it and said it greatly relieved him. He added "I should be perfectly satisfied if I thought that this vast increase of responsibility would not embarrass you." "It is a great relief, sir. I feel as if several tons were taken from my shoulders today. I am now in contact with you, and the Secretary [of War]. I am not embarrassed by intervention.["] "Well" says the Tycoon, "call on me for all the sense I have, and all the information. In addition to your present command, the supreme command of the Army will entail a vast labor upon you." "I can do it all," McC said quietly.

Going to Seward's, *he* [the President] talked long and earnestly about the matter. He had been giving a grave and fatherly lecture to McC. which was taken in good part, advising him to enlarge the sphere of his thoughts and feel the weight of the occasion.

Chapter Five

"THE FAT'S IN THE FIRE"

O**N** November 8, 1861, a shot from the United States sloop of war *San Jacinto* crossed the bow of the British mail steamer *Trent,* as she plowed her way through the Bahama Channel. Refusing to heave to, the *Trent* maintained her speed until a second shot brought her to a halt. Shortly thereafter an American boarding party, following orders from Captain Charles Wilkes, confronted the British commander with a demand for the surrender of James Murray Mason of Virginia and John Slidell of Louisiana, Confederate emissaries bound for London and Paris. Over the violent objections of the British officers, the two rebel agents and their secretaries were removed from the *Trent* as contraband of war and taken to Fort Warren in Boston Harbor.

A jubilant North greeted the news of the Mason-Slidell capture— an incident which touched off one of the most serious Anglo-American crises during the war between the states. Captain Wilkes was hailed as a conquering hero, commended by Navy Secretary Welles, the House of Representatives, the press and the populace. In Washington, members of the diplomatic corps were in a "furious flutter" over the capture. In London, newspapers spouted "as much fiery lava as Vesuvius," as they decried the incident as an affront to the British flag. Henry Adams, son of Charles Francis Adams, American Minister to the Court of St. James, told his brother in America that in the past "we might have preserved our dignity in many ways without going to war with [Britain]. . . . But now all the fat's in the fire." [1]

140

The British accused Seward of masterminding the *Trent* affair; they characterized him as "an ogre fully resolved to eat all Englishmen raw." In fact, however, "the act was done by Commander Wilkes without instructions and even without the knowledge of the government." [2]

How to resolve this threatening situation without losing face or American prestige was the key question before Abraham Lincoln. At the very outset of the *Trent* affair he had felt that "the traitors [Mason and Slidell] will prove to be white elephants." If Britain demanded their release, "we must give them up," he had said.[3] The Cabinet at first had different views and only came around to the President's thinking when public feeling on both sides of the Atlantic had begun to subside. Then these facts came into focus:

Neither the United States nor Great Britain wanted war. Hostilities between the two countries would be a major victory for the South, since they inevitably would produce a Confederate alliance with England and France. Captain Wilkes had acted without authority. While Wilkes, under international law, had the belligerent right to search the *Trent* for contraband, he had no right to make an arrest at sea. He could have ordered the *Trent* into port for adjudication by a prize court, but this he did not do. Instead, he violated the rights of a neutral nation by seizing Mason and Slidell.

As 1861 drew to a close, the Lincoln Government—aided by the moderation and restraint of British diplomacy—agreed to surrender Mason and Slidell. This decision had an "excellent effect" in Paris and a "still better" result in London.[4]

Anglo-American relations had been strained since the outbreak of the Civil War. When the Confederacy was organized, it expected recognition by foreign countries—especially Great Britain and France —principally because it posessed one vital commodity: cotton. One Southerner put it this way to newspaperman Russell: "We know John Bull very well. He will make a great fuss about non-interference at first, but when he begins to want cotton he'll come off his perch." This doctrine of "cotton is king," Russell observed, was "the fixed idea" everywhere in the South.[5] It was, therefore, with a good deal of confidence that the Confederate commissioners—William L. Yancey of Alabama, Pierre A. Rost of Louisiana, and A. Dudley Mann of Georgia—set out in March 1861 for key European capitals. There was a basis for believing cotton diplomacy would be effective.

Trade was a key factor in British-American relations and cotton was vital to England's economy. British aristocracy, reflecting the bent of Europe's ruling classes, sympathized with the Confederacy; they believed the war between the states would sever permanently the American Union. British and French manufacturers looked to their respective governments to protect their interests. The firing on Fort Sumter, Lord Russell, Britain's Foreign Secretary, maintained, would "clinch the separation, but injure trade." Lincoln's blockade proclamations heightened British apprehension, and Lord Lyons, the British Minister at Washington, warned that American interference with British trade could result in his government's recognition of the Confederacy.[6] And, it was known, Britain and France had agreed to act together on problems relating to the American Civil War.

Seward was furious; he knew Yancey, Mann and Rost were about to make a bid for British and French recognition and that worried him. To Russell of the London *Times,* Seward—with "boldness of language"—asserted that "the Southern Commissioners who had been sent abroad could not be received by the Government of any foreign power, officially or otherwise, even to hand in a document or to make a representation, without incurring the risk of breaking off relations with the . . . United States." The American Minister in London, George M. Dallas—soon to be replaced by Charles Francis Adams— was ordered to do all he could to prevent the reception of the rebel agents. But the British Foreign Secretary was determined: "I shall see the Southerners when they come, but not officially, and keep them at a proper distance." [7] Lord Russell did just that, and the Yancey-Mann mission fizzled out. In France, Napoleon III said he would recognize the Confederacy only if Great Britain did. It was to save the situation for the South that Mason and Slidell were sent to Europe in November. The *Trent* affair kept them from arriving at their destinations until January 1862; but they, too, failed in their missions. For unknown to the rebels, Britain had stockpiled a large surplus of raw cotton estimated to last her through most of 1862. In addition, the English had stored considerable quantities of cloth— a premium item in a rising market. Thus, cotton did not succeed as a kingpin of Confederate diplomacy.

Another crisis in British-American relations was due to the Queen's proclamation of neutrality on May 13, 1861—the day before Adams arrived in London to assume his new duties. Again, Seward fumed and stormed. By this proclamation, he declared, Britain "designed to raise the insurgent to the level of a belligerent state." He feared the proclamation was but one step removed from *de facto* recognition of the Confederacy both by London and Paris. Immediately he outlined a course of action to be taken by Minister Adams. In this document of May 21, 1861—sharply edited by Lincoln himself— Seward told Adams to warn the British that a "concession of belligerent rights is liable to be construed as a recognition" of the South and added that "British recognition would be British intervention to create within our own territory a hostile State by overthrowing this Republic itself." [8]

This remonstrance was effective in shaping subsequent American relations not only with Great Britain but with other European governments. Commenting on British neutrality, Henry Adams wrote: "The English are really on our side; of that I have no doubt whatever. But they thought that as a dissolution [of the Union] seemed inevitable . . . their Proclamation was just the thing to keep them straight with both sides, and when it turned out otherwise they did their best to correct their mistake." [9] What was at issue in this international rumpus was that Lincoln and Seward wanted the British to be neutral *for* the Union and not against it.

After his first month in London, Minister Adams perceived that "although there has been and is more or less sympathy with the slaveholders in certain [aristocratic] circles, they are not so powerful as to overbear the general sentiment of the people." [10] Later, he told his son in America:

"People do not quite understand Americans or their politics. They think this a hasty quarrel, the mere result of passion, which will be arranged as soon as the cause of it shall pass off. They do not comprehend the connection which slavery has with it, because we do not at once preach emancipation." [11]

Northerners, too, were of two minds in regard to the war and emancipation. The abolitionists certainly believed the war was being fought to destroy slavery. Gerrit Smith had declared in July 1861: "Let the President . . . proclaim . . . liberation [of the slaves] and the war would end in thirty days." Lincoln's revocation of Frémont's proclamation in September brought a storm of protest down upon his head as abolitionists raged: "A thousand Lincolns and Sewards cannot stop the people from fighting slavery." Charles Sumner summed up abolitionist sentiment by stating that "the Rebellion, & Slavery . . . are mated, so that they will stand or fall together." [12]

Lincoln himself maintained the war to be for the restoration of the Union. His chief concern with slavery was as a military problem and he dealt with it accordingly as it arose in the military departments and in areas occupied by Union forces. Nevertheless, he was concerned also with the broader implications of slavery and the Negro. Even before he became President, Lincoln considered colonization as a solution to the Negro problem. In May 1861, he began examining different Negro colonization schemes; later, he studied plans for outright deportation. As he developed his thinking on the subject, he concluded that unless the Government was prepared to compensate loyal owners for their slaves, the North would be, in effect, punishing these masters for their loyalty. Border state slaveowners should not be deprived of their legal property unless the Government made restitution. From this stemmed Lincoln's concept of gradual, compensated emancipation.

While Lincoln pondered the question of emancipation, Jane Grey Swisshelm, fiery female abolitionist, prodded the Northerners: "Remember those dusky-browed people of the Lord who out of their ignorance and bonds are crying to him for deliverance. Do not forsake them now and range yourelf on the side of the oppressor, but go forward and work, no matter who turns back or falters." [13]

In an attempt to control the war effort, abolitionist members of Congress in December 1861 stimulated the creation of the Joint Committee on the Conduct of the War to investigate the Union disasters at Bull Run and Ball's Bluff. The Jacobin-dominated committee unloosed a vindictive attack upon the Government, revealed its errors and exposed graft, corruption and favoritism in the War Department. This made Lincoln's life more difficult and led to the resignation of Cameron and the appointment in January 1862 of Edwin M. Stanton, former Attorney General in the Buchanan Cabinet, as the new Secretary of War.

Meanwhile, "All quiet on the Potomac" became a slogan for ridiculing the Lincoln Administration. Cameron tried to encourage the North by telling Congress in December that "the army now assembled on the banks of the Potomac, will, under its able leader, soon make such a demonstration as will reestablish its authority throughout all the rebellious States." Zachariah Chandler told the

Senate: "I am informed that a very large number of your generals in command to-day have more sympathy with the enemy than they have with the loyal cause." McClellan continued to proscrastinate. Lincoln moaned: "Delay is ruining us." [14]

"The Policy of Paying"

SUNDAY, DECEMBER 1, 1861

¶ *Late in the afternoon of December 1st, Lincoln discussed compensated emancipation with his good friend Senator Browning, who summarized the conversation in his* Diary: [1]

He is very hopeful of ultimate success. He suggested to me the policy of paying Delaware, Maryland, Kentucky & Missouri $500 a piece for all the negroes they had according to the census of 1860, provided they would adopt a system of gradual emancipation which should work the extinction of slavery in twenty years, and said it would require only about one third of what was necessary to support the war for one year; and agreed with me that there should be connected with it a scheme of colonizing the blacks some where on the American Continent, [*sic*] There was no disagreement in our views upon any subject we discussed[.]

[In November, the President had drafted a bill for compensated emancipation in Delaware. The proposed bill actually had been distributed to members of the Delaware legislature, but it was never introduced.]

"Seward . . . Caused Us Uneasiness"

WEDNESDAY, DECEMBER 4, 1861

¶ *That Seward sought to provoke war with Great Britain had been suspected in Washington diplomatic circles as far back as the Sumter crisis. On October 24th, the Secretary of State issued a circular urging governors of states along the Eastern seaboard and the Great Lakes to fortify their harbor installations against possible invasion.*

In November, when Mason and Slidell were removed from the Trent, there was a view that this seizure was part of Seward's war policy against England. As feeling flared high on both sides of the Atlantic over the Trent *affair, British troops were ordered to Canada.[1] The Canadians, gripped by fear, reasoned that the United States had military might already mobilized to invade a weak British North America and would undoubtedly do so. In this tense atmosphere of suspense, suspicion and distrust, Alexander T. Galt, Canada's Minister of Finance, undertook his first diplomatic mission to the United States.*

Following his arrival in Washington, Galt dined with Lord Lyons, who was "very pleasant, and talked freely on public matters here." Galt also saw Seward, but the Secretary of State "did not impress me much; seemed fidgety, and out of temper." On December 4th, Galt went "by appointment" to see Lincoln and had "a long and satisfactory private interview." "He is very tall, thin, and with marked features, appears fond of anecdote, of which he has a fund," Galt wrote his wife. "I liked him for his straight-forward, strong commonsense." [2]

Ostensibly, Galt had come to Washington to discuss reciprocity. But his memorandum of his interview with Lincoln, written on December 5th, betrays the Canadian's real concern over his country's relations with the United States: [3]

Had interview with the President last evening; [George] Ashmun[4] present. In [the] course of conversation [I] stated that Seward's circular had caused us uneasiness. [The] P[resident] said that when discussed by [the] Cabinet, he alone had supposed that result w[oul]d follow; the rest did not. I said that while we held the most friendly feelings to the U[nited] S[tates], we thought from the indications given of the views of the Gover[nmen]t & the tone of the press, that it was possibly their [the American] intention to molest us, & that the existence of their enormous armed force might be a serious peril hereafter. [The] P.[resident] replied that the press neither here nor in England, as he had the best reason to know, reflected the real views of either Gov[ernmen]t. That no doubt they [the American newspapers] had felt hurt at the early recognition of the South as belligerents, but private explanations of Earl Russell had satisfied him on this point. That he had implicit faith in the steady conduct of the American people even under the trying circumstances of the war, and though the existence of large armies had in other countries placed successful generals in positions of arbitrary power, he did not fear this result, but believed the people would quietly resume their peaceful avocations and submit to the rule of the Gov[ernmen]t. That for himself and his Cabinet, he had never heard from one of his ministers a hostile expression toward us, and he pledged himself as a man of honour, that neither he nor his Cabinet entertained the slightest aggressive designs upon Canada, nor had any desire to disturb the rights of Great Britain on this continent. I said such expressions gave me the greatest pleasure, & with his permission I would convey them to my Colleagues in the [Canadian] Gov[ernmen]t, to which he assented.

Mr. Ashmun then remarked that there was still a possibility of grave difficulty arising out of the M[ason] and S[lidell] affair. To which the P[resident] replied to the effect that in any case that matter could be arranged, intimating that no cause of quarrel would grow out of that.

The conversation then turned upon the Slavery question & American politics [which Galt did not record].

[In concluding his memorandum, the Canadian official added: "The impression left on my mind has been that the President sincerely deprecates any quarrel with England, and has no hostile designs upon Canada, and his statement that his views were those of all his Cabinet is partly corroborated by the statement made to me by Mr. Seward that he [Seward] should be glad to see Canada placed in a position of defence.

"I cannot, however, divest my mind of the impression that the policy of the American Gov[ernmen]t is so subject to popular impulses that no assurance can be, or ought to be, relied on under present circumstances. The temper of the public mind towards England is certainly of doubtful character, and the idea is universal that Canada is most desirable for the North, while its unprepared state would make it an easy prize. The vast military preparations of the North must either be met by corresponding organization in the British provinces, or conflict, if it come, can have but one result.]

"A Monstrous Extravagance"
SATURDAY, DECEMBER 21, 1861

¶ *Even before taking up residence in Washington, Mary Lincoln felt "some anxiety as to the appropriation for refurnishing the White House, & putting new things in the place of the old." For the furniture in the Executive Mansion was in "a deplorably shabby condition" and looked—as Mrs. Lincoln's sister, Elizabeth Todd Grimsley, put it—"as if it had been brought in by the first President."* [1]

After the inauguration, Mary Lincoln, accompanied by Mrs. Grimsley, made several shopping trips to New York and Philadelphia. After all, Mrs. Lincoln later commented, "no one has the interest of the place more at heart than myself." [2]

Congress had appropriated $20,000 to refurnish the White House. When Mary Lincoln, who had no money sense, was through with her purchases, she had exceeded this budget.

Milton Hay used to call Lincoln "an old poke easy"—*a "hen pecked" husband. His nephew, John Hay, thought the President's wife a "Hell-cat."* [3] *But when she received a bill from Wm. H. Carryl & Bro., 719 Chestnut Street, Philadelphia, which brought her purchases to $6,700 in excess of the appropriation, she panicked, fearing that "Mr. Lincoln will not approve it." In her distress, she summoned Major Benjamin Brown French, Commissioner of Public Buildings, and implored him "to see him [her husband] and tell him it is common to overrun appropriations—tell him how* much *it costs to refurnish, he does not know much about it, he says he will pay it out of his own pocket (tears), you know, Major, he cannot afford that, he ought not to do it, Major you must get me out of this difficulty, it is the last, I will always be governed by you henceforth, I will not spend a cent without consulting you." She continued her pleadings: "Now do go to Mr. Lincoln and try and persuade him to approve the bill. Do, Major, for my sake (tears again) but do not let him know that you have seen me."* [4]

French, who described the incident in a chatty letter to his sister-in-law, Pamela French, on December 24, 1861, also reported his interview with the President: [5]

Scene changes to the President's office. *Major.* "Good morning Mr. President." *Prest.* "Good morning, Mr. French." *Maj:* "I have called, Mr. Prest. on a matter about which I have no official concern. A Mr. Car[r]yl has presented a bill of some $7,000 over the appropriation, for furnishing this house, and, before I can ask for an appropriation to pay it, it must have your approval." *Prest.* (A little excited.) "It never can have my approval—I'll pay it out of my own pocket first—it would stink in the nostrils of the American people to have it said that the President of the United States had approved a bill over-running an appropriation of $20,000 for *flub dubs* for this damned old house, when the soldiers cannot have blankets! Who is this Car[r]yl, and how came he to be employed[?]" *Major* (very modestly) "I do not know Sir—the first I ever heard of him he brought me a large bill for room paper. But, as I have nothing to do with the expenditure of the money for furnishing, I know nothing of this, perhaps Mr. Nicolay does." *Prest. rings his bell.* Enter servant. *Prest.* "Tell Nicolay to come here." Enter Nicolay. *Prest.* "How did this man Car[r]yl get into this house?" *Nicolay.* "I do not know sir." *Prest.* "Who employed him[?]" *N[icolay].* "Mrs. Lincoln I suppose." *Prest.* "Yes—Mrs. Lincoln—well I suppose Mrs. Lincoln *must* bear the blame, let her bear it, I swear I won't! Have you Car[r]yl's bill?['] *Nicolay.* "Yes sir." He went out and returning, handed it to the President, who took it and read it thro'— commenting as he went along,—"elegant, grand carpet, $2,500." "I should like to know where a carpet worth $2,500 can be put." I [French] said "probably in the East Room." "No, that [carpet] cost $10,000, a monstrous extravagance." [Lincoln continued:] "It was all wrong to spend one cent at such a time, and I never ought to have had a cent expended, the house was furnished well enough, better than any one we ever lived in, and if I had not been overwhelmed with other business I would not have had any of the appropriation expended, but what could I do? I could not attend to everything," and then he arose and walked the floor, and said many things that I will not undertake to recall, and ended by swearing again that he *never* would approve that bill. So ended that *interesting* morning *call* on the President.

[Commented French at the end of the letter: "They tell a great many stories about Mrs. Lincoln, but I do not believe them—indeed I *know* many of them are false. . . . She is a very imprudent woman

in many things, as I do know, and taking advantage of this the world
delights to add *in a compound ratio, to the reality."*]

"He Would Like to Borrow It"
FRIDAY, JANUARY 10, 1862

¶ *As Congress convened in December, the North's impatience for
action again began mounting in intensity. Roscoe Conkling of New
York, displaying a bellicose mood, told the House: "With six hundred thousand men—more men, I will hazard the assertion, than any
man knows what to do with—with sixty-three thousand cavalry—
although we were told in July we needed none—more cavlary than
any man will ever find a place for; with an outgo of $2,000,000 a
day, we have been for months guarding a beleaguered city [Wash-
ington]. We have been doing something more. We have been making
now and then an advance; and almost as often as we have made one
we have been outnumbered and ignominiously defeated."* [1]

*McClellan remained reluctant to attack. "Nobody knows his
plans," Attorney General Bates complained to his Diary. "The Sec
[retary] of war and the President himself are kept in ignorance of
the actual condition of the army and the intended movements of the
General—if indeed they intend to move at all." When McClellan
came down with typhoid fever in December, "it seemed as if all
military operations were to stop." Lincoln began thinking of "taking
the field himself, and suggested several plans of operations" to his
friend Browning.* [2]

*The evening of January 10th, the President, "in great distress," held
a meeting in the Executive Mansion with two division commanders
—Generals McDowell and William B. Franklin—and members of
the Cabinet. General McDowell took the following minutes of the
session:* [3]

The President was greatly disturbed at the state of affairs. Spoke
of the exhausted condition of the treasury; of the loss of public credit;
of the Jacobinism in Congress; of the delicate condition of our
foreign relations; of the bad news he had received from the West,
particularly as contained in a letter from General Halleck on the
state of affairs in Missouri; of the want of co-operation between

Generals Halleck and [Don Carlos] Buell; but more than all, the sickness of General McClellan.

The President said he was in great distress, and as he had been to General McClellan's house, and the general did not ask to see him; and as he must talk to somebody, he had sent for General Franklin and myself to obtain our opinion as to the possibility of soon commencing active operations with the Army of the Potomac.

To use his own expression, "If something was not soon done, the bottom would be out of the whole affair; and if General McClellan did not want to use the army, he would like to *borrow it,* provided he could see how it could be made to do something."

The Secretary of State stated the substance of some information he considered reliable as to the strength of the forces on the other side, which he had obtained from an Englishman from Fort Monroe, Richmond, Manassas, and Centreville, which was to the effect, that the enemy had twenty thousand men under [Benjamin] Huger, at Norfolk; thirty thousand at Centreville; and in all in our front, an effective force, capable of being brought up at short notice, of about one hundred and three thousand men—men not suffering, but well shod, clothed, and fed. In answer to the question from the President, what could be done with the army, I replied that the question as to the *when* must be preceded by the one as to the *how* and the *where.* That substantially I would organize the army into four army corps, placing the five divisions on the Washington side on the right bank. Place three of these corps to the front—the right at Vienna or its vicinity, the left beyond Fairfax Station, the centre beyond Fairfax Courthouse, and connect the latter place with the Orange and Alexandria Railroad by a railroad now partially thrown up. This would enable us to supply these corps without the use of horses, except to distribute what was brought up by rail, and to act upon the enemy without reference to the bad state of country roads.

The railroads all lead to the enemy's position; by acting upon them in force, besieging his strongholds if necessary, or getting between them if possible, or making the attempt to do so and pressing his left, I thought we should in the first place cause him to bring up all his forces and mass them on the flank most pressed, the left; and possibly, I thought probably, we should again get them out of their works and bring on a general engagement on favorable terms to us; at all events keeping him fully occupied and harrowed.

The Fourth Corps, in connection with a force of heavy guns afloat, would operate on his right flank beyond the Occoquan, get behind the batteries on the Potomac; take Aquia, which being supported by the Third Corps over the Occoquan it could safely attempt, and then move on the railroad from Manassas to the Rappahannock, having a large cavalry force to destroy bridges. I thought by the use of one hundred and thirty thousand men thus employed, and the great facilities which the railroads gave us, and the compact position we should occupy, we must succeed by repeated blows in crushing out the force in our front, even if it were equal in numbers and strength. The road by the Fairfax Courthouse to Centreville would give us the means to bring up siege-mortars and siege materials; and even if we could not accomplish the object immediately, by making the campaign one of positions instead of one of manoeuvres, to do so eventually and without risk. That this saving of wagon transportation should be effected at once by connecting the Baltimore and Ohio Railroad with the Alexandria roads, by running a road over the Long Bridge. That when all this could be commenced, I could better tell when I knew something more definite as to the general condition of the army.

General Franklin being asked, said he was in ignorance of many things necessary to an opinion on the subject, knowing only as to his own division, which was ready for the field. As to the plan of operations, on being asked by the President if he had ever thought what he would do with this army if he had it, he replied that he had, and that it was his judgment that it should be taken, what could be spared from the duty of protecting the capital, *to York River to operate on Richmond*. The question then came up as to the means at hand of transporting a large part of the army by water. The Assistant Secretary of War [John Tucker] said the means had been fully taxed to provide transportation for twelve thousand men. After some further conversation, and in reference to our ignorance of the actual condition of the army, the President wished we should come together the next night at eight o'clock, and that General Franklin and I should meet in the mean time, obtain such further information as we might need, and to do so from the staff of the headquarters of the Army of the Potomac. Immediate orders were to be given to make the railroad over Long Bridge.

[In 1864, General McDowell's manuscript of the above was submitted to Lincoln. The President endorsed it as a true report, with the exception of the phrase, "the Jacobinism of Congress"; he said he had no recollection of using such an expression.[4]]

"Whispering . . . Recommenced"

MONDAY, JANUARY 13, 1862

¶ *By direction of the President, Generals McDowell and Franklin had set about obtaining information about the Army of the Potomac. The next night at the White House, plans of operations again were discussed, when Lincoln desired further data on water transportation for the troops and ordered the generals to obtain details from General Meigs. On January 12th, McDowell and Franklin returned for a meeting with Lincoln and were told of new developments. According to McDowell: "The President and Mr. Seward said that General McClellan had been out to see the President, and was looking quite well, and that now, as he was able to assume the charge of the army, the President would drop any further proceedings with us. . . . Nothing was done but to appoint another meeting the next day, at eleven o'clock, when we were to meet General McClellan and again discuss the question of the movement to be made."* [1]

McClellan, whose malady was presumed more serious than it was, had heard about the White House meetings and felt "McDowell . . . was probably at the bottom of the affair, undertook it con amore, hoping to succeed me in command." [2] *It was, therefore, with an extra chip on his shoulder that McClellan arrived at the White House on January 13th for the council which led to what was to become the Peninsula campaign. Among those present were Lincoln, Seward, Chase, Blair, Generals McClellan, Meigs, McDowell and Franklin. Our report of the proceedings is derived from McDowell's memorandum, McClellan's Own Story, published in 1887, and a reminiscence by Meigs based on his Diary entry. We begin with McDowell's account:* [3]

The President, pointing to a map, asked me to go over the plan I had before spoken to him of. He at the same time made a brief explanation of how he came to bring General Franklin and General McDowell before him. I mentioned in as brief terms as possible what General Franklin and I had done under the President's order, what our investigations had been directed upon, and what were our conclusions as to going to the front from our present base . . . referring also to a transfer of a part of the army to another base further south. That we had been informed that the latter movement could not be commenced under a month to six weeks, and that a movement to the front could be undertaken in all of three weeks. General Franklin dissented only as to the time I mentioned for beginning operations in the front, not thinking we could get the roads in order by that time. I added, *commence* operations in all of three weeks; to which he assented. I concluded my remarks by saying something apologetic in explanation of the position in which we were. To which General McClellan replied somewhat coldly, if not curtly—"You are entitled to have any opinion you please!" No discussion was entered into by him whatever, the above being the only remark he made.

[Meigs recorded: "I moved my chair to the side of McClellan's and urged him, saying, 'The President evidently expects you to speak; can you not promise some movement towards Manassas? You are strong.' He replied, 'I cannot move on them with as great a force as they have.' 'Why, you have near 200,000 men, how many have they?' 'Not less than 175,000 according to my advices.' I said, 'Do you think so?' and 'the President expects something from you.' He replied, 'If I tell him my plans they will be in the New York Herald tomorrow morning. He can't keep a secret, he will tell them to Tad [4] [Lincoln's youngest son].' I said: 'That is a pity, but he is the President,—the Commander-in-Chief; he has a right to know; it is not respectful to sit mute when he so clearly requires you to speak. He is superior to all.' " We now resume with McDowell's report:]

General Franklin said that, in giving his opinion as to going to York River, he did it knowing that it was in the direction of General McClellan's plan. I said that I had acted entirely in the dark. General Meigs spoke of his agency in having us called in by the President. The President then asked what and when any thing could be done, again going over somewhat the same ground he had done with General Franklin and myself. General McClellan said the case was so clear a blind man could see it, and then spoke of the difficulty of ascertaining what force he could count upon; that he did not know whether he could let General Butler go to Ship Island, or whether he could re-enforce [General Ambrose E.] Burnside [who was on his way to Newbern, North Carolina, via Hatteras Inlet and Pamlico

Sound, to operate on Raleigh or Beaufort, or either of them]. Much conversation ensued [McClellan called it whispering], of rather a general character, as to the discrepancy between the number of men paid for and the number effective.

[Here McClellan picks up the narrative:]

The whispering then recommenced, especially between the President and Secretary Chase; . . . at length the latter spoke aloud, for the benefit of all assembled, in a very excited tone and manner, saying that he understood the purpose of the meeting to be that Gen. McClellan should then and there explain his military plans in detail, that they might be submitted to the approval or disapproval of the gentlemen present. The uncalled-for violence of his manner surprised me, but I determined to avail myself of it by keeping perfectly cool myself, and contented myself with remarking—what was entirely true—that the purpose he expressed was entirely new to me; that I did not recognize the Secretary of the Treasury as in any manner my official superior, and that I denied his right to question me upon the military affairs committed to my charge; that in the President and Secretary of War alone did I recognize the right to interrogate me. I then quietly resumed my conversation with Blair and Meigs, taking no further notice of Mr. Chase. . . .

After I had thus disposed of the Secretary of the Treasury he resumed his whispering with the President, who, after a lapse of some minutes, said: "Well, Gen. McClellan, I think you had better tell us what your plans are"—or words to that effect.

To this I replied in substance, that if the President had confidence in me it was not right or necessary to entrust my designs to the judgment of others, but that if his confidence was so slight as to require my opinions to be fortified by those of other persons it would be wiser to replace me by some one fully possessing his confidence; that no general commanding an army would willingly submit his plans to the judgment of such an assembly, in which some were incompetent to form a valuable opinion, and others incapable of keeping a secret, so that anything made known to them would soon spread over Washington and become known to the enemy. I also reminded the President that he and the Secretary of the Treasury knew in general terms what my designs were. Finally, I declined giving further information to the meeting, unless the President gave me the order in writing and assumed the responsibility of the results.

This was probably an unexpected *dénouement*. The President was not willing to assume the responsibility; and, after a little more whispering between him and Mr. Chase, Mr. Seward arose, buttoned his coat, and laughingly said, "Well, Mr. President, I think the meeting had better break up. I don't see that we are likely to make much out of Gen. McClellan."

[In the course of the conversation, McDowell noted, McClellan had said that operations in Kentucky took precedence over those in the East, but refused to develop his plans further. Said McDowell: "The President then asked him [McClellan] if he counted upon any particular time; he did not ask what that time was, but had he in his own mind any particular time fixed when a movement could be commenced. He replied he had. Then, rejoined the President, I will adjourn this meeting."

On January 27th, Lincoln issued his General War Order Number One, directing that all the forces advance on or before February 22nd. Four days later, a Special War Order instructed the Army of the Potomac to move upon Richmond by the same date via Manassas Junction. McClellan submitted a counterplan for a movement by way of Urbana or the Yorktown Peninsula. In a special Council of War, McClellan's strategy was favored by eight of twelve generals assembled and was ultimately adopted by the President.[5]]

"A Frank Confession"

SUNDAY, FEBRUARY 2, 1862

¶ *Early in the war, the great Ralph Waldo Emerson believed Lincoln to be "slow and timid." The President was fighting the war to preserve the Union; Emerson conceived the conflict as a crusade for human equality. However, with the passage of time, Emerson's view underwent change; he began to appreciate Lincoln's position. "Thus the war for the Union is broader than any State policy, or Tariff, or Maritime, or Agricultural, or Mining interest," he wrote on August 5, 1861. "Each of these neutralizes the other. But, at last, Union Party is not broad enough, because of Slavery, which poisons it; and we must come to 'emancipation with compensation to the loyal States,' as the only broad and firm ground." [1]*

When Emerson was in Washington on February 2nd, Seward asked: "Will you go and call on the President? I usually call on him at this hour." Of course, Emerson was glad to go. Later, he wrote in his Journal:²

We found in the President's chamber his two little sons,—boys of seven and eight years, perhaps,—whom the barber was dressing and "whiskeying their hair" as he said, not much to the apparent contentment of the boys, when the cologne got into their eyes. The eldest boy immediately told Mr. Seward, "he could not guess what they had got." Mr. Seward "bet a quarter of a dollar that he could. Was it a rabbit? was it a bird? was it a pig?" He guessed always wrong, and *paid* his *quarter* to the youngest, before the eldest declared it was a rabbit. But he sent away the mulatto to find the President, and the boys disappeared. The President came, and Mr. Seward said, "You have not been to Church to-day." "No," he said, "and, if he must make a frank confession, he had been reading for the first time Mr. Sumner's speech (on the Trent affair)." Something was said of newspapers, and of the story that appeared in the journals, of some one who selected all the articles which Marcy should read, etc. etc. The President incidentally remarked, that for the New York *Herald,* he certainly ought to be much obliged to it for the part it had taken for the Government in the Mason and Slidell business. Then Seward said somewhat to explain the apparent steady malignity of the London *Times.* It was all an affair of the great interests of markets. The great capitalists had got this or that stock. As soon as anything happens that affects their value, this value must be made real, and the *Times* must say just what is required to sell those values, etc., etc. The Government had little or no voice in the matter.

"But what news to-day?" "Mr. [G. V.] Fox [Assistant Secretary of the Navy] has sent none. Send for Mr. Fox." The servant could not find Mr. Fox. The President said he had the most satisfactory communication from Lord Lyons; also had been notified by him, that he had received the Order of the Bath. He, the President, had received two communications from the French minister. France, on the moment of hearing the surrender of the prisoners, had ordered a message of gratification to be sent, without waiting to read the grounds. Then, when the despatches had been read, had hastened to send a fresh message of thanks and gratulation. Spain also had sent a message of the same kind. He [Lincoln] was glad of this

that Spain had done. For he knew that, though Cuba sympathized
with secession, Spain's interest lay the other way. Spain knew that
the secessionists wished to conquer Cuba. Mr. Seward told the
President somewhat of Dr. [Smith] Pyne's sermon, and the President
said he intended to show his respect for him some time by going to
hear him.

We left the President, and returned to Mr. Seward's house.

"The Gallant . . . Ills. Troops"

MONDAY, FEBRUARY 17, 1862

¶ *The quiet along the Eastern front had not extended to the Department of the West, now commanded by General Henry W. "Old
Brains" Halleck. On the Kentucky-Tennessee front, things had begun
to move in November when Brigadier General Ulysses S. Grant of
Galena, Illinois, proceeded against Belmont. On January 17, 1862,
Union forces under General George H. Thomas clashed with General
Felix Zollicoffer's Confederates at Mill Springs. After a blazing
battle, in which Zollicoffer was killed, the Federals had won a
victory which paved the way for their entry into Tennessee. February 6th saw General Grant taking Fort Henry on the Tennessee
River and a week later, he swept across the Cumberland in a drive on
Fort Donelson. When the Donelson commander, Simon B. Buckner,
asked for terms of surrender, Grant replied: "No terms except an
unconditional and immediate surrender can be accepted." Donelson's
fall electrified the country and gave the North a new hero in "Unconditional Surrender" Grant.*[1]

*The night following the victory at Donelson—February 17th—
Nicolay made these notes:*[2]

To-night, the Secretary of War brought over a nomination of Gen.
U. S. Grant to be Major Gen. of Vols, which the Prest signed at
once. Talking over the surrender [of Fort Donelson], and the gallant
behavior of the Ill[inoi]s. troops, the Prest said: "I cannot speak so
confidently about the fighting qualities of the Eastern men, or what
are called Yankees—not knowing myself particularly to whom the
appellation belongs—but this I do know—if the Southerners think
that man for man they are better than our Illinois men, or Western

men generally, they will discover themselves in a grievous mistake."
—"What a great pity that [J. B.] Floyd [who was at Fort Donelson
during the siege] escaped," some one suggested.

"I am sorry he got away," said Stanton. "I want to catch and
hang him."

"It Is a D———d Fizzle"

THURSDAY, FEBRUARY 27, 1862

¶ *February brought deep affliction to the Presidential family with
the death of young Willie Lincoln. During the youngster's illness,
the President and Mrs. Lincoln were unremitting in their attention
to their son, who continued "to sink and grow weaker." Then, about
five o'clock on the afternoon of February 20th, Nicolay wrote, the
President entered "my office" and, choking with emotion, said:
"Well, Nicolay . . . my boy is gone—he is actually gone" and,
bursting into tears, Lincoln left his secretary's room.[1]*

*But personal grief could not be permitted to detract a President
from his duties to the country. While grief over Willie's death cut
sharply into Lincoln's heart, the President continued to wrestle with
a major problem of his Administration—Major General George B.
McClellan. Union victories in the West served to underscore all the
more McClellan's inactivity in the East; February 22nd—the date
Lincoln set for a movement by the Army of the Potomac—had come
and gone and the general was still preparing for the Peninsula campaign.*

*Meanwhile, Lincoln instructed McClellan to reopen the Baltimore
and Ohio Railroad by a movement across the Potomac at Harpers
Ferry and to destroy the enemy batteries on the river.[2] McClellan
gathered a large force at Harpers Ferry and a sufficient number of
canal boats to make a permanent bridge. What happened to this
project is detailed by Nicolay in a memorandum of February 27th:[3]*

This evening, 7 P.M., the Sec. [of] War came in, and after locking
the door, read to the Pres.[ident] two dispatches from the Gen[eral].
[One dispatch reported success in establishing a pontoon bridge
across the Potomac at Harper's Ferry and disclosed that Union troops
had already traversed it in preparation for an attack on Winchester.]

"The next is not so good," remarked the Sec. [of] War. It ran to the effect that the "lift lock" had turned out to be too narrow to admit the passage of the canal boats through the river (as one of the facilities and precautions arrangements had been made to build a permanent bridge of canal-boats across the Potomac, and a large number of canal boats had been gathered for that purpose.) That in consequence of this, he [McClellan] had changed the plan and had determined merely to protect the building of the bridge and the opening of the [Baltimore and Ohio] road—leaving the obvious inference that he proposed to abandon the movement on Winchester. In fact he so stated [because] the impossibility of building the permanent bridge as he had expected would delay him so that Winchester would be reinforced from Manassas, &c. &c.

"What does this mean?" asked the President.

"It means," said the Sec. [of] War, "that it is a d——d fizzle. It means that he [McClellan] doesn't intend to do anything."

The Pres[ident] was much cast down and dejected at the news of the failure of the enterprise. "Why could he not have known . . . [whether] his arrangements were practicable?" &c. &c.

The Sec. [of] State came in and the three had a long conference.

Afterward Gen. [Randolph B.] Marcy [McClellan's father-in-law and his top aide] for whom the Pres[ident] had sent earlier in the evening, came in and the Pres[ident] had a long and sharp talk with him.

"Why in the nation, Gen[eral] Marcy," said he excitedly, "couldn't the General have known whether a boat would go through that lock before spending a million dollars getting them there? I am no engineer, but it seems to me that if I wished to know whether a boat would go through a hole or a lock, common-sense would teach me to go and measure it. I am almost despairing at these results. Everything seems to fail. The general impression is daily growing that the Gen[eral] does not intend to do anything. By a failure like this we lose all the prestige we gained by the capture of Fort Donelson. I am grievously disappointed—almost in despair" &c. &c.

General Marcy endeavored to palliate the failure—said no doubt the Gen[eral] would be able to explain the cause—that other operations would go on, etc., and that he was satisfied—plenty of activity in movements &c.

"I will not detain you any longer now, Gen[eral]," said the Pres [ident], and though Gen Marcy showed a disposition to talk on, the Pres.[ident] repeated the dismissal and the Gen. took his hat and went away.

"A Very Ugly Matter"
SATURDAY, MARCH 8, 1862

¶ *McClellan's inertia was little affected by the growing Northern hostility and distrust harbored against him. Letters to the White House, the Executive Departments and members of Congress as well as to the press contained charges of disloyalty against McClellan. Commented Nicolay and Hay: "Mr. Lincoln felt the injustice of much of this criticism, but he also felt powerless to meet it, unless some measures were adopted to force the general into an activity which was as necessary to his own reputation as to the national cause."* [1] *On March 8th, according to McClellan, "the President sent for me at an early hour in the morning, about half-past seven, and I found him in his office." Here is the general's report of this interview, taken from* McClellan's Own Story:[2]

He appeared much concerned about something, and soon said that he wished to talk with me about "a very ugly matter." I asked what it was; and, as he still hesitated, I said that the sooner and more directly such things were approached the better.

He then referred to the Harper's Ferry affair (the boats being too wide for the lift-locks, etc.), upon which I found that the secretary [Stanton] had deceived me when he said that the President was satisfied. I told him what had passed between the secretary and myself . . . at which he was much surprised. He told me that he had never heard of . . . any explanation on my part. I then gave him my statement of the matter, with which he expressed himself entirely satisfied.

He then adverted to the more serious—or ugly—matter, and now the effects of the intrigues by which he had been surrounded became apparent. He said that it had been represented to him (and he certainly conveyed to me the distinct impression that he regarded these representations as well founded) that my plan of campaign (which was to leave Washington under the protection of a sufficient garrison, its numerous well-built and well-armed fortifications, and the command of Banks, then in the Shenandoah Valley, and to throw the whole active army suddenly by water from Annapolis and Alexandria to the forts on James river, and thence by the shortest route upon Richmond) was conceived with the traitorous intent of removing its defenders from Washington, and thus giving over to the enemy the capital and the government, thus left defenceless.

It is difficult to understand that a man of Mr. Lincoln's intelligence could give ear to such abominable nonsense. I was seated when he said this, concluding with the remark that it did look to him much like treason. Upon this I arose, and, in a manner perhaps not altogether decorous towards the chief magistrate, desired that he should retract the expression, telling him that I could permit no one to couple the word treason with my name. He was much agitated, and at once disclaimed any idea of considering me a traitor, and said that he merely repeated what others had said, and that he did not believe a word of it. I suggested caution in the use of language, and again said that I would permit no doubt to be thrown upon my intentions; whereupon he again apologized and disclaimed any purpose of impugning my motives.

I then informed him that I had called a meeting of the generals of division for that day [March 8th] with reference to the proposed attack upon the enemy's Potomac batteries, and suggested that my plan should be laid before them in order that he might be satisfied. This was done, and I heard no more of treason in that connection.

"Day-Star of a New . . . Dawn"

SUNDAY, MARCH 9, 1862

¶ *"We never printed a State paper with more satisfaction than we feel in giving our readers the Special Message of President* LINCOLN *to Congress," Horace Greeley editorialized in his New York Tribune.[1] He was referring to Lincoln's March 6th proposal that Congress pass a joint resolution "that the United States ought to co-operate with any state which may adopt gradual abolishment of slavery, giving to such state pecuniary aid, to be used by such* state in it's [sic] *discretion, to compensate for the inconveniences public and private, produced by such change of system." The President argued that "initiation of emancipation," as projected by the resolution, would deprive rebels of the hope that "slave states North" would ultimately join the Confederacy. "To deprive them of this hope, substantially ends the rebellion," Lincoln asserted, adding that "I say 'initiation' because, in my judgment, gradual, and not sudden emancipation, is better for all." This proposition, he said, "sets up no claim of a right, by federal authority, to interfere with slavery within state limits." Implementation of the resolution would be "a matter of perfectly free choice" on the part of the Northern slave states.*[2]

Summarizing reaction to Lincoln's recommendation, the New York Herald *declared: "The Message has taken all parties by surprise. A majority of the Senators and Representatives are unprepared to express themselves upon it. All are afraid of it, and all are afraid to oppose it. The radicals look blank. . . . The conservatives . . . are anxious to sustain the policy . . . but they fear that they may be entrapped . . . from their chosen position." Said Greeley: "This Message constitutes of itself an epoch in the history of our country. . . . It is the day-star of a new National dawn. Even if it were no more than a barren avowal by the Chief Magistrate of the Nation that* IT IS HIGHLY DESIRABLE THAT THE UNION BE PURGED OF SLAVERY, *it would be a great fact, of far weightier import than many battles."* [3]

On March 9th—the day after the Confederate ironclad Merrimac *had sunk the* Cumberland and Congress *in Hampton Roads and thrown the North into a panic—Nicolay, in a memorandum, chronicled a conversation between Lincoln and Montgomery Blair, which took place just before the news of the naval engagement reached Washington:* [4]

—I went in this morning to read to the President the additional articles in the Tribune and Herald concerning his Emancipation message—both papers continuing to warmly endorse and advocate it. Before this he had brought me a letter to copy which he wrote and sent to Hon. H. J. Raymond, concerning the [New York] Times' opinion of the impracticability of his scheme on account of expense.[5] After thanking him for the favorable notice of it he [Lincoln] asked if he [Raymond] had studied the fact that one half-days expense of this war would buy all the slaves in Delaware at $400 per head— and that 87 days expense of the war would buy all in Del. Md. D.C.,

Mo. & Ky. at the same price? and whether it would not shorten the war more than 87 days and thus make an actual saving of expense? Think of this, said he, and let there be another article in the Times. While I was still reading to him Mr. Blair came in. "I sent for you, Mr. Blair," said he, "about this: Since I sent in my message, about the usual amount of calling by the Border State Congressmen has taken place; and although they have all been very friendly not one of them has yet said a word to me about it. Garrett Davis [of Kentucky] has been here three times since; but although he has been very cordial he has never yet opened his mouth on the subject. Now I should like very much, sometime soon, to get them all together here, and have a frank and direct talk with them about it. I desired to ask you whether you were aware of any reason why I should not do so."

Mr. Blair suggested that it might be well to wait until the army did something further.

"That is just the reason why I do not wish to wait[,"] said the President. ["]If we should have successes, they may feel and say, the rebellion is crushed and it matters not whether we do anything about this matter. I want them to consider it and interest themselves in it as an auxiliary means for putting down the rebels. I want to tell them that if they will take hold and do this, the war will cease—there will be no further need of keeping standing armies among them, and that they will get rid of all the troubles incident thereto. If they do not the armies must stay in their midst—it is impossible to prevent negroes from coming into our lines; when they do, they [the Border State people] press me on the one hand to have them returned, while another class of our friends will on the other press me not to do so." &c &c. Mr. Blair said he would try and see the border state Congressmen during the day and have them all come and see the President at 9 A. M. tomorrow.

"The Sensibilities of the Slave States"

MONDAY, MARCH 10, 1862

¶ *Montgomery Blair arranged the meeting Lincoln had requested. This interview with the Border State representatives was recorded by Congressman J. W. Crisfield of Maryland immediately thereafter:* [1]

This morning these delegations, or such of them as were in town, assembled at the White House at the appointed time, and after some little delay were admitted to an audience. . . .

After the usual salutations and we were seated, the President said, in substance, that he had invited us to meet him to have some conversation with us in explanation of his Message of the 6th; that since he had sent it in, several of the gentlemen then present had visited him, but had avoided any allusion to the Message, and he therefore inferred that the import of the Message had been misunderstood, and was regarded as inimical to the interests we represented; and he had resolved he would talk with us, and disabuse our minds of that erroneous opinion.

The President then disclaimed any intent to injure the interests or wound the sensibilities of the Slave States. On the contrary, his purpose was to protect the one and respect the other; that we were engaged in a terrible, wasting, and tedious War; immense Armies were in the field, and must continue in the field as long as the War lasts; that these Armies must, of necessity, be brought into contact with Slaves in the States we represented and in other States as they advanced; that Slaves would come to the camps, and continual irritation was kept up; that he was constantly annoyed by conflicting and antagonistic complaints; on the one side, a certain class complained if the Slave was not protected by the Army; persons were frequently found who, participating in these views, acted in a way unfriendly to the Slaveholder; on the other hand, Slaveholders complained that their rights were interfered with, their Slaves induced to abscond, and protected within the lines; these complaints were numerous, loud, and deep; were a serious annoyance to him and embarrassing to the progress of the War; that it kept alive a spirit hostile to the Government of the States we represented; strengthened the hopes of the Confederates that at some day the Border States would unite with them, and thus tend to prolong the War; and he was of opinion, if this Resolution should be adopted by Congress and accepted by our States, these causes of irritation and these hopes would be removed, and more would be accomplished towards shortening the War than could be hoped from the greatest victory achieved by Union Armies; that he made this proposition in good faith, and desired it to be accepted, if at all, voluntarily, and in the same patriotic spirit in which it was made; that Emancipation was a subject exclusively under the control of the States, and must be adopted or rejected by each for itself; that he did not claim nor had this Government any right to coerce them for that purpose; that such was no part of his purpose in making this proposition, and he wished it to be clearly understood; that he did not expect us there to be prepared to give him an answer, but he hoped we would take the subject into serious consideration; confer with one another, and then take such course as we felt our duty and the interests of our constituents required of us.

Mr. [John W.] Noell, of Missouri, said that in his State, Slavery was not considered a permanent Institution; that natural causes were there in operation which would, at no distant day, extinguish it, and he did not think that this proposition was necessary for that; and, besides that, he and his friends felt solicitous as to the Message on account of the different constructions which the Resolution and Message had received. The New York *Tribune* was for it, and understood it to mean that we must accept gradual Emancipation according to the plan suggested, or get something worse.

The President replied, he must not be expected to quarrel with the New York *Tribune* before the right time; he hoped never to have to do it; he would not anticipate events. In respect to Emancipation in Missouri, he said that what had been observed by Mr. Noell was probably true, but the operation of these natural causes had not prevented the irritating conduct to which he had referred, or destroyed the hopes of the Confederates that Missouri would at some time range herself alongside of them, which, in his judgment, the passage of this Resolution by Congress, and its acceptance by Missouri, would accomplish.

Mr. Crisfield, of Maryland, asked what would be the effect of the refusal of the State to accept this proposal, and desired to know if the President looked to any policy beyond the acceptance or rejection of this scheme.

The President replied that he had no designs beyond the action of the States on this particular subject. He should lament their refusal to accept it, but he had no designs beyond their refusal of it.

Mr. [John W.] Menzies, of Kentucky, inquired if the President thought there was any power, except in the States themselves, to carry out his scheme of Emancipation?

The President replied, he thought there could not be. He then went off into a course of remark not qualifying the foregoing declaration, nor material to be repeated to a just understanding of his meaning.

Mr. Crisfield said he did not think the people of Maryland looked upon Slavery as a permanent Institution; and he did not know that they would be very reluctant to give it up if provision was made to meet the loss, and they could be rid of the race; but they did not like to be coerced into Emancipation, either by the direct action of the Government or by indirection, as through the Emancipation of Slaves in this District, or the Confiscation of Southern Property as now threatened; and he thought before they would consent to consider this proposition they would require to be informed on these points.

The President replied that "unless he was expelled by the act of God or the Confederate Armies, he should occupy that house for three years, and as long as he remained there, Maryland had nothing to fear, either for her Institutions or her interests, on the points referred to."

Mr. Crisfield immediately added: "Mr. President, if what you now say could be heard by the people of Maryland, they would consider your proposition with a much better feeling than I fear without it they will be inclined to do."

The President: "That (meaning a publication of what he said), will not do; it would force me into a quarrel before the proper time;" and again intimating, as he had before done, that a quarrel with the "Greeley faction" was impending, he said, "he did not wish to encounter it before the proper time, nor at all if it could be avoided."

Governor [Charles A.] Wickliffe, of Kentucky, then asked him respecting the Constitutionality of his scheme.

The President replied: "As you may suppose, I have considered that; and the proposition now submitted does not encounter any Constitutional difficulty. It proposes simply to co-operate with any State by giving such State pecuniary aid;" and he thought that the Resolution, as proposed by him, would be considered rather as the expression of a sentiment than as involving any Constitutional question.

Mr. [William A.] Hall, of Missouri, thought that if this proposition was adopted at all, it should be by the votes of the Free States, and come as a proposition from them to the Slave States, affording them an inducement to put aside this subject of discord; that it ought not to be expected that members representing Slaveholding Constituencies should declare at once, and in advance of any proposition to them, for the Emancipation of Slaves.

The President said he saw and felt the force of the objection; it was a fearful responsibility, and every gentleman must do as he thought best; that he did not know how this scheme was received by the Members from the Free States; some of them had spoken to him and received it kindly; but for the most part they were as reserved and chary as we had been, and he could not tell how they would vote.

And, in reply to some expression of Mr. Hall as to his own opinion regarding Slavery, he said he did not pretend to disguise his Anti-Slavery feeling; that he thought it was wrong and should continue to think so; but that was not the question we had to deal with now. Slavery existed, and that, too, as well by the act of the North, as of the South; and in any scheme to get rid if it, the North, as well as the South, was morally bound to do its full and equal share. He thought the Institution, wrong, and ought never to have existed; but yet he recognized the rights of Property which had grown out of it, and would respect these rights as fully as similar rights in any other property; that Property can exist, and does legally exist. He thought such a law, wrong, but the rights of Property resulting must be respected; he would get rid of the odious law, not by violating the right, but by encouraging the proposition, and offering inducements to give it up.

Here the interview, so far as this subject is concerned, terminated by Mr. [John J.] Crittenden's assuring the President that whatever might be our final action, we all thought him solely moved by a high patriotism and sincere devotion to the happiness and glory of his Country; and with that conviction we should consider respectfully the important suggestions he had made.

[On April 10, 1862, Lincoln signed his joint resolution after it had been approved by Congress in its original form. The Border Staters had voted against the President's proposition.]

"Yesterday . . . He Shed Tears"

WEDNESDAY, APRIL 2, 1862

¶ *The first real blow at McClellan's prestige was struck by Lincoln on March 11th. That day, by a Presidential war order, Lincoln stripped McClellan of command of all the Union armies; retained him only as the head of the Army of the Potomac.*[1] *How did McClellan take it? "When I left Washington in March . . . to accompany the Army . . . on its march towards Manassas [en route to the Peninsula], I was still commanding general of the United States army, had no reason whatever to suppose that any change was contemplated by the President . . . expected to return in a few days, preparatory to the final movement to the Peninsula," McClellan wrote later to General Grant. "Two or three days after, while at Fairfax Court-House, I, to my complete surprise, received* through the newspapers *the orders relieving me from the command of the United States army."* [2]

Despite McClellan's demotion, rumors as to his loyalty persisted. Senator Browning—who insisted upon calling the general "McClelland"—discussed this matter with the President: [3]

At night I went up to the Presidents and had a talk with him about Genl McClelland whose loyalty is beginning to be questioned in some quarters[.] I asked him if he still had confidence in McClellands fidelity. He assured me he had, and that he had never had any reason to doubt it. That he [McClellan] had now gone to Fortress Monroe with his Command, with orders to move on Richmond without delay, and that only on yesterday when McClelland came to take leave of him preparatory to marching, he [the general] shed tears when speaking of the cruel imputations upon his loyalty, and defending himself against them[.] The President added that Genl Scott, and all the leading military men around him, had always assured him that McClelland possessed a very high order of military talent, and that he did not think they could all be mistaken—yet he was not fully satisfied with his conduct of the war—that he was not sufficiently energetic and aggressive in his measures—that he had studied McClelland and taken his measure as well as he could—that he thought he had the capacity to make arrangements properly for a great conflict, but as the hour for action approached he became nervous and oppressed with the responsibility and hesitated to meet the crisis, but that he had given him peremptory orders to move now, and he must do it. Whilst we were in conversation Mr Secretary Stanton came in.

Supposing he had private business I proposed to leave, but both he and the President insisted that I should remain, and I did so. Stanton then commenced a conversation about McClelland, saying that there was a very general distrust of his loyalty growing up in the Country. He [Stanton] then took from his pocket a letter, which he said he had just received from one of the first men of the Nation, who was known to both the President and myself, but whose name he would not mention, and read from it a passage stating that McClelland some time in 1860 had been initiated as a Knight of the Golden Circle [a subversive organization] by Jeff Davis—that Davis still had great power and influence over him, and that he would do nothing against the rebels which would be inconsistent with his obligations as a Knight of the golden Circle, and that disaster would come upon us as long as he was continued in the Command [of the Army of the Potomac]. Stanton added that he did not believe these imputations of disloyalty, but they were believed extensively and did us injury[.] When we left the President[,] Stanton took me in his carriage and brought me home.

"In . . . Strictest Confidence"

MONDAY, APRIL 14, 1862

¶ *Early in April, as emancipation for the District of Columbia neared the final vote in Congress, Maryland and Virginia Negroes "in scores and hundreds" began rushing into Washington. Opposed to the bill, the* New York Herald *reported District Negroes "are beginning to be alarmed at this influx . . . and . . . are divided upon the question of emancipation."* [1] *Radicals in Congress "with hot haste" agitated for the measure.* [2] *Border State members feared it "as the . . . wedge of an abolition programme embracing all the slave States."* [3] *Lincoln, who said "I would be glad to see . . . [slavery in the District] abolished," was himself "a little uneasy . . . as to the time and manner of doing it."* [4]

Following Senate approval on April 14th, the bill—including compensation and colonization provisions—was brought to Lincoln for signature, by Senator Browning, whose Diary reveals: [5]

At night went to Presidents to lay before him the bill to abolish slavery in the District of Columbia. Had a talk with him. He told me he would sign the bill, but would return it with a special message recommending a supplemental bill making savings in behalf of infants &c. and also some other amendments.[6]

He further told me he regretted the bill had been passed in its present form—that it should have been for gradual emancipation—that now families would at once be deprived of cooks, stable boys &c. and they of their protectors without any provision for them. He further told me that he would not sign the bill before Wednesday —That old Gov Wickliffe had two family servants with him who were sickly, and who would not be benefitted by freedom, and wanted time to remove them, but could not get them out of the City until Wednesday, and that the Gov had come frankly to him and asked for time. He added to me that this was told me in the strictest confidence[.]

"The Next Most Troublesome Subject"
FRIDAY, JUNE 20, 1862

¶ *With approaching summer, abolitionists in Congress stepped up their assaults upon Lincoln. McClellan had won a few battles in the Peninsula, but after more than two months in the field, he had not yet succeeded in taking Richmond; a failure here could cost Republicans the fall elections. In international affairs, there was a new danger of foreign intervention in the American conflict. The Jacobins assailed Lincoln on these issues in violent efforts to induce him "to strike a fatal blow" at slavery. The abolitionists were becoming "remarkably strong"; they were beginning to influence the people.[1]*

June 20th saw Lincoln signing a bill freeing slaves in the territories.[2] That morning, Thomas Garrett, Alice Eliza Hambleton, Oliver Johnson, Dinah Mendenhall, William Barnard, and Eliza Agnew—forming a delegation of Progressive Friends (Quakers)—

entered the White House. They had come to Lincoln with a memorial advocating emancipation. Our record of their talk with the President is derived from two sources: the New York Herald *and* New York Tribune *of June 21, 1862. We begin with the* Herald *material:*

Oliver Johnson read the memorial, prefacing it with the remark that the deputation did not come to seek for office, but to urge the claims of four millions of persons who could not speak for themselves.

[The *Tribune* report follows:]

The President said that, as he had not been furnished with a copy of the memorial in advance, he could not be expected to make any extended remarks. It was a relief to be assured that the deputation were not applicants for office, for his chief trouble was from that class of persons. The next most troublesome subject was Slavery. He agreed with the memorialists, that Slavery was wrong, but in regard to the ways and means of its removal, his views probably differed from theirs. The quotation in the memorial, from his Springfield ["House Divided"] speech, was incomplete. It should have embraced another sentence, in which he indicated his views as to the effect upon Slavery itself of the resistance to its extension.

The sentiments contained in that passage were deliberately uttered, and he held them now. If a decree of emancipation could abolish Slavery, John Brown would have done the work effectually. Such a decree surely could not be more binding upon the South than the Constitution, and that cannot be enforced in that part of the country now. Would a proclamation of freedom be any more effective?

Mr. Johnson replied as follows:

True, Mr. President, the Constitution cannot now be enforced at the South, but you do not on that account intermit the effort to enforce it, and the memorialists are solemnly convinced that the abolition of Slavery is indispensable to your success.

The President further said that he felt the magnitude of the task before him, and hoped to be rightly directed in the very trying circumstances by which he was surrounded.

Wm. Barnard addressed the President in a few words, expressing sympathy for him in all his embarrassments, and an earnest desire that he might, under divine guidance, be led to free the slaves and thus save the nation from destruction. In that case nations yet unborn would rise up to call him blessed, and, better still, he would secure the blessing of God.

The President responded very impressively, saying that he was deeply sensible of his need of Divine assistance. He had sometime[s] thought that perhaps he might be an instrument in God's hands of accomplishing a great work and he certainly was not unwilling to be. Perhaps, however, God's way of accomplishing the end which the memorialists have in view may be different from theirs. It would be his earnest endeavor, with a firm reliance upon the Divine arm, and seeking light from above, to do his duty in the place to which he had been called.

"Nobody Was Hurt"
WEDNESDAY, JUNE 25, 1862

¶ *Late in June, Lincoln hastened to West Point to consult General Scott on military matters. Although the old general issued a statement on his talks with the President, full knowledge of what transpired at these conferences still remains a matter of conjecture.*[1] *Lincoln's unexpected appearance at West Point "created the most intense excitement and curiosity." Was Scott to resume "the chief command" of Union armies? Was he to replace Stanton? The "quidnuncs" were "in a muddle," while "Old Abe himself, all smiles and good nature, declared that 'nobody was hurt.' "* [2]

When Lincoln, accompanied by Scott, boarded the train at Garrison's Station on July 25th for the return trip to Washington, a New York Herald *correspondent went along in an attempt to get his story. His report appeared in the* Herald *on June 26, 1862:*

Exactly at ten minutes before nine o'clock [in the morning] . . . the West Point boys fired a salute . . . to the President. The train started off without a moment's delay, at the rate of very little less than fifty miles an hour. At this station the morning papers were received, and Old Abe was observed very intently pouring [*sic*] over a leader in the NEW YORK HERALD devoted to an explanation of his sudden visit to West Point. Before the train departed a poor woman threw a bouquet of Sweet Williams into the car for the President. Mr. [Samuel] Sloan [president of the Hudson River Railroad] picked it up and presented it to Old Abe, who remarked, with a smile, "Very rich, but not much variety." "It is an offering of the heart," suggested one of the party. "The widow's mite," put in General Scott. "As such I accept it," answered the President.

During the trip the conversation turned upon the capture of Norfolk and the President threw some light upon the subject. [Lincoln had been at Fortress Monroe at the time and helped direct the operations which led to the city's fall.] "I knew," he remarked, "that Saturday night that the next morning the Merrimac would either be in the James river or at the bottom. Mr. Stanton, Commodore [L. M.] Goldsborough and myself had a long conversation on the subject. I knew that, Norfolk in our possession, the Merrimac would have no place to retire to, and therefore I took the step which resulted in the capture of that place. The result proved my figuring correct." . . .

In conversation with our reporter, Mr. Lincoln declared that there was nothing at all alarming going on, and seemed to be very unreserved in his conversation. General Scott likewise spoke in the same terms, asserting that Mr. Lincoln's visit [to the Point] was not on account of any disaster, past or expected. The old chief declared he had no idea of going to Washington again, as his health would not bear so much labor. From this [added the reporter] it is fair to infer, though the General [who accompanied the President only as far as Jersey City] seemed unwilling to admit it, that the whole object of the President's visit was to consult General Scott relative to the conduct of the war. . . .

"The Blow Must Fall"

SUNDAY, JULY 13, 1862

¶ *Lincoln first divulged his inclination to emancipate the slaves to Gideon Welles and William H. Seward on Sunday, July 13th. Up to that time, the President had always disclaimed any intention of interfering with slavery in the states, where he considered it protected by the Constitution. On this particular Sunday, however, as the three* men rode in the Presidential carriage *"to the funeral of an infant child of Secretary Stanton,"* Lincoln himself raised the subject of emancipation.

Welles, writing for The Galaxy *in December 1872, tells us what happened on this solemn ride:* [1]

It was on this occasion . . . that he first mentioned to Mr. Seward and myself that he had about come to the conclusion that, if the rebels persisted in their war upon the Government, it would be a necessity and a duty on our part to liberate their slaves. He was convinced, he said, that we could not carry on a successful war by longer pursuing a temporizing and forbearing policy toward those who disregarded law and Constitution, and were striving by every means to break up the Union. Decisive and extensive measures must be adopted. His reluctance to meddle with this question, around which there were thrown constitutional safeguards, and on which the whole Southern mind was sensitive, was great. He had tried various expedients to escape issuing an executive order emancipating the slaves, the last and only alternative, but it was forced upon him by the rebels themselves. He saw no escape. Turn which way he would, this disturbing element which caused the war rose up against us, and it was an insuperable obstacle to peace. He had entertained hopes that the border States, in view of what appeared to him inevitable if the war continued, would consent to some plan of prospective and compensated emancipation; but all his suggestions, some made as early as March, met with disfavor, although actual hostilities had then existed for a year. Congress was now about adjourning, and had done nothing final and conclusive—perhaps could do nothing on this question. He had since his return from the army the last week called the members of Congress from the border States together, and presented to them [this was on the previous day, July 12, 1862] the difficulties which he encountered, in hopes they would be persuaded, in the gloomy condition of affairs, to take the initiative step toward emancipation; but they hesitated, and he apprehended would do nothing. Attached as most of them and a large majority of their constituents were to what they called their labor system, they felt it would be unjust for the Government which they supported to compel them to abandon that system, while the States in flagrant rebellion retained their slaves and were spared the sacrifice. A movement toward emancipation in the border States while slavery was recognized and permitted in the rebel States would, they believed, detach many from the Union cause and strengthen the insurrection. There was, he presumed, some foundation for their apprehension. What had been done and what he had heard satisfied him that a change of policy in the conduct of the war was necessary, and that emancipation of the slaves in the rebel States must precede that in the border States. The blow must fall first and foremost on them [the rebels]. Slavery was doomed. This war, brought upon the country by the slave-owners, would extinguish slavery, but the border States could not be induced to lead in that measure. They would not consent to be convinced or persuaded to take the first step. Forced emancipation in the States which continued to resist the Government would of course be followed by voluntary emancipation in the loyal States, with the aid we might give them. Further efforts with the border States would, he thought, be useless. That was not the road to lead us out of this difficulty. We must take a different path. We wanted the army to strike more vigorous blows. The Administration must set an example, and strike at the heart of the rebellion. The country, he thought, was prepared for it. The army would be with us. War had removed constitutional obligations and restrictions with the declared rebel communities. The law required us to return the fugitives who escaped to us. This we could and must do with friends, but not with enemies. We invited all, bond and free, to desert those who were in flagrant war upon the Union and come to us; and uniting with us they must be made free from rebel authorities and rebel masters.

If there was no constitutional authority in the Government to emancipate the slaves, neither was there any authority, specified or reserved, for the slaveholders to resist the Government or secede from it. They could not at the same time throw off the Constitution and invoke its aid. Having made war upon the Government, they were subject to the incidents and calamities of war, and it was our duty to avail ourselves of every necessary measure to maintain the Union. If the rebels did not cease their war, they must take the consequences of war. He dwelt earnestly on the gravity, importance, and delicacy of the movement, which he had approached with reluctance, but he saw no evidence of a cessation of hostilities; said he had given the subject much thought, and had about come to the conclusion that it was a military necessity, absolutely essential to the preservation of the Union. We must free the slaves or be ourselves subdued. The slaves were undeniably an element of strength to those who had their service, and we must decide whether that element should be with us or against us. For a long time the subject had lain heavy on his mind. His interview with the representatives of the border States had forced him slowly but he believed correctly to this conclusion, and this present opportunity was the first occasion he had had of mentioning to any one his convictions of what in his opinion must be our course. He wished us to state frankly, not immediately, how the proposition of emancipation struck us, in case of the continued persistent resistance to Federal authority.

Mr. Seward remarked that the subject involved consequences so vast and momentous, legal and political, he should wish to bestow on it mature reflection before advising or giving a decisive answer; but his present opinion inclined to the measure as justifiable, and perhaps he might say expedient and necessary. These were essentially my views, more matured perhaps, for I had practically been dealing with slavery from the beginning as a wrecked institution. During that ride the subject was the absorbing theme, and before separating the President requested us to give it early, especial, and deliberate consideration, for he was earnest in the conviction that the time had arrived when decisive action must be taken; that the Government could not be justified in any longer postponing it; that it was forced upon him as a necessity—it was thrust at him from various quarters; it occupied his mind and thoughts day and night. He repeated he had about come to a conclusion, driven home to him by the conference of the preceding day, but wished to know our views and hear any suggestions either of us might make.

Chapter Six

"THE GASES OF PUBLIC EXASPERATION"

T HE Peninsula campaign, begun with so much fanfare, ended in a fizzle. But if McClellan had failed to take Richmond, Robert E. Lee failed to destroy McClellan's army. Lincoln believed McClellan had been overcautious, prone to overestimating the enemy's numbers and effectiveness. During the campaign, the President's major concern had been for the safety of Washington, which he considered inadequately protected. When McClellan called for reinforcements, they were not sent swiftly enough. Lincoln was fast losing confidence in his "Little Napoleon." If Washington were captured while troops were being sent to McClellan, what would the country say?

The Federal disasters in Virginia threw the North into "a depressed, dismal, asthenic state of anxiety and irritability." Said one prominent New Yorker: "We are beat back by superior forces but not destroyed. The enemy was superior because we have been outgeneralled. The blame rests, probably, on the War Department." And he added: "Prevailing color of people's talk is blue. What's very bad, we begin to lose faith in Uncle Abe." [1]

In Detroit, the *Free Press* blamed the Peninsula failure on "Stanton and the abolition politicians," asserting: "It has come solely from the mean partisan hatred of McClellan." Cried the *New York Herald:* "The late advance of General McClellan . . . if rightly supported at Washington, would have given us the rebel capital. . . ." It was "the embeciles [sic] from the Navy and War departments, who have brought such disgrace upon our arms," the *Herald* charged, declaring: "Public opinion . . . demands a change or two" in the Cabinet.

178

After it was all over, McClellan maintained: "A little of the nerve at Washington which the Romans displayed . . . against Hannibal would have settled the fate of Richmond in very few weeks."[2]

Despite the attacks upon the Administration's conduct of the war, Lincoln made no Cabinet changes. By July, he had created the short-lived Army of Virginia—dissolved after Second Manassas—from some of McClellan's original forces and had placed Major General John Pope at its head. Following his return from a "flying visit" to Harrison's Landing for personal talks with McClellan and his generals, Lincoln named Henry W. Halleck general in chief of all the Union armies. McClellan was subsequently ordered to remove his forces to Aquia Creek, south of Bull Run.[3]

"It had got to be," Lincoln later recalled, "midsummer, 1862. Things had gone on from bad to worse, until I felt that we had reached the end of our rope on the plan of operations we had been pursuing; that we had about played our last card, and must change our tactics, or lose the game!" It was at this point that Lincoln "determined upon the adoption of the emancipation policy."[4]

For Lincoln, this was no snap judgment. When he took the Presidential oath, he had promised not to interfere with slavery where it then existed. When Frémont tried to abolish slavery in the Department of the West, Lincoln promptly rescinded the general's order. When Major General David Hunter on May 9, 1862, declared "forever free" persons "heretofore held as slaves" in Georgia, Florida and South Carolina, Lincoln also repudiated this *pronunciamento,* stating that granting freedom to slaves was a responsibility "I reserve to myself, and which I can not feel justified in leaving to the decision of commanders in the field." Lincoln knew full well that "in repudiating Hunter's proclamation, "I gave dissatisfaction, if not offence, to many whose support the country can not afford to lose." The "pressure" in favor of emancipation "is still upon me, and is increasing," he told Border State representatives in July.[5]

In his approach to the slavery question, Lincoln was concerned with keeping the Border States from joining the Confederacy. He had felt they "must be conciliated and kept in the Union by pleasant promises." On the other hand, "Border State Conservatives . . . looked upon the President's policy of conciliation as an evidence of weakness, and treated his concessions, not as grateful acts of mercy and condescension, but as surrenders to their just demands, and, consequently, deputations of borderers, impudent in their exactions, have visited the White House, presuming upon the conciliatory policy of the President, to secure their growing demands." Lincoln's advocacy of compensated, voluntary emancipation was an attempt to reconcile the conflicting abolitionist and conservative viewpoints. Instead, both groups regarded it with suspicion. Refusal of the Border States to accept this plan demonstrated Lincoln's "Border State" policy to be "a failure." [6]

As Lincoln wrestled with the slavery issue, the radicals kept hammering away at him with a vindictive ferocity. To the fiery Wendell Phillips, Lincoln was "a first rate second rate man." This discontented abolitionist warned: "As long as you keep the present turtle at the head of the government, you make a pit with one hand and fill it with the other." [7] William Lloyd Garrison had become "skeptical as to the 'honesty' of Lincoln," whom he characterized as "nothing better than a wet rag." Lincoln reportedly told Senator John B. Henderson of Missouri: "Stevens, Sumner and Wilson, simply haunt me . . . with their importunities for a Proclamation of Emancipation. Wherever I go and whatever way I turn, they are on my trail, and still in my heart, I have the deep conviction that the hour has not yet come." The editor of the *North American* feared "that the President is rapidly alienating his friends and will soon find himself without a party, if not without a country." The eccentric Polish Count Adam Gurowski opined: "Lincoln acts . . . [only] when the gases of public exasperation rise powerfully and strike his nose." [8]

The less organized, less vocal conservatives were hardly a match for the radicals. Lincoln's boyhood friend, Joshua Fry Speed, was deeply aware of conservative need for leadership. He suspected "mischief brewing" among the Jacobins; that a "large and powerful party of . . . ultra men" was "being formed to make war upon the President and upon his conservative policy." Speed urged that conservatives must "beat" the radicals "at every point from the picket skirmish to the grand charge," in "parliamentary movements as in the field." James Gordon Bennett of the *New York Herald* called for "an organization of the conservative majority in the House for a systematic resistance to the radical revolutionary measures of the abolition disunionists." Citing Jacobinism as "the only danger . . . we have now to fear," Bennett declared that "in President

Lincoln we have found the man who has thus far been able to grapple it successfully." "The time has come . . . when conservative Union men of Congress and the country should rally . . . to his support." Commented Judge David Davis of Illinois: "If . . . [Lincoln] preserves his conservatism inflexibly & makes himself the breakwater ag[ains]t the radicalism that is rampant—then his fame will be undying . . . & his deeds of omission & commission will be buried out of sight." [9]

Between these elements, said Noah Brooks, "the President . . . failed to ride easily." [10]

Lincoln himself was a moderate liberal, who wished "all men to be free." He hated slavery; hated "to see the poor creatures hunted down, and caught, and carried back to their stripes, and unrewarded toils;" hated it "because it deprives our republican example of its just influence in the world—enables the enemies of free institutions, with plausibility, to taunt us as hypocrites—causes the real friends of freedom to doubt our sincerity, and especially because it forces so many really good men amongst ourselves into an open war with the very fundamental principles of civil liberty—criticizing the Declaration of Independence, and insisting that there is no right principle of action but *self-interest.*" He had seen slavery in New Orleans as a young man. In 1841, while returning by steamboat from Louisville to Springfield, he was horrified at the sight of "ten or a dozen slaves" aboard ship, "shackled together with irons." "That sight was a continual torment to me," he told Speed. Yet, as a citizen of a slave nation, he had to "bite my lip and keep quiet." [11]

While Lincoln despised slavery, he was willing to condone it where it existed in the states. But he was vehemently opposed to permitting its extension to the territories.

He professed no prejudice against the Southerners. "They are just what we would be in their situation," he had declared in a speech in Peoria in 1854. "When southern people tell us they are no more responsible for the origin of slavery, than we; I acknowledge the fact. When it is said that the institution exists; and that it is very difficult to get rid of it, in any satisfactory way, I can understand and appreciate the saying. . . . If all earthly power were given me, I should not know what to do, as to the existing institution." [12]

Despite his belief that slavery was a "monstrous injustice," he never favored "bringing about in any way the social and political equality of the white and black races." He did not favor "making voters or jurors of negroes, . . . [or] qualifying them to hold office." He could never advocate that the colored "intermarry with the white people." [13] In his Charleston debate with Douglas, he argued:

"I do not understand that because I do not want a negro woman for a slave I must necessarily want her for a wife. . . . My understanding is that I can just let her alone." [14]

These were Lincoln's early views about racial discrimination, and although he modified them considerably later on, he was not an abolitionist. He maintained that "abolition doctrine tends rather to increase than to abate" the "evils" of slavery. The abolitionist radicals were intent upon wreaking havoc upon the South; they were determined to make the slaveowner pay for the sin of enslaving human beings. Lincoln approached the problem differently. "As an anti-slavery man," he said, "I have a motive to desire emancipation, which pro-slavery men do not have; but even they have strong enough reason to . . . place themselves . . . under the shield of the Union." [15] The slaveowners had rights under the Constitution; rights he was willing to respect. With war's end, Lincoln meant to seek a peace with justice for all; the radicals craved subjugation of the South with a vengeance.

As the events of the conflict converged upon the summer of 1862, Lincoln's "cold, calculating, unimpassioned reason" told him: "This government cannot much longer play a game in which it stakes all, and its enemies stake nothing. Those enemies must understand that they cannot experiment for ten years trying to destroy the government, and if they fail still come back into the Union unhurt." [16]

There were some to argue that an emancipation proclamation was unconstitutional. Lincoln differed with such a view: "I . . . understand . . . that my oath to preserve the constitution to the best of my ability, imposed upon me the duty of preserving, by every indispensable means, that government—that nation—of which that constitution was the organic law. Was it possible to lose the nation, and yet preserve the constitution? . . . I felt that measure, otherwise unconstitutional, might become lawful, by becoming indispensable to the preservation of the constitution, through the preservation of the nation." On this basis, Lincoln submitted that "the constitution invests its commander-in-chief, with the laws of war, in time of war." [17]

Robert Dale Owen, the social reformer, took a different approach in favoring emancipation—a view brought to Lincoln's attention by Secretary Chase:

"Conceive reunion with slavery still in existence. Imagine Southern sympathizers in power among us, offering compromises. Suppose the South, exhausted by military reverses, and desiring a few years armistice to recruit, decides to accept it under the guise of peace and reconstruction? What next? Thousands of slaves, their excited hopes of emancipation crushed, fleeing across the border. A fugitive slave law, revived by peace, demanding their rendition. Popular opinion in the North opposed to the law and refusing the demand. Renewed war the certain consequence. . . .

"With all the advantages of a just cause over our enemies, we have suffered them to outdo us in earnestness. We lack the enthusiasm which made irresistible the charge of Cromwell's Ironsides. We need the invincible impulse of a sentiment. We want, above all, leaders who know and feel what they are fighting for. This is a war in which mercenaries avail not. There must be a higher motive than the pay of a Swiss—a holier duty urging on, than the professional pride or the blind obedience of a soldier. By parliamentary usage a proposed measure is intrusted, for fostering care, to its friends. So should this war be. Its conduct should be confided to men whose hearts and souls are in it." [18]

Lincoln prepared the original draft of the emancipation proclamation "without consultation with, or the knowledge of the Cabinet." Late in July, "after much anxious thought," the President "called a Cabinet meeting upon the subject." There it was agreed to withhold the proclamation until the North had gained a military victory. And Lincoln, placing the draft proclamation in his desk drawer, agreed to postpone this action.[19]

The year 1862 had been ushered in with a series of Union victories —Mill Springs in Kentucky, Roanoke Island in North Carolina, Forts Henry and Donelson in Tennessee, Pea Ridge in Arkansas, Shiloh in Tennessee, Island No. 10 in the Mississippi River, Forts Jackson and St. Philip in the lower Mississippi, and the capture of New Orleans. Then the tide reversed. McClellan's campaign against Richmond—another hoped-for gain—collapsed. Recruiting had fallen off during the Peninsula campaign; officers and men in the Army of the Potomac were demoralized. Then came another disaster at the Second Battle of Bull Run. The dates: August 29-30. The North was shaken by the news. Casualties were heavy. The Federals lost nearly 15,000 men; the Confederates 10,000. Lincoln's anxiety heightened.

In September, a new campaign was opening in Maryland. Lee's triumph over Pope at Bull Run enabled the Confederate forces to cross the Potomac into that state, and occupy Frederick. McClellan's army engaged him and ultimately ousted the rebels from Maryland at Antietam. This was not a decisive victory, but it was a victory. Lincoln "determined to wait no longer." The time had come for him to issue the emancipation proclamation.[20]

"The . . . Hands to Ethiopia"

TUESDAY, JULY 22, 1862

¶ *Four days after his talk with Welles and Seward, the President— with some misgivings—signed the Second Confiscation Bill, which freed the slaves of all rebels, and which he considered unconstitu- tional because it declared "forfeiture, extending beyond the lives of the guilty persons; whereas the Constitution . . . declares that 'no attainder of treason shall work corruption of blood, or forfeiture, except during the life of the person attained.'* "[1]

On July 22nd, the President formally informed the Cabinet of his contemplated emancipation policy. Almost two years later, Lincoln described this meeting to Francis B. Carpenter, the artist, who re- corded the conversation in Six Months at the White House with Abraham Lincoln, *published in 1866. Our account of this Cabinet session is based on the Carpenter report as well as upon Chase's* Diary *entry for that day, which fails to recognize the importance of the President's proposal. We begin with Lincoln's statement to Car- penter:* [2]

". . . All were present, excepting Mr. Blair, the Postmaster- General, who was absent at the opening of the discussion, but came in subsequently. I said to the Cabinet that I had resolved upon this step, and had not called them together to ask their advice, but to lay the subject-matter of a proclamation before them; suggestions as to which would be in order, after they had heard it read. . . ."

[The President then proceeded to read as follows:]

In pursuance of the sixth section of the act of congress entitled "An act to suppress insurrection and to punish treason and rebellion, to seize and confiscate property of rebels, and for other purposes" Approved July 17, 1862, and which act, and the Joint Resolution explanatory thereof, are herewith published, I, Abraham Lincoln, President of the United States, do hereby proclaim to, and warn all persons within the contemplation of said sixth section to cease participating in, aiding, countenancing or abetting the existing rebellion, or any rebellion against the government of the United States, and to return to their proper allegiance to the United States, on pain of the forfeiture and seizures, as within and by said sixth section provided.

And I hereby make known that it is my purpose, upon the next meeting of congress, to again recommend the adoption of a practical measure for tendering pecuniary aid to the free choice or rejection, of any and all States which may then be recognizing and practically sustaining the authority of the United States, and which may then have voluntarily adopted or thereafter may voluntarily adopt, gradual abolishment of slavery within such State or States—that the object is to practically restore, thenceforward to be maintain[ed], the constitutional relation between the general government, and each, and all the states, wherein that relation is now suspended, or disturbed; and that, for this object, the war, as it has been, will be, prossecuted [*sic*]. And, as a fit and necessary military measure for affecting this object, I, as Commander-in-Chief of the Army and Navy of the United States, do order and declare that on the first day of January in the year of Our Lord one thousand, eight hunderd and sixty-three, all persons held as slaves within any state or states, wherein the constitutional authority of the United States shall not then be practically recognized, submitted to, and maintained, shall then, thenceforward, and forever, be free.[3]

[According to Lincoln:]

". . . Various suggestions were offered. Secretary Chase wished the language stronger in reference to the arming of the blacks."

[As Chase recalled this point:]

I said that I should give to such a measure my cordial support, but

I should prefer that no new expression on the subject of compensation should be made, and I thought that the measure of Emancipation could be much better and more quietly accomplished by allowing Generals to organize and arm the slaves (thus avoiding depredation and massacre on the one hand, and support to the insurrection on the other) and by directing the Commanders of Departments to proclaim emancipation within their Districts as soon as practicable; but I regarded this as so much better than inaction on the subject, that I should give it my entire support.

[Lincoln continues the narrative:]

"Mr. Blair, after he came in, deprecated the policy, on the ground that it would cost the Administration the fall elections. Nothing, however, was offered that I had not already fully anticipated and settled in my own mind, until Secretary Seward spoke. He said in substance: 'Mr. President, I approve of the proclamation, but I question the expediency of its issue at this juncture. The depression of the public mind, consequent upon our repeated reverses, is so great that I fear the effect of so important a step. It may be viewed as the last measure of an exhausted government, a cry for help; the government stretching forth its hands to Ethiopia, instead of Ethiopia stretching forth her hands to the government.' His idea," said the President, "was that it would be considered our last *shriek, on the retreat.*" (This was his *precise* expression.) " 'Now,' continued Mr. Seward, 'while I approve the measure, I suggest, sir, that you postpone its issue, until you can give it to the country supported by military success, instead of issuing it, as would be the case now, upon the greatest disasters of the war!' " Mr. Lincoln continued: "The wisdom of the view of the Secretary of State struck me with very great force. It was an aspect of the case that, in all my thought upon the subject, I had entirely overlooked. The result was that I put the draft of the proclamation aside, as you do your sketch for a picture, waiting for a victory. . . ."

"Two Colored Regiments"

MONDAY, AUGUST 4, 1862

¶ *Radicals and conservatives had been locked in conflict for some time over another issue: recruitment of Negro troops. Repeated at-*

tempts were made to "coerce" the President to accept colored soldiers, but to him the time had not yet come "for the adoption of such a plan." [1]

Lincoln's attitude toward enlisting Negroes is stated in his interview on August 4th with a "deputation of Western gentlemen," who came "to offer two colored regiments from . . . Indiana." Heading the group were two members of Congress; one of them was the fiery James H. Lane of Kansas. [2] *Our account of this interview is taken from the* New York Tribune *of August 5, 1862:*

A deputation of Western gentlemen waited upon the President this morning. . . . The President received them courteously, but stated to them that he had not prepared to go the length of enlisting negroes as soldiers. He would employ all colored men offered as laborers, but would not promise to make soldiers of them.

The deputation came away satisfied that it is the determination of the Government not to arm negroes unless some new and more pressing emergency arises. The President argued that the nation could not afford to lose Kentucky at this crisis, and gave it as his opinion that to arm the negroes would turn 50,000 bayonets from the loyal Border States against us that were for us.

Upon the policy of using negroes as laborers, the confiscation of Rebel property, and the feeding of National troops upon the granaries of the enemy, the President said there was no division of sentiment. He did not explain, however, why it is that the Army of the Potomac and the Army of Virginia carry out this policy so differently. The President promised that the war should be prosecuted with all the rigor he could command, but he could not promise to arm slaves or to attempt slave insurrections in the Rebel States. The recent enactments of Congress on emancipation and confiscation he expects to carry out.

"What the Executive Had to Say"

THURSDAY, AUGUST 14, 1862

¶ *Lincoln's contemplation of emancipation raised the question of what to do with the freed Negroes. Liberated "darkies" were proving a problem in Federal military districts—a problem that might* *well become more serious as more slaves secured their freedom. One solution could be colonization of the freed Negroes "at some place, or places, in a climate congenial to them." Lincoln had recommended this in his annual message to Congress in December 1861. Since then, Congress had appropriated $600,000 for colonization.[1] He himself had favored such a scheme as far back as 1854, and, as President, had given mature consideration to the Chiriqui Project which, together with subsequent colonization programs, were to be abandoned.*

In August 1862, Lincoln sought to influence free colored people to emigrate voluntarily from the United States. On the 14th, a selected delegation of five free Negroes were welcomed to the White House by Presidential invitation. Our report of this interview —during which Lincoln did almost all the talking—comes to us from the New York Tribune *of August 15, 1862:* [2]

They were introduced by the Rev. J. Mitchell, Commissioner of Emigration. E. M. Thomas, the Chairman, remarked that they were there . . . to hear what the Executive had to say to them. Having all been seated, the President, after a few preliminary observations, informed them that a sum of money had been appropriated by Congress, and placed at his disposition for the purpose of aiding the colonization in some country of the people, or a portion of them, of African descent, thereby making it his duty, as it had for a long time been his inclination, to favor that cause; and why, he asked, should the people of your race be colonized, and where? Why should they leave this country? This is, perhaps, the first question for proper consideration. You and we are different races. We have between us a broader difference than exists between almost any other two races. Whether it is right or wrong I need not discuss, but this physical difference is a great disadvantage to us both, as I think your race suffer very greatly, many of them by living among us, while ours suffer from your presence. In a word we suffer on each side. If this is admitted, it affords a reason at least why we should be separated. You here are freemen I suppose.

A VOICE: Yes, sir.

The President—Perhaps you have long been free, or all your lives. Your race are suffering, in my judgment, the greatest wrong inflicted on any people. But even when you cease to be slaves, you are yet far removed from being placed on an equality with the white race. You are cut off from many of the advantages which the other race enjoy. The aspiration of men is to enjoy equality with the best when free, but on this broad continent, not a single man of your race is made the equal of a single man of ours. Go where you are treated the best, and the ban is still upon you.

I do not propose to discuss this, but to present it as a fact with which we have to deal. I cannot alter it if I would. It is a fact, about which we all think and feel alike, I and you. We look to our condition, owing to the existence of the two races on this continent. I need not recount to you the effects upon white men, growing out of the institution of Slavery. I believe in its general evil effects on the white race. See our present condition—the country engaged in war!— our white men cutting one another's throats, none knowing how far it will extend; and then consider what we know to be the truth. But for your race among us there could not be war, although many men engaged on either side do not care for you one way or the other. Nevertheless, I repeat, without the institution of Slavery and the colored race as a basis, the war could not have an existence.

It is better for us both, therefore, to be separated. I know that there are free men among you, who even if they could better their condition are not as much inclined to go out of the country as those, who being slaves could obtain their freedom on this condition. I suppose one of the principal difficulties in the way of colonization is that the free colored man cannot see that his comfort would be advanced by it. You may believe you can live in Washington or else-where in the United States the remainder of your life, perhaps more so than you can in any foreign country, and hence you may come to the conclusion that you have nothing to do with the idea of going to a foreign country. This is (I speak in no unkind sense) an ex-tremely selfish view of the case.

But you ought to do something to help those who are not so fortunate as yourselves. There is an unwillingess on the part of our people, harsh as it may be, for you free colored people to remain with us. Now, if you could give a start to white people, you would open a wide door for many to be made free. If we deal with those who are not free at the beginning, and whose intellects are clouded by Slavery, we have very poor materials to start with. If intelligent colored men, such as are before me, would move in this matter, much might be accomplished. It is exceedingly important that we have men at the beginning capable of thinking as white men, and not those who have been systematically oppressed.

There is much to encourage you. For the sake of your race you should sacrifice something of your present comfort for the purpose of being as grand in that respect as the white people. It is a cheering thought throughout life that something can be done to ameliorate the condition of those who have been subject to the hard usage of the world. It is difficult to make a man miserable while he feels he is worthy of himself, and claims kindred to the great God who made him. In the American Revolutionary war sacrifices were made by men engaged in it; but they were cheered by the future. Gen. Washington himself endured greater physical hardships than if he had remained a British subject. Yet he was a happy man, because he was engaged in benefiting his race—something for the children of his neighbors, having none of his own.

The colony of Liberia has been in existence a long time. In a certain sense it is a success. The old President of Liberia, [Joseph Jenkins] Roberts, has just been with me—the first time I ever saw him. He says they have within the bounds of that colony between 300,000 and 400,000 people, or more than in some of our old States, such as Rhode Island or Delaware, or in some of our newer States, and less than in some of our larger ones. They are not all American colonists, or their descendants. Something less than 12,000 have been sent thither from this country. Many of the original settlers have died, yet, like people elsewhere, their offspring outnumber those deceased.

The question is if the colored people are persuaded to go any-where, why not there? One reason for an unwillingness to do so is that some of you would rather remain within reach of the country of your nativity. I do not know how much attachment you may have toward our race. It does not strike me that you have the greatest reason to love them. But still you are attached to them at all events.

The place I am thinking about having for a colony is in Central America. It is nearer to us than Liberia—not much more than one-fourth as far as Liberia, and within seven days' run by steamers. Unlike Liberia it is on a great line of travel—it is a highway. The country is a very excellent one for any people, and with great natural resources and advantages, and especially because of the similarity of climate with your native land—thus being suited to your physical condition.

The particular place I have in view is to be a great highway from the Atlantic or Caribbean Sea to the Pacific Ocean, and this particular place has all the advantages for a colony. On both sides there are harbors among the finest in the world. Again, there is evidence of very rich coal mines. A certain amount of coal is valuable in any country, and there may be more than enough for the wants of the country. Why I attach so much importance to coal is, it will afford an opportunity to the inhabitants for immediate employment till they get ready to settle permanently in their homes.

If you take colonists where there is no good landing, there is a bad show; and so where there is nothing to cultivate, and of which to make a farm. But if something is started so that you can get your daily bread as soon as you reach there, it is a great advantage. Coal land is the best thing I know of with which to commence an enterprise.

To return, you have been talked to upon this subject, and told that a speculation is intended by gentlemen, who have an interest in the country, including the coal mines. We have been mistaken all our lives if we do not know whites as well as blacks look to their self-interest. Unless among those deficient of intellect everybody you trade with makes something. You meet with these things here as elsewhere.

If such persons have what will be an advantage to them, the question is whether it cannot be made of advantage to you. You are intelligent, and know that success does not as much depend on external help as on self-reliance. Much, therefore, depends upon yourselves. As to the coal mines, I think I see the means available for your self-reliance.

I shall, if I get a sufficient number of you engaged, have provisions made that you shall not be wronged. If you will engage in the enterprise I will spend some of the money intrusted to me. I am not sure you will succeed. The Government may lose the money, but we cannot succeed unless we try; but we think, with care, we can succeed.

The political affairs in Central America are not in quite as satisfactory condition as I wish. There are contending factions in that quarter; but it is true all the factions are agreed alike on the subject of colonization, and want it, and are more generous than we are here. To your colored race they have no objection. Besides, I would endeavor to have you made equals, and have the best assurance that you should be the equals of the best.

The practical thing I want to ascertain is whether I can get a number of able-bodied men, with their wives and children, who are willing to go, when I present evidence of encouragement and protection. Could I get a hundred tolerably intelligent men, with their wives and children, to "cut their own fodder," so to speak? Can I have fifty? If I could find twenty-five able-bodied men, with a mixture of women and children, good things in the family relation, I think I could make a successful commencement.

I want you to let me know whether this can be done or not. This is the practical part of my wish to see you. These are subjects of very great importance, worthy of a month's study, [not] of a speech delivered in an hour. I ask you then to consider seriously not pertaining to yourselves merely, nor for your race, and ours, for the present time, but as one of the things, if successfully managed, for the good of mankind—not confined to the present generation, but as

> "From age to age descends the lay,
> To millions yet to be,
> Till far its echoes roll away,
> Into eternity."

The above is merely given as the substance of the President's remarks.

The Chairman of the delegation briefly replied that "they would hold a consultation and in a short time give an answer." The President said: "Take your full time—no hurry at all."

The delegation then withdrew.

[Subsequently, Thomas conferred "with leading colored men in Phila New York and Boston" only to find "our friends" hostile to the colonization scheme.[3]]

"Distressed . . . Exceedingly"

TUESDAY, SEPTEMBER 2, 1862

¶ The North winced painfully in the wake of Second Bull Run. The disaster forced Pope to admit: "You have hardly an idea of the *demoralization among officers of high rank." And there was demoralization, too, among the soldiers themselves, many of whom were deserting. It was argued but never proved that McClellan had withheld vital reinforcements from Pope during the heat of battle. Later, he blamed the Union defeat on "a total absence of brains" in planning and executing the Bull Run action."* [1]

At Washington, "disorder reigned unchecked and confusion was everywhere" as the residents, fearing Lee would soon capture the capital, prepared to flee the city. [2] *It was under these circumstances that McClellan was ordered to take command of the defenses of Washington.*

Chase's Diary *reveals the Cabinet's reaction to McClellan's new appointment:* [3]

Cabinet met, but neither the President nor Secretary of War were present. Some conversation took place concerning Generals. Mr. F. W. Seward (the secretary of State being out of town) said nothing. All others agreed that we needed a change in Commander of the Army. Mr. Blair referred to the report [support?] he had constantly given McClellan, but confessed that he now thought he could not wisely be trusted with the chief command. Mr. Bates was very decided against his [McClellan's] competency, and Mr. Smith equally so. Mr. Welles was of the same judgment, though less positive in expression.

After some time, while the talk was going on, the President came in, saying that not seeing much for a Cabinet Meeting to-day, he had been talking at the Department and Head Quarters about the War. The Secretary of War came in. In answer to some inquiry, the fact was stated, by the President or the Secretary, that McClellan had been placed in command of the forces to defend the Capital—or rather, to use the President's own words, he "had set him to putting these troops into the fortifications about Washington," believing that he could do that thing better than any other man. I remarked that this could be done equally well by the Engineer who constructed the Forts; and that putting Genl. McClellan in command for this purpose was equivalent to making him second in command of the entire army. The Secretary of War said that no one was now responsible for the defense of the Capital;—that the Order to McClellan was given by the President direct to McClellan, and that Genl. Halleck considered himself relieved from responsibility, although he acquiesced, and approved the Order;—that McClellan could now shield himself, should anything go wrong, under Halleck, while Halleck could and would disclaim all responsibility for the Order given. The President thought Gen. Halleck as much responsible as before, and repeated that the whole scope of the Order was, simply, to direct McClellan to put . . . troops into the fortifications and command them for the defense of Washington. I remarked that this seemed to me equivalent to making him Commander in Chief for the time being, and that I thought it would prove very difficult to make any substitution hereafter, for active operations;—that I had no feeling whatever against Genl. McClellan;—that he came to the command with my most cordial approbation and support;—that until I became satisfied that his delays would greatly injure our cause, he possessed my full confidence;—that, after I had felt myself compelled to withhold that confidence, I had (since the President, notwithstanding my opinion that he should, refrained from putting another in command) given him all possible support in every way, raising means and urging reinforcements;—that his experience as a military commander had been little else than a series of failures;—and that his omission to urge troops forward to the battles of Friday and Saturday [Second Bull Run], evinced a spirit which rendered him unworthy of trust, and that I could not but feel that giving the command to him was equivalent to giving Washington to the rebels. This and more I said. Other members of the Cabinet expressed a general concurrence, but in no very energetic terms. (Mr. Blair must be excepted, but he did not dissent.)

The President said it distressed him exceedingly to find himself differing on such a point from the Secretary of War and Secretary of the Treasury; that he would gladly resign his plan; but he could not see who could do the work wanted as well as McClellan. I named [Joseph] Hooker, or [Edwin V.] Sumner, or [Ambrose E.] Burnside —either of whom, I thought, would be better.

At length the conversation ended and the meeting broke up, leaving the matter as we found it.

"I Can Never Feel Confident"

MONDAY, SEPTEMBER 8, 1862

¶ *Almost a week later, Lincoln freely aired his views on McClellan and Bull Run in a conversation with Gideon Welles. The Secretary recorded it as follows in his* Diary:[1]

The President called on me to know what authentic [news had been received] of the destruction of the Rebel steamer in Savannah river. He expresses himself very decidedly concerning the management or mismanagement of the army. Said he, "We had the enemy in the hollow of our hands on Friday if our Generals, who are vexed with Pope had done their duty. All of our present difficulties and reverses have been brought upon us by these quarrels of the Generals." These were, I think, his very words. While we were conversing Collector [Hiram] Barney of N. Y. came in. The President said, perhaps before [Barney] came in, that Halleck selected McClellan to command the troops against the Maryland invasion. ["]I could not have done it,["] said he, ["]for I can never feel confident that he [McClellan] will do any thing.["] He went on, freely commenting and repeating some things before B. joined us. Of Pope he spoke in complimentary terms as brave, patriotic, and as having done his whole duty in every respect in Virginia,—to the entire satisfaction of himself and Halleck, who both knew and watched, day by day, every movement. On only one point had Halleck doubted any order P.[ope] had given, which was, in directing one division, I think Hinselmans [Samuel P. Heintzelman's] to march for the Chain bridge, by which the flanks of that division were exposed. When that order reached him by telegraph, Halleck was uneasy for he could not countermand it in season, because the dispatch would have to go part of the way by courier. However all went well [and] the division was not attacked.

Pope, said the President, did well, but there was an army prejudice against him, and it was necessary he should leave. He had gone off very angry, and not without cause, but circumstances controlled us.

Barney said he had mingled with all descriptions of persons, and particularly with men connected with the army, and perhaps could speak from actual knowledge of public sentiment better than either of us. He was positive that no one but McClellan could do anything just now with this army. He had managed to get its confidence and meant to keep it, and use it for his own purposes. Barney proceeded to disclose a conversation he had with [S. L. M.] Barlow, some months since. Barlow, a prominent Democratic lawyer and politician of New York had been to Washington to attend one of McClellan's grand reviews, when he lay here inactive on the Potomac. McClellan had specially invited Barlow to be present, and during this visit opened his views—said he did not wish the Presidency,—would rather have his place at the head of the army, etc., etc., intimating he had no political views or aspirations. All with him was military, and he had no particular desire to close this war immediately, but would pursue a line of policy of his own, regardless of the Administration, and its wishes and objects.

The combination against Pope was, Barney says, part of the plan and the worst feature to him was the great demoralization of the soldiers. They were becoming reckless and untamable. In these remarks the President concurred, and he was shocked to find that of 140,000 whom we were paying for in Pope's army, only 60,000 could be found. McClellan brought away 93,000 from the Peninsula, but could not to day count on over 45,000 and as regarded demoralization [the President said] there was no doubt that some of our men permitted themselves to be captured in order that they might leave on parole, get discharged, and go home. Where there is such rottenness, is there not reason to fear for the country?

"The Pope's Bull Against the Comet"

SATURDAY, SEPTEMBER 13, 1862

¶ *Greeley renewed his clamor for emancipation with his August 20th editorial, "The Prayer of Twenty Millions." Lincoln replied: "My paramount object in this struggle is to save the Union, and is not either to save or destroy slavery. If I could save the Union without freeing any slave I would do it, and if I could save it by freeing all the slaves I would do it; and if I could save it by freeing some and leaving others alone I would also do that. What I do about slavery, and the colored race, I do because I believe it helps to save the Union; and what I forbear, I forbear because I do not believe it would help save the Union."* [1]

Raymond of The New York Times *editorialized: "The chief difference between Mr. Lincoln and Mr. Greeley seems to be this: that the former is President and was sworn on his own conscience, and must be governed by his own sense of oath, honor and duty, as to the time and manner of his actions. On the other hand Mr. Greeley having clearer conceptions, it may be, of right, policy and statesmanship, wishes to substitute his conscience for Mr. Lincoln's in the present National perplexity. The President not yet seeing the propriety of abdicating in behalf of our neighbor, consoles him with a letter that assures the country of abundant sanity in the White House."* [2]

Lincoln won few friends by following a noncommittal course on the slavery issue as he waited for the right moment to issue his emancipation proclamation. George Templeton Strong confided to his Diary: *"Disgust with our present government is certainly universal. Even Lincoln himself has gone down at last, like all our popular idols of the last eighteen months. This honest old codger was the last to fall, but he has fallen. Nobody believes in him any more."* The New York Times *was urging "a responsible cabinet . . . clear in its aims and distinct in principles."* [3]

The President's remarks to a religious deputation from Chicago on September 13th were to plague him even after he had issued his preliminary emancipation proclamation. Reverend William W. Patton and Reverend John Dempster, who had been delegated to present Lincoln with a petition urging emancipation, wrote a report of this conference eight days later, which was published in a number of newspapers: [4]

The President received us courteously, and gave the fullest opportunity to discharge the duty assigned. He listened with fixed attention while the memorial was read by the chairman of the delegation, who added a few words to express the deep interest felt in the President by the religious community, as manifested in the many prayers offered in his behalf from the day of his election to the present hour, and to explain the pressure of feeling that caused those prayers to be followed by a memorial expressive of their solemn conviction of national duty and necessity. He observed that in doing this the memorialists believe that they discharge their solemn obligations as Christian citizens, which is all they seek, having no desire to dictate to their Chief Magistrate, who has his own responsibility to God, the nation and the world. The time of presenting the memorial might seem inauspicious, in view of recent disasters, which make the authority of the government in the slave States less extensive and influential than before. But the memorialists believe these disasters to be tokens of Divine displeasure, calling for new and advanced action by the President in behalf of the country, such as would indicate national repentance for the sin of oppression; and he must see that, if success in our military affairs was supposed to render such action unnecessary, and defeat to make it unavailing, then duty becomes an idle word, and God's voice of remonstrance and warning are an unmeaning utterance.

The delegation presented, at the same time, a memorial of similar import, drawn in German and in English, and signed by a number of our German citizens, which was placed in their [the delegates'] hands on leaving home.

After a moment's silence the President answered, and, as we waited upon him in a public capacity, as a delegation from a large body of the people, to learn his views on a grave political and moral subject which is profoundly agitating the nation, we suppose the reply belongs as properly to those whom we represented as to ourselves. We give it, therefore, with some degree of fulness, accurately in substance, and often in the very words which fell from his lips. The President made his observations deliberately and with well chosen language, speaking in an earnest and often solemn manner, as one impressed with the weight of the theme, yet at times making a characteristically shrewd remark with a pleasant air.

THE PRESIDENT'S ANSWER—DIVINE REVELATIONS.

The subject presented in the memorial is one upon which I have thought much for weeks past, and I may even say for months. I am approached with the most opposite opinions and advice, and that by religious men, who are equally certain that they represent the Divine will. I am sure that either the one or the other class is mistaken in that belief, and perhaps in some respects both. I hope it will not be irreverent for me to say that, if it is probable that God would reveal his will to others on a point so connected with my duty, it might be supposed he would reveal it directly to me. For, unless I am more deceived in myself than I often am, it is my earnest desire to know the will of Providence in this matter. And, if I can learn what it is, I will do it. These are not, however, the days of miracles, and I suppose it will be granted that I am not to expect a direct revelation. I must study the plain, physical facts of the case, ascertain what is possible, and learn what appears to be wise and right.

DIFFERENCES OF OPINION ON THE SUBJECT.

The subject is difficult, and good men do not agree. For instance, the other day four gentlemen of standing and intelligence from New York called, as a delegation, on business connected with the war; but before leaving two of them earnestly beset me to proclaim general emancipation, upon which the other two immediately attacked them. You know, also, *that the last session of Congress had a decided majority of anti-slavery men, yet they could not unite on this policy.* And the same is true of the religious people. Why, the rebel soldiers are praying with a great deal more earnestness, I fear, than our own troops, and expecting God to favor their side; for one of our soldiers, who had been taken prisoner, told Senator [Henry] Wilson a few days since, that he met with nothing so discouraging as the evident sincerity of those he was among in their prayers. But we will talk over the merits of the case.

WHY AN EMANCIPATION PROCLAMATION SHOULD NOT BE ISSUED.

What good would a proclamation of emancipation from me do, especially as we are now situated? I do not want to issue a document that the whole world will see must necessarily be inoperative, like the Pope's bull against the comet. Would my word free the slaves, when I cannot even enforce the constitution in the rebel States? Is there a single court, or magistrate, or individual that would be influenced by it there? And what reason is there to think it would have any greater effect upon the slaves than the late law of Congress, which I approved, and which offers protection and freedom to the slaves of rebel masters who come within our lines? Yet I cannot learn that that law [the Second Confiscation Act] *has caused a single slave to come over to us. And suppose they could be induced, by a proclama-*

tion of freedom from me, to throw themselves upon us, what should we do with them? How can we feed and care for such a multitude? General Butler wrote me, a few days since, that he was issuing more rations to the slaves who have rushed to him than to all the white troops under his command. They eat, and that is all; though it is true, General Butler is feeding the whites also by the thousands, for it nearly amounts to a famine there [in the Department of the Gulf].

WHAT IS TO PREVENT THE REBELS FROM ENSLAVING THE NEGROES AGAIN.

If now, the pressure of the war should call off our forces from New Orleans to defend some other point, what is to prevent the masters from reducing the blacks to slavery again, for I am told that whenever the rebels take any blacks prisoners, free or slave, they immediately auction them off. They did so with those they took from a boat that was aground on the Tennessee river a few days ago.

HOW MR. LINCOLN IS BLAMED.

And then I am very ungenerously attacked for it. For instance, when, after the late battles at and near Bull Run, an expedition went out from Washington under a flag of truce to bury the dead and bring in the wounded, and the rebels seized the blacks who went along to help, and sent them into slavery, Horace Greeley said in his paper that the government would probably do nothing about it. What could I do?

WHAT GOOD WOULD AN EMANCIPATION PROCLAMATION DO?

Now, then, . . . what possible result of good would follow the issuing of such a proclamation as you desire? Understand, I raise no objection against it on legal or constitutional grounds; for, as Commander-in-Chief of the army and navy, in time of war, I suppose I have a right to take any measure which may best subdue the enemy. Nor do I urge objections of a moral nature, in view of possible consequences of insurrection and massacre at the South. I view the matter as a practical war measure, to be decided upon according to the advantages or disadvantages it may offer to the suppression of the rebellion.

. . . I admit that slavery is the root of the rebellion, or at least its sine qua non. The ambition of politicians may have instigated them to act, but they would have been impotent without slavery as their instrument. I will also concede that emancipation would help us in Europe, and convince them that we are incited by something more than ambition. I grant further that it would help somewhat at the North, though not so much, I fear, as you and those you represent imagine. Still, some additional strength would be added in that way to the war. And then unquestionably it would weaken the rebels by drawing off their laborers, which is of great importance. *But I am not so sure we could do much with the blacks. If we were to arm them, I fear that in a few weeks the arms would be in the hands of the rebels;* and indeed thus far we have not had arms enough to equip our white troops.

MR. LINCOLN HAS FEARS FOR THE BORDER SLAVE STATES.

I will mention another thing, though it meet only your scorn and contempt. *There are fifty thousand bayonets in the Union armies from the border slave States. It would be a serious matter if, in consequence of a proclamation such as you desire, they should go over to the rebels.* I do not think they all would—not so many indeed as a year ago, or as six months ago—not so many to-day as yesterday. Every day increases their Union feeling. They are also getting their pride enlisted, and want to beat the rebels. Let me say one thing more:—I think you should admit that we already have an important principle to rally and unite the people in the fact that constitutional government is at stake. This is a fundamental idea, going down about as deep as anything.

. . . REPLY FROM THE DELEGATION—A CONVERSATION.

We answered that, being fresh from the people, we were naturally more hopeful than himself as to the necessity and probable effect of such a proclamation. The value of constitutional government is indeed a grand idea for which to contend; but the people know that nothing else has put constitutional government in danger but slavery; that the toleration of that aristocratic and despotic element among our free institutions was the inconsistency that has nearly wrought our ruin and caused free government to appear a failure before the world; and, therefore, the people demand emancipation to preserve and perpetuate constitutional government. Our idea would thus be found to go deeper than this and to be armed with corresponding power.

Mr. LINCOLN—Yes, that is the true ground of our difficulties.

DELEGATION—That a proclamation of general emancipation, giving "liberty and Union" as the national watchword, would rouse the people and rally them to his support beyond anything yet witnessed— appealing alike to conscience, sentiment and hope. He must remember, too, that present manifestations are no index to what would then take place. If the leader would but utter a trumpet call, the nation will respond with patriotic ardor. No one can tell the power of the right word from the right man to develop the latest fire and enthusiasm of the masses.

Mr. LINCOLN—I know it.

DELEGATION—That good sense must, of course, be exercised in drilling, arming and using black as well as white troops, to make them efficient; and that, in a scarcity of arms, it was at least worthy of inquiry whether it were not wise to place a portion of them in the hands of those nearest to the seat of the rebellion, and able to strike the deadliest blow. That, in case of a proclamation of emancipation, we had no fear of serious injury from the desertion of border State troops. The danger was greatly diminished, as the President had admitted. But, let the desertions be what they might, the increased spirit of the North would replace them two to one. One State alone, if necessary, would compensate the loss, were the whole fifty thousand to join the enemy. The struggle has gone too far, and cost too much treasure and blood to allow of a partial settlement. Let the line be drawn at the same time between freedom and slavery and between loyalty and treason. The sooner we know who are our enemies the better.

In bringing our interview to a close, after an hour of earnest and frank discussion, of which the foregoing is a specimen, Mr. Lincoln remarked:—"Do not misunderstand me, because I have mentioned those objections. They indicate the difficulties that have thus far prevented my action in some such way as you desire. I have not decided against a proclamation of liberty to the slaves, but hold the matter under advisement. And I can assure you that the subject is on my mind, by day and night, more than any other. Whatever shall appear to be God's will I will do. I trust that, in the freedom with which I have canvassed your views, I have not in any respect injured your feelings."

We assured him that he had not, and expressed our hope that, in honest endeavors to express and defend our convictions, we had not been wanting in due respect for our Chief Magistrate. Bidding him farewell, we commended him to the gracious guidance of God, having faith that, if the memorial and our added interview had thrown into the trembling scales but a single grain of truth that might aid in the preponderance of justice and humanity, our mission would not prove to be in vain.

"Desire to Do You Justice"

MONDAY, SEPTEMBER 22, 1862

¶ *The battle of Antietam Creek—"the most severe ever fought on this continent," said McClellan—cost the Union 12,000 casualties. Mc-Clellan had bested Lee and turned back the Confederate invasion of the North. "I feel some little pride in having, with a beaten and demoralized army, defeated Lee so utterly and saved the North so completely," boasted "Little Mac." Lincoln, too, considered Antietam a significant gain; called for "three hearty cheers for all" who had fought there. The Yanks had forced Lee to retreat into Virginia. But McClellan—overcautious as usual—gave no chase to the rebels. This failure on McClellan's part rankled the President. "Are you not over-cautious when you assume that you can not do what the enemy is constantly doing?" Lincoln asked his general. "Should you not claim to be at least his equal in prowess, and act upon the claim? . . . You know I desired, but did not order, you to cross the Potomac [in pursuit of Lee] . . ." Lincoln wanted McClellan at least to "try," observing that "if we never try, we shall never succeed."* [1]

A few days after Antietam, McClellan, anxious to know how Lincoln felt about the action, sent Detective Allan Pinkerton to Washington. Pinkerton, now intelligence officer of the Army of the Potomac, has been blamed for feeding McClellan faulty information on the Confederates. While in the capital, Pinkerton kept "tabs" on the President, reporting the latter's movements and conversations to McClellan. [2] *The morning of September 22nd, the detective had an unexpected talk with the President about McClellan. Lincoln, apparently conversing "tongue in cheek," conveyed the impression that he was entirely gratified with McClellan and appreciated the general's motivations in not pressing Lee after Antietam. Pinkerton, in a letter to McClellan that day, gave an account of this meeting:* [8]

Lincoln was very friendly at the start and continued so all the time. He said he was glad I had called. That he wanted to learn all I knew in relation to the movements of Genl. McClellan's Army —And that before proceeding further, he would say that in talking with me whatever he might say was not meant to criticize anything relating to Genl. McClellan, but simply for the purpose of eliciting what I knew or supposed caused certain things to be done and not for the purpose of seeking aught against you. That in reference to the Battle of South Mountain & Antietam he thought those great and decisive victories—victories achieved under great difficulty and in themselves of the greatest value to the nation and that you had accomplished all you had set out to do viz—to push the Rebels back of Maryland . . . and free the Capitol from danger. Admitting that all this had been accomplished and that he felt that to you, your officers and men, . . . the nation, owed you a deep debt of gratitude —and that he personally owed you more. That you had taken the Command of the Army at a time of great peril and when the army was suffering under great defeats. That with that same army you had gone out to meet the same victorious foe—that he owed you for this what he never could repay you, but that placed as he is— he was desirous of knowing some things which he supposed from the pressure on your mind, you had not advised him on or that you considered was of minor importance, not sufficiently worthy of notice for you to send to him, and if I knew anything about these matters and my duty to Genl. McClellan permitted of it—He would like to ask me . . . [about them]. I said that there was doubtless many things transpiring in regard to the movements of the Army which you did not deem of importance enough to report to him or trouble him with. Skirmishes, reconnaissances and such as that you did not think of importance enough. Except where important results followed [you did not wish] to trouble the Pres. . . . That you relied upon having the full confidence of the President and relying so, did not deem it necessary to burden him with such detail, etc. etc.

He then alluded to the surrender of Harpers Ferry and enquired if everything had been done . . . I assured him it [was]. . . . He said that many had endeavored to impress him with the belief that you *might* have done more than you had done for the relief of the Ferry. That he had always felt confident that you would do all in your power to aid the extrication of that force. . . .

He next referred to the battle of Antietam, enquiring into the number of the enemy and conditions, as also your numbers & condition. I stated the Rebel Force to be 140,000 and yours about 90,000. He said that he thought you had about 100,000 and admitted that he believed the rebels had the number I said. As for the condition of the two Armies I said that I believed the one was fully as anxious to fight as the other. I explained fully to him in relation to what had been done from the time you forced the enemy in position on the Antietam on Monday afternoon up till the time I left headquarters (Saturday P.M.) at least so far as I knew of them. He enquired the reason why the Army did not fight on Thursday and I explained to him the position of our Army on Wednesday evening after the battle had closed & the fact that the enemy still remained in line of battle all day Thursday—recalled to his mind the exhausted condition of our Army. The large number of dead & wounded which lay on the field and the necessity of disposing of them ere fighting the field over again. As also that large or long range ammunition was short and the fact that the enemy had punctured their line of battle well all the previous day and the necessity of great caution on your part or the largely superior force of the rebels might have obtained some partial success. I described . . . [your?] indefatigable suspension of every disposition on the field— and he at once frankly said that he had no doubt—not any—but that you had fought the battle skillfully . . . much more so than any General he knew of could have done, and again repeated enquiring as he was about these details—he was not criticizing anything which you had done—for on the contrary you had his confidence, but he was seeking to learn all I could tell him—without betraying Genl. McClellan's confidence.

He next enquired regarding the Rebels escaping across the Potomac and I explained to him the position of the Rebel line of battle on

Thursday in reference to the river. The stage of water. The fact that infantry and cavalry could cross almost anywhere. That the enemy had been . . . on the Maryland shore and the numerous fords in that vicinity which might be made available for crossing artillery on water. Also the fact that the citizens of Sharpsburg informed us that wave[s] of the Rebels commenced crossing into Virginia until about 9 P.M. Thursday . . . Arguing from this that if you had commenced the engagement you would have to have done it in the face of many very great obstacles. That all day Thursday was spent in burying the dead—Taking care of the wounded. . . .

I explained on Friday morning the rapid advance of your army to the shore and the crossing of Genl. [Alfred] Pleasanton's in rapid pursuit as also the movement of Banks Corps to occupy Maryland Heights & . . . march to Williamsport and assured him that you would drive them as rapidly as could be done. . . .

I must say General that I never saw a man feel better than he did with these explanations. He expressed himself as highly pleased and gratified with all you had done (. . . commending your caution) and frankly admitted that you had done everything which could or ought to be expected of you. . . . For myself you know I am rather prejudiced against him—but I must confess that he impresses me more at this interview with his honesty towards you & his desire to do you justice than he has ever done before and I would respectfully suggest that whenever you can consistently give him information regarding your movements, skirmishes, . . . etc. it would be very acceptable. For instance, he knew nothing of the . . . [difficulties?] of Antietam Creek which lay between you and the enemy except what he had learned from newspapers.

"Promise . . . to My Maker"

MONDAY, SEPTEMBER 22, 1862

¶ *After Pinkerton had left the White House, the Cabinet convened. All members were present. Two of them, Chase and Welles, recorded the proceedings of this historic event in their respective diaries.*[1]

Lincoln opened the meeting by announcing that he had received a book from Artemus Ward, which contained an extremely humorous chapter, "High Handed Outrage at Utica." It was so funny that the President felt impelled to read it to the Cabinet:

In the Faul of 1856, I showed my show in Utiky, a trooly grate sitty in the State of New York.

The people gave me a cordyal recepshun. The press was loud in her prases.

1 day as I was givin a descripshun of my Beests and Snaiks in my usual flowry stile what was my skorn & disgust to see a big burly feller walk up to the cage containin my wax figgers of the Lord's Last Supper, and cease Judas Iscarrot by the feet and drag him out on the ground. He then commenced fut to pound him as hard as he cood.

"What under the son are you abowt?" cried I.

Sez he, "What did you bring this pussylanermus cuss here fur?" & he hit the wax figger another tremenjis blow on the hed.

Sez I, "You egrejus ass, that air's a wax figger—a representashun of the false 'Postle."

Sez he, "That's all very well fur you to say, but I tell you, old man, that Judas Iscarrot can't show hisself in Utiky with impunerty by a darn site!" with which observashun he kaved in Judassis hed. The young man belonged to 1 of the first famerlies in Utiky. I sood him, and the Joory brawt in a verdick of Arson in the 3d degree.[2]

Secretary Chase, in his Diary, *takes it up from here:*

The President then took a graver tone and said:—

"Gentlemen; I have, as you are aware, thought a great deal about the relation of this war to Slavery; and you all remember that, several weeks ago, I read you an Order I had prepared on this subject, which, on account of objections made by some of you, was not issued. Ever since then, my mind has been much occupied with this subject, and I have thought all along that the time for acting on it might very probably come. I think the time has come now. I wish it were a better time. I wish that we were in a better condition. The action of the army against the rebels has not been quite what I should have best liked. But they have been driven out of Maryland, and Pennsylvania is no longer in danger of invasion. When the rebel army was at Frederick, I determined, as soon as it should be driven out of Maryland, to issue a Proclamation of Emancipation such as I thought most likely to be useful. I said nothing to any one; but I made the promise to myself, and (hesitating a little)—to my Maker. The rebel army is now driven out, and I am going to fulfill that promise. I have got you together to hear what I have written down. I do not wish your advice about the main matter—for that I have determined for myself. This I say without intending any thing but respect for any one of you. But I already know the views of each on this question. They have been heretofore expressed, and I have considered them as thoroughly and carefully as I can. What I have written is that which my reflections have determined me to say. If there is anything in the expressions I use, or in any other minor matter, which anyone of you thinks had best be changed, I shall be glad to receive the suggestions. One other observation I will make. I know very well that many others might, in this matter, as in others, do better than I can; and if I were satisfied that the public confidence was more fully possessed by any one of them than by me, and knew of any Constitutional way in which he could be put in my place, he should have it. I would gladly yield it to him. But though I believe that I have not so much of the confidence of the people as I had some time since, I do not know that, all things considered, any other person has more; and, however this may be, there is no way in which I can have any other man put where I am. I am here. I must do the best I can, and bear the responsibility of taking the course which I feel I ought to take."

The President then proceeded to read his Emancipation Proclamation, making remarks on the several parts as he went on, and showing that he had fully considered the whole subject, in all the lights under which it had been presented to him.

After he had closed, Gov. Seward said: "The general question having been decided, nothing can be said further about that. Would it not, however, make the Proclamation more clear and decided, to leave out all references to the act being sustained during the incumbency of the present President; and not merely say that the Government 'recognizes,' but that it will maintain, the freedom it proclaims?"

I followed, saying: "What you have said, Mr. President, fully satisfies me that you have given to every proposition which has been made, a kind and candid consideration. And you have now expressed the conclusion to which you have arrived, clearly and distinctly. This it was your right, and under your oath of office your duty, to do.

The Proclamation does not, indeed, mark out exactly the course I should myself prefer. But I am ready to take it just as it is written, and to stand by it with all my heart. I think, however, the suggestions of Gov. Seward very judicious, and shall be glad to have them adopted."

The President then asked us severally our opinions as to the modifications proposed, saying that he did not care much about the phrases he had used. Everyone favored the modification and it was adopted. Gov. Seward then proposed that in the passage relating to colonization, some language should be introduced to show that the colonization proposed was to be only with the consent of the colonists, and the consent of the States in which colonies might be attempted. This, too, was agreed to; and no other modification was proposed. . . .

[Here, Secretary Welles takes up the discussion in his *Diary:*]

It [the Proclamation] was then handed to the Secretary of State to publish to-morrow. After this, Blair remarked that he did not concur in the expediency of the measure at this time, though he approved of the principle, and should therefore wish to file his objections. He stated at some length his views, which were that we ought not to put in greater jeopardy the patriotic element in the border States,—that the results of this Proclamation would be to carry over those States *en masse* to the Secessionists as soon as it was read, and that there was a class of partisans in the free States endeavoring to revive old parties, who would have a club put into their hands of which they would avail themselves to beat the Administration.

The President said he had considered the danger to be apprehended from the first objection, which was undoubtedly serious, but the objection was certainly as great not to act;—as regarded the last, it had not much weight with him. The question of power, authority in the Government was not much discussed at this meeting, but had been canvassed individually by the President in private conversation with the members. Some thought legislation advisable but Congress was clothed with no authority on this subject—nor is the Executive, except under the war power,—military necessity, martial law—when there can be no legislation.

"Would You . . . Shake Hands with Me . . . ?"

SATURDAY, OCTOBER 4, 1862

¶ *Early in October, Lincoln went to Maryland to visit the Army of the Potomac "and satisfy himself by a personal inspection of the troops and interview with General McClellan, in regard to the necessity for temporary delay and the utility of future movements." While there, the President "went through the different encampments, reviewed the troops, and went over the battle-fields of South Mountain and Antietam." He also appeared at the rebel hospital at Sharpsburg—a "remarkable scene," chronicled by a Baltimore newspaperman:* [1]

Passing through one of the hospitals devoted exclusively to Confederate sick and wounded, President Lincoln's attention was drawn to a young Georgian—a fine noble looking youth—stretched upon a humble cot. He was pale, emaciated and anxious, far from kindred and home, vibrating, as it were, between life and death. Every stranger that entered [was] caught in his restless eyes, in hope of their being some relative or friend. President Lincoln observed this youthful soldier, approached and spoke, asking him if he suffered much pain. "I do," was the reply. "I have lost a leg, and feel I am sinking from exhaustion." "Would you," said Mr. Lincoln, "shake hands with me if I were to tell you who I am?" The response was affirmative. "There should," remarked the young Georgian, "be no enemies in this place." Then said the distinguished visitor, "I am Abraham Lincoln, President of the United States." The young sufferer raised his head, looking amazed, and freely extended his hand, which Mr. Lincoln took and pressed tenderly for some time. There followed an instinctive pause. The wounded Confederate's eyes melted into tears, his lips quivered, and his heart beat full. President Lincoln bent over him motionless and dumb. His eyes, too, were overflowing, thus giving utterance to emotions far beyond the power of any language to describe. It was a most touching scene. Not a dry eye was present. Silence was subsequently broken by a kind conciliatory conversation between the President and this young Confederate, when they parted, there being but slim hope of the latter's recovery.

Chapter Seven

"LIKE A CHINAMAN BEATING HIS SWORDS"

ON December 2nd, War Secretary Stanton told the President that regardless of the disasters "our armies may have suffered at particular points, a great advance has nevertheless been made since the commencement of the war." When war began, the rebels controlled Norfolk and every port on the Southern coast; they were in possession of the Mississippi from Cairo to New Orleans. "Now," Stanton reported, "the blockaded ports of Charleston and Mobile only remain to them on the sea-board, and New Orleans and Memphis have been wrested from them." Confederate possession of Vicksburg still obstructed the Mississippi, but it was of no commercial use to the enemy. Rebel strongholds on the Tennessee and Cumberland were now in Union hands.

"General Andrew Johnson, as military governor of Tennessee, holds Nashville," said Stanton. "The enemy have been driven from Kentucky, West Tennessee, Missouri, part of Arkansas; are fleeing before Grant in Mississippi, and all their hopes of Maryland are cut off." [1]

But Lincoln's big problem was still in Maryland—was still George B. McClellan. As Halleck put it: "From the sixteenth of September [when the Battle of Antietam was fought] till the twenty-sixth of October, McClellan's main army remained on the north bank of the Potomac, in the vicinity of Sharpsburgh [sic] and Harper's Ferry. The long inactivity of so large an army in the face of a defeated foe, and during the most favorable season for rapid movements and a

211

vigorous campaign, was a matter of great disappointment and regret." [2]

After Antietam, McClellan claimed his forces were exhausted.
He kept calling for new men, for more supplies. Lincoln had tried
everything to compel McClellan to move. He even outlined a plan
to his general for "going to Richmond on the inside track." But now
the President was becoming increasingly irritated with "Little Mac."
Nicolay noted that Lincoln kept poking "sharp sticks under Mc-
Clellan's ribs." McClellan "is an admirable engineer," Lincoln
quipped, "but he seems to have a special talent for a stationary
engine." [3]

It was not until October 26th that McClellan's army began crossing the Potomac in pursuit of Lee. For nine days the Yanks kept
crossing the river. Then, on November 5th, Lincoln wrote an order
relieving McClellan from command of the army. "I said I would
remove him if he let Lee's army get away from him, and I must
do so." [4]

Major General Ambrose E. Burnside, a thirty-eight-year-old
West Pointer, "a brave soldier within his sphere," who was to prove
himself an incompetent commander, was placed at the head of the
Potomac Army. It was Burnside who, disregarding Lincoln's suggested plan, moved against the rebels at Fredericksburg in mid-
December and was responsible—as he himself admitted—for the
last great Union disaster of 1862. [5]

In the Army of the Potomac, morale hit an unprecedented low after
Fredericksburg. Wrote Charles Francis Adams, Jr.: "There is a
great deal of croaking, no confidence, plenty of sickness, and desertion is the order of the day. This arises from various causes; partly
from the defeat at Fredericksburg . . . but mostly from the change
of commanders of late. You or others may wonder or agree, as you
choose, but it is a fact that McClellan alone has the confidence of this
army." [6]

Senator Fessenden sized up the situation this way:

"Many of our poor soldiers have not had a dime for months. . . .
Nobody can blame them for deserting. I am heartsick when I think
of the miserable mismanagement of our army. In what is called the
'Convalescent Camp' thousands are almost without shelter, and
miserably provided with food—all through the stupidity of our
officers, for there have been ample means provided. If I was

secretary of war, wouldn't heads fall? The simple truth is, there never was such a shambling, half and half set of incapables collected in one government before or since the world began." [7]

Attacks upon the Administration gained momentum as "doubt and discouragement" enveloped the North. In a Chase-inspired Senatorial movement, Lincoln and Seward were assailed "very bitterly," and the latter was charged "with all the disasters which had come upon our arms alleging that he was opposed to a vigorous prosecution of the war—controlled the President and thwarted the other members of the Cabinet." They demanded Seward's dismissal from the Cabinet, and Senator Wade advocated "the creation of a Lieutenant Genl with absolute and despotic powers, and said he would never be satisfied until there was a Republican at the head of our armies." [8]

In the midst of this "uncomfortable excitement," Burnside began planning another attack. Upon learning this, two of his subordinate generals—John Newton and John Cochrane—on December 30th hastened to warn the President of "the dispirited condition of the army, and the danger there was in attempting any movement against the enemy at that time." Lincoln thereupon told Burnside not to make a general movement "without letting me know." [9]

Late in January 1863, "Fighting Joe" Hooker superseded Burnside and fast began earning the name of "Working Joe Hooker." Upon assuming command, he began reorganizing and disciplining the army. "He has issued the most stringent orders concerning furloughs and leaves of absence, and will deal summarily with deserters," ran one newspaper account. "He is taking measures to sift out disloyal, disobedient, disaffected and demoralized officers, who have so long cursed the Potomac army." [10] The North looked to Hooker for victories.

Reaction to Lincoln's emancipation proclamation had set in against this background of military disaster and Cabinet crisis. It was a swift reaction which followed party lines. One New England newspaper opined that while it might be difficult to foresee the effect of the proclamation on the South, in Europe, "it will immediately benefit our cause." England and France "will hesitate to intervene, when intervention would plainly be to throw their influence in favor of slavery." [11]

This view was corroborated by the Paris correspondent of the

New York Herald. However, while liberal elements in Europe applauded the proclamation, official news organs in England and France derided it. Said the London *Star:* "The fiat has gone forth, and the heart of humanity will hail its execution." Wrote the London *Times:* "Where he has no power Mr. LINCOLN will set the negroes free; where he regains power he will consider them as slaves. . . . This is more like a Chinaman beating his two swords together to frighten his enemy than like an earnest man pressing on his cause in steadfastness and truth." [12]

In the United States, the proclamation was a major issue in the fall elections of 1862, the results of which were a great blow to the Administration. But it was not the only key issue of the campaign. On September 24th, Lincoln had proclaimed the suspension of the writ of habeas corpus throughout the North to cope with those who sought to hinder the draft or indulge in other disloyal practices against the government.[13] A series of arbitrary arrests by military authorities followed, in which the guilty and the innocent were often imprisoned on mere suspicion of wrongdoing.

The writ's suspension was considered an aggression upon personal freedom and constitutional rights. Cried Kentucky's Garrett Davis: "Every traitor, every felon, every sympathizer with rebellion is entitled to every right which the Constitution and the law give him." New York's Congressman Burt Van Buren declared: "Men all over the country have thrown obstacles in the way of the war and its prosecution; have given their influence against enlistments to fill up our armies, and in some cases have declared openly and defiantly that if they had to fight . . . they would fight upon the side of our enemies." However, Representative John W. Menzies of Kentucky maintained: "It is a great mistake to suppose that the Constitution is too weak for the emergency. If the Constitution is too weak, the rebels are too strong for us under any plan of operation." [14]

In his post-mortem on the elections, Pennsylvania Congressman Hendrick B. Wright concluded that "the great change in public opinion . . . results . . . from a want of confidence in the manner in which the war has been conducted, and the blunders of the Administration. The people . . . have not abandoned the idea of saving their country, but they have adopted the idea of changing their rulers." [15]

On the other hand, Congressman S. S. "Sunset" Cox of Ohio

insisted the elections had demonstrated that "the people have condemned the edict of emancipation. . . . The people desired the war to be continued on one line of policy, . . . for the Constitution and the Union." [16]

Lincoln had been warned that issuing his emancipation proclamation would invite a Republican disaster at the polls. Now, with the election over, the President was being pressured to cancel the edict. The people wondered what he would do in spite of his declaration "that the result of the election had in no way modified his views regarding the wisdom of emancipating all the slaves within the rebel lines on the 1st of January." [17] When his December Message to Congress focused primarily upon his plan for compensated emancipation, doubts as to whether the proclamation would be forthcoming grew still more intense.

However, on January 1, 1863, Lincoln kept his word. "I am a slow walker," he observed afterward in commenting upon the emancipation proclamation, "but I never walk back." [18]

"Tell Me Frankly . . ."

FRIDAY, OCTOBER 17, 1862

¶ *Many radicals—especially in Pennsylvania—attributed the Republican defeat in the fall elections "to the President's retention of McClellan . . . after he [the general] had proven himself unwilling or incompetent to conduct an aggressive campaign against the Confederate army." Judge William D. Kelley had been McClellan's friend; for years had known his father and uncle, "who ranked high among Philadelphia's distinguished surgeons and physicians." Early in the war, Kelley had greeted McClellan's appointment to the supreme command of the armies "with enthusiasm." But before the end of 1861, says Kelley, "I had taken my place with those who denounced his course in selecting his intimate associates from the ranks of those who were most hostile to the administration that had placed him in command of an army which was charged with the duty of conquering embattled rebellion, and in wasting the entire summer and autumn in inaction." [1]*

Nevertheless, in the October election, Kelley had managed to pile up a majority in a strongly conservative Pennsylvania district. Three

days after that contest, he had "a memorable interview with the
President." Kelley described this event in an article in Rice's Reminiscences of Abraham Lincoln by Distinguished Men of His Time
(1886):[2]

I presented myself to the President as his first visitor, [and] he
advanced with extended hand to greet me, exclaiming, "Kelley, you
know how sincerely I congratulate you. Come, sit down and tell me
how it is that you, for whose election nobody seemed to hope, are
returned with a good majority at your back, while so many of our
friends, about whom there was no doubt, have been badly beaten."

Admitting that I would have been beaten had the election occurred
six months earlier, I said that my triumph was due to my loyalty to
him and his administration, coupled with my known independence
of both in demanding the substitution of a fighting general for
McClellan. Without pausing for a reply, I continued: It is the
desire to secure this change that has brought me here at such an
early hour this morning. I am, as you know, not a soldier, and have
rendered no military service, yet it happens that, as one of a squad
of emergency men, I was in charge of the spare guns and sick horses
of a battery of regular artillery in a camp between Hagerstown and
Sharpsburg, and heard the fire of musketry that opened the battle of
Antietam in the gray dawn of the morning; that by a detail from
Dr. [H. H.] Smith, the Surgeon-General of Pennsylvania, I had been
the bearer of a communication to General [John F.] Reynolds touching the reserves, or "Home Guard" of Philadelphia, who, having
volunteered as "emergency men" for duty within our State, had,
without rest, drill, or other preparation for field duty, been ordered
to the front immediately on their arrival at the State line; and that
I could therefore tell him, from personal observation, that the
sacrifices of that long day's fighting had been surrendered by Mc-
Clellan, who, while it was not only daylight, but while the sun was
still high and Fitz-John Porter's corps was in reserve, and other
troops were comparatively fresh, had silenced his guns, and permitted Lee to withdraw his forces from a *cul-de-sac,* in which they
were practically imprisoned. At this moment we were interrupted by
a messenger with a card, which proved to be that of my colleague
from the Gettysburg district, Hon. Edward McPherson. He had just

been beaten in what had been regarded as a certain district. With the most sympathetic manner, Mr. Lincoln, who had advanced toward the threshold to meet him, asked "how he accounted for so unhappy and so unexpected a result in his district." I had not conversed with Mr. McPherson on the subject, but knew that his friends were outspoken in charging the loss of the district to the President; and when, with the gentleness of his nature, he [McPherson] was suggesting specious causes for the sweeping reverse, I interrupted him by saying: "Mr. President, my colleague is not treating you frankly; his friends hold you responsible for his defeat." "If that be true," rejoined the President, "I thank you for the suggestion;" and turning to McPherson, said: "Tell me frankly what cost us your district. If ever there was an occasion when a man should speak with perfect candor to another it is now, when I apply to you for information that may guide my course in grave national matters." "Well, Mr. President," said McPherson, "I will tell you frankly what our friends say. They charge the defeat to the general tardiness in military movements, which result, as they believe, from McClellan's unfitness for command. The enforcement of the draft occurred during the campaign, and of course our political enemies made a great deal of capital out of it; but, in my judgment, not enough to change the complexion of the district. But the persistent refusal of McClellan and his engineers to protect our borders from invasion, by the construction of works to command the fords of the Potomac, had a very positive effect; for, as a result of the neglect of this duty, [J. E. B.] Stuart, with his cavalry, raided through my district on the Friday and Saturday before the election; paroled sick and wounded Union soldiers whom he found in hospital at Chambersburg; burnt the railroad station, machine shops, and several trains of loaded cars, and destroyed thousands of muskets and large quantities of army clothing."

The President was not permitted to reply to these suggestions, for the main door on the broad landing at the head of the stairs opened without knock or other premonition, and the sturdy form of Hon. J. K. Moorhead, who represented the Pittsburg district, advanced toward the President, who met him with extended hand, saying, "And what word do you bring, Moorhead; you, at any rate, were not defeated?" "No," exclaimed Moorhead, in a voice at a high pitch and tremulous with nervous excitement—"no, Mr. President, but I am sorry to say it was not your fault that we were not all beaten;" and continuing in the same nervous manner he proceeded to the performance of a duty which, knowing the gentleness of Mr. Lincoln's nature, he felt to be a most ungracious one, and said: "Mr. President, I came as far as Harrisburg yesterday, and passed the evening with a number of the best and most influential men of our State, including some of those who have been your most earnest supporters, and they charged me to tell you that when one of them said, 'he would be glad to hear some morning that you had been found hanging from the post of a lamp at the door of the White House,' others approved the expression."

The manner of the President changed. He was perfectly calm, and in a subdued voice said: "You need not be surprised to find that that suggestion has been executed any morning; the violent preliminaries to such an event would not surprise me. I have done things lately that must be incomprehensible to the people, and which cannot now be explained." I met the President's admission of such a possibility with what, as I remember it at this distance of time, seems to me to have been a most indecorous display of earnestness. I could not retain my seat, and pacing the floor with quick and violent step, begged him to permit no other person to hear that he had ever entertained the thought of so fearful a possibility. I charged upon him a lack of self-appreciation, and said "he had but to assert his position by showing himself master of the military department, as he did of all other departments of the administration, to command a following in the Northern States such as even Andrew Jackson had never had; that he enjoyed a greater share of the personal affection of his fellow-citizens than any public man but Washington had done; that within twenty-four hours of the time it should come to be known that he had put a soldier in McClellan's place, he would find that he could command the moral, social, and financial resources of the country as no other President had done;" to all of which, after they had recovered their surprise at my impulsive outburst, my colleagues assented. The kind-hearted President, who had not been offended by my manner, turned to me and said: "Kelley, if it were your duty to select a successor to McClellan, whom would you name?" I evaded a direct reply, and said: "My advice to you, Mr. President, would be to make up your mind to change, and to let it be known that the loss of a great battle would be to the general the loss of his command, and to go on changing until you find the right man, though he prove to be a private with a marshal's baton in his knapsack." "Well," said he, "but you are talking about an immediate successor to McClellan, and I ask you whom you would name for his position if the duty were yours." "I think, sir," said I, "my judgment would incline to Hooker, whose sobriquet of 'Fighting Joe' would convey the impression to the impatient country that the change meant 'fight,' which the people would believe to be synonymous with ultimate and early success." "Would not Burnside do better?" said the President. "I don't think so," said I; "you know I have great respect for Burnside, but he is not known to the country as an aggressive man, and in that respect I think Hooker would be better in the present conjunction of affairs." "I think," said he, "Burnside would be better, for he is the better housekeeper." With uncontrollable impatience I exclaimed with an expletive, which I hope was pardoned elsewhere as freely as it was by the President. "You are not in search of a housekeeper or a hospital steward, but of a soldier who will fight, and fight to win." "I am not so sure," said Mr. Lincoln, quietly, "that we are not in search of a housekeeper. I tell you, Kelley, the successful management of an army requires a good deal of faithful housekeeping. More fight will be got out of well-fed and well-cared-for soldiers and animals than can be got out of those that are required to make long marches with empty stomachs, and whose strength and cheerfulness are impaired by the failure to distribute proper rations at proper seasons." This was so true, so kindly, so thoroughly expressive of Mr. Lincoln's nature, that it commanded unqualified assent, and this part of the interview closed with a renewal of the joint suggestion that change should follow change until the right man had been found, and the expression of a hope that the first change would be promptly made. The President's thoughtful but evasive response to all of which was, "We shall see what we shall see."

[In less than three weeks, McClellan was replaced by Burnside.]

"What Do These Men Want?"

THURSDAY, DECEMBER 18, 1862

¶ On December 13th, Union forces suffered disaster at Fredericksburg, characterized as "a pitting of breastbones against breastworks."
Days later, Lincoln faced what a Washington correspondent described
as "the most serious Cabinet crisis that has ever occurred in the
history of this country." [1] Set afoot by the radicals, their objective
was to oust Seward from the Cabinet.

Triggered by the Federal defeat at Fredericksburg, the radical
campaign to remove Seward had deeper roots. The Jacobins had
been gunning for Seward—a man of conservative ideas—since the
inception of the Lincoln Administration. Charles Sumner maintained
Seward "lost his head after he lost the nomination at Chicago and
has done nothing but blunder since. He never understood our war."
Cried Joseph Medill of the Chicago Tribune: "He has been President
de facto, and has kept a sponge saturated with chloroform to Uncle
Abe's nose all the while." Another abolitionist claimed that Lincoln,
"guided by the baleful councils of Seward & the Border State men,"
would never carry out the emancipation proclamation.[2]

Senator Browning, himself a conservative, made this analysis of
the Cabinet crisis:

"These ultra, radical, unreasoning men who raised the insane cry
of on to Richmond in July 1861, and have kept up a war on our
generals ever since—who forced thro the confiscation bills, and
extorted from the President the proclamations and lost him the
confidence of the country are now his bitterest enemies, and doing
all in their power to break him down. They fear the indignation of
the people will break in fury upon their own heads, as it should,
and they are intent upon giving it another direction." [3]

For two days—December 16-17—the Republican Senators had
met in secret caucus, assailing the Administration and denouncing
Lincoln and Seward. Some Senators were willing to vote for a
resolution asking Lincoln to resign. But this was never considered.
They refused to call pointedly for Seward's removal from the Cabinet.
Ultimately, they agreed to a resolution asserting that the Administration would regain public confidence "by a . . . partial reconstruction of the Cabinet." The caucus adjourned after instructing its chairman, Senator Jacob Collamer, to seek an interview with the President.[4]

Despite the implicit secrecy of these proceedings, Senator Preston King on December 17th reported on them to Seward and the President. Seward and his son, Frederick, Assistant Secretary of State, upon hearing King's narrative, immediately wrote out their resignations and requested the Senator to deliver the documents to the President.[5]

It was after Senator King had seen Lincoln that Browning arrived at the White House. His conversation with Lincoln is recorded in his Diary:[6]

In the evening went with Mr D W Wise of Boston [probably Daniel Wise, editor of *Zion's Herald*] to the Presidents[.] The Servant at the door reported that he was not in his office—was in the house but had directed them to say that he could not be seen to night.

I told the boy to tell him I wished to see him a moment and went up in to his room. He soon came in. I saw in a moment that he was in distress—that more than usual trouble was pressing upon him. I introduced Mr Wise who wished to get some items for the preparation of a biography, but soon discovered that the President was in no mood to talk upon the subject. We took our leave. When we got to the door the President called to me saying he wished to speak to me a moment. Mr Wise passed into the hall and I returned. He [Lincoln] asked me if I was at the caucus yesterday. I told him I was and the day before also. Said he "What do these men want?" I answered "I hardly know Mr President, but they are exceedingly violent towards the administration, and what we did yesterday was the gentlest thing that could be done. We had to do that or worse." Said he "They wish to get rid of me, and I am sometimes half disposed to gratify them." I replied ["]Some of them do wish to get rid of you, but the fortunes of the Country are bound up with your fortunes, and you stand firmly at your post and hold the helm with a steady hand—To relinquish it now would bring upon us certain and inevitable ruin." Said he "We are now on the brink of destruction. It appears to me the Almighty is against us, and I can hardly see a ray of hope." I answered "Be firm and we will yet save the Country. Do not be driven from your post. You ought to have crushed the ultra, impracticable men last summer. You could then have done it, and escaped these troubles. But we will not talk of the past. Let us be hopeful and take care of the future[.] Mr Seward appears now to be the especial object of their hostility. Still I believe he has managed our foreign affairs as well as any one could have done. Yet they are very bitter upon him, and some of them very bitter upon you." He then said ["]Why will men believe a lie, an absurd lie, that could not impose upon a child, and cling to it and repeat it in defiance of all evidence to the contrary." I understood this to refer to the charges against Mr Seward.

He then added "the Committee is to be up to see me at 7 O'clock. Since I heard last night of the proceedings of the caucus I have been more distressed than by any event in my life." I bade him good night, and left him[.]

"To Tender . . . Their Friendly Counsel"

THURSDAY, DECEMBER 18, 1862

¶ Before their 7:00 P.M. meeting at the White House, the Senators decided to draw up a paper, expressing their views, for submission to the President. The document finally agreed to was prepared by a special committee consisting of Collamer, Wade, Grimes, Fessenden, Trumbull, Sumner, Harris, Pomeroy, and Howard. It stated:

A meeting of the Republican members of the Senate of the United States at which they were all present but two [Solomon Foot of Vermont, and John C. Ten Eyck of New Jersey], after full consultation, came unanimously to the following conclusion (one present not voting [Preston King of New York]):—

1st. The only course of sustaining this government and restoring and preserving national existence, and perpetuating the national integrity, is by a vigorous and successful prosecution of the war, the same being a patriotic and just war on the part of this nation, produced by and rendered necessary to suppress a causeless and atrocious rebellion.

2d. The theory of our government, and the early and uniform political construction thereof is, that the President should be aided by a Cabinet council, agreeing with him in political principles and general policy, and that all important public measures and appointments should be the result of their combined wisdom and deliberation. This most obviously necessary condition of things, without which no administration can succeed, we and the public believe does not now exist, and therefore such selections and changes in its members should be made as will secure to the country unity of purpose and action, in all material and essential respects, more especially in the present crisis of public affairs.

3d. The Cabinet should be exclusively composed of statesmen who are the cordial, resolute, unwavering supporters of the principles and purposes first above stated.

4th. It is unwise and unsafe to commit the direction, conduct, or execution of any important military operation or separate general command or enterprise in this war to any one who is not a cordial believer and supporter of the same principles and purposes first above stated.

The Republican senators of the United States, entertaining the most unqualified confidence in the patriotism and integrity of the President, identified as they are with the success of his administration, profoundly impressed with the critical condition of our national affairs, and deeply convinced that the public confidence requires a practical regard to the above propositions and principles, feel it their duty, from the positions they occupy, respectfully to present them for executive consideration and action.[1]

An account of the meeting at which this paper was presented to Lincoln was written by Senator Fessenden shortly thereafter:[2]

At the hour appointed for our reception we waited upon the President. He received us with his usual urbanity, and after we were seated Mr. Collamer rose and read to him our paper. Mr. Collamer then stated that the paper contained all he had to say on the part of the Republican senators, and that he had nothing to say on his own account—observing also that whatsoever others of the committee might see fit to add, they and not the Senate would be responsible for.

Mr. Wade then rose and addressed the President, mainly on the conduct of the war, and the fact that it was left in the hands of men who had no sympathy with it or the cause, commenting at some length on the recent elections in the West, imputing the defeat of the Republicans to the fact that the President had placed the direction of our military affairs in the hands of bitter and malignant Democrats.

To this the President made no response.

Mr. Grimes and Mr. Howard followed, both expressing their entire want of confidence in Secretary Seward, and their belief that he had entirely lost the confidence of their constituents. They also expressed the belief that we should have no success until the command of our armies was in different hands.

Mr. Fessenden began by expressing the confidence of the Senate in the patriotism and integrity of the President and disclaiming any wish on the part of senators to dictate to him with regard to his Cabinet. They claimed, however, the privilege, as his constitutional advisers, to tender him their friendly counsel when, in their judgment, it was rendered necessary by an emergency of sufficient importance —such as the present. The paper read covered all the points suggested by the Republican senators as a body. Mr. Fessenden had no new points to suggest, but would state some matters by way of illustration.

A belief existed in the community that the Cabinet were not consulted as a council—in fact, that many important measures were decided upon not only without consultation, but without the knowledge of its members. It was believed, also, that the Secretary of State was not in accord with the majority of the Cabinet and exerted an injurious influence upon the conduct of the war. Such was common rumor. The Republican senators believed that if such a state of things existed it could not fail to be attended with evil consequences.

Again, it was thought that the war was not sufficiently in the hands of its friends. Perhaps at the outset this was unavoidable, as the officers of the regular army had little sympathy with the Republican party. They were largely pro-slavery men and sympathized strongly with the Southern feeling. It was singularly unfortunate that almost every officer known as an anti-slavery man had been disgraced. He instanced General Frémont, Hunter, and Mitchel,[3] and others. It was time to change this condition of affairs. The war should be conducted by its friends. The administration must protect itself. It was evident that it had nothing to expect from the Democracy. General McClellan had been used for party purposes and was now busy in making an attack upon the government, as was obvious from his statement in the McDowell case. The government had the power to show the falsity of his statements, and it was due to the country and the party that the government should make known the true state of the facts.

At this point the President rose and said the explanation was very simple. Mr. Fessenden stopped speaking, and the President produced a large bundle of papers and read several letters to General McClellan, showing that he had been sustained by the government to the utmost of its power. Some half hour was thus spent, and Mr. Fessenden did not resume his remarks.

Mr. Sumner next addressed the President, and commented freely upon Mr. Seward's official correspondence, averring that he had subjected himself to ridicule in diplomatic circles at home and abroad; that he had uttered statements offensive to Congress and spoken of it repeatedly with disrespect in the presence of foreign ministers; that he had written offensive dispatches which the President could not have seen or assented to. Mr. Sumner instanced a dispatch shortly after the passage of the Confiscation Act, placing the Confederates and the majority of Congress upon the same levels. It was dated (I think) July 5.

[On that date, Seward said in a dispatch to Charles Francis Adams: "It seems as if the extreme advocates of African slavery and its most vehement opponents were acting in concert together to precipitate a servile war—the former by making the most desperate attempts to overthrow the Federal Union, the latter by demanding an edict of universal emancipation, as a lawful and necessary, if not, as they say, the only legitimate way of saving the Union." [4]]

The President said it was Seward's habit to read his dispatches to him before they were sent, but they were not usually submitted to a Cabinet council. He did not recollect that to which Mr. Sumner alluded.

Mr. Trumbull also made some remarks, but their tenor has escaped my memory.

Some three hours were spent in conversation with the President, but no definite action was discussed. The President said he would carefully examine and consider the paper submitted, expressed his satisfaction with the tone and temper of the committee, and we left him apparently in cheerful spirits, and so far as we could judge, pleased with the interview.

[At a special meeting the following morning, Lincoln told his Cabinet what had occurred during his interview with the Senators. As Gideon Welles reported Lincoln's version in the *Diary:* [5]]

The President in reply to the committee stated how this movement shocked and grieved him. That the Cabinet he had selected in view of impending difficulties and of all the responsibilities upon him that the members and himself had gone on harmoniously—that there had never been serious disagreements though there had been differences—that in the overwhelming troubles of the country which had borne heavily upon him he had been sustained and consoled by the good feeling and the mutual and unselfish confidence and zeal that pervaded the Cabinet.

He expressed a hope that there would be no combined movement on the part of other members of the Cabinet to resist this assault whatever might be its termination. [Continuing his remarks, which were addressed to those present at the Cabinet meeting, the President] Said the movement was uncalled for—that there was no such charge, admitting all that was said, as should break up or overthrow a Cabinet—nor was it possible for him to go on with a total abandonment of old friends.

Lincoln's Fear: "A General Smash-Up"
FRIDAY, DECEMBER 19, 1862

¶ *On Friday, Lincoln notified the Republican Senators that he desired another meeting with them that evening. But unknown to them, the President had also invited his Cabinet—with the exception of Seward—to attend the session at 7:30 P.M. Senator Fessenden again gives us a report of what took place:* [1]

Arriving, I found several members of the committee and several members of the Cabinet in the anteroom [of the President's office]. In a few moments all of the Cabinet but Mr. Seward and all of the committee but Mr. Wade (who had gone to Falmouth) were assembled. The committee then proceeded to the President's office, when he stated that he had invited the Cabinet, with the exception of Mr. Seward, to meet the committee for a free and friendly conversation in which all, including the President, should be on equal terms; and he desired to know if the committee had any objection to talk over matters with the Cabinet. Having no opportunity for consultation, the committee made no objection, and the Cabinet, excepting Mr. Seward, came in.

The President opened with a speech, admitting that the Cabinet had not been very regular in its consultations, but excusing it for want of time. He thought that most questions of importance had received a reasonable consideration—was not aware of any divisions or want of unity. Decisions had, so far as he knew, received general support after they were made. He thought Mr. Seward had been earnest in the prosecution of the war, and had not improperly interfered—had generally read him his official correspondence, and had sometimes consulted with Mr. Chase. He called on the members of the Cabinet present to say whether there had been any want of unity or of sufficient consultation.

It was remarkable that in the course of his speech, which was quite long, the President, while averring that there had been a sufficient reasonable consultation, stated several instances in which most important action was had not only without consultation with his Cabinet, but without the knowledge of several: such as the appointment of McClellan and Halleck, the sending for General Halleck to act as commander-in-chief, placing the army under McClellan's command after his return from the Peninsula, and the Banks expedition [to New Orleans in mid-December].

After the President had concluded, Mr. Chase said that he should not have come here had he known that he was to be arraigned before a committee of the Senate. He went on to say that questions of importance had generally been considered by the Cabinet, though perhaps not so fully as might have been desired, and that there had been no want of unity in the Cabinet, but a general *acquiescence* on public measures; no member had opposed a measure after it had once been decided on.

Mr. Fessenden then said it should be understood what the positions of senators was, and repeated what he had before told the President with regard to the desire to offer friendly advice, and not to dictate to him, or interfere with his prerogative. In answer to what Mr. Chase had said about being arraigned, Mr. Fessenden stated what had previously occurred between the President and the committee on the subject of meeting the Cabinet. It was no movement of ours, nor did we suspect or come here for that purpose. Mr. Fessenden further said that he thought all important questions should be discussed in Cabinet council, though the President was not bound by any decisions made by his Cabinet, but might act on his own judgment.

Mr. Blair followed in a long and somewhat rambling speech, in which he contended that the Cabinet had and ought to have no voice except when the President called for it. . . . Mr. Blair, had differed much with Mr. Seward, but believed him as earnest as any one in the war: thought it would be injurious to the public service to have him leave the Cabinet, and that the Senate had better not meddle with matters of that kind.

Mr. Grimes followed with some comments on Mr. Seward, expressing his entire want of confidence in him, and the belief that his presence in the Cabinet was injurious to the public interests.

Mr. Sumner again spoke of Mr. Seward as a diplomatist, and condemned his correspondence in very strong terms.

Mr. Trumbull called attention to the fact that from the President's own admissions most important questions had been decided without sufficient consideration.

Mr. Collamer said a few words in support of the views of Republican senators, or rather in explanation of the paper submitted.

Whereupon Mr. Bates entered into a constitutional argument to show that the President need not consult his Cabinet unless he pleased. Mr. Bates spoke of himself as a "garrulous old man," and I think there was a general acquiescence in the correctness of the description.

The President made several speeches in the course of the evening, and related several anecdotes, most of which I had heard before. In remarking upon the Proclamation with regard to emancipation, he said that Mr. Seward had fully concurred after it had been resolved upon by him (it appeared without previous consultation with his Cabinet), whereupon

Mr. Chase called his attention to the fact that Mr. Seward had suggested amendments which strengthened it, such as the pledge to *maintain* the freedom of those emancipated.

After a long conversation the President desired senators present to give him their opinions upon the point whether Mr. Seward ought to leave the Cabinet, and to advise him what their constituents thought about it, observing that all the senators present had not given him their opinions on that point.

Mr. Collamer said he did not know what his constituents thought about it, and he was not prepared to go beyond the paper submitted.

Mr. Grimes said he had already given his opinion.

Mr. Harris made a speech in which he said that considering the state of parties in New York, and Mr. Seward's influence and friends, he thought his removal would be injurious, and he advised against it.

Mr. Pomeroy said he had thought highly of Mr. Seward, studied law in his office; but he had lost confidence in him, and so had his constituents, and he thought he ought not to remain.

Mr. Fessenden: "I believe I am the only member of the committee who has not expressed an opinion."

The President: "Yes, sir."

Mr. Howard: "No, sir; I have not."

The President: "I believe I understood Mr. Howard's opinion."

Mr. Howard: "Not from anything I have said this evening. I do not feel called upon to express an opinion here."

Mr. Fessenden: "I was about remarking that this subject has not, that I am aware of, been discussed in Maine, and I cannot answer for my constituents. I believe, however, that many who were formerly most zealous friends of Mr. Seward have lost their confidence in him. As to myself, I do not think this is the time or place to discuss the subject. Before doing so, I should wish to know whether the President means to follow the wishes of the Republican senators when ascertained. If so, and he desires it, I am willing to try and ascertain what those wishes are. At present I am not instructed to answer for them. Nor do I think it proper to discuss the merits or demerits of a member of the Cabinet in the presence of his associates —especially when I am not informed how far our opinions would be regarded. That is precisely my position."

Whereupon Mr. Chase said, "I think the members of the Cabinet had better withdraw." And they did so.

After some further conversation Mr. Collamer and Mr. Harris also left, and it was continued between the President and the senators remaining. Then Mr. Fessenden said to the President, "You have asked my opinion upon Mr. Seward's removal. There is a current rumor that Mr. Seward has already resigned. If so, our opinions are of no consequence on that point."

The President: "I thought I told you last evening that Mr. Seward had tendered his resignation. I have it in my pocket, but have not yet made it public or accepted it."

Mr. Fessenden: "Then, sir, the question seems to be whether Mr. Seward shall be requested to withdraw his resignation."

The President: "Yes."

Mr. Fessenden: "As the fact of his resignation cannot be concealed, and its cause cannot but be well understood, my opinion is that all the harm which can be done in dividing the Republicans of New York has been done. The breach has been made and the withdrawal of his resignation will not heal it. Under these circumstances I feel bound to say that as Mr. Seward has seen fit to resign, I should advise that his resignation be accepted. Mr. Seward lost my confidence before he became secretary of state, and had I been consulted I should not have advised his appointment. . .[."]

The President: "I had no opportunity to consult you."

Mr. Fessenden: "No, sir; but my opinion at the time was, as expressed to Mr. Trumbull, that before forming your Cabinet you should come to Washington, where you could advise with senators. I am sorry you did not do so. Do you wish us to advise with our fellow-senators on the point suggested?"

The President: "I think not."

We then withdrew, at one A.M. Saturday morning.

It was observed by senators that the President did not appear to be in so good spirits as when we left him on the preceding evening, and the opinion was expressed that he would make no change in his Cabinet. He said that he had reason to fear "a general smash-up" if Mr. Seward was removed, and he did not see how he could get along with an entire change in his Cabinet. To an inquiry as to the grounds of his apprehension, he replied that he thought Mr. Chase would seize the occasion to withdraw, and it had been intimated that Mr. Stanton would do the same, and he could not dispense with Mr. Chase's services in the Treasury just at this time. It was replied that everybody in Congress and out was entirely satisfied with Mr. Chase, and if he withdrew it would be because he desired a pretext for doing so.

. . . Secretaries Stanton, Smith, and Welles did not say a word during our interview with the President.

"This . . . Cuts the Gordian [K]not"
SATURDAY, DECEMBER 20, 1862

¶ *The first thing Saturday morning, Gideon Welles hastened to the White House to present his views to the President on the Cabinet crisis. "In short," said Welles, "I considered it for the true interest of the country, now as in the future, that this scheme should be defeated." Seward must remain in the Cabinet.*[1]
    With Lincoln's blessing, Welles hurried to convince Seward to retract his resignation. Upon his return to the White House, Welles found Chase and Stanton in the President's office; Lincoln was out. In a brief exchange "on the great topic in hand," Welles was emphatically against Seward's resignation; Chase and Stanton, while expressing no opinion on the subject, "both wished to be understood as acquiescing," thought the Navy Secretary. Welles' Diary gives us the rest of the story:[2]

    When the President came in, which was in a few moments, his first address was to me, asking if I "had seen the man." I replied that I had, and that he assented to my views. He then turned to Chase and said ["]I sent for you, for this matter is giving me great trouble.["] At our first interview [before Welles went off to see Seward] he [the President] rang and directed that a message be sent to Mr. Chase [apparently summoning Chase to the White House].
    Chase said he had been painfully affected by the meeting last evening, which was a total surprise to him, and after some, not very explicit remarks as to how he was affected, informed the President he had prepared his resignation. ["]Where is it[?"] said the President quickly, his eye lighting up in a moment. ["]I brought it with me,["] said Chase,—taking it from his pocket—["]I wrote it this morning.["] ["]Let me have it,["] said the President,—reaching his long arm and fingers towards C. who held on,—seemingly reluctant to part with the letter which was sealed, and which he apparently hesitated to surrender. Something further he wished to say, but the President was eager and did not perceive it, but took the letter.
    ["]This[,"] said he, looking towards me with a triumphal laugh

[,"]cuts the Gordian [k]not.["] An air of satisfaction spread over his countenance, such as I have not seen for some time. ["]I can dispose of this subject now[,"] he added, as he turned on his chair and broke the seal. ["]I see my way clear.["]

Chase sat by Stanton fronting the fire—the President beside the fire his face towards them—Stanton nearest him. I was on the Sofa near the east window. While the President was reading the note which was brief, Chase turned round towards me a little perplexed and would, I think have been better satisfied could this interview with the President been without the presence of others, or at least if I was away. The President was delighted and saw not how others were affected.

["]Mr. President,["] said Stanton with solemnity, ["]I informed you day before yesterday that I was ready to tender you my resignation. I wish you sir to consider my resignation at this time in your possession.["]

["]You may go to your Department[,"] said the President, ["]I don't want yours. This,["] holding out Chase's letter[,"]is all I want—this relieves me—my way is clear—the trouble is ended. I will detain neither of you longer.["] We all rose to leave, but Stanton held back as we reached the door. Chase and myself came downstairs together. He was moody and taciturn.

[The next day, Lincoln requested both Seward and Chase to withdraw their resignations. They agreed. The Cabinet remained intact. Lincoln, with great aplomb, had ended the Cabinet crisis.]

"The President . . . Expressed Misgivings"

THURSDAY, JANUARY 1, 1863

¶ *Early on New Year's Day, General Burnside hastened to Washington for an urgent conference with Lincoln. The Army of the Potomac had been poised for another expedition against the rebels along the Rappahannock, when the President restrained the movement. "I could not imagine at the time," Burnside said, "what reasons the President had for sending this telegram." At Murfreesboro, Tennessee, Braxton Bragg was pounding away at the Army of the Cumberland, commanded by William S. Rosecrans. There was anx-*

iety in Washington over the outcome of this battle, eventually to end
in Union victory. Perhaps, thought Burnside, Lincoln's instructions
"related in some way to some important military movements in other
parts of the country, in which it was necessary to have co-operation." [1]

Burnside ascertained Lincoln's motives during this conference,
which he recounted to the Joint Committee on the Conduct of the
War, on February 7, 1863: [2]

I came up to Washington, saw the President, and he frankly
told me that some general officers of my command had called upon
him, and represented that I was on the eve of another movement;
that the order for the preparation of rations, ammunition, &c., had
already been issued, and all the preliminary arrangements made;
and that they were satisfied that if the movement was made, it
would result in disaster. That was about the substance of what the
President told me, although he said a great deal more. I was so
much surprised at the time at what I heard that it did not make
an active impression on my mind as to the exact words. But I am
sure that was the nature of it; and I think he said that he had
understood that no prominent officer of my command had any
faith in my proposed movement.

I then sat down and gave the President a detailed account of
my plans for this movement, at the same time telling him that I
was satisfied there was some misgiving on the part of some of my
general officers as to making any movement at all at that time.
But I said that I was myself satisfied that that movement ought to
be made, and I had come to that conclusion without any consultation
with the other generals.

The President still expressed misgivings as to the feasibility of
making the entire movement, but expressed some regret at the
cavalry portion of it being stopped. I told him that that was a portion
of the general movement, and that if these picked men were to go
around Richmond without having any general movement in co-
operation with them, and were to meet with disaster and be captured,
it would be a very serious loss to us; and even if they were to meet
with success, it would not compensate for the risk, unless we were
to take advantage of that success by a general movement; and,

besides, if the details of this cavalry movement could be kept quiet—kept secret—it might yet be made in conjunction with the general movement, as I had proposed.

The President then said that he did not feel willing to authorize a continuous movement without consultation with some of his advisers. He sent for General Halleck and Mr. Stanton, and the matter was very fully talked over. He told them what they then for the first time heard of—that these officers had called upon him and made these representations to him, resulting in his telegram to me. I asked him if he would give me the names of those officers. He said he could not. I expressed some opinions in reference to what ought to be done with them, but at the same time said that I should not insist upon having the names, as he had a right to withhold them. General Halleck at the same time expressed the opinion that officers making representations of that kind should have been dismissed [from] the service at once, or arrested at once, or something of that kind. My view was that they should have been dismissed [from] the service.

No definite conclusion was come to during that conference, in reference to the subject of a movement.

"My Whole Soul Is In It"

THURSDAY, JANUARY 1, 1863

¶ *There were no ceremonies for signing the final Emancipation Proclamation. When Burnside had gone, the President took up his post in the Blue Room to receive New Year's greetings at a public reception. Afterwards, he hurried to his office to perform that momentous act in Ameriman history. John W. Forney, editor of the* Washington Chronicle *and* Philadelphia Press, *a Lincoln crony who happened to be at the White House at that time, talked about this act in 1865:*[1]

The roll containing the Emancipation Proclamation was taken to Mr. Lincoln . . . by Secretary Seward and his son Frederick. As it lay unrolled before him, Mr. Lincoln took a pen, dipped it in ink, moved his hand to the place for the signature, held it a moment, and then removed his hand and dropped the pen. After a little hesitation he again took up the pen and went through the same movement as before. Mr. Lincoln then turned to Mr. Seward, and said:—

"I have been shaking hands since nine o'clock this morning, and my right arm is almost paralyzed. If my name ever goes into history it will be for this act, and my whole soul is in it. If my hand trembles when I sign the Proclamation, all who examine the document hereafter will say, 'He hesitated.' "

He then turned to the table, took up the pen again, and slowly, firmly wrote that "Abraham Lincoln" with which the whole world is now familiar. He looked up, smiled, and said: "That will do."

"Stronger with the Country"

SATURDAY, JANUARY 24, 1863

¶ *Lincoln, on January 8th, cautiously permitted Burnside to proceed against the enemy, despite objections of some military men, including the rambunctious Hooker. Result: the famous "mud march" and another failure. After this fiasco, Burnside drafted an order—subject to Lincoln's approval—dismissing, among others, Hooker for criticisms, and Newton and Cochrane for complaining to the President.[1] Lincoln refused to acquiesce; he had to consult his advisors. Burnside tendered his resignation. Lincoln rejected it. Burnside hurried to his friend Henry J. Raymond. On hearing Burnside's story, Raymond went to see the President. Later, the editor wrote in his* Journal: [2]

I . . . found a great crowd surrounding Mr. Lincoln. [There was a "levee" at the White House.] I managed, however, in brief terms, to tell him that I had been with the army, and that many things were occurring there which he ought to know. I told him of the obstacles thrown in Burnside's way by his subordinates, and especially of General Hooker's habitual conversation. He put his hand on my shoulder and said in my ear, as if desirous of not being overheard, "That is all true—Hooker does talk badly; but the trouble is, he is stronger with the country to-day than any other man." I ventured to ask him how long he [Hooker] would retain that strength when his real conduct and character should be understood. "The country," he answered, "would not believe it; they would say it is all a lie."

"No Reason . . . to Resign"
SUNDAY, JANUARY 25, 1863

¶ After leaving Raymond, General Burnside returned to his command at Falmouth. The next morning Burnside came back to the White House to learn the President's decision concerning the proposed order to dismiss the subordinate generals. Burnside told the Joint Committee on the Conduct of the War about this interview with Lincoln: [1]

[T]he President told me that he had concluded to relieve me from the command of the army of the Potomac, and place General Hooker in command. I told him that I was willing to accept that as the best solution of the problem; and that neither he nor General Hooker would be a happier man than I would be if General Hooker could gain a victory there. The President also said that he intended to relieve General [E. V.] Sumner and General [William B.] Franklin. I said that I thought it would be wise to do so, if he made the change he proposed to make. General Sumner was a much older officer than General Hooker, and ought not to be asked to serve under him. [As for Franklin, he had been slated for removal by Burnside.[2]]

I then said to him, "I suppose, Mr. President, you accept my resignation, and all I have to do is to go to my home." He replied, "General, I cannot accept your resignation . . ." I replied that I had some private business to attend to; that it was absolutely necessary it should be attended to, it had been neglected so long. He said, "You can have as much time as you please for your private business, but we cannot accept your resignation." I replied, "You can say whether I shall stay in the service or not; but if I stay in, I wish to be employed." And I took the liberty of saying to the President that if all general officers whom it was found necessary to relieve should resign, it would be better for him, as it would free him from the applications of their friends. He said that was true. "But," said he, "there is no reason for you to resign."

Mr. Stanton and General Halleck had come in in the mean time. The President said I could have the department of North Carolina. I said that it was now under command of an officer who had served there under me for a long time; that he was an efficient man, and now knew more about that department than I did, and I did not think it would be just to him to give the department to me. They then spoke of combining the two departments of North Carolina and South Carolina, and giving them to me. I said that they had just sent General Hunter there; that he had scarcely got there; that he ranked me, and I did not think it would be wise to supersede him by me. That seemed to strike them at once; and I do not think they seriously intended to say what they did say with reference to General Hunter. They then said that General [John G.] Foster [commander of the Department of North Carolina] had applied to have me come down there; that he would rather serve under me than to have command of the department. That coincided with a letter that I had myself received from General Foster, and which I had thought was of rather a complimentary nature. I said that that was all very well; but it might create trouble for me to go there, and General Foster certainly was able to command the department.

They then said, "General, make your application for a leave of absence, and we will give it to you." I said, "Very well, I will make application for thirty days of absence."

[Burnside was subsequently appointed commander of the Department of the Ohio.]

"He Had to Make Way for Joshua"

SUNDAY, JANUARY 25, 1863

¶ *The Sunday of January 25th, a group of New England abolitionists —Wendell Phillips, Dr. S. G. Howe, Francis Bird, George L. Stearns, J. H. Stevenson, Elizur Wright, and Reverend Moncure D. Conway— went to parley with the President. They were concerned over his emancipation policy. They were especially concerned over Edward Stanly, military governor of North Carolina, who was doing everything possible to thwart Lincoln's emancipation program and—in spite of this—was being condoned by the President. Conway, who earlier that day preached in the Senate Chamber on "The Negro,*

the Savior of the Nation," wrote a hostile account of this conference
for England's Fraser's Magazine, *published in January 1865:*[1]

Mr. Lincoln received us at the appointed hour with what seemed
to me a forced cordiality, and with a story of doubtful elegance, mis-
chievously meant, I was sure, as a kind of humorous defiance of the
'Boston set,' which the Western men regard as fearfully fastidious
and puritanical. The substantial conversation was introduced by
Mr. Wendell Phillips, who, with the courtesy for which he is remarkable, thanked the President for his proclamation, and asked
him how it was working. The President said that he had not
expected much from it at first, and consequently had not been
disappointed; he had hoped and still hoped that something would
come of it after a while. This remark made us all feel uneasy; it
was plain from his manner, even more than his words, that it had
not occurred to him that our interest was in anything but the
military aspects of his proclamation. Mr. Phillips then alluded to
the deadly hostility that the proclamation had awakened among
the pro-slavery, and gently hinted that the anti-slavery masses were
not satisfied. The President replied that he had no doubt that the
general dissatisfaction in the country was due, so far as the masses
were concerned, to the want of military successes alone; as for the
rest, he continued somewhat bitterly, 'most of us here present have
been all our political lives working in minorities, and have got into a
habit of being dissatisfied. At any rate it has been very rare that
an opportunity of "running" this administration has been lost.' To
this Mr. Phillips good-humouredly said, 'If we see this administration
earnestly working to free the country from slavery and its rebellion,
we will show you how we can "run" it into another four years of
power.' The President was restored to a better humour by this, I
thought; but he said, 'Oh, Mr. Phillips, I have long ceased to have
any personal feeling or expectation in this matter, if I ever had it,
so abused and borne upon as I have been.' 'Nevertheless,' replied
Phillips, 'what I have said is true.' After this there came a pause, which
was at last broken by some one bringing forward the particular
matter [dissatisfaction with Governor Stanly] that had brought us.
Mr. Lincoln listened carefully to the presentation of the facts showing
that Stanly[2] was resisting freedom in North Carolina, and setting aside

his (Lincoln's) proclamation. It was evident, however, that he knew all about the case; *nor did he deny one of these allegations*. At the end he simply said, 'Well, gentlemen, whom would you put in Stanly's place?' Some one present replied with warmth, 'Would it not be better to have nobody there at all than one subverting the declared policy of the President and the country?' To this the President made no reply.³ Some one then suggested Mr. Frémont,⁴ who had at that time no command, as a natural representative of the proclamation, which he had anticipated in Missouri, as a good substitute for Stanly. The President said that he had the greatest respect for Mr. Frémont and his abilities; 'but,' he added, 'the fact is, gentlemen, that the pioneer in any movement is generally not the best man to carry that movement to a successful termination. It was so in old times—wasn't it? Moses began the emancipation of the Jews, but he had to make way for Joshua to complete the work. The fact is, the first reformer has to meet such a hard opposition, and gets so battered and bespattered, that afterwards, when people find they have to accept the reform, they will accept it more gracefully from another man.' (This philosophic utterance of the President's seemed to me worth writing down as soon as we left the White House. . . .) In reply to what he said we intimated that Frémont was scarcely a pioneer reformer, but that he and his proclamation had been so universally popular, that the first voice publicly heard against them had not come from the people but from the White House! Nay, we were unanimous in dating the resuscitation now so formidable to the President of the pro-slavery [anti-slavery?] party in the North (even then too insignificant to justify the President's humouring of it) from the President's revocation of Frémont's proclamation. Of course we knew beforehand that this was bearing hard upon the President, and were fully prepared for the anger with which he replied, 'Well, gentlemen, the people have entrusted the conduct of this matter to *me*, and I must do what *I* think best, and take the responsibility.' 'Of course,' said Mr. Phillips; 'but, nevertheless, Mr. President, it is well not to forget that if the ship goes down, it will not be *you alone* that shall go down with it—all of us are equally in it!' It was the voice that has held millions spell-bound that said this; there was no wonder that the President quailed under it. Recovering presently his good nature, which rarely deserts him, he said, 'Well, gentlemen, suppose I should put in the South these anti-slavery generals and governors, *what could they do with the slaves that would come to them?'*

That the recent proclaimer of liberty to three millions of negroes should at that date thus confess that he was putting forward in the South generals and governors who would *not* carry it out in good faith by freeing practically as many as possible of those declared free; that he should be genuinely exercised in mind on so rudimentary a question as to what should be done with a people who had always supported themselves and their masters, and who had already flocked northward by thousands without adding an iota to the burthen of any one, but helped the nation bear its burthen; were considerations that produced in the minds of all present at that interview a conviction that the President, though superficially quick, was profoundly dull, that there was not a particle of heroism in him, that he was incapable of an idea, and, in fact, that the nation, like Issachar of old, was a strong ass bound between two burthens—slavery in arms, and an administration two years behind the mind of the country. As we went away it was with this conclusion in every mind: 'At least we have got him on our hands until 1865, and must make the best of him that we can. He is at least dragable; we must hitch our horses before him and put our drivers behind him.'

"He Did Not Know What Better to Do"

MONDAY, JANUARY 26, 1863

¶ *Lincoln knew Hooker's faults. In placing the colorful, hotheaded "Fighting Joe" in command of the Army of the Potomac, the President, in a unique letter, had told the general that "there are some things in regard to which, I am not quite satisfied with you." Hooker was a brave and skillful soldier, who mixed no politics with his "profession." That was good. He had self-confidence which, "within reasonable bounds, does good rather than harm." But, continued the President, "I think that during Gen. Burnside's command . . . you . . . thwarted him as much as you could, in which you did a great wrong to the country, and to a most meritorious and honorable brother officer. I have heard . . . of your recently saying that both the Army and the Government needed a Dictator. Of course it was not for this, but in spite of it, that I have given you the command. . . . What I now ask of you is military success, and I will risk the dictatorship."* [1]

The Monday after Hooker's appointment, rumor swept the Senate that G:nerals Sumner and Franklin had been arrested for refusing to fight under him. Senator Browning continues our story: [2]

I was uneasy about it [the rumor], and . . . at night went to the Presidents to learn the facts. He told me that on Saturday Burnside was here, and informed him that various causes had contributed to lose him the confidence of the army, and that he was satisfied the service would suffer by it if he continued longer in command, and he desired to relinquish it, which he did. That he the President did not know what better to do than to appoint Hooker, altho he was not satisfied with his conduct—for he was one of those who had thwarted Burnside—but he appointed him, and knowing that Sumner and Franklin did not wish to be under his [Hooker's] command, and would not probably co operate heartily with him, he [Lincoln] had simply relieved them of their commands, but that they had not been arrested. I remarked that from all I could learn from such men and officers of the army as I had seen Genl Mc Clelland [3] possessed their confidence to a greater extent than any other man, and I thought they would fight under him better than under any other Genl we had. He said McClellan stood very high with all educated military men, but the fact was he would not fight[.]

I expressed the apprehension I felt from the difficulty to be encountered in recruiting our army. We must keep it up to the maximum allowed by law to enable us to suceed—that I feared we could not now raise soldiers by enlistment, and we were so divided, and party spirit was so rancorous that an attempt to draft would prob-ably be made the occasion of resistance to the government. He replied that the rebel army was diminishing as fast as ours—I answered that they were united as one man, and we were fatally divided—that their government, call it what they would, was an absolute despotism to which every one yielded unquestioning obedience, and that they could put their whole force in the field—but we were and must be dependent upon the will of the people, and unless we could, in some way, regain their confidence, I feared the democrats would soon begin to clamor for compromise, and even make an effort to carry the Western states off with the South. To this he said that whenever they proposed either[,] the people would leave them,. and they would be effectually broken down &c.

"As Water Bubbling"

EARLY IN 1863

¶ *Reverend Cornelius Van Santwood, former chaplain of the Eighth New York Infantry and one-time college mate of Lincoln's pastor, Phineas D. Gurley, saw the President "stripped of ceremony . . . easily accessible . . . to all classes of citizens." Shortly after the Emancipation Proclamation had been issued, Van Santwood—at the White House on one of Lincoln's "public days"—was impressed by a Chief Magistrate "in playful vein, whose ebullitions were as spontaneous as water bubbling from a fountain." Years later, working from notes made at the time, the clergyman wrote an account of this "informal audience given to the people." Entitled "A Reception by President Lincoln," the article was published in* The Century *Magazine, in April 1883:* [1]

He was clad plainly, but becomingly, in a black broadcloth suit, nothing in all his dress betokening disregard of conventionality, save, perhaps, his neat cloth slippers, which were doubtless worn for comfort. He was seated beside a plain, cloth-covered table, in a commodious arm-chair. [Van Santwood had stationed himself in a corner near the President, "where I could see and hear all that was going on."]

The first to get the President's eye and ear was a dapper, smooth-faced, boyish-looking little person, intent apparently on obtaining a clerkship in one of the departments. Encouraged by a friendly nod and smile and a "Well, what can I do for you?" which seemed to show that he was not quite unknown, nor seen there for the first time, the youth approached the President, and spoke *sotto voce,* as. if afraid that some one else would hear a syllable he had to say.

"Well," said Mr. Lincoln, "I will consider the matter and see what can be done," with a manner that implied that nothing further need be said and that this closed the interview. The applicant,.

however, did not seem to understand it so, but continued to press the matter in earnest half whispers until interrupted by the President with an emphatic "Yes, yes, I know all about it, and will give it proper attention." This ended the colloquy. The young man vanished, and was succeeded by an older man in military dress, wearing lieutenant's shoulder-straps, who desired to be appointed colonel of a colored regiment. The experiment of employing colored troops had not yet been fully tested, was, in fact, hardly begun, and its success may have been doubted, at this time, by Mr. Lincoln, as by many others. In answer to the request he said, "The whole thing amounts only to a colonelcy for the applicant, as, should a regiment be raised, in six months there would be a colonel without a negro left in the command."

"But my purpose is not that," said the lieutenant, "it is to serve the cause, not myself."

"That may be your purpose," said the President, "but the certain *effect* none the less will be what I have described." And as further argument seemed unnecessary the would-be colonel took his leave, with a countenance indicating anything but satisfaction at the result of his patriotic overture.

He was followed by a sturdy, honest-looking German soldier, minus a leg, who hobbled up to the President on crutches. In consideration of his disabled condition, he wanted some situation about Washington, the duties of which he might be able to discharge, and he had come to the President, hoping that he would provide the desired situation for him. On being interrogated as to how he had lost his leg, he answered that it was the effect of a wound received in battle, mentioning the time and the place.

"Let me look at your papers," said Mr. Lincoln.

The man replied that he had none, and that he supposed his word would be sufficient.

"What!" exclaimed the President, "no papers, no credentials, nothing to show how you lost your leg! How am I to know that you lost it in battle, or did not lose it by a trap after getting into somebody's orchard?" This was spoken with a droll expression which amused the bystanders, all except the applicant, who, with a very solemn visage, earnestly protested the truth of his statement, muttering something about the reasons for not being able to produce his papers. "Well, well," said the President, "it is dangerous for an army

man to be wandering around without papers to show where he belongs and what he is, but I will see what can be done for you." And
taking a blank card from a little pile of similar blanks on the table,
he wrote some lines upon it, addressed it, and handing it to the
man bade him deliver it to a certain Quartermaster, who would
attend to his case.

Then a striking scene occurred. A person apparently of sixty
years of age, with dress and manner which showed that he was
acquainted with the usages of good society, whose whole exterior,
indeed, would have impressed people who form opinions from ap-
pearances, approached the President, asking his aid in some commission project, for the success of which Mr. Lincoln's favor was
regarded as essential. The President heard him patiently, but demurred against being connected with or countenancing the affair,
suggesting mildly that the applicant would better set up an office
of the kind described, and run it in his own way and at his own
risk. The man plead his advanced years and obscurity as a reason
for not attempting this, but said that if the President would only
let him use his name to advertise and recommend the enterprise,
he would then, he thought, need nothing more. At this the eyes
of the President flashed with sudden indignation, and his whole
aspect and manner underwent a portentous change. "No!" he broke
forth, with startling vehemence, springing from his seat under the
impulse of emotion. "No! I'll have nothing to do with this business,
nor with any man who comes to me with such degrading propositions.
What! Do you take the President of the United States to be a
commission broker? You have come to the wrong place, and for you
and every one who comes for such purposes, there is the door!"
The man's face blanched as he cowered and slunk away confounded,
without uttering a word. The President's wrath subsided as speedily
as it had risen.

A white-haired, gentlemanly-looking person, in company with
his daughter, who seemed quite young and was certainly very pretty
and prepossessing, though she had a shy, bashful, and even
frightened look, met with a most courteous and friendly reception.
The gentleman said he had no business to transact and would not
trespass on the President's time, that he had come simply to see and
salute him, and to present his daughter, who had longed to have

this honor before returning to their distant home. Mr. Lincoln greeted them very cordially, rising and shaking hands with them, and with the frank, bland, and familiar manner which made strangers feel unconstrained and at ease in his presence, he chatted pleasantly, even playfully, with them for some minutes, to the evident delight of both visitors. When they were about to go away, he politely escorted them to a door opening into the hall, and different from that through which the visitors entered, and dismissed them with charming courtesy.

Coming back to his chair, he found a gentleman from the "land o' cakes and brither Scots," with letters of introduction in hand, awaiting an audience. Being pleasantly received, the visitor, after some preliminaries, proceeded to say that he had but recently come from Scotland, and had called to present, in the name of numbers of his Scotch friends (mentioning Dr. Guthrie in particular), congratulations and greetings on the issuing of the Emancipation Proclamation. He said that the great act met with warmest sympathy among his countrymen, and all trusted and prayed that the President would stand firm in maintaining the principles it promulgated. "Well," replied the President, "I am inclined to remain firm, but do not say I will, certainly, though all others should fail, as Peter once said and repeated with so much confidence, and only saw his folly and weakness as the cock crew—yet, God helping me, I trust to prove true to a principle which I feel to be right, of which the public sentiment approves, and which the country is prepared to support and maintain. Tell this to your friends at home with my acknowledgments for their sympathy and good wishes."

When this visitor had withdrawn, an immense specimen of a man presented himself. Broad-shouldered, robust, with thews and sinews to match his great height, and withal an honest, good-natured countenance—all seemed to mark him as belonging to the hardy yeomanry of the West. He sidled up awkwardly to the President, seeming almost afraid to accost him, but after some hesitation contrived to say, that being on a visit to Washington, he simply wanted before leaving to see the President, and have the honor of shaking hands with him. He found a kindly reception, and after some introductory civilities, Mr. Lincoln ran his eye curiously over his huge caller, surveying him from head to foot, and then saying with a humorous look and accent it would be hard to describe, "I rather think you have a little advantage of me in height; you are a taller man than I am."

"I guess not, Mr. President," replied the visitor, with the self-abnegating air of one who seemed to regard any claim on his part, of possessing an *advantage* over the Chief Magistrate, as an offense little short of treason—"the advantage cannot be on my side."

"Yes, it is," was the rejoinder, "I have a pretty good eye for distances, and I think I can't be mistaken in the fact of the advantage being slightly with you. I measure six feet three and a half inches in my stockings, and you go, I think, a little beyond that."

The man demurred, insisting very respectfully that the precedence in the matter lay on the President's side.

"It is very easily tested," said the President, and rising briskly from his chair and taking a book from the table, he placed it edgewise against the wall, just higher than his head. Then, turning to his doubting competitor for the nonce, he bade him "Come under." This the man did not do at once, pausing, with flushed face and irresolute look, as if not certain how far he might venture to trust the lion in his playful mood,—his countenance the while wearing a bewildered, half-frightened, and yet half-smiling expression that was really comical to see.

"Come under, I say," repeated the President, in a more peremptory tone, and then the visitor slowly complied. "Now straighten yourself up, and move your head in this way,"—suiting the action to the word. This being done, Mr. Lincoln added, "Now you hold the book, and be sure not to let it slip down a hair-breadth, and I will try." Planting himself accordingly underneath the book, and moving his head from right to left, it was found that he fell a trifle short of the other's measurement. "There," said he, "it is as I told you. I knew I couldn't be mistaken. I rarely fail in taking a man's true altitude by the eye."

"Yes, but Mr. President," said the man, his courage, amid the merriment of the company, beginning to return, "you have slippers on and I boots, and that makes a difference."

"Not enough, to amount to anything in *this* reckoning," was the reply. "You ought at least to be satisfied, my honest friend, with the proof given that you actually *stand higher* to-day than your President."

With this scene the reception, which had lasted about an hour, came to an end.

"Evils of Being So Far Apart"
SATURDAY, FEBRUARY 7 [?], 1863

¶ *In February, a young English girl—who was to become Lady Agnes Harrison Macdonnel—went to a White House reception, and there, for the first time, met Abraham Lincoln. "He did not look grand or aristocratic, or even like a very cultivated man, but you knew he was great," she wrote her parents that month, adding: "One felt that he said what he meant to say, neither more nor less." Of her brief chat with the President, she reported:* [1]

In the Blue Room . . . , the President stood receiving the stream that flowed towards him, and thence passed into the great East Room, and so out. While the others were busy talking to a number of their friends I watched the President. He shook hands and bowed, only occasionally speaking to someone he knew, or chose to distinguish by his notice. Sometimes he answered a remark made to him. But it was generally, "Good morning, Mrs. Jones." "Mr. Smith, how do you do?" (You see how carefully I write this that you may note the pleasing difference of your daughter's reception!) "Miss ————, of England." "Ah," said the President, and he stooped his great height to look into my face. He looked so kind that I forgot to be frightened. I forgot what he first talked of. Then I blurted out, "Mr. Lincoln, may I tell you how earnestly my people at home are with you in heart and soul, especially since the 1st of January." "I am very glad to hear it; very glad, though I may not know them personally. That is one of the evils of being so far apart. We have a good deal of salt water between us. When you feel kindly towards us we cannot, unfortunately, be always aware of it. But it cuts both ways. When you, in England, are cross with us, we don't feel it quite so badly." He smiled as he said this, and then he went on quite gravely, "I wish England were nearer, and in full understanding with us." Colonel Davies said something about my having been unhappy over the *Trent* matter, and the prospect of war between

England and the United States. Mr. Lincoln said that he thought
there were three parties in England, an aristocratic party, which
will not be sorry to see the Republic break up, a class allied to the
South through trade relations, and a third, larger, or if not larger,
of more import, which sympathises warmly with the cause of the
North. He turned to me again, and took my hand in his—it *was*
a large hand!—and said with great kindness, "Tell your friends in
England this, and tell them I am obliged to them for their good
wishes. It is pleasant to have good wishes, and," he added, smiling,
"I take it there will be no war." That was all. We courtseyed [*sic*] and
shook hands with Mrs. Lincoln. She was dressed in black velvet,
black gloves and fan, in mourning for her little boy. . . . We stood
not far from the President for some time, and I watched him with
all my eyes. . . .

On the staircase was a boy of about twelve who was doing his
best to upset the gravity of the servants handing up guests, and
playing pranks. Mrs. M. spoke to him and he replied politely, and behaved at once with the dignity and propriety proper in the son of
a President. I think they called him Thad.

"The Tail of the Army"

WEDNESDAY, MARCH 4 [?], 1863

¶ *James M. Stradling, a native of Mechanicsville, Pa., had joined
a New Jersey cavalry regiment at the age of nineteen. Before enlisting, he lived in Greenville as an apprentice tanner at the home
of John W. Gilbert. Early in March, after spending part of his
furlough with the Gilberts, the young cavalryman found himself in
Washington, unable to obtain river transportation back to the front
at Aquia Creek. Afraid of being picked up as a deserter, Stradling
—whose naïveté was so apparent that White House guards took one
look at him and called him "Country" and "Greeny"—turned to
the President for assistance.*

*In a letter to John Gilbert, dated March 6, 1863, Stradling de-
scribed his adventure with the President of the United States:* [1]

I did not have long to wait . . . [after arriving at the White
House], for in a few minutes Mr. [John] Hay . . . said, "The

President will see you." I followed him into the President's room, where he announced, "Sergeant Stradling," and passed out. As I came abreast of the people in the room, there sat Ben Wade and two other gentlemen I did not recognize, and General Hooker was standing up and saying good-by to the President.

As I approached, the President hesitated a moment and asked me to take a seat, when he went on and said good-by to General Hooker, and said, "General, we shall expect to have some good news from you very soon." I saluted the general, which he returned and then passed out.

In my efforts to acknowledge the President's invitation to take a seat I had finally blurted out that I would rather stand. The President then arose, and I did not think he would ever stop going up. He was the tallest man, John, I think I ever saw. He then turned around to me and extended a hand which was fully three times as large as mine, and said, "What can I do for you, my young friend?"

He had a grip on him like a vise, and I felt that my whole hand would be crushed. I had a small fit of coughing, during which time I regained my composure. Then I told him my case briefly as I could. He then signed my furlough, on which Mr. Hay had written across the face of it: "To any steamboat captain going to the front, please give bearer transportation," and handed it to me and said, "If I have any influence with the steamboat captains, I think that will take you to the front."

I thanked him and was taking my leave, when he said to Senator Wade, "Senator, we have had the head of the Army here a few minutes ago, and learned from him all he cared to tell. Now we have here the tail of the Army, so let us get from him how the rank and file feel about matters. I mean no reflection on you, Sergeant, when I say the tail of the Army."

I said I understood him and knew what he was driving at. He said a great many men had deserted in the last few months, and he was endeavoring to learn the cause. He said there must be some good reason for it. Either the Army was opposed to him, to their Generals or the Emancipation Proclamation, and he was very desirous of learning from the rank and file about the conditions in the Army. "None of the Generals desert or resign, and we could spare a number of them better than we can spare so many privates."

Turning around to me, he asked if I could enlighten him on any of these points. In the meantime I had become perfectly cool, perfectly composed. The weakness had disappeared from my knees and the heat from under my collar. I braced myself to tell him things which I knew would not be pleasing to him. I however determined to tell him frankly and truthfully all I knew about the feeling in the Army, as far as I knew it.

First I said, "Mr. President, so far as I know, the Army has the utmost confidence in your honesty and ability to manage this war. So far as I can learn, the army had no faith in the ability of General Burnside. In fact it had but very little faith in him, and no respect for his ability. He appeared to us as a general who had no military genius whatever, and fought his battles like some people play the fiddle, by main strength and awkwardness. Not the most approved way of fighting a battle, surely."

The President asked me if I was in the battle of Fredericksburg. I replied in the affirmative. "Did you see much of the battle?" I replied that when the fog lifted we could see nearly the whole line. I explained to him that the battleground consisted of a long and level plain and was what they call in Virginia "bottom land." The rebels were entrenched on a number of low hills skirting this plain on the south while at the foot of Mary[e]'s Heights was a sunken road. Their batteries and more infantry were entrenched on the heights proper, while the sunken road was full of infantry and sharp-shooters. This was the position against which General Burnside launched General Hooker's corps, the flower of the army. "You know too well the result, for I can observe the great gloom which still hangs around you on account of that battle."

Senator Wade then asked me if I thought there was any excuse for such a blunder. I replied that if it was agreeable, I would give my views about the matter. The President spoke up and said, "This is very interesting to me, so please go ahead."

I said the country was an open one. There was no mountains or large rivers to cross, but both flanks of the field army were susceptible of being turned, and Lee flanked out of his strong position. Even we privates wondered why such an attack was made. General Burnside must have known of the sunken road, for we of the cavalry had been over this road with General [D.] Bayard in 1862, and he must have informed General Burnside all about it. If General Burnside had possessed any military genius, he would have flanked Lee out of that strong position, and fought him where he could have had at least an equal chance.

All of those present listened very attentively, when the President said, "What you have stated, Sergeant, seems very plausible to me. When General Hooker left us but a few minutes ago he said, 'Mr. President, I have the finest army that was ever assembled together, and I hope to send you good news very soon.' That is just the language General Burnside used when he left me shortly before the battle of Fredericksburg. And such a disaster that followed still makes my heart sick." (I wonder if the President has visions of future disasters to follow.)

I said, "Mr. President, even privates when on the ground cannot help seeing and wondering why certain movements are made. I refer to the charge of General Hooker on our right. Our duty, however, is not to criticize, but to obey even if we get our heads knocked off. I have found that soldiers are willing to obey without hesitation and take the chances when they feel that their show is equal to that of the enemy."

The President said, "You have said nothing about how the soldiers feel towards the Emancipation Proclamation."

I replied, "Mr. President, I approach the Emancipation Proclamation with great reluctance, for I know how your heart was set on issuing that document. So far as I am personally concerned, I heartily approve of it. But many of my comrades said that if they had known the war would free the 'niggers' they would never have enlisted, so many of them deserted. Others said they would not desert, but would not fight any more, and sought positions in the wagon trains; the Ambulance Corps; the Quartermaster's Department, and other places, to get out of fighting. In fact, the 'nigger in the woodpile' is an old saying, but a very true one in this instance.

"I was born a Quaker, and was therefore an anti-slavery young man when I entered the army. When I was a boy I attended from two to three debating societies a week, and the slavery question was always under debate in one form or another. I had heard the question debated and helped debate it for two or three years before I entered the army, and was therefore a full-blooded abolitionist, and welcomed the proclamation with open arms. The issuing of the proclamation caused many to desert, no doubt, and the presence of General Burnside at the head of the army caused many others to leave the army."

I suppose the President and Senator Wade and the other two

gentlemen wondered what they had before them, but, John, I had been invited to the feast and had my say.

The President sat still a moment or two, when he said, "Sergeant, I am very glad indeed to have had your views. I am glad to know how many of your comrades feel about slavery, and I am exceedingly glad you have mentioned the Emancipation Proclamation, for I shall take this opportunity to make a few remarks which I desire you to convey to your comrades.

"The proclamation was, as you state, very near to my heart. I thought about it and studied it in all its phases long before I began to put it on paper. I expected many soldiers would desert when the proclamation was issued, and I expected many who care nothing for the colored man would seize upon the proclamation as an excuse for deserting. I did not believe the number of deserters would materially affect the army. On the other hand, the issuing of the proclamation would probably bring into the ranks many who otherwise would not volunteer.

"After I had made up my mind to issue it, I commenced to put my thoughts on paper, and it took me many days before I succeeded in getting it into shape so that it suited me. Please explain to your comrades that the proclamation was issued for two reasons. The first and chief reason was this, I felt a great impulse moving me to do justice to five or six millions of people. The second reason was that I believed it would be a club in our hands with which we could whack the rebels. In other words, it would shorten the war. I believed that under the Constitution I had a right to issue the proclamation as a 'Military Necessity.' I have faith that it will shorten the war by many months. How does the rank and file view General Hooker?"

I replied that General Hooker was a hard fighter. "The boys have great respect for him, as well as great faith in his ability."

The President then extended his hand and said, "I thank you very much, and I trust you will reach the front in the morning."

"Because They Cultivate the Earth"
FRIDAY, MARCH 27, 1863

¶ *The East Room of the White House was like a great wigwam that Friday morning, as a group of "fine-looking" Indian chiefs, on a visit to Washington, came for a formal interview with the Great White Father. As a reporter for the* Washington Daily Morning Chronicle *told it for posterity: "The Indians were all seated on the floor in a line, and around them the spectators formed a ring which, notwithstanding the assiduous yet polite efforts of Mr. Nicolay, was still too contracted to permit all to see the principal actors." Despite the "hard and cruel lines in their faces which we might expect of savages," said this observer, the Indians "evidently" were "men of intelligence and force of character. They were both dignified and cordial in their manner, and listened to every thing with great interest." Their decorum was sharply contrasted by the noisy, "restless and eager crowd of visitors," including Secretaries Seward, Chase, and Welles; Daniel S. Dickinson, anti-Weed Republican from New York; Professor Joseph Henry, Superintendent of the Smithsonian Institution; and "other distinguished personages." Noted the* Chronicle *man: "Everybody seemed to find some one's bonnet or shoulder in the way, and to think himself or herself entitled to the best and most conspicuous place. The ladies, too, could not refrain from audible comments on the speeches."*

The next day, Washington subscribers to the Chronicle *read:* [1]

At half-past eleven the President entered the circle, and each one of the chiefs came forward and shook him by the hand, some of them adding a sort of salaam or salutation by spreading out the hands, and some contenting themselves with a simple shake of the hand and the inevitable "how" of the Indians of the Plains. The following is a list of the chiefs:

Chayennes [sic].—Lean Bear, War Bonnet, and Standing Water.
Kiowais [sic].—Yellow Buffalo, Lone Wolf, Yellow Wolf, White Bull, and Little Heart.
Arapahoes.—Spotted Wolf and Nevah.
Comanches.—Pricked Forehead and Ten Bears.

Apache.—Poor Bear.

Caddo.—Jacob.

Mr. [Indian] Commissioner [William P.] Dole introduced them, saying:

"Mr. President: We have here some of the chiefs belonging to the wild tribes of the West, who desire to have a talk with you on subjects of mutual interest to you and themselves. These chiefs have expressed a great desire to express their sentiments to you, and to have the benefit of your advice and counsel.

"The interpreter will introduce each of them by name, and give you, also, the name of the tribe to which he belongs."

The President said:

"Say to them I am very glad to see them, and if they have anything to say, it will afford me great pleasure to hear them."

Lean Bear, the chief spokesman, then said that he felt nervous, and would be glad to have a chair, whereupon a chair was placed for him, and being seated in it, he addressed the President, through the interpreter, as follows:

"Lean Bear (through the interpreter) expressed his thanks to the Great Chief for his kindness, and the great pleasure it was to him to have this interview. The chiefs who had come with him were of different tribes, but they were all glad to see the Great Chief of the white people and shake him by the hand, and speak their hearts to him. They had come a long way, and wanted his advice and counsel on many matters concerning their condition. He would hear all the Great Chief had to say; and when he went away he would not carry it in his pocket, but in his heart, out of which it could not be lost. The President is the Great Chief of the white people; he (Lean Bear) was the Great Chief of the Indians. Their wigwams are not so fine as this; they are small and poor. He hoped the Great Chief would look upon his people with favor, and say in his wisdom what would be best for them to do. They were here to listen to his advice and carry it in their hearts. Where he lives many white people have come to settle. He always wished to be at peace with them. He feared these white men on the plains were not so ready to keep peace towards them as they were towards the white people. He would always endeavor to prevent his people from doing anything to incur their ill-will; and if there was trouble, it would not be owing to bad conduct on the part of the Indians. They were sorry that there was great trouble in this country now between the white people. They understood the white men were fighting each other. His nation . . . did not desire to take sides with either party. They wanted nothing but peace towards the white people, and they hoped it would last as long as they lasted. He and his comrades were now far away from their homes. Their families were alone, with nobody to protect them. He hoped the Great Chief would send them back as soon as he could. They wanted to get home."

These remarks were delivered with much animation and a profusion of gestures. At the conclusion he [Lean Bear] rose from his seat, and Spotted Wolf of the Arapahoes took the chair. He saluted the President with a shake of the hand and a "how," and spoke nearly as follows:

"He was very glad to have the opportunity of seeing the Great Chief. They had come a long way to speak with their Great Father. They lived on the great plains, they were one people, and lived in peace and friendship. They had come all the way here to get some good counsel from their Great Father. He hoped, when they went back to their nation, they would have something good to tell their people. They would listen to what was told them as he and his comrades would listen to the Great Chief.

"He had been treated with great kindness all the way along his journey; the white people treated them with kindness wherever they met them; until finally they were here in the Great Wigwam, in the presence of their Great Father. He had met nothing but brothers and friends ever since he came among the whites. He had seen a great many white men; they were all his friends. He hoped they would always remain friends. It appeared to him like a dream that he was here. When he looked around him and saw all these fine things, it seemed like some kind of magic; he could not tell how he got here, so far away from home. It seemed to him that he must have come on wings—that he must have flown as a bird flies through the air."

This chief having concluded his remarks, the President said:

"You have all spoken of the strange sights you see here, among your pale-faced brethren; the very great number of people that you see; the big wigwams; the difference between our people and your own. But you have seen but a very small part of the pale-faced people. You may wonder when I tell you that there are people here in this wigwam, now looking at you, who have come from other countries a great deal farther off than you have come.

"We pale-faced people think that this world is a great, round ball, and we have people here of the pale-faced family who have come almost from the other side of it to represent their nations here and conduct their friendly intercourse with us, as you now come from your part of the round ball.

[Here a globe was introduced, and the President, laying his hand upon it, said:[2]]

"One of our learned men will now explain to you our notions about this great ball, and show you where you live."

Professor Henry then gave the delegation a detailed and interesting explanation of the formation of the earth, showing how much of it was water and how much was land; and pointing out the countries with which we had intercourse. He also showed them the position of Washington and that of their own country, from which they had come.

The President then said:

"We have people now present from all parts of the globe—here, and here, and here. There is a great difference between this pale-faced people and their red brethren, both as to numbers, and the way in which they live. We know not whether your own situation is best for your race, but this is what has made the difference in our way of living.

"The pale-faced people are numerous and prosperous because they cultivate the earth, produce bread, and depend upon the products of the earth rather than wild game for a subsistence.

"This is the chief reason of the difference; but there is another. Although we are now engaged in a great war between one another, we are not, as a race, so much disposed to fight and kill one another as our red brethren.

"You have asked for my advice. I really am not capable of advising you whether, in the providence of the Great Spirit, who is the great Father of us all, it is best for you to maintain the habits and customs of your race, or adopt a new mode of life.

"I can only say that I can see no way in which your race is to become as numerous and prosperous as the white race except by living as they do, by the cultivation of the earth.

"It is the object of this Government to be on terms of peace with you, and with all our red brethren. We constantly endeavor to be so. We make treaties with you, and will try to observe them; and if our children should sometimes behave badly, and violate these treaties, it is against our wish.

"You know it is not always possible for any father to have his children do precisely as he wishes them to do.

"In regard to being sent back to your own country, we have an officer, the Commissioner of Indian Affairs, who will take charge of that matter, and make the necessary arrangements."

The President's remarks were received with frequent marks of applause and approbation. "Ugh," "Aha" sounded along the line as the interpreter proceeded, and their countenances gave evident tokens of satisfaction.

The President then advanced and passed along the line, shaking hands with each chief, who rose to his feet as Mr. Lincoln came along. When he came to the two squaws they evidently did not expect to be noticed, but as the President passed before them they rose and shook him by the hand with every expression of delight. These girls will go home highly elated by the honor thus unexpectedly conferred upon them, and will probably boast all their days that they shook hands with the great Chief of the Pale faces. We cannot forbear noticing that Yellow Wolf, of the Kiowas also "smiled all over," quite against Indian proprieties, when he saluted the President; but what he lost among his brethren, he gained in the good will of the audience, for a buzz ran around the circle, "he is a good fellow," "there, now, I like that one," at which, if he had understood it, he must have felt highly complimented. The ceremonies being closed, the President retired, and the visitors flocked around the Indians, asking questions of the interpreter, and gazing at their strange attire. We heard Secretary Chase ask the interpreter what proportion of his translation was words and what proportion gestures. The answer was that about two thirds was language.

"Full Length 'Landscape'"

MID-APRIL 1863

¶ *John L. Cunningham was twenty-two years old when he became a lieutenant in the 118th New York Volunteer Infantry at Platts-burg on August 20, 1862. Seven months later, based at Camp Adirondack north of Washington—near Findley Hospital—he was detailed to special duty at the Old Capitol Prison, in charge of the prison guard. This gave him an opportunity to spend some time in the nation's capital and pay a visit to the White House in company with Congressman Orlando Kellogg, an old friend of Lincoln's. Then, on Sunday, April 12, 1863, the 118th "received orders to be pre-pared to move." Marching orders came on Monday, April 20th. Between these two dates, Cunningham saw Lincoln again, this time by chance at Matthew Brady's photographic gallery.*

More than a half century after the war, going through his diaries and other memoranda, Cunningham came across his notes on his meeting with Lincoln at Brady's. They were included in the veteran's Three Years with the Adirondack Regiment, 118th New York Volunteer Infantry:[1]

Just before we left Washington and when we were under orders to be ready to move, Lieutenants Riggs, Carter and myself went to Brady's celebrated photographic gallery to leave our negatives from which we might order photographs when wanted. Our officers had started an exchange of photos so that each one might have one of each. . . .

We found no one ahead of us and while registering and getting our numbered cards, Mr. Nicolay, one of the President's secretaries, came in and said to the man in charge that the President had been asked by Mr. Brady to pose for a standing, full-length photo and that he was in his carriage outside and would come in if the matter could have immediate attention.

We waited no longer, hurried upstairs, to be in the operating rooms when the President came. Shortly after the office man appeared with President Lincoln and requested that we waive our priority in his behalf. Lieutenant Riggs replied, rather dramatically: "Certainly, our Commander-in-Chief comes first everywhere." Mr. Lincoln thanked us and said, in substance: "Soldiers come first everywhere, these days. Black-coats are at a discount in the presence of the blue and I recognize the merit of the discount."

The operator was a Frenchman, with a decided accent. He said to the President that there was considerable call for a full-length standing photograph of him. The President jokingly inquired whether this could be done with a single negative, saying: "You see, I'm six feet four in my stockings." The operator replied that it could be done all right and left to arrange for the "standing."

The President then said to us that he had lately seen a very long, or rather, a very wide landscape photograph and that he wondered if there was a camera large enough to take in such an area; but on close examination he found that it had been taken in parts and nicely joined together, and he thought, perhaps, this method might be necessary for all his "full length 'landscape.'"

The operator announced that he was ready and they went into the camera room, but the President stood where we could see and hear him. He asked whether he should stand as if addressing a jury "with my arm like this," stretching out his right arm. The operator came to him several times, placing the President's arms by his side, turning his head, adjusting his clothing, etc. "Just look natural," said the operator. "That is what I would like to avoid," Mr. Lincoln replied.

In the meantime each of us tried on the President's tall hat and it fitted Lieutenant Riggs finely.

The President came back to us and told us of a custom saw-mill built in the early days out in his part of the country, a very up-to-date single-gate mill, of which the owner was proud. One day a farmer brought from some distance an oak log, by ox team, to be sawed into plank and waited for the product. The log was adjusted and the saw started and all went lovely—for a while. A crash came! It proved that in the early days of this oak tree an iron spike had been driven into it and covered from sight by later growth, but the saw found it. The saw was broken and other damage done to the mill, to the grief of the owner. He shut off the water and while sorrowfully investigating the cause of the disaster, the farmer anxiously inquired, "Say, yer ain't spiled the plank, hev yer?" "Goll dern yer old log—just look what it has done to the mill!" replied the mill man.

"That camera man," continued the President, "seemed anxious about the picture; but, boys, I didn't know what might happen to the camera."

The operator came from the dark room, holding the negative up to a window, and asked the President to look at it, suggesting that it was very natural. "Yes," said the President, "that is my objection. These cameras are painfully truthful," saying this with an assumed solemnity.

Two other negatives, with little change in pose, were taken, and the President was asked if he had any choice. He replied, "They look about alike as three peas."

The operator mentioned that Secretary Seward had recently visited the gallery for a sitting and the President asked, "Did he tell you any stories?" The operator said he did not, and the President said: "I did not suppose he did, for Mr. Seward is limited to a couple of stories which from repeating he believes are true." He then said he had recently heard a story about Mr. Seward that, whether true or not, was "a good one on him." He related it and, in substance, to the effect that during the then last presidential campaign Mr. Seward engaged to speak at a "pole raising and mass meeting" affair and was asked to make a later date because the pole couldn't be made ready for the raising; the point being that they evidently considered the raising of the pole of more consequence than Mr. Seward's presence and speech. He told the story with some animation and with bits of interspersed humor.

Mr. Lincoln seemed happy and care-free that morning and we thought he really enjoyed his hour or so at the gallery. Mr. Nicolay, who had driven away with the carriage, returned for the President. Mr. Lincoln again thanked us for our courtesy in waiving our first claim to gallery service, trusted that we would live through the war, and giving each of us a hearty handshake departed.

"What Will the Country Say!"

WEDNESDAY, MAY 6, 1863

¶ *In April, Hooker felt his army ready for battle. Early that month, Lincoln returned from a visit to the Potomac Army "somewhat cheered and comforted by . . . indications that the coming battle . . . would result fortunately for the cause of the Union." Hooker had the rebels "just where he wanted them," wrote a war correspondent. The 130,000 "lion-hearted" Yanks were certain to annihilate the 60,000 "half-starved ragamuffins" in the Confederate Army.[1] This was the talk before Chancellorsville (May 2-4), in which 17,287 Union soldiers fell before the "murderous volleys" of the insurgents. Confederate losses were 12,463.[2]*

Noah Brooks, who wrote under the name of "Castine" as Washington correspondent for the Sacramento Daily Union, *and another close friend of Lincoln's, Dr. Anson G. Henry, were at the White House when news of Hooker's defeat arrived. Brooks, in his volume,* Washington in Lincoln's Time, *describes the President's reaction:* [3]

[T]he President, who seemed anxious and harassed beyond any power of description, said that while still without any positive information as to the result of the fighting at Chancellorsville, he was certain in his own mind that "Hooker had been licked." He was only then wondering whether Hooker would be able to recover himself and renew the fight. The President asked me to go into the room then occupied by his friend Dr. Henry, who was a guest in the house, saying possibly we might get some news later on.

In an hour or so, while the doctor and I sat talking, say about three o'clock in the afternoon, the door opened, and Lincoln came into the room. I shall never forget that picture of despair. He held a telegram in his hand, and as he closed the door and came toward us I mechanically noticed that his face, usually sallow, was ashen in hue. The paper on the wall behind him was of the tint known as "French gray," and even in that moment of sorrow and dread expectation I vaguely took in the thought that the complexion of the anguished President's visage was almost exactly like that of the wall. He gave me the telegram, and in a voice trembling with emotion, said, "Read it—news from the army." The despatch was from General [Daniel] Butterfield, Hooker's chief of staff, . . . to the War Department, and was to the effect that the army had been withdrawn from the south side of the Rappahannock, and was then "safely encamped" in its former position. The appearance of the President, as I read aloud these fateful words, was piteous. Never, as long as I knew him, did he seem to be so broken, so dispirited, and so ghostlike. Clasping his hands behind his back, he walked up and down the room, saying, "My God! my God! What will the country say! What will the country say!"

He seemed incapable of uttering any other words than these, and after a little time he hurriedly left the room. Dr. Henry, whose affection for Lincoln was deep and tender, burst into a passion of tears. I consoled him as best I could, and while we were talking . . . , I saw a carriage drive up to the entrance of the White House, and, looking out, beheld the tall form of the President dart into the vehicle, in which sat General Halleck, and drive off.

"Whose Wife Will I Take?"

SATURDAY, MAY 30, 1863

¶ *At war's end, the North had 166 colored regiments comprising 178,000 men—about one-eighth of the Federal army—officered by whites. During the rebellion, the Negro had fought gallantly at Port Hudson, Vicksburg, the Wilderness Campaign, Petersburg; he had been massacred at Fort Pillow—he had been in at the finish at Appomattox. Once the black man sang, "Do you think I'll make a soldier?" Having been given a chance to fight for freedom, he declared: "When God made me, I wasn't much, but I's a man now."* [1]

For the privilege of fighting in Mr. Lincoln's Army, the Negro had to overcome Northern prejudice as well as officers who refused to recognize him as a soldier. In 1862, Lincoln, although authorized to employ Negroes for any purpose, was cool to the idea of enlisting colored men. With the issuance of the final Emancipation Proclamation, the President began to realize that "the colored population is the great available *and yet* unavailed *of, force for restoring the Union."* [2]

Negro troops had been used earlier by Butler in Louisiana and

Hunter in South Carolina. A number of governors—to offset difficulties in raising their quotas—began enlisting colored men. However, it was in 1863 that the Federal Government began recruiting Negroes as part of national policy—a policy opposed by New York's Democratic Governor Horatio Seymour. In protest against the governor's position, a committee—backed by Horace Greeley, George Opdyke, and William Cullen Bryant, among others—sent a delegation to Lincoln with a plea for help. A report of the interview with Lincoln was given at a meeting in New York on June 11, 1863.

Our account is taken from articles in the Sacramento Daily Union *and* New York Herald.[3] *We begin with material from the* Union:

The memorial presented to the President . . . declared that 3,000 blacks had already signified their readiness to enlist—and closed by praying the President to give the command to General Frémont. The Committee believed that 10,000 colored recruits could be raised in sixty days. The President listened to the statements of the Committee, and then stated that the policy of the Government, so far as he represented it or constituted it, was to use all proper influences to secure the co-operation of the blacks for putting down the rebellion. He heartily desired this, and he frankly stated that he had been disappointed in the blacks, who had not rallied as he supposed they would when his proclamation [of emancipation] was issued, or when able Generals tried to get them to enlist with them. He said to the Committee, "You ask a suitable command for General Frémont. There I see difficulty. General Frémont is the second officer in the active service of the United States; a suitable command would certainly mean a department. I have not a department vacancy to give him. I do not think I would be justifiable in dismissing any commander of a department for the purpose of placing him [Frémont] upon duty as contemplated in your memorial." He discussed the portion of the memorial referring to the troops being commanded by any particular officers contemplated in the petition, and said that contingencies were liable to occur in which it would be necessary to transfer them to another officer—as, for example, in defense of the Capital, or any threatened point.

[Here the *Herald* takes up the story:]

In this the President found himself in the position of the English gentleman who had a rake for a son, whom he told to take a wife.

When the hopeful replied, "Well, father, whose wife will I take?" [4] The President took a map, pointing to the colored parts representing the sections of the rebel States largely peopled by colored people. He noticed that bordering on Vicksburg in particular, remarking that he hoped for co-operation from the negroes in that section to take Vicksburg and hold it. He had urged upon many generals to take the work of raising an army of colored men; [5] but he could not prevail on them, because they had stars on their shoulders. He further informed the committee that he believed Frémont to be the man to do this work and give it effect, on account of his peculiarities and those of the colored people. [6] He assured them that he would do all in his power to forward the movement. Mr. Chase was present during the interview, but never spoke. Senator Sumner was also present, and stated that he believed the greatest name to be written in these times will be written by the hand of that man who organizes the colored people into an army for their own deliverance and the restoration of the Union.

"A Very Long Grace for a Thin Plate of Soup"

LATE SPRING OR EARLY SUMMER, 1863

¶ *General James S. Wadsworth used to marvel at Lincoln's grasp of military matters. After one interview at the White House, the general said the President "argued the point with much skill & even knowledge of military language as well as technics."* [1] *But "Old Brains" Halleck apparently thought differently.*

Early in 1863, Union attempts were under way to take Charleston. Admiral Samuel F. DuPont had made protracted preparations for his attack on the city—preparations Lincoln characterized as "a very long grace for a thin plate of soup." [2] *That assault and subsequent efforts to capture Charleston at that time ended in failure. Lincoln had some ideas for remedying the situation, if Halleck would only listen. Noah Brooks, in an article, "Personal Reminiscences of Lincoln,"* *published in* Scribner's Monthly *in March 1878, and later, in his volume,* Washington in Lincoln's Time, *tells of the "foggy night" in the late spring or early summer when Lincoln and Halleck talked strategy; he also notes the danger to which the President habitually*

exposed himself in his night walks to and from Army Headquarters.[8]
We quote first from the article in Scribner's:

[B]eing at the White House, Lincoln asked me if I would not
walk over to General Halleck's headquarters with him; as we passed
out of the family part of the house, the President turned back and
from a number of walking-sticks in a corner, selected a heavy one,
shod and tipped with historic iron bolts from some ship [the rebel
ram *Merrimac*], I believe. He never used a cane in walking, and
as he took this he said, dropping his voice to a serio-comic and confidential whisper, "Mother has got a notion into her head that I
shall be assassinated, and to please her I take a cane when I go over
to the War Department at nights—when I don't forget it."

The precaution, though taken almost in a spirit of fun, made me
a little nervous, especially as the night was dark and gloomy, and
the way to Halleck's headquarters lay through the park between the
War Department and the White House. Crossing the street beyond
the department building, the slouching figure of a man near the
Winder building attracted my notice and I scarcely paid any attention
to the President's chat, distracted as I was by the apparition.

[Brooks continues the narrative in *Washington in Lincoln's Time:*]
Soon after our arrival [at headquarters], the President and General
Halleck fell into a discussion as to the possibility of landing a strong
force of artillery and infantry on Morris Island, Charleston Harbor,
under cover of the gunboats, to cooperate with the navy in an
attack upon the rebel fortifications on Cummings Point. The
President said he thought that Fort Sumter might be reduced in this
way, and that, by gradual approaches, we could get within range
of the city of Charleston. He illustrated his theory of gradual approaches by means of three or four lead-pencils and pen-handles,
which he arranged in parallels, shifting them from time to time
to show how, according to his notion of military strategy, our lines
could be advanced in the desired direction. Halleck would not say
that it was impracticable to land troops on the southeast end of
the island, but he insisted that they could do nothing after they got
there; and he made a strong point of the statement that the strip of
land between Fort Wagner and the place of landing was so narrow
that the zigzag parallel lines laid out by the President, according to

scientific rules, could not be made. Assistant-Secretary Fox of the Navy Department came in during the conference, and the President appealed to him for his opinion. Captain Fox agreed with Lincoln that the movement could be made, but whenever the President pressed this view upon Halleck, the general invariably replied: "If it were practicable it would have been done; but the plan would be utterly futile for the reason that there is not room enough for the approaches which must be made." Halleck, although he treated the suggestions of Lincoln with great respect, evidently entertained profound contempt for his military knowledge. When he went away Lincoln (whose common-sense view of the situation appeared to me, an amateur, to be sensible and feasible) expressed himself as discouraged with what he called "General Halleck's habitual attitude of demur."

That night, as we walked back to the White House through the grounds between the War Department buildings and the house, I fancied that I saw in the misty moonlight a man dodging behind one of the trees. My heart for a moment stood still, but, as we passed in safety, I came to the conclusion that the dodging figure was a creature of the imagination.

[We now revert to Brooks' earlier article:]

The President noticed this [Brooks' sense of apprehension], perhaps, for when we had reached the house . . . , he said, "Now own up that I scared you by putting plots and assassinations into your head, when we went out." I confessed that I was worried and that I should not have thought of danger if he had not mentioned it. He laughed and said that that was human nature. Then he added more seriously, "I long ago made up my mind that if anybody wants to kill me, he will do it. If I wore a shirt of mail and kept myself surrounded by a body-guard, it would be all the same. There are a thousand ways of getting at a man if it is desirable that he should be killed. Besides, in this case, it seems to me, the man who would come after me [Vice-President Hamlin] would be just as objectionable to my enemies—if I have any."

"Hooker Had Taken Umbrage"

SUNDAY, JUNE 28, 1863

¶ *In June, as Lee pressed his invasion of Maryland and Pennsylvania —and the North was again in panic—Hooker called for the evacuation of Maryland Heights at Harpers Ferry as a means of securing additional troops. When Halleck refused Hooker's demand, "Fighting Joe" tendered his resignation.*

Gideon Welles tells of the Cabinet meeting at which Lincoln announced Hooker's resignation and the appointment was disclosed of the relatively unknown Major General George Gordon Meade— a West Pointer, whose men called him "a damned old goggle-eyed snapping turtle"—as the new commander of the Army of the Potomac: [1]

[The] President drew from his pocket a telegram from Genl Hooker asking to be relieved. The President said he had, for several days as the conflict became imminent, observed in Hooker the same failings that were witnessed in McClellan after the battle of Antietam, A want of alacrity to obey, and a greedy call for more troops which could not, and ought not to be taken from other points. He [Hooker] would, said the President, strip Washington bare—had demanded the force at Harper's ferry, which Halleck said could not be complied with—he (Halleck) was opposed to abandoning our position at Harper's ferry. Hooker had taken umbrage at the refusal—or at all events had thought it best to give up the command.

Some discussion followed, chiefly in regard to a successor. The names of Meade, [John] Sedgwick and [Darius N.] Couch were introduced. I soon saw this review of names was merely a feeler to get an expression of opinion—a committal—or to make it appear that all were consulted and it shortly became obvious that the matter had already been settled, and the President finally remarked, he supposed Genl Halleck had issued the orders. He asked Stanton if it was not so. Stanton replied affirmatively—that Hooker had been ordered to Baltimore and Meade succeeded him.

Chase was disturbed more than he cared should appear. Seward and Stanton were obviously cognizant of the fact before the meeting took place,—had been consulted—perhaps advised proceedings, but, doubtful of results, wished the rest to confirm their act. Blair and Bates were not present with us.

Instead of being disturbed, like Chase, I experienced a feeling of relief, and only regretted that Hooker had not been relieved immediately after the Battle of Chancellorsville. . . .

Chase immediately interested himself for the future of Hooker. Made a special request that he should be sent to Fortress Monroe and take charge of a demonstration upon Richmond via James River. The President did not give much attention to the suggestion. I enquired what was done, or doing, with [John A.] Dix's command,— whether that considerable force was coming here, going to Richmond, or to remain inactive. The President thought a blow might at this time be struck at Richmond, but had not faith much could be accomplished by Dix. But, though not much of a General, there were reasons why he did not like to supersede him. [John G.] Foster he looked to as a rising General, who had maintained himself creditably at Washington, North Carolina. Chase admitted F.[oster] was deserving of credit but claimed credit was due [Colonel Henry T.] Sisson [of the 5th Rhode Island Volunteers], who relieved him, also [during the siege of Washington, North Carolina].

Chapter Eight

"ANYTHING BUT A BED OF ROSES"

EARLY in March 1863, Seward summed up the situation in philosophic terms, declaring: "The wheel of American civilization is grinding on its gudgeon—that is all. It is not broken, and once repaired it will move faster and stronger than ever." [1]

Lincoln shared this confidence in the nation's future. But as he surveyed "this great trouble"—as he called the rebellion—he had to confess his inability to fully understand it. Nevertheless, he maintained, "I am placed here where I am obliged to the best of my poor ability to deal with it. And that being the case I can only go just as fast as I can see how to go." [2]

As "President of one part of this divided country," he was constantly burdened by military, civil and political perplexities that would throw him into fits of despondency. "Look at me!" he would say to Ward Lamon. "I wish I had never been born! . . . With a fire in my front and rear; having to contend with the jealousies of the military commanders, and not receiving the cordial co-operation and support from Congress which could reasonably be expected; with an active and formidable enemy in the field threatening the very life-blood of the government,—my position is anything but a bed of roses." [3]

On May 5th, General Burnside, commanding the Department of the Ohio, gave Lincoln a new headache to worry about. Without consulting the President, Burnside had arrested former Ohio Congressman Clement L. Vallandigham, a vicious Peace Democrat (or Copperhead) leader, who had been denouncing the Administration

269

for waging a "wicked abolition war," and urging immediate armistice and foreign mediation to restore the Union as it was. Charged with sympathizing with the rebels and publicly "declaring disloyal sentiments," Vallandigham was court-martialed and sentenced to imprisonment; Lincoln commuted the sentence to banishment from the Union. Subsequently, Vallandigham made his way to Niagara Falls, Canada, "there to await coming events." [4]

For this episode in Administration activity, Lincoln had to bear the brunt of stinging criticisms levied upon him in the name of liberty and free speech, while the Copperheads glorified Vallandigham as a martyr.

In defending the government's position, Lincoln had this to say: Vallandigham was not arrested for exercising his right to free speech or for injuring the Administration's political prospects. He was seized because he was hampering enlistments and encouraging desertions, thereby striking at "the life of the nation." Said Lincoln:

"Must I shoot a simple-minded soldier boy who deserts, while I must not touch a hair of a wiley agitator who induces him to desert? This is none the less injurious when effected by getting a father, or brother, or friend, into a public meeting, and there working upon his feelings, till he is persuaded to write the soldier boy, that he is fighting in a bad cause, for a wicked administration of a contemptable government, too weak to arrest and punish him if he shall desert. I think that in such a case, to silence the agitator, and save the boy, is not only constitutional, but, withal, a great mercy." [5]

The day following Vallandigham's arrest, the "utter rout and annihilation of the Army of the Potomac" at Chancellorsville threw the North into "almost the blackest period of the war." Once more civic and military morale hit a new low, and as a *New York Tribune* writer remembered: "There was groping for a General, and groping so far as the East was concerned, in the dark." There were cries for McClellan's reinstatement, but as Lincoln reasoned it: "Do we gain anything by opening one leak to stop another?" Hooker was given a chance to vindicate himself. When Lee invaded the North and again "out-generaled" Hooker, Meade was placed in command of the Army of the Potomac. [6]

On July 3rd, Meade brought the Union a great Eastern victory at Gettysburg. The next day, word came from the Southwest that Grant had triumphed at Vicksburg. This was the turning point in the war. As Grant moved ahead with his campaign plans, Lincoln expected Meade to pursue and, to use Halleck's expression, "cut up" the enemy. Instead, Meade permitted Lee's army to escape "without another battle," creating "great dissatisfaction in the mind of the President." Welles quipped: "Meade is watching the enemy as fast as he can since he let them slip and get away from him." And the *New York Herald* was needling Meade—and the Administration— by referring to his "masterly inactivity." [7]

As summer wore on, John Hay noted that "The Tycoon" was "in fine whack. I have rarely seen him more serene & busy. He is managing this war, the draft, foreign relations, and planning a reconstruction of the Union, all at once. I never knew with what tyrannous authority he ruled the Cabinet, till now. The most important things he decides & there is no cavil." Although "well-meaning" journals advised Lincoln "to keep his fingers out of the military pie," Hay believed "if he did, the pie would be a sorry mess." There was something comforting about being able to say: "The old man sits here and wields like a backwoods Jupiter the bolts of war and the machinery of government with a hand equally steady & equally firm." [8]

Chauncey Depew claimed that Lincoln "knew the whole situation better than any man in the administration, and virtually carried on in his own mind not only the civic side of the government, but all the campaigns." But, said Noah Brooks: "It was this incessant demand upon his time, by men who sought place or endeavored to shape his policy, that broke down his courage and his temper, as well as exhausted his strength." Often, he became suspicious of "the motives of men"; he would observe: "Sitting here, where all the avenues to public patronage seem to come together in a knot, it does seem to me that our people are fast approaching the point where it can be said that seven-eighths of them were trying to find out how to live at the expense of the other eighth." On another occasion, the President remarked: "I sometimes fancy that every one of the numerous grist ground through here daily, from a Senator seeking a war with France down to a poor woman after a place in the Treasury Department, darted at me with thumb and finger, picked out their especial piece of my vitality, and carried it off. When I get through with such a day's work there is only one word which can express my condition, and that is—*flabbiness*." [9]

Even on the street, Lincoln was frequently "waylaid by soldiers importunate to get their back-pay, or a furlough, or a discharge; and if the case was not too complicated," he "would attend to it then and there." [10]

The President, said Seward, "had no notion of recreation as such." At times, he sought refuge from official pressures by running off to visit the Potomac Army. "It is a great relief to get away from Washington and the politicians," he would say. "But nothing touches the tired spot." [11] At times, he found "temporary respite" from "care and worry" by sneaking into a theatre with Tad and a friend, and watching the performance hidden from the audience. At times, he found "such a relief from politicians" by visiting the Navy Yard. His youngest son, Tad, was a joy and Lincoln indulged the lad extravagantly, much to the chagrin of some onlookers. "Let him run," Lincoln would say, "he will have time enough to learn his letters and get poky." [12] He would tell stories about Tad and his older brother, Robert—stories like:

"I heard my little Tad making an outcry as though some one was abusing him . . . and, looking into the room, saw him hanging on to Bob and demanding a knife which Bob had in his hand. 'Oh, let him have the knife, Bob, to keep him quiet,' said I; but Bob replied, 'No; it's my knife, and I need it to keep me quiet.' " [18]

Even his little dog, Jip, helped relieve Lincoln of "some portion of the burden, for the little fellow was never absent from the Presidential lunch. He was always in Mr. Lincoln's lap to claim his portion first, and was caressed and petted by him through the whole meal." [14]

But the "weary & care worn" Lincoln found his greatest escape in telling anecdotes; he could tell a story at any time of day or night to illustrate a point in conversation with Congressman, foreign diplomat, Billy Yank, or Mr. John Doe Citizen. And it was not only in the telling, it was also in the listening to a new story that he derived great enjoyment. John Forney said: "When I go to see him he asks me what is the last good joke I have heard." [15] David R. Locke, the humorist who wrote under the pseudonym "Petroleum V. Nasby," recalled:

"Grave and reverend Senators who came charged to the brim with important business—business on which the fate of the nation depended—took it ill that the President should postpone the consideration thereof while he read them a letter from 'Saint's Rest, wich is in the state uv Noo Jersey,' especially as grave statesmen, as a rule, do not understand humor, or comprehend its meaning or effect." [16]

Forney noted that Lincoln "liked the short farce." [17] Brooks said the President particularly relished jokes at the expense of some high dignitary:

"Anything that savored of the wit and humor of the soldiers was especially welcome to Lincoln. His fondness for good stories is a well-accepted tradition, but any incident that showed that 'the boys' were mirthful and jolly in all their privations seemed to commend itself to him. He used to say that the grim grotesqueness and extravagance of American humor were its most striking characteristics. . . . Lincoln, relating these . . . stories . . . , said, 'It seems as if neither death nor danger quench the grim humor of the American soldier.' " [18]

More stories were attributed to Lincoln than he could honestly claim as his own. "You speak of Lincoln stories," the President said to Brooks. "I don't think that is a correct phrase. I don't make the stories mine by telling them. I am only a retail dealer." Once he reckoned that "only about one-sixth" of all the stories credited to him had ever been told by him.[19]

And when the stories had been told and the laughter had faded, Lincoln returned "to his gloom and his melancholy," while his critics scorned him as "the national joker" in the White House.[20]

"Here Goes for Two Years More"

TUESDAY, JULY 14, 1863

¶ *Elated over his Gettysburg victory, General Meade had issued an order thanking his army for defeating "an enemy, superior in numbers, and flushed with the pride of a successful invasion." Meade, however, pointed out: "Our task is not yet accomplished, and the commanding general looks to the army for greater efforts to drive from our soil every vestige of the . . . invader." This last sentence rankled the President, who saw in it no intention on Meade's part to pursue and destroy "Lee's traitor army." To Lincoln, this was "a dreadful reminiscence of McClellan." [1]*

Meade had intended pursuing the Confederates, who were moving "as rapidly as possible towards Richmond, without order or arrange-

ment." But he yielded to a council of his officers and permitted Lee to make good his escape.[2]

Word that the rebels had crossed the Potomac without hindrance reached Lincoln on July 14th. Deeply grieved at the news, Lincoln told Hay: "We had them within our grasp. . . . We had only to stretch forth our hands & they were ours." And in the Potomac Army, Meade's soldiers grumbled: "Well, here goes for two years more."[3]

That day, a few Cabinet members—including John P. Usher, who became Secretary of the Interior when Smith resigned in January— came to the White House for a scheduled meeting. This is the way Welles reported it to his Diary:[4]

Two or three of us were there, when Stanton came in with some haste and asked to see the President alone. The two were absent about three minutes in the library. When they returned, the President's countenance indicated trouble and distress—Stanton was disturbed—disconcerted. Usher asked Stanton if he had bad news— he [Stanton] said, ["]No.["] Something was said of the report that Lee had crossed the river. Stanton said abruptly and curtly he knew nothing of Lee's crossing. *"I do,"* said the President emphatically, with a look of painful rebuke to Stanton. "If he has not got all of his men across—he soon will."

The President said he did not believe we could take up anything in Cabinet to day. Probably none of us were in a right frame of mind for deliberation—he was not. He wanted to see Genl Halleck at once. Stanton left abruptly. I retired slowly. The President hurried and overtook me. We walked together across the lawn and stopped and conversed a few moments at the gate. He said with a voice and countenance which I shall never forget, that he had dreaded yet expected this—that there has seemed to him for a full week, a determination that Lee should escape with his force and plunder,—["]and that, my God, is the last of this Army of the Potomac. There is bad faith somewhere.—Meade has been pressed and urged but only one of his Generals was for an immediate attack —was ready to pounce on Lee—the rest held back—What does it mean, Mr Welles—Great God, what does it mean?["] I asked what orders had gone from him [Lincoln], while our troops had been quiet with a defeated army in front, and an impassable river to prevent their escape. He could not say that any thing positive had been done, but both Stanton and Halleck professed to agree with him and he thought Stanton did [something positive]. Halleck was all the time wanting to hear from Meade. ["]Why,["] said I, ["]he [Halleck] is within four hours of Meade—is it not strange that he [Halleck] has not been up there to advise and encourage him [Meade?"] I stated I had observed the inertness, if not incapacity of the Genl in Chief and had hoped that he [Lincoln], who had better and more correct views would issue peremptory orders. [Welles disliked Halleck intensely; he believed "Halleck sits, and smokes, and swears, and scratches his arm . . . but exhibits no mental capacity or intelligence." [5]] The President immediately softened his tone and said Halleck knew better than he [Lincoln] what to do—he [Halleck] was a military man—had a military education, he [the President] had brought him here to give him (the President) military advice. ["]His views and mine are widely different. It is better that [I,] who am not a military man should defer to him, rather than he to me.["] I told the President I did not profess to be a military man, but there were some things on which I could form perhaps as correct an opinion as Genl Halleck, and I believe that he, the President could more correctly direct military movements than Halleck, who it appeared to me could originate nothing, and was as now, all the time waiting to hear from Meade or whoever was in command.

"The First Great Man"

MONDAY, AUGUST 10, 1863

¶ One August day in 1863, a bearded, bushy-headed mulatto in his mid-forties entered the White House, "chaperoned" by Senator Pomeroy of Kansas.[1] Frederick (Bailey) Douglass was ready for his "first" interview with Abraham Lincoln.

Born in Maryland of a Negro mother and a white father, Douglass had known the meaning of slavery. As a boy, he had himself been sold to a Baltimore man. There, despite his master's disapproval, young Fred had taught himself to read and write before escaping to the North. In the Land of Freedom—Pennsylvania, New York and Massachusetts—he became active in the abolitionist crusade and

*before long rose to prominence as the spokesman for his people.
After his marriage to a free Negro woman, his home in Rochester,
New York, became a refuge for escaped slaves.*

*During the rebellion, Douglass was active in recruiting Negro
troops in Massachusetts. As editor and publisher of* Douglass'
Monthly, *he had declared as early as May 1861: "Every consideration
of justice, humanity and sound policy confirms the wisdom of calling
upon black men just now to take up arms in behalf of their country."
To him, it was a war to bring about "the end of slavery."* [2] *He
welcomed Lincoln's Emancipation Proclamation. And although opponents of the edict claimed it to be "inoperative," Douglass quipped:
"I approve the one-spur-wisdom of Paddy, who thought that if he
could get one side of his horse to go, he could trust the speed of
the other side."* [3]

*Now, in the summer of 1863, shortly after the Confederacy had
declared that captured colored soldiers would be treated as insurgents
and that it was the rebel purpose "not to treat any such soldiers as
prisoners of war subject to exchange like other soldiers," Douglass
was anxious to discuss this "threat" with Lincoln—"the first great
man that I talked with in the United States freely, who in no single
instance reminded me of the difference between himself and myself,
of the difference of color, and I thought that all the more remarkable
because he came from a State where there were black laws." Douglass
wrote several accounts—each with some variations—of his talk with
Lincoln. Our report of this occasion is taken from his article in the*
New York Tribune, July 5, 1885: [4]

I was somewhat troubled with the thought of meeting one so
august and high in authority, especially as I had never been in the
White House before and had never spoken to a President of the
United States before. But my embarrassment soon vanished when
I met the face of Mr. Lincoln. When I entered he was seated in a
low chair, surrounded by a multitude of books and papers, his feet
and legs were extended in front of his chair. On my approach he
slowly drew his feet in from the different parts of the room into
which they had strayed, and he began to rise, and continued to
rise until he looked down upon me, and extended his hand and gave
me a welcome. I began, with some hesitation, to tell him who I was
and what I had been doing, but he soon stopped me, saying in a sharp,
cordial voice: "You need not tell me who you are, Mr. Douglass, I

know who you are, Mr. [Samuel E.] Sewell has told me all about you." He then invited me to take a seat beside him. Not wishing to occupy his time and attention, seeing that he was busy, I stated to him the object of my call at once. I said "Mr. Lincoln I am recruiting colored troops. I have assisted in fitting up two regiments in Massachusetts, and am now at work in the same way in Pennsylvania, and have come to say this to you, sir, if you wish to make this branch of the service successful you must do four things.

"First, you must give colored soldiers the same pay that you give white soldiers.

"Second, you must compel the Confederate States to treat colored soldiers, when taken prisoners, as prisoners of war.

"Third, when any colored man or soldier performs brave meritorious exploits in the field, you must enable me to say to those that I recruit that they will be promoted for such service, precisely as white men are promoted for similar service.

"Fourth, in case any colored soldiers are murdered in cold blood and taken prisoners you should retaliate in kind."

To this little speech Mr. Lincoln listened with earnest attention and with very apparent sympathy, and replied to each point in his own peculiar forcible way. First he spoke of the opposition generally to employing negroes as soldiers at all, of the prejudice against the race, and of the advantage to colored people that would result from their being employed as soldiers in defence of their country. He regarded such an employment as an experiment, and spoke of the advantage it would be to the colored race if the experiment should succeed. He said that he had difficulty in getting colored men into the United States uniform; that when the purpose was fixed to employ them as soldiers, several different uniforms were proposed for them, and that it was something gained when it was finally determined to clothe them like other soldiers.

Now, as to the pay, we had to make some concession to prejudice. There were threats that if we made soldiers of them at all white men would not enlist, would not fight beside them. Besides, it was not believed that a negro could make a good soldier, as good a soldier as a white man, and hence it was thought that he should not have the same pay as a white man. But said he, "I assure you, Mr. Douglass, that in the end they shall have the same pay as white soldiers." As to the exchange and general treatment of colored soldiers when taken prisoners of war, he should insist to their being entitled to all privileges of such prisoners. Mr. Lincoln admitted the justice of my demand for the promotion of colored soldiers for good conduct in the field, but on the matter of retaliation he differed from me entirely. I shall never forget the benignant expression of his face, the tearful look of his eye and the quiver of his voice, when he deprecated a resort to retaliatory measures. "Once begun," said he, "I do not know where such a measure would stop." He said he could not take men out and kill them in cold blood for what was done by others. If he could get hold of the persons who were guilty of killing the colored prisoners in cold blood, the case would be different, but he could not kill the innocent for the guilty.

Before leaving Mr. Lincoln, Senator Pomeroy said:

"Mr. President, Mr. Stanton is going to make Douglass Adjutant-General to General Thomas, and is going to send him down the Mississippi to recruit."

Mr. Lincoln said in answer to this: "I will sign any commission that Mr. Stanton will give Mr. Douglass." At this we parted.

"More Angry Than I Ever Saw Him"

MONDAY, SEPTEMBER 14, 1863

¶ *Early in 1863, Charles Sumner recorded: "The President tells me that he now fears 'the fire in the rear'—meaning the Democracy, especially at the Northwest—more than our military failures." The Copperheads, as the seditionists were called, were active in undermining public morale, hindering the war effort by thwarting enlistments and inducing army desertions. It had reached a point where "parents, wives, brothers, and sisters" were so anxious "to relieve their kindred that they filled the express trains to the army with packages of citizen clothing to assist them in escaping from the service."* [1]

The urgent need for fresh troops impelled Congress to enact a national draft law, which was at once attacked as "unconstitutional." It was the first instance, observed Lincoln, "in which the power of congress to a thing has ever been questioned, in a case when the power is given by the constitution in express terms." [2] *Public reaction to the draft was to become a serious Administration concern. There*

*were not only verbal protests, enrollment officers were beaten and—
in some instances—murdered.*[3] *In July, a series of riots broke out
in Boston, Troy, Newark and New York. There was "a widespread
and organized determination to resist the draft."* [4]

*When the civil courts began interfering with the draft by misusing
the privilege of the writ of habeas corpus, Lincoln summoned his
Cabinet to a special meeting. And Bates noticed that the President
was "more angry than I ever saw him."* [5] *Secretary Chase, a major
participant in the Cabinet discussion that day, gives us his version
of the meeting:* [6]

I went with . . . [Governor John A. Andrew of Massachusetts]
to the President, where I found Secretary Stanton, to whom I recommended "Scotty" [Private James "Scottie" Gray, of the 50th Ohio Infantry, who had fought with distinction at Port Republic and Cedar
Mountain] for a medal, as I had promised him. Stanton said he
would order one engraved, as soon as I sent him the name and inscrip-
tion. At eleven a meeting of Heads was held. The President said that
the applications for discharges by drafted men and deserters were
very numerous, and were granted under circumstances which show
that the Judges are disposed to defeat the objects of the law. He
expressed the opinion that State Courts had no authority to issue
a Writ of Habeas Corpus for any person in the custody of United
States officers,—claiming to act under the national law. He proposed, therefore, to direct officers holding persons in such custody,
to make a return of the fact that they were so held, and to refuse
to obey the writ, and if force should be used to overcome it by
force. Mr. Seward favored this action, and there was no expression
against it, till I remarked that I had always been accustomed to
regard the Writ of Habeas Corpus as a most important safeguard of
personal liberty. "It has been generally conceded," I went on to
say, "or at least such has been the practice, that State Courts may
issue Writs of Habeas Corpus for persons detained as enlisted soldiers,
and to discharge them. Several cases of this kind have occurred in
Ohio, and the proceeding of the State Court was never questioned,
to my knowledge. Of course, a proper exercise of the power does not
justify its improper exercise. If the Writ is abused with a criminal
purpose of breaking up the Army, the persons who abuse it should
be punished as any other criminals are. But before taking any action,

which even seems to set aside the writ, a clear case should be made, which will command the concurrence of the people and their approval. I suggest, therefore, that the Secretary of War should make a statement of the number of persons discharged from military service under the Writ, with such notes of the circumstances as will show the abuse of it. After which such action can be taken as the case requires." Mr. Blair and Mr. Usher coincided substantially with these views, Mr. Blair remarking that he had often, when a judge in Missouri, discharged soldiers on Habeas Corpus. The President thought there was no doubt of the bad faith in which the Writ was now being used; Mr. Seward thought it indispensable to assert the authority of the Government at once; and Mr. Bates expressed the opinion that the President as head of the Army could not be interfered with by any civil authority, whatever; but was in his action as Commander-in-Chief superior to any process, and might properly instruct his officers and disregard such process; and this without any suspension of the Writ of Habeas Corpus, except as incidental to the exercise of his legitimate authority.—Mr. Stanton thought prompt action necessary. The President ended the discussion by saying he would prepare such an order as he thought best, and would see us again tomorrow at half-past two. The conversation then turned upon Writs of Habeas Corpus issued from Federal courts, when it appeared that the number of discharges made by two Federal Judges in Pennsylvania, [John] Cadwalader at Philadelphia, and [Wilson] McCandless at Pittsburgh, largely exceeded the number discharged by all the State Courts put together. So it at once became evident that an order to reach the State Courts only would be inefficient.

"Our Military Horoscope Is . . . Clouded"

MONDAY, SEPTEMBER 21, 1863

¶ *There were "gleams of evil tidings from the Southwest" as Lincoln visited Welles the afternoon of September 21st. Noah Brooks told his readers about this time: "Rosecrans has been met in his advance upon the rebel stronghold of Atlanta by an overpowering host" of Confederate forces. Washington was beginning to buzz with "dark rumors of a great defeat of the Union army, and the President was fain to declare that he believed that Rosecrans had*

been badly whipped." As Brooks summed up matters: "Our military
horoscope is at . . . present . . . somewhat clouded." [1]
   From Welles' Diary we learn about his conversation with the
President: [2]

The President came to me this afternoon with the latest news. He
is feeling badly. Tells me a dispatch was sent to him at the Soldiers'
Home shortly after he got asleep, and so disturbed him that he had
no more rest, but arose and came to the City and passed the remainder of the night awake and watchful. He has a telegram this
P.M. which he brings me that is more encouraging. Our men stood
well their ground and fought like Union heroes for their country and
cause. We conclude the rebels have concentrated a large force to
overpower Rosecrans and recapture Chattanooga. While this was
being done, Halleck frittered away time and dispersed our forces.
Most of Grant's effective force appears to have been sent across
the Mississippi where a large force is not needed. Burnside is in
North Eastern Tennessee, two hundred miles away from Chattanooga.
While our men are thus scattered, a large division from Lee's army
in our front has been sent under Longstreet to Bragg; and Hill's and
Ewell's corps, it is reported [are] there also. I trust this account is
exaggerated though the President gives it credence. I do not learn,
nor can I ascertain that Genl Halleck was apprised of, or even suspected what was being done—certainly he has made no preparation.
The President is, I perceive, not satisfied, but yet he does not
censure nor complain. Better perhaps if he did.
   I expressed surprise to the President at the management and
his forbearance, and it touched him. I asked what Meade was doing
with his immense army and Lee's skeleton and depleted show in
front. He said he could not learn that Meade was doing any thing,
or wanted to do anything. ["]It is,["] said he, ["]the same old story
of this Army of the Potomac. Imbecility, inefficiency—don't want
to *do*—is defending the Capital. I enquired of Meade,["] said he,
["]what force was in front. Meade replied he thought there were
40,000 Infantry. I replied he might add fifty thousand and if Lee
with sixty thousand could defend their capital against our ninety
thousand—and if defense is all our armies were to do,—we might,
I thought, detach fifty thousand from his command, and leave him
with forty thousand to defend us. Oh!["] groaned the President—

["]it is terrible, terrible, this weakness, this indifference of our Potomac Generals, with such armies of good and brave men.["]

["]Why[,"] said I[, "]not rid yourself of Meade who may be a good man and good officer, but is not a great general—certainly is not the man of the position he occupies[?] The escape of Lee with his army across the Potomac has distressed me almost beyond any occurrence of the War. And the impression made upon me, in the personal interview shortly after, was not [what] I wished—had inspired no confidence.["]

The President assented to all I said, but "What can I do,["] he asked, ["]with such generals as we have? Who among them is any better than Meade? To sweep away the whole of them from the Chief Command would cause a shock, and be likely to lead to combinations and troubles greater than we now have. I see all the difficulties as you do. They oppress me."

Alluding to the failures of the generals, particularly those who commanded the armies of the Potomac, he thought the selections, if unfortunate, were not imputable entirely to him. The Generals-in-Chief and the Secretary of War should know the men better than he. The Navy Department had given him no trouble in this respect,—perhaps naval training was more uniform and equal than the military. I thought not, that we had our troubles, but they were less conspicuous. In the selection of [David G.] Farragut and Porter, I thought we had been particularly fortunate, and DuPont had merit also. He thought there had not been, take it all in all, so good an appointment in either branch of the Service as Farragut, whom he did not know or recollect when I gave him command. DuPont he classed, and has often, with McClellan, but Porter he considers a busy schemer, bold but not of high qualities as a chief. For some reason he has not so high an appreciation of Porter as I think he deserves, but no man surpasses Farragut with him.

"Beware of Being Assailed by One"
WEDNESDAY, SEPTEMBER 30, 1863

¶ *Missouri had been "a thorn in the side of the President" from the outbreak of the war. To manage the military and political affairs "of that annoying little State," Lincoln had appointed—in succession—*

Generals Harney, Frémont, Hunter and Curtis. All had failed, principally because each had become tangled up in what Lincoln called the "pestilent factional quarrel" between the Claybanks (conservatives) and Charcoals (radicals) of Missouri. The political controversy between the Blair and Frémont factions had been growing in intensity, with conservative elements supporting Governor Hamilton R. Gamble against General Samuel B. Curtis, who had radical backing. Lincoln had to try to "reconcile the difficulty," and, as he said, "as I could not remove Gov. Gamble, I had to remove Gen. Curtis." [1]

Curtis' replacement was thirty-two-year-old General John M. Schofield—"a firm, competent, energetic & eminently fair man." Lincoln instructed the new Missouri commander "to exercise your own judgment, and do right for the public interest," adding: "Let your military measures be strong enough to repel the invader and keep the peace, and not so strong as to unnecessarily harrass [sic] and persecute the people. It is a difficult role, and so much greater will be the honor if you perform it well. If both factions, or neither, shall abuse you, you will probably be about right. Beware of being assailed by one, and praised by the other."* [2]

In the summer of 1863, the Missouri Constitutional Convention adopted gradual emancipation, but the plan was "of such an uncertain and dilatory character, that public opinion in the State promptly rejected it." On the heels of this action—complicated still further by William C. Quantrill's forays into Missouri and Kansas—the Jacobins raised the cry that Schofield was too soft with traitors and "identified himself with . . . Gamble's pro-slavery and conservative views." [3] *Schofield, they announced, must go.*

Late in September, a Missouri-Kansas delegation arrived in Washington to press for a new commander "to aid the cause of Freedom in Missouri." Their choice: Benjamin F. Butler, "the Hero of New Orleans," who "would restore peace in less than sixty days." [4]

On September 30th, at 10:00 A.M., *the 70-member Missouri-Kansas delegation—"his little army," as Senator James H. Lane called it—assembled in the East Room of the White House to present their memorial to President Lincoln. Newsmen were barred, and the* New York Herald *complained that "for the first time perhaps during all this administration, the front doors of the Presidential mansion were closed and locked against all intruders." That was the way the radicals wanted it; Lincoln acceded to this request.*

Our report of the conference comes to us from the pen of John Hay, who summarized his notes of the proceedings in Abraham Lincoln: A History: [5]

It [the delegation] was a compact phalanx of devoted political soldiers, officered by a few leaders of great ability. Mr. Lincoln never appeared to better advantage than in this interview, which lasted something over two hours, partly spent in speech-making and partly in desultory talk. Though the President well knew how great the danger was to his political hopes from the unreasoning anger of the committee, he never cringed to them for an instant. The chairman, Hon. C. D. Drake of St. Louis, impressively read their long, studied address, and though no reporters were present, one of the President's secretaries [Hay] took full notes of his reply, from which we have room to quote only a small portion. Said he [Lincoln]: "It would not be consistent, either with a proper respect for you or a fair consideration of the subject involved, to give you a hasty answer. I will take your address, carefully consider it, and respond at my earliest convenience. I shall consider it without partiality for, or prejudice against, any man or party. No painful memories of the past and no hopes for the future, personal to myself, shall hamper my judgment."

The President then took up their points of complaint in detail. He told them that while they did not appear to relish his having characterized their troubles in Missouri as a "pestilent factional quarrel," Governor Gamble liked it a great deal less; that Gamble had been chosen governor by their own State Convention, seemingly with the universal consent of the Union people of the State; that he, the President, had uniformly refused to give the Governor exclusive control of the Missouri State Militia; that, on the other hand, the Enrolled Militia existed solely under State laws with which he had no right to interfere, either in Missouri or elsewhere; and if that organization were inconsistent with their State laws, he, as President, had no power over it. He was sorry they had not been more specific in their complaints about Schofield; they had only accused him vaguely of sympathy with their enemies. "I cannot," continued he, "act on vague impressions. Show me that he has disobeyed orders; show me that he has done something wrong, and I will take your request for his removal into serious consideration. He has never protested against an order—never neglected a duty with which he has been intrusted, so far as I know. When General Grant was struggling in Mississippi and needed reënforcements, no man was so active and efficient in sending him troops as General Schofield. I know nothing to his disadvantage. I am not personally acquainted with him. I have with him no personal relations. If you will allege a definite wrong-doing, and, having clearly made your point, prove it, I shall remove him. You object to his order on my recent proclamation suspending the privilege of the writ of *habeas corpus*. I am at a loss to see why an order executing my official decree should be made a ground of accusation to me against the officer issuing it. You object to its being used in Missouri. In other words, that which is right when employed against opponents is wrong when employed against yourselves. Still, I will consider that. You object to his muzzling the press; as to that, I think when an officer in any department finds that a newspaper is pursuing a course calculated to embarrass his operations and stir up sedition and tumult, he has the right to lay hands upon it and suppress it, but in no other case. I approved the order in question after the 'Missouri Democrat' had also approved it."

Here an unwary delegate replied: "We thought then it was to be used against the other side."

Lincoln: "Certainly you did. Your ideas of justice seem to depend on the application of it.

"You have spoken of the consideration which you think I should pay to my friends as contra-distinguished from my enemies. I suppose, of course, that you mean by that those who agree or disagree with me in my views of public policy. I recognize no such thing as a political friendship personal to myself. You will remember that your State was excluded from the operations of that decree [the Emancipation Proclamation] by its express terms. The proclamation therefore can have no direct bearing upon your State politics. Yet you seem to insist that it shall be made as vital a question as if it had. You seem to be determined to have it executed there."

Delegate: "No, sir; but we think it is a national test question."

Lincoln: "You are then determined to make an issue with men who may not agree with you upon the abstract question of the propriety of that act of mine. Now let me say that I, who issued the proclamation, after more thought on the subject than probably any one of you has been able to give it, believe it to be right and expedient. I am better satisfied with those who believe with me in this than with those who hold differently. But I am free to say that many good men, some earnest Republicans, and some from very far North, were opposed to the issuing of that proclamation, holding it unwise and of doubtful legality. Now, when you see a man loyally in favor of the Union—willing to vote men and money—spending his time and money and throwing his influence into the recruitment of our armies, I think it ungenerous, unjust, and impolitic to make his views on abstract political questions a test of his loyalty. I will not be a party to this application of a pocket inquisition."

In the desultory talk which followed the speech-making Mr. Lincoln was as fair and as firm on all collateral points and issues, meeting every statement of grievance with a quick counter-statement so brief and so clinching that the several volunteer spokesmen who came forward to support the main address retired, one by one, disconcerted and overwhelmed. The interview finally closed with a little rejoinder from him, intended more especially for the marplots in the delegation. After stating that he appreciated perfectly the difference between the ultimate value of Conservatives and Radicals in the long controversy, he continued: "My Radical friends will therefore see that I understand and appreciate their position. Still you appear to come before me as my friends, if I agree with you, and not otherwise. I do not here speak of mere personal friendship. When I speak of my friends I mean those who are friendly to my measures, to the policy of the Government. I am well aware that by many, by some even among this delegation—I shall not name them—I have been in public speeches and in printed documents charged with 'tyranny and willfulness,' with a disposition to make my own personal will supreme. I do not intend to be a tyrant. At all events I shall take care that in my own eyes I do not become one. I have no right to act the tyrant to mere political opponents. If a man votes for supplies of men and money, encourages enlistments, discourages desertions, does all in his power to carry the war on to a successful issue, I have no right to question him for his abstract political opinions. I must make a dividing line somewhere between those who are the opponents of the Government, and those who only approve peculiar features of my Administration while they sustain the Government."

[Commenting to Hay about the Missouri radicals, Lincoln said on October 28th: "They are nearer to me than the other side, in thought and sentiment, though bitterly hostile personally. They are utterly lawless—the unhandiest devils in the world to deal with—but after all their faces are set Zionwards." [6]]

Chapter Nine

"A LEADER TO SPEAK THE BOLD WORD"

THE Lincoln Administration faced a crucial test in the fall elections of 1863, especially in Ohio and Pennsylvania. In Ohio, Vallandigham was the Democratic candidate for governor by "unanimous nomination" while he was "yet in the confederate States." [1] Heading the Union ticket in the "Buckeye State" was John Brough, a War Democrat. In Pennsylvania, Andrew G. Curtin, running for re-election, squared off against Judge George W. Woodward, the pro-South candidate.

The Ohio canvass was "even more bitter than that in Pennsylvania, and in many instances . . . led to serious breaches of the peace and bloodshed." Said the *New York Herald:* "The issue, for the first time since the commencement of the war in any loyal State, is clearly and plainly between the war and peace parties, or, in other words, the conservative democrats and republicans against the copperheads." Said the *New York Tribune:* "Not only the people of the loyal but those of the disloyal States and of England feel that the fate of the Union rests upon the result of the election in Ohio." [2]

From his Canadian haven—"almost within sight of my native State"—Vallandigham poured campaign letters and addresses into Ohio, denouncing the "arbitrary power" and "despotism" of Abraham Lincoln, and proclaiming that the South was "resolved to perish rather than yield to the pressure of arms even in the most desperate extremity." Cried Vallandigham: "When the war shall have ceased and invading armies been withdrawn," the South will be ready "to consider and discuss the question of reunion." [3]

In Washington, a "nervous" Lincoln said "he had more anxiety in regard to the election results . . . than he had in 1860 when he was chosen." [4]

It was important for the issues to be placed squarely before the people. This Lincoln did in a letter read at a mass meeting in Springfield on September 3rd, to offset Copperhead influence in Illinois.

"There are those who are dissatisfied with me," wrote Lincoln. "To such I would say: You desire peace; and you blame me that we do not have it." There were three ways in which peace could be secured: First, by suppressing the rebellion by force of arms; this Lincoln was trying to do. Second, by forsaking the Union; he was against this. Third, by a compromise, to which the South would not agree unless its independence were guaranteed.

"You say you will not fight to free negroes," said the President. "Some of them seem willing to fight for you; but, no matter. Fight you, then, exclusively to save the Union. I issued the proclamation [of emancipation] on purpose to aid you in saving the Union. Whenever you shall have conquered all resistance to the Union, if I shall urge you to continue fighting, it will be an apt time, then, for you to declare you will not fight to free negroes."

However, he pointed out, "negroes, like other people, act upon motives." Why should Negroes do anything for the whites if the whites will do nothing for them? If Negroes "stake their lives for us, they must be prompted by the strongest motive—even the promise of freedom." That promise, once made, must be kept.

Lincoln continued:

"The signs look better. The Father of Waters again goes unvexed to the sea. Thanks to the great North-West for it. Nor yet wholly to them. Three hundred miles up, they met New-England, Empire, Key-Stone, and Jersey, hewing their way right and left. . . . The job was a great national one; and let none be banned who bore an honorable part in it. And while those who have cleared the great river may well be proud, even that is not all. It is hard to say that anything has been more bravely, and well done, than at Antietam, Murfreesboro, Gettysburg, and on many fields of lesser note. Nor must Uncle Sam's Web-feet [a reference to the Navy] be forgotten. At all the watery margins they have been present. Not only on the deep sea, the broad bay, and the rapid river, but also up the narrow muddy bayou, and wherever the ground was a little damp, they have been, and make their tracks. . . ."

Peace was nearer now than ever before, said Lincoln. "I hope it will come soon, and come to stay; and so come as to be worth the keeping in all future time. It will then have been proved that, among free men, there can be no successful appeal from the ballot to the bullet. . . . And then, there will be some black men who can remember that, with silent tongue, and clenched teeth, and steady eye, and well-poised bayonet, they have helped mankind on to this great consummation; while, I fear, there will be some white ones, unable to forget that, with malignant heart, and deceitful speech, they have strove to hinder it."

He cautioned against overconfidence in a speedy final triumph. "Let us be quite sober," he said. "Let us diligently apply the means, never doubting that a just God, in his own good time, will give us the rightful result." [5]

The Springfield meeting was "a magnificent success"; some 50,000 to 75,000 persons "applauded most vociferously every sentiment in favor of the vigorous prosecution of the war until the rebellion was subdued—the Proclamation of Emancipation and the arming of negro soldiers and every allusion" to Lincoln and his policy. John Hay hailed the letter as "a great thing." Despite some "hideously bad rhetoric—some indecorums that are infamous," the whole Cabinet, said Hay, "could not have tinkered up a letter which could have been compared with it. He can snake a sophism out of its hole, better than all the trained logicians of all schools." [6]

The London *Times* debunked the letter: "That such a man should have been called upon to guide the destinies of a mighty nation during a grand historical crisis is surely strange enough, but that he should have blundered and vacillated as he has, without for a moment losing confidence in himself, or altogether forfeiting that of his countrymen, is stranger still." How any man "in his sober senses" could have "compose[d] such a rhapsody as this, or having composed it could have read it over with gravity and ordered it to be printed, passes our comprehension." [7]

To the London *Star,* however, the Presidential document placed "in the clearest, strongest light, the wicked unreasonableness of the rebellion and the religious duty of all loyal citizens." It was a vindication of the Washington Cabinet; a masterpiece of cogent argument.

"As an appeal to the spirit of the nation, it is sublime in the dignified simplicity of its eloquence." This was "the manifesto of a truly great man in an exigency of almost unequaled moment." Worthy of a Cromwell or a Washington, Lincoln's letter, addressed "to friends and neighbors, to supporters and opponents, . . . is open to the world to read." [8]

On October 13th, Ohio and Pennsylvania gave their Union tickets overwhelming support. Brough swamped Vallandigham with a 101,-000 majority. In Pennsylvania, Curtin beat Woodward 269,000 to 254,000, and Stanton observed: "Pennsylvania must be a damned loyal State to give such a victory to Curtin." In other October and November elections, all the Northern states—except New Jersey—went for the Union. There was great rejoicing everywhere, as Lincoln told Senator Chandler privately: "I am very glad the elections this autumn have gone favorably, and that I have not, by my native depravity, or under evil influences, done anything bad enough to prevent the good result." [9]

Noah Brooks said the election result was being hailed "not because it is a party triumph, but because all true and honest men feel that notwithstanding the false representations of Northern traitors, the North is yet loyal to the Government and to the Administration, and that, too, to the core." Lincoln was credited with the political victory. To James K. Moorhead, it meant that Ohio and Pennsylvania "now declare for *A Lincoln* in 1864." Elihu Washburne told Lincoln "you ought to let some of your confidential friends know your wishes" regarding "the question of our next presidential candidate." And Lincoln replied: "A second term would be a great honor and a great labor, which together, perhaps I would not decline, if tendered." [10]

The "heart of the nation" beat high with hope; its purpose strengthened, its religious faith deepened. "The war was never more popular" as Lincoln—following a two-hour oration by Edward Everett—rose to speak "a few appropriate remarks" at ceremonies on November 19th, dedicating part of the Gettysburg battlefield as a national cemetery. Little over four months had passed since "the champions of Slavery and Freedom met here in deadly strife, and already the name of Gettysburgh has become historical, and its soil . . . classic ground." [11]

With simple eloquence, the President spoke not only for the present but for the future: "We have come to dedicate a portion"

of "a great battle-field." But, "in a larger sense, we can not dedicate
—we can not consecrate—we can not hallow—this ground. The
brave men, living and dead, who struggled here, have consecrated
it, far above our poor power to add or detract." He summoned the
nation to dedicate itself "to the great task remaining before us—
that from these honored dead we take increased devotion to that
cause for which they gave the last full measure of devotion—that
we here highly resolve that these dead shall not have died in vain—
that this nation, under God, shall have a new birth of freedom—
and that government of the people, by the people, for the people,
shall not perish from the earth." [12]

The President's "calm but earnest utterances" stirred "the deepest
fountains of feeling and emotion in the hearts of the vast throng
before him, and when he had concluded, scarcely could an untearful
eye be seen, while sobs of smothered emotion were heard on every
hand." The *Ohio State Journal* man reported:

"At our side stood a stout, stalwart officer, bearing the insignia
of a captain's rank, the empty sleeve of his coat indicating that he
had stood where death was revelling, and as the President, speaking
of our Gettysburg soldiers, uttered that beautifully touching sentence,
so sublime and so pregnant of meaning—'The world will little note,
nor long remember what we here SAY, but it can never forget what
they here DID:'—the gallant soldier's feelings burst over all restraint,
and burrying [*sic*] his face in his handkerchief, he sobbed aloud while
his manly frame shook with no unmanly emotion. In a few moments,
with a stern struggle to master his emotions, he lifted his still
streaming eyes to heaven and in low and solemn tones exclaimed,
'God Almighty, bless Abraham Lincoln!' And to this spontaneous
invocation a thousand hearts around him silently responded,
'*Amen.*' "[13]

Editorial comment on Lincoln's Gettysburg Address followed
party lines. To the Copperhead *Chicago Times,* Lincoln's were "silly,
flat and dish-watery utterances." Massachusetts' *Springfield Republican* called the address "a perfect gem, deep in feeling, compact in
thought and expression," and *Harper's Weekly* commented: "The
few words of the President were from the heart to the heart." Lincoln
himself thought "that speech won't *scour.*" [14]

Less than a week later, Lincoln, "sick in bed," worried about the
fighting at Knoxville and Chattanooga, as he pondered his message

to Congress, scheduled to convene early in December. In some two years, the Yankees had recaptured nearly every important point held by the rebels on the seacoast; the Federals had reconquered and now held more than 250,000 square miles of territory once occupied by Confererate armies. "The extent of country thus recaptured and occupied by our armies," according to Halleck, "is as large as France or Austria, or the entire peninsula of Spain and Portugal, and twice as large as Great Britain, or Prussia, or Italy. Considering what we have already accomplished, the present condition of the enemy, and the immense and still unimpaired military resources of the loyal States, we may reasonably hope, with the same measure of success as heretofore, to bring this rebellion to a speedy and final termination." [15]

Lincoln turned to thoughts of peace—a sound, enduring peace. There must be, as Horace Greeley put it, "no vengeance—no military execution—no confiscation—no more devastation—let us all be friends, equals, brothers, once more. But Slavery, the wicked fomenter of this horrible strife, must die, or the Peace will be a hollow delusive truce, to be soon followed by another desolating war." [16] With Louisiana, Arkansas and Tennessee under military governments since 1862, means must now be provided for bringing them back into the Union as loyal states. To facilitate such a move, the President issued a proclamation of Amnesty and Reconstruction, appended to his annual message to Congress. Under the proclamation, he offered a pardon to all Southerners who would take an oath to support, protect and defend the Constitution and the Union, and to abide by and uphold all Congressional acts and Presidential proclamations concerning slaves made during the rebellion. But, he stressed, "no man" is to be "coerced to take" the oath. He further provided for the restoration of loyal government in a seceded state when a number equal to one-tenth of those qualified to vote in that state in 1860—"having taken the oath"—should form a government. [17]

John Hay recorded: "I never have seen such an effect produced by a public document. Men acted as if the millennium had come." Radicals were delighted. Conservatives thought it "highly satisfactory." Henry Wilson said: "The President has struck another great blow." Boutwell observed quietly: "It is a very able and shrewd paper. It has great points of popularity: & it is right." Owen Lovejoy exclaimed that he should now live "to see slavery ended in America." And Forney declared: "We only wanted a leader to speak the bold word. It is done and all can follow." [18]

"Pursuit of the Presidency"
SUNDAY, OCTOBER 18, 1863

¶ *While the North was preparing for the fall elections, aspirants for the Presidency in 1864 were marshaling their forces. In October, Washington, "that vortex of the political maelstrom," was beginning to seethe "with the petty jealousies and ambitions of rival factions and divers interests."* [1]

Horace Greeley deprecated such maneuverings "on the back of our present National convulsions," and called upon Americans to unite "in the resolve to save the Nation first, if possible, and make the next President afterward." Of the Cabinet, all but Chase had relinquished their claims to the Presidency. "I'm afraid Mr. Chase's head is turned by his eagerness in pursuit of the presidency," Attorney General Bates told his Diary. "For a long time back he has been filling all the offices in his own vast patronage, with extreme partizans, and contrives also to fill many vacancies, properly belonging to other departments." Chase was "working like a beaver" and one of his "special confidential" agents had sought the support of former Ohio Governor William Dennison. John Hay had this right from Dennison's mouth. But Dennison was "pledged to Lincoln"; he told Hay that in the West there was "a widespread and constantly increasing concurrence of sentiment in favor of the reelection of Mr. Lincoln." [2]

When Hay returned to Washington from the West, he reported the conversation with Dennison to the President: [3]

On presenting myself to the President this morning, I told him what Govr. Dennison had told me. He rejoined by telling me that Gov. D. had been here and repeated what he had said to me.

I gave him my impression of the unmanly conduct of Mr. C.[hase] in trying to cut under in the way he is doing, instancing what Den[n]ison . . . had related. He [Lincoln] said "it was very bad taste,["] but that he had determined to shut his eyes to all these performances: that Chase made a good Secretary and that he would keep him where he is: ["]if he becomes Prest., all right. I hope we may never have a worse man. I have all along clearly seen his plan of strengthening himself. Whenever he says that an important matter is troubling me, if I am compelled to decide it in a way to give offense to a man of some influence he always ranges himself in opposition to me and persuades the victim that he has been hardly dealt by and that he (C) would have arranged it very differently. It was so with Gen. Frémont [4]—with Genl. Hunter when I annulled his hasty proclamation—with Gen. Butler, when he was recalled from New Orleans—with these Missouri people when they called the other day. I am entirely indifferent as to his success or failure in these schemes, so long as he does his duty as the head of the Treasury Department."

He talked of the Missouri matter and read to me the letter he had written Drake for the Committee. As it will probably be published, I forbear synopsis. It is a superb affair, perfectly just and frank, courteous but immovable. He will not be bullied even by his friends. He tries to reason with those infuriated people. The world will hear him if they do not. He read to me a letter which he has today written to Governor Gamble, who it seems, is anxious to have the Prest. espouse his side of the quarrel and to recognize him as the State Government and use the Federal authority to crush out the Radicals, who, he says, meditate Revolution and civil war in Missouri. The President answering says he will be at all times ready to extend to Missouri the protection guaranteed by the Constitution against domestic violence, whenever he (the Prest.) shall see cause to suspect such violence as imminent. He does not so regard it at present. He thinks the instructions given to Genl. Schofield cover the case.[5]

We got into this vein of talk through my telling him what Joe Gillespie [an Illinois friend of Lincoln] says and what I myself observed, of the tendency of public opinion in the West, almost universally in favor of the Radicals as against the Conservatives in Missouri.

"Controversy Between the Two Sets"

SUNDAY, NOVEMBER 1, 1863

¶ *On October 3rd, Montgomery Blair—"the meanest man in the Cabinet"—unleashed a scathing attack upon the Jacobins in a speech at Rockville, Maryland.[1] Angered by the ultra Republicans who were pressing for immediate emancipation in Maryland, and furious over Chase's scheming for the Presidential nomination, Blair lashed out at the radicals, whose "despotic . . . tendencies" he likened to "the slavocrats of the South." He warned that abolitionists sought "to make a caste of another color by amalgamating the black element with the free white labor of our land, and would make the manumission of the slaves the means of infusing their blood into our whole system by blending with it* amalgamation, equality and fraternity."[2] *Blair, the self-styled Administration spokesman, assured his listeners that the Federal Government would not molest their slaves.*

The speech touched off a political firecracker. Thad Stevens said it was "so vulgar, so infamous that I think it becomes necessary for the true men of the party to bring it to the attention of the President with a request for his [Blair's] removal—He has done us more harm in our election than all the copperhead speeches of the campaign—" Said a Washington correspondent for the Sacramento Daily Union: *"Blair . . . excites attention here only as the development of his carefully prepared policy for a coalition between Border State Peace Democrats and other fag-ends of parties, by which he hopes to make his brother (Frank) Speaker of the next House, and probably pave the way for higher honors for the Blair family."*[3]

Lincoln's comments on the Rockville speech were recorded by John Hay in his Diary *on November 1st:*[4]

I handed the President Blair's Rockville Speech, telling him I had read it carefully, and saving a few intemperate and unwise personal expressions against leading Republicans which might better have been omitted, I saw nothing in the speech which could have given rise to such violent criticism.

"Really" says the President "the controversy between the two sets of men [the radical and conservative elements of the Republican

Party], represented by him [Blair] and by Mr. Sumner is one of mere form and little else. I do not think Mr Blair would agree that the states in rebellion are to be permitted to come at once into the political family & renew the very performances which have already so bedeviled us. I do not think Mr. Sumner would insist that when the loyal people of a state obtain the supremacy in their councils & are ready to assume the direction of their affairs, that they should be excluded. I do not understand Mr. Blair to admit that Jefferson Davis may take his seat in Congress again as a Representative of his people; I do not understand Mr. Sumner to assert that John Minor Botts may not. So far as I understand Mr. Sumner he seems in favor of Congress taking from the Executive the power it at present exercises over insurrectionary districts, and assuming it to itself. But when the vital question arises as to the right and privilege of the people of these states to govern themselves, I apprehend there will be little difference among loyal men. The question at once is presented in whom this power is vested: And the practical matter for decision *is how* to keep the rebellious populations from overwhelming and outvoting the loyal minority."

I asked him if Blair was really opposed to our Union ticket in Maryland. He said he did not know anything about it—had never asked: he says Crisfield plainly told him he was opposed to the Administration.

I spoke of Fox having said that Union men must divide on the question of the Blair and Sumner theories & that I could see no necessity for it. He agreed. He says Montgomery Blair came to him today to say that Frank has no idea or intention of running for Speaker—that Frank wishes to know what the President desires him to do & he will do it. The President will write to Frank his ideas of the best thing to do: For Frank to come here at opening of Congress: say publicly he is not candidate for Speaker: assist in organization of the House on Union basis & then go back to the field.[5]

"It Secures Us Tennessee"
MONDAY, DECEMBER 7, 1863

¶ *Grant's victory at Chattanooga on November 25th hinged upon his ability to take the rebel strongholds on Missionary Ridge and Lookout Mountain, overlooking the city. Hooker's forces, enveloped by fog, clambered up the rugged slopes of Lookout Mountain to decisive victory in the famous "battle above the clouds" on November 23rd. That night, Sherman's men successfully assailed the rebels on Missionary Ridge in a bloody encounter. After three days' fighting in the face of the "supernatural armies" of the Union, Braxton Bragg's demoralized troops fled in panic and despair.[1]*

Grant pursued the enemy for twenty miles before halting to dispatch Sherman with reinforcements to relieve Burnside, then besieged by James Longstreet at Knoxville. However, before Sherman reached Knoxville, Burnside had repulsed Longstreet, who headed for Virginia.[2]

The night of December 7th, Nicolay made this memorandum:[3]

The President this evening read me a telegram from [John G.] Foster saying that Sherman had reached and joined Burnside at Knoxville[,] that Longstreet was in full retreat up the valley into Va.—that he Foster would obey orders received and vigorously follow up the pursuit &c.

"Now[,]" said the President, "if this Army of the Potomac was good for anything—if the officers had anything in them—if the Army had any legs, they could move thirty thousand men down to Lynchburg and catch Longstreet. Can anybody doubt, if Grant were here in command that he would catch him. There is not a man in the whole Union who would for a moment doubt this. But I do not think it would do to bring Grant away from the West. I talked with Gen. Halleck this morning about the matter, and his opinion was the same. But you know Mr. President, said the General, how hard we have tried to get this Army to move towards the enemy and we cannot succeed."

—"This" said the Prest. (referring to Sherman's junction with

Burnside, and Longstreet's retreat) "is one of the most important gains of the war—the difference between Burnside saved and Burnside lost is one of the greatest advantages of the war—it secures us East Tennessee."

"Stay with Her as Long as You Can"

SECOND WEEK OF DECEMBER 1863

¶ *The second week in December, the Lincolns had a special visitor in the White House—Emilie Todd Helm, widow of Confederate General Ben Hardin Helm, who died in battle south of Chattanooga. Emilie was Mary Lincoln's half sister. A mother of three small children, she was almost penniless when she arrived at the White House, hopeful that "Brother Lincoln"—who did not wish her visit known—would help her reach Lexington, Kentucky.*[1]

After her arrival in Washington, Emilie wrote in her Diary: *"Mr. Lincoln and my sister met me with the warmest affection, we were all too grief-stricken at first for speech. I have lost my husband, they have lost their fine little son Willie and Mary and I have lost three brothers in the Confederate service." During Emilie's stay at the White House, the sisters "dined intimately, alone." They talked about "immaterial things," such as old friends in Springfield or Kentucky. "Sister and I cannot open our hearts to each other as freely as we would like," Emilie noted in despair. "This frightful war comes between us like a barrier of granite closing our lips but not our hearts, for though our tongues are tied, we weep over our dead together and express through our clasped hands the sympathy we feel for each other in our mutual grief." Yet, she found a touching tenderness in the White House, where "Sister Mary" and "Brother Lincoln pet me as if I were a child, and, without words, try to comfort me."*[2]

On one occasion, Emilie told her Diary:[3]

Sister Mary was sitting in a drooping despondent attitude as I came across the room to kiss her good morning; the newspaper she had been reading dropped to the floor as she held her arms out to me and said, "Kiss me, Emilie, and tell me that you love me! I seem to be the scape-goat for both North and South!" Then suddenly as if she had thrown off a dark cloak and stood revealed in a gay costume, she held her head up and smiled. I was marveling at the transformation but instantly understood the cause as Brother Lincoln's voice came to us, "I hope you two are planning some mischief." Mischief—I am sure he saw Mary's despondency and heard what she said to me and that his cheerfulness was forced, for later in the day he said: "Little Sister, I hope you can come up and spend the summer with us at the Soldiers' Home, you and Mary love each other—it is good for her to have you with her—I feel worried about Mary, her nerves have gone to pieces; she cannot hide from me that the strain she has been under has been too much for her mental as well as her physical health. What do you think?" he asked me anxiously. I answered him as I knew he wished me to do, candidly. "She seems very nervous and excitable and once or twice when I have come into the room suddenly the frightened look in her eyes has appalled me. She seems to fear that other sorrows may be added to those we already have to bear. I believe if anything should happen to you or Robert or Tad it would kill her." Brother Lincoln said, as he shook his head sorrowfully: "Stay with her as long as you can."

[Later that day, Emilie wrote:]

She [Mary] is frightened about Robert going into the Army. She said to-day to Brother Lincoln (I was reading in another part of the room but could not help hearing the conversation): "Of course, Mr. Lincoln, I know that Robert's plea to go into the Army is manly and noble and I want him to go, but oh! I am so frightened he may never come back to us!"

Mr. Lincoln said sadly, "Many a poor mother, Mary, has had to make this sacrifice and has given up every son she had—and lost them all." "Don't I know that too well?" cried Mary; "before this war is ended I may be like that poor mother, like my poor mother in Kentucky, with not a prop left her in her old age." I heard no more, for feeling the conversation was not meant for me to hear I left the room.

[Robert Lincoln subsequently entered the army and served with General Grant as a captain.]

"Fully Apprehensive of the Schemes"

SATURDAY, FEBRUARY 13, 1864

¶ *With the dawn of 1864, the Presidential contest began "with a vengeance." Before the end of 1863, it was known that while Lincoln was not seeking renomination, he really desired it "as an approval of the policy with which he has conducted an Administration through a long and arduous struggle." A change of administration would be "virtually voting him a failure."* [1]

Lincoln's major opposition for the Republican nomination was Salmon P. Chase, who had Jacobin support. Greeley believed the Treasury Secretary possessed "the largest brain and the steadiest arm." In December, Chase—"with Presidency glaring out of both eyes"—claimed to have all the Republican machines with him, except those in New York, Illinois and New Jersey. However, said James Gordon Bennett: "Chase overestimates his own resources and underrates the President's powers of self-defense. . . . Ordinarily Honest Abe does not display much energy and spirit. So long as he is left in peace to read Artemus Ward's book and crack his own little jokes he is happy; but when the emergency comes Old Abe is generally prepared to meet it." [2]

Despite the political gymnastics of the Republican factions, "the masses" had "an abiding faith" in Lincoln's "honesty and ability." And Harper's Weekly commented at the turn of the year: "If the Presidential election took place next week, Mr. Lincoln would undoubtedly be returned by a greater majority than any President since Washington." [3]

On February 13th, Lincoln talked politics with Attorney General Bates, who recorded: [4]

Called on the President and had a private conversation, of some ½ hour, chiefly about the presidential election. He is fully apprehensive of the schemes of the Radical leaders. When I suggested some of their plots, he said they were almost *fiendish*. He is also fully aware that they would strike him at once, if they durst; but they fear that the blow would be ineffectual, and so, they would fall under his power, as *beaten enemies;* and, for that only reason the hyprocrit[e]s try to occupy equivocal ground—so that, when they fail, as *enemies,* they may still pretend to be *friends.*

He told me (what I partly knew before) that the extremists (Chase men?) had called several caucuses in the hope of finding it safe to take open ground ag[ain]st[5] L[incoln]'s re-nomination, but had never found one in three of the M.[embers of] C[ongres]s that would go against him—⟨I tried to impress upon him the important fact, that they need him quite as much as he does them—that they are cunning and unscrupluous, and when they find that they dare not openly oppose him, their effort will *then* be to commit him to as many as possible, of their extreme measures, so as to drive off his other friends, until he is weakened down to their level, and it becomes *safe to cast him off*—I think he sees it plainly[.]⟩[6]

He told me also, that the Editor of the Mo. Democrat . . . sometime ago, wrote a letter to Jim Lane, sharply censuring him for voting for the confirmation of Gen Schofield—and declaring that *Lincoln must be defeated, at all hazards*—But that it is not *prudent yet, to declare openly against him*!! This letter, *Lane* himself shewed to the President—Such is the faith that those knaves keep with each other!! . . .

I remarked to him [Lincoln] that if he stood out manfully against the unprincipled designs of the Radicals, I thought it would be easy to bring all the old Whigs to his support—He answered—I suppose so, and added that many of the better sort of Democrats were in the same condition—saying that [Lieutenant] Gov[erno]r. [Willard P.] Hall[7] of Mo. had written to his brother, Judge [William A.] Hall,[8] M.[ember of] C.[ongress] that the Dem[ocrat]s. of Mo. would go for L.[incoln] of necessity, and that he, the Judge w[oul]d. have to take the pill, however bitter.

Upon the whole, the President seems very hopeful that the machinations of the Radicals will fail, and that, in the matter of the nomination, his friends will be able to counteract them effectually.

"If It Is All the Same to You"

WEDNESDAY, MARCH 2, 1864

¶ *Reaction to Federal activities in Florida—a relatively minor war theatre—was disconcerting to Lincoln. In January, the President, believing "an effort" was being made "by some worthy gentlemen to reconstruct a loyal state government in Florida," notified General*

Quincy A. Gillmore, commander of the Department of the South: "I wish the thing done in the most speedy way possible" within the terms of the Amnesty Proclamation. On February 20th, General Truman Seymour, outnumbered by the rebels, suffered a disastrous defeat at the Battle of Olustee, near Jacksonville. Gillmore blamed Seymour for the disaster. Halleck dissociated himself from the engagement. The press attributed the "fiasco" to Lincoln, charging that the expedition was undertaken because "he wanted Florida . . . to be restored in time to vote in the Baltimore Convention," scheduled by the Republicans for early June.[1]

Shortly thereafter, Francis B. Carpenter, the artist, who spent six months at the White House painting a canvas of the Cabinet discussing the Emancipation Proclamation, had "an unusually long and interesting sitting" with Lincoln. Also present that March 2nd, was Samuel Sinclair, business manager of the New York Tribune. *Carpenter, in his* Six Months at the White House with Lincoln, *published in 1867, reports the talk on this occasion:*[2]

Mr. Lincoln was deeply wounded by these charges [concerning the Florida battle]. He referred to them during the sitting; and gave a simple and truthful statement of the affair, which was planned, if I remember rightly, by General Gillmore. A few days afterward, an editorial appeared in the New York "Tribune," which was known not to favor Mr. Lincoln's renomination, entirely exonerating him from all blame. I took the article to him in his study, and he expressed much gratification at its candor. It was, perhaps, in connection with the newspaper attacks, that he told, during the sitting, this story.—"A traveller on the frontier found himself out of his reckoning one night in a most inhospitable region. A terrific thunderstorm came up, to add to his trouble. He floundered along until his horse at length gave out. The lightning afforded him the only clew to his way, but the peals of thunder were frightful. One bolt, which seemed to crash the earth beneath him, brought him to his knees. By no means a praying man, his petition was short and to the point, —'O Lord, if it is all the same to you, give us a little more light and a little less noise!'[3] ["]

Presently the conversation turned upon Shakespeare, of whom it is well known Mr. Lincoln was very fond. He once remarked, "It matters not to me whether Shakespeare be well or ill acted; with him the thought suffices." Edwin Booth was playing an engagement at this time at Grover's Theatre. He had been announced for the coming evening in his famous part of *Hamlet*. The President had never witnessed his representation of this character, and he proposed being present. The mention of this play, which I afterward learned had at all times a peculiar charm for Mr. Lincoln's mind, waked up a train of thought I was not prepared for. Said he,—and his words have often returned to me with a sad interest since his own assassination,—"There is one passage of the play of 'Hamlet' ⁴ which is very apt to be slurred over by the actor, or omitted altogether, which seems to me the choicest part of the play. It is the soliloquy of the king, after the murder. It always struck me as one of the finest touches of nature in the world."

Then, throwing himself into the very spirit of the scene, he took up the words:—

"O my offence is rank, it smells to heaven;
It hath the primal eldest curse upon 't,
A brother's murder!—Pray can I not,
Though inclination be as sharp as will;
My stronger guilt defeats my strong intent;
And, like a man to double business bound,
I stand in pause where I shall first begin,
And both neglect. What if this cursed hand
Were thicker than itself with brother's blood?
Is there not rain enough in the sweet heavens
To wash it white as snow? Whereto serves mercy
But to confront the visage of offence;
And what's in prayer but this twofold force—
To be forestalled ere we come to fall,
Or pardoned, being down? Then I'll look up;
My fault is past. But O what form of prayer
Can serve my turn? Forgive me my foul murder?—
That cannot be; since I am still possessed
Of those effects for which I did the murder,—
My crown, my own ambition, and my queen.
     May one be pardoned and retain the offence?
In the corrupted currents of this world,
Offence's gilded hand may shove by justice,
And oft 't is seen the wicked prize itself
Buys out the law; but 't is not so *above*.

There is no shuffling; there the action lies
In its true nature; and we ourselves compelled,
Even to the teeth and forehead of our faults,
To give in evidence. What then? what rests?
Try what repentance can; what can it not?
Yet what can it when one cannot repent?
O wretched state! O bosom black as death!
O bruised soul that, struggling to be free,
Art more engaged! Help, angels, make assay!
Bow, stubborn knees! And heart with strings of steel,
Be soft as sinews of the new-born babe;
All may be well!"

He repeated this entire passage from memory, with a feeling and appreciation unsurpassed by anything I ever witnessed upon the stage. Remaining in thought for a few moments, he continued:—

"The opening of the play of 'King Richard the Third' seems to me often entirely misapprehended. It is quite common for an actor to come upon the stage, and, in a sophomoric style, to begin with a flourish:—

" 'Now is the winter of our discontent
Made glorious summer by this sun of York,
And all the clouds that lowered upon our house,
In the deep bosom of the ocean buried!'

Now," said he, "this is all wrong. Richard, you remember, had been, and was then, plotting the destruction of his brothers, to make room for himself. Outwardly, the most loyal to the newly crowned king, secretly he could scarcely contain his impatience at the obstacles still in the way of his own elevation. He appears upon the stage, just after the crowning of Edward, burning with repressed hate and jealousy. The prologue is the utterance of the most intense bitterness and satire."

Then, unconsciously assuming the character, Mr. Lincoln repeated, also from memory, Richard's soliloquy, rendering it with a degree of force and power that made it seem like a new creation to me. Though familiar with the passage from boyhood, I can truly say that never till that moment had I fully appreciated its spirit. I could not refrain from laying down my palette and brushes, and applauding heartily, upon his conclusion, saying, at the same time, half in earnest, that I was not sure but that he had made a mistake in the

choice of a profession, considerably, as may be imagined, to his
amusement. Mr. Sinclair has since repeatedly said to me that he
never heard these choice passages of Shakespeare rendered with
more effect by the most famous of modern actors.

"This Is General Grant, Is It?"
TUESDAY, MARCH 8, 1864

¶ *Ulysses S. Grant, "the hero of Donelson, Vicksburg and Missionary
Ridge," was being hailed as "the first soldier of the times." Since
his Chattanooga victories, the "rather slightly built" man with
"stooping shoulders, mild blue eyes and light brown hair and
whiskers, with a foxy tinge to his mustache," was being boomed as
Lincoln's successor. But Grant, almost always chewing a cigar, bore
his laurels modestly. The Presidency, he said, "is the last thing in
the world I desire." To politicians he would say: "I never aspired
to but one office in my life. I should like to be mayor of Galena—
to build a new sidewalk from my house to the depot."* [1]

*Grant was concerned with doing his duty to help suppress the
rebellion. This attitude was a relief to Lincoln, who had worried
about the general as a possible rival. When Congress revived the
rank of Lieutenant General—previously held only by George Washington and Winfield Scott—Lincoln unhesitatingly conferred it upon
Grant. And Stanton summoned the general to Washington to receive
the commission from the President himself.*

*The day before the scheduled presentation ceremonies, Grant
arrived in the capital. "By some sort of negligence," Nicolay recalled,
"there was no one at the Depot to receive him but he found his way
to Willards with the two members of his staff who accompanied
him."* [2] *That evening, he went to see the President, unaware that a
levee was in progress at the White House. Nicolay, in a memorandum
penned the same night, recorded:* [3]

[T]he "Republican" having announced that Grant would attend
the reception it brought out a considerable crowd. At about 9½ P.M.,
the General came in—alone . . . excepting his staff—and he and
the President, met for the first time. The President expecting him
knew from the buzz and movement in the crowd that it must be him;

and when a man of modest mien and unimposing exterior presented himself, the President said "This is General Grant, is it?" The General replied "Yes!" and the two greeted each other more cordially, but still with that modest deference—felt rather than expressed by word or action—so appropriate to both—the one the honored Ruler and the other the honored Victor of the nation and the time. The crowd too partook of the feeling of the occasion—there was no rude jostling—or pushing or pulling, but unrestrained the circle kept its respectful distance, until after a brief conversation the President gave the General in charge of Seward to present to Mrs. L. at the same time instructing me to send for the Secretary of War. After paying his respects to Mrs. Lincoln the General was taken by Seward to the East Room where he was greeted with cheer after cheer by the assembled crowd, and where he was forced to mount a sofa from whence he could shake hands with those who pressed from all sides to see him. It was at least an hour before he returned, flushed heated and perspiring with the unwanted exertion.

After a promenade in the East Room—the Prest with Mr Seward and Gen Grant with Mrs L. [—] the party returned to the Blue Room and sat down. The President went up stairs and returning in a little while sat down where the General the Sec of War and myself were sitting[.]

"Tomorrow," said the Prest to the Genl. "at such time as you may arrange with the Sec of War, I desire to make to you a formal presentation of your commission as Lieut. Genl. I shall then make a very short speech to you to which I desire you to reply for an object; and that you may be properly prepared to do so I have written what I shall say—only four sentences in all—which I will read from my MSS. as an example which you may follow and also read your reply, as you are perhaps not as much accustomed to speaking as I myself—and I therefore give you what I shall say that you may consider it and frame your reply. There are two points that I would like to have you make in your answer: 1st To say something which shall prevent or obviate any jealousy of you from any of the other generals in the service, and secondly, something which shall put you on as good terms as possible with this Army of the Potomac. Now consider whether this may not be said to make it of some advantage; and if you see any objection whatever to doing it be under no restraint whatever in expressing that objection to the Secretary of War who will talk further with you about it." The General asked at what time this presentation should take place.

"The Secretary of War and yourself may arrange the time to suit your convenience[.] I am ready, whenever you shall have perpared your reply."

"I can be ready in thirty minutes," said the General.

One oclock tomorrow was finally fixed as the hour, after which the General took his leave, accompanied by the Sec of War.

—The President as I learned in reply to a question to him, is contemplating bringing the General east to see whether he cannot do something with the unfortunate army of the Potomac.

[The formal ceremonies were held on March 9th. The following day, Grant was assigned to the command of the armies of the United States; Halleck was named to the newly created post of "Chief of Staff of the Army, under the direction of the Secretary of War" and assigned to duty in Washington.⁴ Less than a month later, Grant, who had gone West to consult with Sherman, was back in Washington reorganizing the Potomac Army for the spring campaign.]

"I Have a Clear Conscience"

THURSDAY, APRIL 7, 1864

¶ *George Thompson, the noted British anti-slavery leader, addressed a large audience—including Lincoln and Hamlin—in the House of Representatives the night of April 6th. "The* tout ensemble *was extremely brilliant," Thompson said, adding: "My mention of the names of Garrison and Phillips called forth loud cheers—so did an allusion to John Brown." The* New York Herald's *Washington correspondent called the meeting "a gathering of the faithful [radicals] only," observing: "Even Old Abe looked ill at ease and out of place where only his most radical utterances were applauded, and the names of all the apostles of radicalism, from mad John Brown all the way down to Horace Greeley, were received with cheers."* ¹

The next day, "Mr. Thompson and party," consisting of Rev. John Pierpont, Oliver Johnson, former president of the New York Anti-Slavery Society, and Hon. Lewis Clephane, of Washington, called at the White House. Carpenter, who was present at this interview, wrote about it in his book: [2]

The President was alone when their names were announced, with the exception of myself. Dropping all business, he ordered the party to be immediately admitted. Greeting them very cordially, the gentlemen took seats, and Mr. Thompson commenced conversation by referring to the condition of public sèntiment in England in regard to the great conflict the nation was passing through. He said the aristocracy and the "money interest" were desirous of seeing the Union broken up, but that the great heart of the masses beat in sympathy with the North. They instinctively felt that the cause of liberty was bound up with our success in putting down the Rebellion, and the struggle was being watched with the deepest anxiety.

Mr. Lincoln thereupon said: "Mr. Thompson, the people of Great Britain, and of other foreign governments, were in one great error in reference to this conflict. They seemed to think that, the moment I was President, I had the power to abolish slavery, forgetting that, before I could have any power whatever, I had to take the oath to support the Constitution of the United States, and execute the laws as I found them. When the Rebellion broke out, my duty did not admit of a question. That was, first, by all strictly lawful means to endeavor to maintain the integrity of the government. I did not consider that I had a *right* to touch the 'State' institution of 'Slavery' until all other measures for restoring the Union had failed. The paramount idea of the constitution is the preservation of the Union. It may not be specified in so many words, but that this was the idea of its founders is evident; for, without the Union, the constitution would be worthless. It seems clear, then, that in the last extremity, if any local institution threatened the existence of the Union, the Executive could not hesitate as to his duty. In our case, the moment came when I felt that slavery must die that the nation might live! I have sometimes used the illustration in this connection of a man with a diseased limb, and his surgeon. So long as there is a chance of the patient's restoration, the surgeon is solemnly bound to try to save both life *and* limb; but when the crisis comes, and the limb must be sacrificed as the only chance of saving the life, no honest man will hesitate.

"Many of my strongest supporters urged *Emancipation* before I thought it indispensable, and, I may say, before I thought the country ready for it. It is my conviction that, had the proclamation been issued even six months earlier than it was, public sentiment would not have sustained it. Just so, as to the subsequent action in reference to enlisting blacks in the Border States. The step, taken sooner, could not, in my judgment, have been carried out. A man watches his pear-tree day after day, impatient for the ripening of the fruit. Let him attempt to *force* the process, and he may spoil both fruit and tree. But let him patiently *wait,* and the ripe pear at length falls into his lap! We have seen this great revolution in public sentiment slowly but *surely* progressing, so that, when final action came, the opposition was not strong enough to defeat the purpose. I can now solemnly assert," he concluded, "that I have a clear conscience in regard to my action on this momentous question. I have done what no man could have helped doing, standing in my place."

Oliver Johnson, speaking, as he said, for the old Anti-Slavery party, assured the President that they had fully appreciated the difficulties and embarrassments of his position; but when they realized the importance of the grand issue, and observed the conflicting influences that were surging around him, they were in an agony of anxiety lest he should somehow be led to take a false position. If, in the months preceding the issue of the Emancipation Proclamation, they had seemed impatient and distrustful, it was because their knowledge of his character had not been sufficient to assure them that he would be able to stand up manfully against the opposing current. He thanked God that the result had shown that we had a President who was equal to the emergency; and for *his* part he was willing to sink all minor issues in the grand consummation he believed then in sight!

A characteristic incident occurred toward the close of the interview. When the President ceased speaking the Rev. Mr. Pierpont, impressed with his earnestness, turned to Mr. Thompson, and repeated a Latin quotation from the classics. Mr. Lincoln, leaning forward in his chair, looked from one to the other inquiringly, and then remarked, with a smile, *"Which,* I suppose you are both aware, *I* do not understand."

As the party rose to take leave, the President remarked, motioning toward me, "We have a young man here who is painting a picture down-stairs, which I should be glad to have you see." The gentlemen expressed their acknowledgments of the courtesy, and Mr. Lincoln led the way by the private staircase to the state dining-room. In the passage through the hall he jocularly remarked to Mr. Thompson, "Your folks made rather sad work of this mansion when they came up the Potomac in 1812. Nothing was left of it but the bare walls." I do not remember the reply to this sally, save that it was given and received in good part. Briefly going over the portraiture and composition of the picture, then in too early a stage for criticism, Mr. Lincoln presently excused himself, and returned to his duties. And thus ended an interview doubtless indelibly stamped upon the memory of each individual privileged in sharing it.

"Beehive . . . Kicked Over"

MONDAY, APRIL 25, 1864

¶ *Chase was presented openly as a Presidential candidate in a "secret circular"—extensively distributed among prominent Republicans—that found its way into print late in February. Signed by Kansas Senator Samuel C. Pomeroy, Chase's manager, the document asserted that even if Lincoln's re-election were "desirable," it was "practically impossible." A second term for Lincoln—who was prone to "compromises and temporary expedients of policy"—would injure "the cause of human liberty and the dignity and honor of the nation," the circular charged, stressing that the "one term principle" was "absolutely essential to the certain safety of our republican institutions." The man best qualified for the Presidency in 1864 was Salmon P. Chase, the "Pomeroy manifesto" proclaimed.[1]*

The circular "produced a perfect convulsion" in Republican ranks. In a letter of explanation, Chase told the President: "I do not wish to administer the Treasury Department one day without your entire confidence." Lincoln, for his part, absolved Chase of any blame in the matter.[2]

Lincoln's friends became more resolute in their support of the President after the circular appeared. Members of the Republican caucus in the Ohio Legislature were "so indignant" over this affair that early in March they expressed their preference for Lincoln. On the heels of this action, Chase asked that his name be withdrawn

as a Presidential candidate, moaning: "Our Ohio folks don't want
me enough, if they want me at all." ³

But all this did not satisfy Frank Blair. With venomous hatred
for Chase, the Missourian, speaking in the House, viciously attacked
the Secretary on February 27th, charging that Chase was using
Treasury Department patronage to secure the Presidential nomination. On April 23rd, Blair fired a second volley at Chase as talk
swept political circles that Frémont was being boomed as an anti-
Lincoln candidate by the ultra abolitionists, who had scheduled a
nominating convention at Cleveland for the end of May.

"Nobody is simple enough to believe that the distinguished Secretary has really retired from the canvass," cried Blair, alleging: "The
Cleveland convention is a whip convention which will say to the
Union convention to be held at Baltimore, 'If you insist on the
nomination of Lincoln we will nominate Frémont against him as
an independent candidate.' " Thus, as Blair saw it, Chase planned
to secure the nomination as a "compromise candidate." ⁴

Chase, furious over the Blair assault, believed it had Lincoln's
sanction. The Secretary was ready to resign. However, he agreed to
hold back until Congressman Albert G. Riddle of Ohio had had an
opportunity to see Lincoln to determine under what circumstances
Blair had made that speech.

On April 25th, Riddle, accompanied by his successor in the House,
Rufus P. Spalding—"the personal and confidential friend nearest
the Secretary"—met with the President. This, according to Riddle,
is what happened at the conference: ⁵

Mr. Lincoln received us politely but with no pretence of cordiality.
After brief salutations he passed around to the other side of the
long wide table and sat down by a bundle of papers, grimly awaiting
my assault.

"Mr. President," I said, "I am one of the personal and political
friends of Mr. Chase, who believes that the safety of the Union
cause requires that you should be unanimously nominated at the
June Convention, and should receive in November the eagerly cast
ballot of every man devoted to our country. It is this conviction
which brings me here to remove, if I can, a most seriously disturbing
cause which threatens to render this consummation impossible.

"As you are aware, on last Saturday, General Frank Blair, a
Republican representative from Missouri, repeated on the floor of

the House his attack of the early part of the session upon the Secretary of the Treasury, and this with added acrimony. You are aware of the unfortunate occurrence between General Blair and the Executive, in reference to the resumption by Mr. Blair of this Government's commission and his assignment to one of the highest commands in the army, and you are also aware of his departure, following immediately upon the close of the speech. These events, coincident with his attack, seemed as if planned for dramatic effect, as parts of a conspiracy against a most important member of the Cabinet and Administration. The always alert, jealous, and somewhat exacting abolitionists, forgetting how impossible it is that you can be guilty of an attack upon your Secretary—upon your own administration, believe that Blair must have had at least your countenance in this wretched business, and they demand the instant resignation of Mr. Chase. It is only by the strenuous exertions of one or two persons that this has been delayed.

"Mr. President, Mr. Chase's abrupt resignation now would be equal in its effects to a severe set-back of the army under Grant. It would foretell the defection of his friends at Baltimore, equal in effect to the defeat of that army in a pitched battle. Their defection in November might be the destruction of our cause.

"I pray you remember who these abolitionists are. They are the first, the oldest anti-slavery men—the abolitionists who conquered, foot by foot, the pro-slavery North, and who, with later allies, have conducted this great struggle to the issue of war—who made your accession to power possible. I know they have at times been over-hasty. Have I not personally heard their demands upon you and your answers? They were, however, the first to leap to your side, and who have pressed most closely after you, nay, would push you forward.

"Mr. President, I am not the emissary of these men, come to demand terms; I am not the agent of Mr. Chase. I have said to them, that I would return to them your word that you were in no way a party to or responsible for a word uttered by Mr. Blair. He was an independent representative of his constituency and spoke for them and himself, and could no more be dictated to by the President than you could think of dictating to him; and, having spoken, he was not responsible to you for his utterances.

"I invited Judge Spalding to be present, to hear your assurances, and with me bear them to our waiting friends."

Spalding, a handsome "personable" man, of fine manner, added a few words to the effect that he coincided with me in position and sentiment.

I had addressed the President standing, as had Spalding. The effect was marked; he arose, came round, and with great cordiality took each of us by the hand and evinced the greatest satisfaction at our presence and the sentiments we had expressed. Mr. Lincoln then returned, took up his papers and standing, addressed us for nearly half an hour. He spoke in his best manner, as if before a very select audience. He said—

"Gentlemen, I am glad to meet you, glad for your mission, and especially for your way of executing it. It makes my statement easier than I expected. I nevertheless will say about what I intended. Your frankness and cordiality shall be fully responded to."

Taking up some papers—"Have you seen my letter to Mr. Chase of Feb. 29th, in reply to his on the 22d, concerning his candidacy, and offering his resignation?"

MR. SPALDING—"I have."

MR. RIDDLE—"I have not."

Mr. Lincoln read it:

WASHINGTON, D. C., February 29, 1864.

". . . I should have taken time to answer sooner yours of the 22d, but that I did not suppose any evil could result from the delay, especially as, by a note, I promptly acknowledged the receipt of yours, and promised a fuller answer. Now, on consideration, I find there is really very little to say. My knowledge of Mr. Pomeroy's letter having been made *public* came to me only the day you wrote; but I had in spite of myself known of its *existence* several days before. I have not yet read it, and I think I shall not. I was not shocked or surprised by the appearance of the letter, because I had had knowledge for several weeks of Mr. Pomeroy's committee, of the secret issue which I supposed came from it, and of secret agents who I supposed were sent out by it. I have known just as little of these things as my friends have allowed me to know. They bring the documents to me, but I do not read them; they tell me what they think fit to tell me, but I do not inquire for more.

"I fully concur with you that neither of us can be justly held responsible for what our respective friends may do without our instigation or countenance, *and I assure you, as you have assured me, that no assault has been made upon you by my instigation, or with my countenance.*

"Whether you shall remain at the head of the Treasury Department is a question which I do not allow myself to consider from any standpoint other than my judgment of the public service, and in that view I do not perceive occasion for change.

"ABRAHAM LINCOLN."

MR. LINCOLN.—"The Blairs are, as you know, strong, tenacious men, having some peculiarities, among them the energy with which their feuds are carried on."

MR. RIDDLE.—"Yes, Montgomery says that when the Blairs go in for a fight they go in for a funeral."

MR. LINCOLN.—"Exactly. As you know, they labored for ten years to build up an anti-slavery party in Missouri, and in an action of ejectment to recover that party in the State, they could prove title in any common law court. Frank has in some way permitted himself to be put in a false position. He is in danger of being kicked out of the house built by himself, and by a set of men rather new to it. You know that they contributed more than any twenty men to bring forward Frémont [6] in 1855. I know that they mainly induced me to make him a Major-General and send him to Missouri."

He spoke of the quarrel between Frémont and Frank Blair, and said he did not know the actual facts of that matter. . . .

Mr. Lincoln said that, on Frank's arrival in Washington, he called on him on some business, and that as he was leaving, he, Frank, said that he wanted to make a speech in the House on the Mississippi Trade Regulations, to which he, Mr. Lincoln, replied:

"If you will do the subject justice, showing fairly the workings of the regulations, and will collect and present all the information on the subject, you will doubtless render a service to the country and do yourself much credit; but if you intend to make it the occasion of pursuing a personal warfare, you had better remain silent."

The President used stronger expressions than I can recall. He was annoyed and mortified by the speech. The trade regulations themselves were revised and arranged in Cabinet council, and he and each member of the Cabinet was as much responsible as was the Secretary of the Treasury. The speech was an assault on the

Government, and when it assailed Mr. Chase for the workings of the machinery it undoubtedly did him injustice. He had never been called upon in the premises, and did not know that he could interfere. Shortly before Frank left for the army, he called and asked that the arrangement with him should be carried out, and Mr. Lincoln sent an order to the War Office to have the order of his restoration made, and supposed it had been done. He heard no more of it till about noon of the day on which Frank made the last of that series of speeches, when he called on him [the President] and said he must leave that evening, and that the all-important order had not been made. The President then sent a messenger to the Adjutant-General, who replied that Mr. Blair was not known in the Department as an officer; whereupon the President ordered his resignation to be cancelled, which was done.[7]

"Within three hours," said Mr. Lincoln, "I heard that this speech had been made, when I knew *that another beehive was kicked over.* My first thought was to have cancelled the orders restoring him to the army and assigning him to command. Perhaps this would have been best. On such reflection as I was able to give to the matter, however, I concluded to let them stand. If I was wrong in this, the injury to the service can be set right.

"And thus you see how far I am responsible for Frank Blair's assaults on Mr. Chase."

Mr. Lincoln appealed several times to proofs of his statements, and concluded with re-assertions of their accuracy.

MR. SPALDING.—"Mr. President, spare us all other evidence. We only ask your word."

MR. RIDDLE.—"Your word, Mr. President, is the highest human evidence."

Mr. Lincoln also spoke of Maryland politics, in so far as this was essential to a full understanding of the present position of men and things. He said that in the formation of his Cabinet, he was for some days balancing between Montgomery Blair and Henry Winter Davis, and finally settled on Mr. Blair. He added that in the disposition of the Maryland patronage, he had, as far as possible, met the wishes of Mr. Davis. Subsequently he regarded Mr. Davis as holding ground not the most favorable to the best interests of the country. Still later, that gentleman made a speech in the House which wholly disabused his mind, and he was greatly rejoiced to find his first opinion of him correct. In Mr. Davis's contest for Congress, he had rendered him all the aid he consistently could. He also understood that Mr. Chase favored Mr. Davis's Union opponent. Since that election, Mr. Davis had desired some aid in the Maryland Constitutional election, which he could not see his way to afford him, and Mr. Davis had become very cool towards him. In fact, the President believed he was now an active friend of the Secretary of the Treasury.

At the close of his [the President's] statement Mr. Spalding said:

"Mr. President, I desire to know whether your letter to Mr. Chase, just read by you, expresses your present views and wishes in reference to the continuance of Mr. Chase in your Cabinet?"

MR. LINCOLN.—"It does most fully. I cannot see now, as I could not then, how the public service could be advanced by his retirement."

Mr. Lincoln was fully an hour in making his statement—his explanation, as he called it. He was plain, sincere, and most impressive.

Mr. Spalding expressed himself as perfectly satisfied, and was sure Mr. Chase and his friends would be also. I certainly was.

Mr. Lincoln expressed great satisfaction, and with many cordial expressions we withdrew. The interview occupied nearly two hours.

"Pity to Spoil So Good a Story"

MONDAY, APRIL 25, 1864

¶ *From the top of the east portico of Willard's Hotel, Lincoln—on April 25th—"standing with uncovered head" reviewed Burnside's command of 30,000 troops as they marched through Washington, en route from Annapolis to reinforce the Army of the Potomac. Sensing a campaign in the offing, the review "drew a numerous concourse of spectators, and the coming movement was everywhere the absorbing topic of conversation."* [1] *That evening, Pennsylvania's Governor Curtin, with a friend, came into Lincoln's office. Carpenter was there, too. Here is his report of the conversation:* [2]

As he [Curtin] sat down he referred to the fine appearance of Burnside's men; saying, with much emphasis, "Mr. President, if there is in the world one man more than another worthy of profound respect, it is the volunteer citizen soldier." To this Mr. Lincoln assented, in a quiet way,—the peculiar dreaminess of expression so remarkable at times, stealing over his face as his mind reverted to the thousands whose lives had been so freely offered upon the altar of their country, and the myriad homes represented by the thronging columns of the day's review, in so many of which there was henceforth to be weary watching and waiting for footsteps which would return no more.

I took this opportunity to get at the truth concerning a newspaper story which went the rounds a year or two previous, purporting to be an account of a meeting of the loyal Governors in Washington, early in the war. It was stated that the President laid the condition of the country before such a council, convened at the White House, and anxiously awaited the result. An oppressive silence followed. Curtin was represented as having been standing, looking out of one of the windows, drumming unconsciously upon a pane of glass. Mr. Lincoln, at length addressing him personally, said: "Andy, what is Pennsylvania going to do?" Turning around, Curtin replied: "She is going to send twenty thousand men to start with, and will double it, if necessary!" "This noble response" [quoted from memory] [3] "overwhelmed the President, and lifted the dead weight which seemed to have paralyzed all present."

I repeated this account substantially as here given; but both parties smiled and shook their heads. "It is a pity to spoil so good a story," returned the President, "but, unfortunately, there is not a word of truth in it. I believe the only convocation of Governors that has taken place during the war," he added, looking at Curtin, "was that at Altoona—was it not?"

Subsequently the two gentlemen proposed to visit my room, and Mr. Lincoln accompanied them. Sitting down under the chandelier on the edge of the long table, which ran the whole length of the apartment, swinging back and forth his long legs, passing his hand occasionally over his brow and through his rough hair (his appearance and manner come back to me most vividly, as I write), he listened abstractedly to my brief explanation of the design of the picture. When I ceased, he took up the record in his own way. "You see, Curtin," said he, "I was brought to the conclusion that there was no dodging this negro question any longer. We had reached the point where it seemed that we must avail ourselves of this element, or in all probability go under." He then went over the circumstances attending the step, in much the same language he had used upon the occasion of my first interview with him. Governor Curtin remarked that the impression prevailed in some quarters that Secretary Seward opposed the policy. "That is not true," replied Mr. Lincoln; "he advised postponement, at the first meeting, which seemed to me sound. It was Seward's persistence which resulted in the insertion of the word 'maintain,' which I feared under the circumstances was promising more than it was quite probable we could carry out."

The bill empowering the Secretary of the Treasury to sell the surplus gold had recently passed, and Mr. Chase was then in New York, giving his attention personally to the experiment. Governor Curtin referred to this, saying, "I see by the quotations that Chase's movement has already knocked gold down several per cent." This gave occasion for the strongest expression I ever heard fall from the lips of Mr. Lincoln. Knotting his face in the intensity of his feeling, he said, "Curtin, what do you think of those fellows in Wall Street, who are gambling in gold at such a time as this?" "They are a set of sharks," returned Curtin. "For my part," continued the President, bringing his clinched [clenched] hand down upon the table, "I wish every one of them had his *devilish* head shot off!"

Chapter Ten

"IT IS NOT BEST TO SWAP HORSES"

THE night of May 3rd, Ulysses Grant—"one of the simplest, stillest men"—began leading the 122,000-man Potomac Army across the Rapidan. Confidently, the Yanks advanced into the Virginia Wilderness to grapple with Lee's 62,000 warriors. "Lee's army will be my objective point," said Grant. "Wherever he goes I will go also." And Lincoln said: "Grant has gone to the Wilderness, crawled in, drawn up the ladder, and pulled in the hole after him." [1]

On May 5th—as Sherman was preparing for his march through Georgia—the opposing armies of Grant and Lee clashed in what the Union general later called "the bloodiest swath ever made on this globe." Locked in desperate conflict in the wild, tangled pine woods, the fighting was at close range. There was no room for maneuvering in that jungle; "no possibility of a bayonet charge, no help from artillery; no help from cavalry; nothing but close, square, severe, face-to-face volleys of fatal musketry." One war correspondent wrote: "No man can claim that he saw this battle; and although undoubtedly it had a line and formation of its own, it would puzzle even the commanding General to lay it down on the map." [2]

The indecisive Battle of the Wilderness, the operations at Spotsylvania, North Anna River and the great slaughter at Cold Harbor —the assault Grant "always regretted . . . was ever made"—cost the Union 54,000 casualties, including 7,621 killed. [3]

Lincoln, during the darkest days of the Wilderness Campaign, went to the opera. "People may think strange of it," he explained, "but

319

I *must* have some relief from this terrible anxiety, or it will kill me." The "grave and anxious" President could not bear seeing the long lines of wounded. "This suffering, this loss of life is dreadful," he moaned. Grant said: "Without a greater sacrifice of life than I was willing to make, all could not be accomplished that I had designed north of Richmond." [4]

Grant had failed to defeat Lee. But Lee had failed to turn back the Army of the Potomac as he had done in the past. When Grant went into the Wilderness, the North was elated. Now, the public was decidedly dejected, and Noah Brooks noted, "everybody forgetting apparently, that reverses, great and small, must form a part of every campaign. . . . The great public, like a spoiled child, refuses to be comforted, because Richmond is not taken forthwith, and because we do not meet with an unbroken success at every point." [5] The Lincoln Administration began weathering anew a wave of criticism as Grant, on June 19th, buckled down to his siege of Petersburg. Cox of Ohio declared that there was "no denying that since Grant's failure or seeming failure," the public had manifested "an increase of the peace sentiment—irrespective of consequence." From Buffalo came word that "among the masses of the people a strong reaction is setting in, in favor of the Democrats & against the war." [6]

Interwoven with the Union's military fortunes—especially with Grant's on the Virginia front—was Lincoln's political fate in this Presidential year. By spring 1864, Chase's Presidential boom was virtually deflated. Republican radicals continued their abuse of Mr. Lincoln, who was "severely censured" for his "conservatism and timidity in dealing with the emancipation question." A Hartford man wrote Welles: "I am unable to see our way out of our National troubles through the drifting conciliatory and temporizing policy of Mr. Lincoln, but believe its continuance would ruin us." And a supporter of Thad Stevens asserted that "there are a very large class of earnest men who will feel very little interest in this contest [unless Lincoln changes his policy]. . . . It makes me sick to think what we have lost & the prospect of having nearly five years more of this thing." [7]

A majority of Republican leaders were averse to Lincoln's renomination, but as Horace Greeley put it: "The People think of him by night & by day & pray for him & their *hearts* are where they have made so heavy investments." James A. Garfield said that in the West, "the people are Lincoln-crazy." One Washington observer concluded: "The great majority are in favor of the re-election of Mr. Lincoln . . . [He] can get more votes than any other man." And a New Jersey lass wrote Lincoln that "no other President has come so near our hearts." [8]

Most vociferous in their antagonism toward Lincoln were the ultra abolitionists, who were united primarily by their hatred of him. They styled themselves the "Radical Democracy," called a convention at Cleveland for May 31st, and nominated General John C. Frémont for President and General John Cochrane, of New York, as his running mate. The "Radical Democracy," said James Gordon Bennett, had "boldly" entered the Presidential field "upon the broad and commodious platform of the Union, the constitution and the laws, the suppression of the rebellion by gunpowder, free speech, a free press, the habeas corpus, the right to asylum, the one term principle, the Monroe Doctrine, emancipation and confiscation, and 'liberty, equality and fraternity.' " [9]

However, while no one in well-informed circles believed that the Frémont party had any expectation of success, this movement could not be regarded with indifference "when we know that it is supported by a powerful body of honest and inflexible radicals," including the Frémont German Legion.

"Their object," said Bennett, "is not the election of Frémont, but the defeat of Lincoln." Frémont himself, in accepting the nomination, declared that if the Republicans *"will nominate any man whose past life justifies a well-grounded confidence in his fidelity to our cardinal principles, there is no reason why there should be any division among the really patriotic men of the country.* To any such I shall be most happy to give a cordial and active support. . . . But *if Mr. Lincoln should be nominated*—as I believe *it would be fatal to the country* to indorse a policy and renew a power which has cost us the lives of thousands of men, and needlessly put the country on the road to bankruptcy—there will remain no other alternative but to organize against him every element of conscientious opposition with the view to prevent the misfortune of his re-election." [10]

Even before the Frémont convention, the abolitionists were split on a Presidential candidate. The conservative *New York Herald* crowed over the schism: "Mr. [William Lloyd] Garrison and Mr.

[Wendell] Phillips . . . are at variance upon the Presidential question. Mr. Garrison believes that President Lincoln ought to be reelected, while Mr. Phillips denounces the President as a 'tortoise,' a 'fool' and a 'hyprocrite.' Mr. Phillips thinks that Frémont ought to be our next President, while Mr. Garrison denounces the Pathfinder as unfaithful to the abolition creed since his Missouri proclamation." [11]

Enemies and unfriendly critics of the Lincoln Administration were predicting "all sorts of disasters, political and military," should the President be "forced upon the people," Brooks remembered. "The commonest forecast of the situation made by these pessimists was that if the military movements of 1864 were successful, Grant would be the next President; if they were unsuccessful, neither Grant nor Lincoln could be elected that year." [12]

The *New York Herald* was constantly boosting Grant for the White House as "the man who knows how to tan leather, politicians and the hides of rebels." Lincoln, said Bennett, "is a joke incarnate," adding: "His intrigues to secure a renomination and the hopes he appears to entertain for a re-election are, however, the most laughable jokes of all." Lincoln himself declared: "If Grant could be more useful than I in putting down the rebellion, I would be quite content. He is fully committed to the policy of emancipation and employing negro soldiers; and with this policy faithfully carried out, it will not make much difference who is President." But so far as Grant was concerned: "Lincoln is just the man of all others whom the country needs, and his defeat would be a great national calamity." [13]

For days before the National Union Party Convention opened in Baltimore on June 7th, Lincoln was busy entertaining various delegations, "consulting with the leading wirepullers." Wrote one Washington correspondent: "The organization of the Convention and the choice of the candidate for the Vice Presidency are the topics discussed. It is believed that these points will be definitely decided here . . . so that the Convention will have nothing to do except to ratify the programme thus agreed upon." But the newsman did not have all his facts straight. Lincoln refused to give even a "confidential suggestion" regarding a Vice-Presidential candidate—a point disputed in later years—nor did he wish to interfere on convention organization. He made only one proposal: That the platform call for an amendment to the Constitution "abolishing and prohibiting slavery forever." This was a concession to the Republican radicals, who—unable to find a satisfactory candidate after Chase's withdrawal —went to Baltimore resigned to Lincoln's renomination.[14]

Every delegate—except the Missourians—voted for Lincoln on the first ballot. Rival delegations had come from Missouri and the anti-Blair radicals won the right to be seated in convention. On the first ballot, they cast their 22 votes for Grant and then voted to make Lincoln's nomination unanimous. Attorney General Bates was chagrined at the public and behind-the-scenes conduct of the convention delegates. "I shall tell the Prest: in all frankness," he confided to his *Diary,* "that his best nomination is not that at Baltimore, but his nomination spontaneously, by the People, by which the convention was constrained to name him." [15]

The Vice-Presidential nomination was the most absorbing theme of the convention in selecting the ticket. Hannibal Hamlin was seeking renomination. Against him were pitted such War Democrats as General John A. Dix and Daniel S. Dickinson, both of New York; Joseph Holt of Kentucky; and Andrew Johnson of Tennessee, the tailor who had become a senator and was now military governor of his state. After a good deal of maneuvering, the convention ultimately united in making Johnson its candidate for the Vice-Presidency.

The platform upon which Messrs. Lincoln and Johnson were mounted included a series of resolutions endorsing the President's course in the conduct of the war, calling for suppression of the rebellion by force of arms and enactment of a Thirteenth Amendment to the Constitution that would utterly extirpate slavery "from the soil of the United States." Another plank called for harmony in the Administration's councils and approved "only those officials whose sentiments and conduct are in full accord with the salient measures of the administration." This vaguely worded resolution was meant to serve notice upon Lincoln that his Cabinet must be reshuffled; it was aimed primarily at Seward and Blair, although Bates was also intended as a target.[16]

Being human, Lincoln desired a second term to "see this thing through." If he had not been nominated, he told Brooks, he should have returned "to private life with absolute content." To a delegation from the National Union League, he said on June 9th: "I have not permitted myself . . . to conclude that I am the best man in the country; but I am reminded, in this connection, of a story of the old Dutch farmer, who remarked to a companion once that 'it was not best to swap horses when crossing streams.' " [17]

The period between Lincoln's renomination and the convening of the Democrats at Chicago on August 29th saw the resignation of Chase as Treasury Secretary; the pocket vetoing of the radical Reconstruction Bill, championed by Benjamin F. Wade and Henry Winter Davis; Jubal Early's swift raid on Washington and his successful retreat over the Potomac; and Horace Greeley—with Lincoln's consent—rushing to Niagara Falls in a fruitless attempt at peace with the rebels.

Once again, the war was flagging; people were discontented, and the finances were running low. Lincoln was uncertain whether "the people would pronounce for peace or war." Brooks wrote: "If he was to be defeated, he said, the verdict of the people must be accepted as final against further prosecution of the war." In August, the Copperhead *New York World* editorialized: "It would be difficult to determine which are more damaging to the prospects of Mr. Lincoln in his candidacy for reelection—the heavy blows in front which his manly opponents are dealing, or the stabs in the back inflicted by his professed friends." These "professed friends" were now talking of dropping Lincoln as their standard-bearer.[18]

When the Democratic convention was about to assemble, Lincoln told Brooks: "That convention must put a war man on a peace platform, or a peace man on a war platform, I don't care much which." McClellan's nomination was almost a foregone conclusion. As his running mate, the Democrats chose George H. Pendleton, whom the Republicans charged with having "persistently pursued in Congress that course most calculated to encourage the armed enemies of the country and to foster secession and treason of all kinds and grades." Taking into account the mood of the times, newsman Whitelaw Reid commented: "We think McClellan and Pendleton a very strong ticket and fear the result." [19]

The Democratic platform, which called for an end to war and restoration of peace "at the earliest possible moment," was an embarrassment to McClellan.[20] It made treason a major issue of the campaign. *The New York Times* alleged that the convention was made up of "black hearted traitors," while the *New York Tribune* shouted that the Democratic platform was "concocted by Rebels in Richmond . . . was agreed to by disloyal politicians at the North in a conference with Rebels at Niagara Falls . . . and was taken to Chicago and adopted by a convention expressly chosen to adopt it." The *Chicago Tribune* reported that "treason to the government has for hours at a time cascaded over the balconies of the hotels, spouted and squirted, dribbled and pattered, and rained on our out of door listeners and pedestrians" from the mouths of the Democratic delegates. And it was "noticeable," said the *Cincinnati Daily Gazette,* "that not one word has been uttered in condemnation of the rebellion." [21]

The political battle lines had been drawn for the Presidential campaign of 1864.

"He Was . . . Non-Committal"

MONDAY, JUNE 6, 1864

¶ *The night before the National Republican Convention assembled in Baltimore, Brooks talked with Lincoln at the White House. In his* Washington in Lincoln's Time, *Brooks recounts:* [1]

He requested me to come to him when I should return from Baltimore, and bring him the odd bits of political gossip that I might pick up in the convention, and which, as he said, would not get into the newspapers. I had hoped to see Mr. Hamlin renominated, and had anxiously given Mr. Lincoln many opportunities to say whether he preferred the renomination of the Vice-President; but he was craftily and rigidly non-committal, knowing, as he did, what was in my mind concerning Mr. Hamlin. He would refer to the matter only in the vaguest phrase, as, "Mr. Hamlin is a very good man," or, "You, being a New Englander, would naturally like to see Mr. Hamlin renominated; and you are quite right," and so on. By this time Lincoln's renomination was an absolute certainty, and he cheerfully conceded that point without any false modesty. But he could not be induced to express any opinion on the subject of the selection of a candidate for vice-president. He did go so far as to say that he hoped that the convention would declare in favor of the

constitutional amendment abolishing slavery as one of the articles
of the party faith. But beyond that, nothing.

"What! Am I Renominated?"

THURSDAY, JUNE 9, 1864

¶ *Brooks went to the White House after his return from the Baltimore
convention. Of this interview with the President, he wrote:* [1]

I made a verbal report to the President, and entertained him with
an account of some of its [the convention's] doings of which he had
not previously heard; and he was then willing to admit that he would
have been gratified if Mr. Hamlin could have been renominated.
But he said: "Some of our folks [referring, as I believed, to Republican leaders] [2] had expressed the opinion that it would be wise
to take a War Democrat as candidate for vice-president, and that,
if possible, a border-State man should be the nominee." Mr. Lincoln
appeared to have accepted the result, saying, "Andy Johnson, I think,
is a good man." Nevertheless, I have always been confident that
Lincoln, left to himself, would have chosen that the old ticket of
1860—Lincoln and Hamlin—should be placed in the field. . . .

I was astonished by his jokingly rallying me on my failure to
send him word of his nomination. It appeared that nobody had
apparently thought it worth while to telegraph him the result of
the balloting for the presidential nominee of the convention. . . .
[Brooks erred in making this statement. A telegram announcing his
renomination had been sent to Lincoln, but he was not at the
White House when it arrived.[3]]

It turned out that the President, having business at the War
Department, met Major [Thomas T.] Eckert, superintendent of the
military bureau of telegraphs, who congratulated him on his nomination. "What! Am I renominated?" asked the surprised chief. When
assured that this had been done, Mr. Lincoln expressed his gratification, and asked Major Eckert if he would kindly send word over to
the White House when the name of the candidate for vice-president
should have been agreed upon.

"They Had Touched His Clothes"
TUESDAY, JUNE 21, 1864

¶ *Lincoln made his first visit to Grant's army at City Point on June 21st. "We get no good army news from Petersburg," Welles told his Diary. "Our troops have suffered much and accomplished but little, so far as I can learn." There had been little news from Grant. "Were the news favorable it would be otherwise." In his "intense anxiety," Lincoln, accompanied by Assistant Navy Secretary Fox and Tad Lincoln, went down to the front "to see for himself what is the real state of the case, and what the prospects are."* [1]

General Horace Porter, aide-de-camp to Grant—who was in the habit of making extensive notes of the conversations he heard— describes Lincoln's sojourn with the army in his volume Campaigning With Grant: [2]

As the boat neared the shore, the general [Grant] and several of us who were with him at the time walked down to the wharf, in order that the general-in-chief might meet his distinguished visitor and extend a greeting to him as soon as the boat made the landing. As our party stepped aboard, the President came down from the upper deck, where he had been standing, to the after-gangway, and reaching out his long, angular arm, he wrung General Grant's hand vigorously, and held it in his for some time, while he uttered in rapid words his congratulations and expressions of appreciation of the great task which had been accomplished since he and the general had parted in Washington. The group then went into the after-cabin. General Grant said: "I hope you are very well, Mr. President." "Yes, I am in very good health," Mr. Lincoln replied; "but I don't feel very comfortable after my trip last night on the bay. It was rough, and I was considerably shaken up. My stomach has not yet entirely recovered from the effects." An officer of the party now saw that an opportunity had arisen to make this scene the supreme moment of his life, in giving him a chance to soothe the digestive organs of the Chief Magistrate of the nation. He said: "Try a glass of champagne, Mr. President. That is always a certain cure for seasickness." Mr. Lincoln looked at him for a moment, his face lighting up with a smile, and then remarked: "No, my friend; I have seen too many fellows seasick ashore from drinking that very stuff." This was a knockdown for the officer, and in the laugh at his expense Mr. Lincoln and the general both joined heartily.

General Grant now said: "I know it would be a great satisfaction for the troops to have an opportunity of seeing you, Mr. President; and I am sure your presence among them would have a very gratifying effect. I can furnish you a good horse, and will be most happy to escort you to points of interest along the line." Mr. Lincoln replied: "Why, yes; I had fully intended to go out and take a look at the brave fellows who have fought their way down to Petersburg in this wonderful campaign, and I am ready to start at any time."

General Grant presented to Mr. Lincoln the officers of the staff who were present, and he had for each one a cordial greeting and a pleasant word. There was a kindliness in his tone and a hearty manner of expression which went far to captivate all who met him. The President soon stepped ashore, and after sitting awhile at head-quarters mounted the large bay horse "Cincinnati," while the general rode with him on "Jeff Davis." Three of us of the staff accompanied them, and the scenes encountered in visiting both Butler's and Meade's commands were most interesting. . . . The soldiers rapidly passed the word along the line that "Uncle Abe" had joined them, and cheers broke forth from all the commands, and enthusiastic shouts and even words of familiar greeting met him on all sides. After a while General Grant said: "Mr. President, let us ride on and see the colored troops, who behaved so handsomely in Smith's attack on the works in front of Petersburg last week." "Oh, yes," replied Mr. Lincoln; "I want to take a look at those boys. I read with the greatest delight the account given in Mr. [Charles A.] Dana's despatch to the Secretary of War of how gallantly they behaved. He [Dana, who was Assistant Secretary of War] said they took six out of the sixteen guns captured that day. I was opposed on nearly every side when I first favored the raising of colored regiments; but they have proved their efficiency, and I am glad they have kept pace with the white troops in the recent assaults. When we wanted every able-bodied man who could be spared to go to the front, and my opposers kept objecting to the negroes, I used to tell them that at such times it was just as well to be a little color-blind. I think, general, we can say of the black boys what a country fellow who was an old-time abolitionist in Illinois said when he went to the theatre in Chicago and saw [Edwin] Forrest playing *Othello*. He was not very well up in Shak[e]spe[a]re, and did n't know that the tragedian was a white man who had blacked up for the purpose. After the play was over the folks who had invited him to go to the show wanted to know what he thought of the actors, and he said: 'Waal, layin' aside all sectional prejudices and my partiality I may have for the race, derned if I don't think the nigger held his own with any on 'em.' " The Western dialogue employed in this story was perfect.

The camp of the colored troops of the Eighteenth Corps was soon reached, and a scene now occurred which defies description. They beheld for the first time the liberator of their race—the man who by a stroke of his pen had struck the shackles from the limbs of their fellow-bondmen and proclaimed liberty to the enslaved. Always impressionable, the enthusiasm of the blacks now knew no limits. They cheered, laughed, cried, sang hymns of praise, and shouted in their negro dialect, "God bress Massa Linkum!" "De Lord save Fader Abraham!" "De day ob jubilee am come, shuah." They crowded about him and fondled his horse; some of them kissed his hands, while others ran off crying in triumph to their comrades that they had touched his clothes. The President rode with bared head; the tears had started to his eyes, and his voice was so broken by emotion that he could scarcely articulate the words of thanks and congratulation which he tried to speak to the humble and devoted men through whose ranks he rode.

"Better Let It Alone This Time"

WEDNESDAY, JUNE 29, 1864

¶ *Lincoln had always had his troubles with Salmon P. Chase. But from the time of the "Pomeroy circular" until his final exit from the Treasury Department, "Salmon the Solemn" was "continually in hot water" with the President.[1] The rupture finally came over the appointment of the Assistant Treasurer at New York.*

John J. Cisco, the Assistant Treasurer at New York, resigned his office in June, after more than ten years of efficient service in that influential post. Chase demanded that Maunsell B. Field, Assistant Secretary of the Treasury, should succeed Cisco. The President refused to make the appointment "principally because of Senator [Edwin D.] Morgan's very firm opposition to it." Chase, who had determined to have his own way in the matter, tendered his resignation. Lincoln accepted.²

The evening of June 29th—Chase had resigned earlier that day— Ohio Governor John Brough arrived in Washington. On his way to the War Department, Brough ran into the President. Their conversation was recorded by Brough, who, on July 12, 1864, dictated a "third person" memorandum of the proceedings: ³

[T]he President, who seemed very glad to see him [Brough], . . . insisted on his stepping into the White House. "The truth is, Brough, I have a little matter on hand which concerns the State of Ohio"—[So, in they went the President continuing the sentence⁴] "and which I have a notion to tell you, though you must remember that it is not public until tomorrow." The Governor assured Mr. Lincoln that he never desired such confidences, as they usually proved ugly customers. As the President manifested some anxiety to communicate with him, the Governor enquired—"What is it, another Treasury embroglio?"

Mr. Lincoln. "Right—hit it at first, it is a Treasury embroglio."

Gov. Brough. "Well Mr. President, before going further, I have a question to ask, Is it beyond mediation?"

Mr. Lincoln.—"Well—[hesitating⁵] perhaps and perhaps not. What do you propose?"

Gov. Brough.—"First tell me the nature of the difficulty."

Mr. Lincoln.—"It is about Cisco."

Gov. Brough. "I do not wish to intrude, but for the interest of the country, and it being nothing more serious than that, if you will delay action until tomorrow morning when I can get the Ohio men together, I think it can be arranged."

Mr. Lincoln.—"But this is the third time he [Chase] has thrown this [a resignation] at me, and I do not think I am called on to continue to beg him to take it back, especially when the country would not go to destruction in consequence."

Gov. Brough.—"This is not simply a personal matter. The people will not understand it. They will insist that there is no longer any harmony in the Councils of the nation, and that the retiracy [retirement?] of the Sec'y of the Treasury is a sure indication that the bottom is about to fall out. Therefore, to save the Country from this backset, if you will give me time, I think Ohio can close the breach and the world be none the wiser."

Mr. Lincoln.—"I know you doctored the matter up once, but on the whole, Brough, I reckon you had better let it alone this time."

Gov. Brough.—["]Then I have but one more question to ask: Have you settled who is to be the Successor; or is the matter open to advisement?"

Mr. Lincoln.—"Well—[in a hesitating manner as before[6]]—not— certainly, and yet I have one in view;—but I think I wont tell you that."

Gov. Brough.—["]Then I will go and see Stanton."

Mr. Lincoln.—["]Remember, Brough, not a word of this to any one."

Gov. Brough.—"I shall respect the confidence."

"He Knows the Ropes"

FRIDAY, JULY 1, 1864

¶ *When Brough returned to the White House the next day (June 30th), Washington was agog with the news of Chase's resignation. Lincoln had nominated David Tod, ex-governor of Ohio, for the Treasury portfolio. The Senate Finance Committee was flabbergasted and requested the President to withdraw the nomination. While Lincoln pondered the issue, Tod telegraphed his inability to accept the post because of ill health.*

On July 1st, as Senator William Pitt Fessenden, chairman of the Senate Finance Committee, waited to see the President, Lincoln slipped John Hay a new nomination to be taken immediately to the Senate. Said Lincoln: "I have determined to appoint Fessenden himself." Said Hay: "Fessenden is in my room waiting to see you." Commanded the President: "Send him in & go at once to the Senate."

Fessenden's nomination met with universal approval and he was, despite his attempts to refuse the office, "instantly confirmed." Later that day, Hay noted in his Diary:[1]

The President says—"It is very singular, considering that this appointment of F.'s is so popular when made, that no one ever mentioned his name to me for that place. Thinking over the matter two or three points occurred to me. *First* he knows the ropes thoroughly: as Chairman of the Senate Committee on Finance he knows as much of this special subject as Mr. Chase. *2nd,* He is a man possessing a national reputation and the confidence of the country. 3d. he is a radical—without the petulent [*sic*] and vicious fretfulness of many radicals. On the other hand I considered the objections: the Vice President & Sec. Treasury coming from the same small state—though I thought little of that: then that Fessenden from the state of his health is of rather a quick & irritable temper: but in this respect he should be pleased with this incident; for, while for some time he has been running in rather a pocket of bad luck—such as the failure to renominate Mr. Hamlin which makes possible a contest between him & the V.P. the most popular man in Maine for the election which is now imminent—& the fact of his recent spat in the Senate where Trumbull told him his ill-temper had left him no friends—this thing has developed a sudden & very gratifying manifestation of good feeling in his appointment, his instant confirmation, the earnest entreaties of every body that he may accept & all that. It cannot but be very grateful to his feelings. This morning he came into this room just as you left it. He sat down & began to talk about other things. I could not help being amused by seeing him sitting there so unconscious and you on your way to the Capitol. He at last began to speak of this matter, rather supporting [Hugh] McCulloch for Secretary. I answered, 'Mr. Fessenden I have nominated you for that place. Mr. Hay has just taken the nomination to the Senate.' 'But it hasn't reached there—you must withdraw it—I cant accept.' 'If you decline' I replied 'you must do it in open day: for I shall not recall the nomination.' We talked about it for some time and he went away less decided in his refusal. I hope from the long delay, that he is making up his mind to accept. If he would only consent to accept & stay here and help me for a little while, I think he would be in no hurry to go." . . . [Fessenden ultimately accepted the post.]

The President says, what Chase ought to do is to help his successor through his installation as he professed himself willing to do in his letter to me: go home without making any fight and wait for a good thing hereafter, such as a vacancy on the Supreme Bench or some such matter.

"I Doubt the Authority"

TUESDAY, JULY 4, 1864

¶ *It was not much like the "old-fashioned" Independence Day in Washington; there was no formal attempt at celebration. The "tide of holiday makers who were out tended toward the Capitol as the only place where there was any excitement." Adjournment of Congress—slated for twelve noon—had been extended ten minutes. In the House, pages darted to and fro with messages and bills; government department heads "were buzzing among the members; lobbyists squeezed in upon the floor . . . and a general scene of disorder spread over the hall." At the other end of the Capitol sat President Lincoln, signing bills "with might and main." The radicals were in suspense. The Wade-Davis Reconstruction Bill had gone to Lincoln for signature. It called for the abolition of slavery in the states and provided that a seceded state might apply for readmission to the Union by a majority vote of its white citizens, excluding active rebels. This was in direct contradiction to Lincoln's ten per cent plan.*[1] *Would the President endorse this legislation? Sumner was intensely anxious; Boutwell feared the bill would be "pocketed."*

What took place in the President's room on this subject is described by John Hay:[2]

Chandler came in and asked if it was signed. "No." He said it would make a terrible record for us to fight if it were vetoed: the President talked to him a moment. He said, "Mr. Chandler, this bill was placed before me a few minutes before Congress adjourns. It is a matter of too much importance to be swallowed in that way." [Chandler replied:] "If it is vetoed it will damage us fearfully in the North West. It may not in Illinois, it will in Michigan and Ohio. The important point is that one prohibiting slavery in the reconstructed states."

Pres. "That is the point on which I doubt the authority of Congress to act."

Chandler. "It is no more than you have done yourself."

President. "I conceive that I may in an emergency do things on military grounds which cannot be done constitutionally by Congress."

Chandler. "Mr. President I cannot controvert y[ou]r position by argument, I can only say I deeply regret it."

Exit Chandler.

The President continued, "I do not see how any of us now can deny and contradict all we have always said, that congress has no constitutional power over slavery in the states." Mr. Fessenden, who had just come into the room, said "I agree with you there, sir. I even had my doubts as to the constitutional efficacy of your decree of emancipation, in such cases where it has not been carried into effect by the actual advance of the army."

Prest. ["]This bill and this position of these gentlemen seems to me to make the fatal admission (in asserting that the insurrectionary states are no longer in the Union) that States whenever they please may of their own motion dissolve their connection with the Union. Now we cannot survive that admission, I am convinced. If that be true I am not President, these gentlemen are not Congress. I have laboriously endeavored to avoid that question ever since it first began to be mooted & thus to avoid confusion and disturbance in our own counsels. It was to obviate this question that I earnestly favored the movement for an Amendment to the Constitution abolishing slavery, which passed the Senate and failed in the House. I thought it much better, if it were possible, to restore the Union without the necessity of a violent quarrel among its friends, as to whether certain states have been in or out of the Union during the war: a merely metaphysical question and one unnecessary to be forced into discussion."

Seward, Usher, and Fessenden seemed entirely in accord with this.

After we left the Capitol I said I did not think Chandler, man of the people and personally popular as he was had any definite comprehension of popular currents and influence—that he was out of the way now especially—that I did not think people would bolt their ticket on a question of metaphysics.

The Prest. answered, "If they choose to make a point upon this

I do not doubt that they can do harm. They have never been friendly to me & I don't know that this will make any special difference as to that. At all events, I must keep some consciousness of being somewhere near right: I must keep some standard of principle fixed within myself."

[On July 8th, Lincoln issued a proclamation explaining why he refused to sanction the Wade-Davis bill. On August 5th, Benjamin Wade and Henry Winter Davis blasted the President for his "pocket veto," charging it was "a blow at the friends of his Administration," against the "rights of humanity" and the "principles of Republican Government." There was no doubt, as an Albany politician had reported: "The radical portion of the Republican party" was "entirely *out* with Mr. Lincoln." [8]]

"The People with the Governing Power"
TUESDAY, JULY 19[?], 1864

¶ *An interesting view of President Lincoln is provided by a Canadian editor—probably Josiah Blackburn of the* London *Free Press, who visited Washington in the summer of 1864—which was reprinted in the American press:* [1]

The President's private room is just over the reception room, and is entered from a sort of square hall, about which there are many waiting rooms for persons seeking audiences with the President. Upon entering this room I saw persons walking to and fro in waiting. I at once placed in the hands of a messenger my card and letters (previously procured from friends in New York and Cincinnati), to deliver to the President, and with scarcely a moment's delay I was ushered into his presence, when he arose and stepped forward in a stooping position, extended his hand and shook mine kindly, but rather loosely, as if he was afraid of hurting it, remarking at the same time, "I am glad to see you sir; be seated." I replied, "I am a stranger to the Capital, and have sought an interview with you, Mr. President, and have been much pleased with the easy means of access."

President—"Yes, this ready means of access is, I may say, under our form of government, the only link or cord which connects the people with the governing power; and, however unprofitable much of it is, it must be kept up; as, for instance, a mother in a distant part, who has a son in the army who is regularly enlisted, has not served out his time, but has been as long as she thinks he ought to stay, will collect together all the little means she can to bring her here to entreat me to grant him his discharge. Of course, I cannot interfere, and can only see her and speak kindly to her. How far is your place from Detroit, sir?"

"About one hundred miles east from Detroit; we have no water communications, but have a very nice little inland city. I intend remaining in Washington for a few days; all seems stir and commotion here."

President—"Yes, there never was anything in history to equal this."

"Your position must indeed be responsible and trying, President."

"Yes, to think of it, it is very strange that I, a boy brought up in the woods, and seeing, as it were, but little of the world, should be drifted into the very apex of this great event."

"I read your proclamation of this morning calling for more men; it will, no doubt, be filled up." [Lincoln, on July 18th, called for 500,000 volunteers.]

President—"Yes, sir, it will be filled up."

I then arose, saying—"I thank you, Mr. President, for your kindness and courtesy."

President shakes hands again, and says: "I am most happy to have made your acquaintance."

These words are given exactly as expressed by the President, written down a few moments after they were uttered.

"Am I to Be the Mere Puppet of Power . . . ?"

SATURDAY, AUGUST 13 [?], 1864

¶ *During the dark days of August, Lincoln's defeat at the polls appeared certain. "The want of any decided military successes thus far, and the necessity of the new draft . . . has materially dis-*

couraged many of our friends, who are inclined to be a little weak-kneed, and croakers are talking everywhere about the impossibility of re-electing Mr. Lincoln 'unless something is done,'" Nicolay recorded. Farragut's important naval victory in Mobile Bay failed to stem the national despondency. A political movement was under way to dump Lincoln and nominate a new Presidential candidate in a September convention at Cincinnati. Conservative elements charged Lincoln with favoring the radicals. Republican extremists accused the President of being too conservative. The President was attacked for countenancing the Blairs. "Tens of thousands of men will be lost to you or will give a reluctant vote on account of the Blairs," Massachusetts' Senator Henry Wilson told the Chief Magistrate.[1] The radicals were in a tough mood; the clamor was for Cabinet changes.

One evening about mid-August, Thad Stevens tried to pressure Lincoln into dropping Montgomery Blair from the Cabinet. Simon Cameron and Colonel R. M. Hoe of New York were present at the interview. Years later, Hoe told Nicolay about this "noteworthy" meeting and the man who had been Lincoln's secretary took down the words in shorthand:[2]

Some preliminary business having been transacted, Mr. Stevens introduced the main topic of the evening:

"Mr. President," said he[,] "our Convention at Baltimore has nominated you again, and, not only that, but we are going to elect you. But the certainty of that will depend very much on the vote we can give you in P[ennsylvani]a in October; and in order that we may be able in our State to go to work with a good will we want you to make us a promise; namely that you will reorganize your Cabinet and leave Montgomery Blair out of it."

Mr. Stevens then went on to elaborate his reasons, and a running fire of criticism [and] of comment was entered upon between the three gentlemen gradually rising in warmth and interest, the whole interview lasting some two or three hours. As the discussion proceeded, Mr. Lincoln rose from his seat and walked up and down the room.

The issue being made up the President finally gave his answer, in substance as follows, towering up to his full height, and delivering his words with emphatic gestures, and intense earnestness of speech:

"Mr. Stevens, I am sorry to be compelled to deny your request to make such a promise. If I were even myself inclined to make it, I have no right to do so. What right have I to promise you to remove Mr. Blair, and not make a similar promise to any other gentleman of influence to remove any other member of my Cabinet whom he does not happen to like? The Republican party, wisely or unwisely has made me their nominee for President, without asking any such pledge at my hands. Is it proper that you should demand it, representing only a portion of that great party? Has it come to this that the voters of this country are asked to elect a man to be President —to be the Executive—to administer the government, and yet that this man is to have no will or direction of his own[?] Am I to be the mere puppet of power—to have my constitutional advisers selected for me beforehand, to be told I must do this or leave that undone? It would be degrading to my manhood to consent to any such bargain —I was about to say it is equally degrading to your manhood to ask it.

"I confess that I desire to be re-elected. God knows I do not want the labor and responsibility of the office for another four years. But I have the common pride of humanity to wish my past four years Administration endorsed; and besides I honestly believe that I can better serve the nation in its need and peril than any new man could possibly do. I want to finish this job of putting down the rebellion, and restoring peace and prosperity to the country. But I would have the courage to refuse the office rather than accept it on such disgraceful terms, as not really to be the President after I am elected."

"I Vote for Massa Lincoln"

FRIDAY, AUGUST 19, 1864

¶ *War Democrat Charles D. Robinson, editor of the* Advocate *in Green Bay, Wisconsin, had sustained Lincoln's "war policy" as "the only available method of putting down the rebellion." But now the editor was concerned. "The Niagara Falls 'Peace' movement was of no importance whatever, except that it resulted in bringing out your declaration, as we understand it, that no steps can be taken*

towards peace . . . unless accompanied with an abandonment of
slavery," he wrote the President on August 7th. "This puts the
whole war question on a new basis, and takes us War Democrats
clear off our feet. . . . If we sustain the war and war policy, does
it not demand the changing of our party politics?" Robinson was
not "finding fault" with Lincoln's policy. But he did want the Presi-
dent to suggest "some interpretation of it, as will . . . make it
tenable ground on which we War Democrats may stand." Robinson
said his friend, former Governor Alexander W. Randall, personally
would deliver the letter. Randall could vouch for Robinson's "entire
good faith." 1

Ten days later, Lincoln drafted a reply to Robinson, reconsidered
the matter and decided not to send it. On August 19th, Randall,
accompanied by Judge Joseph T. Mills, visited the President at the
Soldiers' Home. Lincoln talked about his war policy. That night,
Judge Mills wrote in his Diary *about it:* 2

The President was free & animated in conversation. I was astonished at his Elasticity of Spirits. Says Gov Randall, ["]why cant you
Mr P.[resident] seek some place of retirement for a few weeks.[?] You
would be reinvigorated—["] ["]Aye[,"] said the President, ["]3
weeks would do me no good—my thoughts[,] my solicitude for this
great country follow me where ever I go—I don't think it is personal
vanity, or ambition—but I cannot but feel that the weal or woe of
this great nation will be decided in the approaching canvas [*sic*]—
My own experience has proven to me, that there is no program intended by the democratic party but that will result in the dismember-
ment of the Union.["] [Said Randall: "]But Genl McClellan is in
favor of crushing out the rebellion, & he will probably be the Chicago
Candidate—["] [President Lincoln declared: "]The slightest acquaintance with arithmetic will prove to any man that the rebel armies
cannot be destroyed with democratic Strategy[.] It would sacrifice all
the white men of the north to do it— There are now between 1 & 200
thousand black men now in the service of the Union. These men will
be disbanded, returned to slavery & we will have to fight two nations
instead of one. I have tried it— You cannot conciliate [*sic*] the
South, when the mastery & control of millions of blacks makes them
sure of ultimate success— You cannot conciliate [*sic*] the South,
when you place yourself in such a position, that they see they can

achieve their independence. The war democrat depends upon conciliation. He must confine himself to that policy entirely— If he fights at all in such a war as this[,] he must economise [*sic*] life & use all the means which God & nature puts in his power— Abandon all the posts now garrisoned by black men[,] surrender all these advantages to the enemy, & we would be compelled to abandon the war in 3 weeks. We have to hold territory— Where are the war democrats to do it[?]The field was open to them to have enlisted & put down this rebellion by force of arms, by concilliation [*sic*], long before the present policy was inaugurated— There have been men who have proposed to me to return to Slavery the black warriors of Port Hudson & Olustee to their masters to conciliate the South. I should be damned in time & in eternity for so doing. The world shall know that I will keep my faith to friends & enemies, come what will. My enemies say I am now carrying on this war for the sole purpose of abolition. It is & will be carried on so long as I am President for the sole purpose of restoring the Union— But no human power can subdue this rebellion without using the Emancipation lever as I have done. Freedom has given us control of 200 000 able bodied men, born & raised on Southern soil. It will give us more yet. Just so much it has sub[t]racted from the Strength of our enemies, & instead of alienating the South from us, there are evidences of a fraternal feeling growing up between our own & rebel Soldiers— My enemies condemn my emancipation policy— Let them prove by the history of this war, that we can restore the Union without it—["] The President appeared to be not the pleasant joker I had expected to see, but a man of deep convictions & an unutterable yearning for the Success of the Union Cause. His voice was pleasant—his manner earnest & cordial. As I heard a vindication of his policy from his own lips, I could not but feel that his mind grew in Stature like his body, & that I stood in the presence of the great guiding intellect of the age, & that those huge Atlantian shoulders were fit to bear the weight of mightiest monarchies . . . C[o]m[missione]r. Dole then came in. We were about to retire, but he [the President] insisted on our remaining longer— Dismissing the present state of the country, he entertained us with reminiscences of the past—of the discussions between himself & Douglas[3]— He said he was accused of . . . joking— In his later Speeches, the Seriousness of the theme prevented him from using anecdotes. [Lincoln said: "]Mr.[Thomas L.] Harris[,] a democratic orator of Ill, once appealed to his audience in this way. If these republicans get into power, the darkies will be allowed to come to the polls & vote— Here comes forward a white man, & you ask him who will you vote for—[?] I will vote for S A Douglas.[4] Next comes up a sleek[,] pampered negro— Well Sambo, who do you vote for—[?] I vote for Massa Lincoln— Now[,] asked the orator, what do you think of that—[?] Some old farmer cried out, I think the darkey show[e]d a dam[ne]d sight of more Sense than the white man.["] It is such social tete a tetes among his friends that enables Mr Lincoln to endure mental toils & application that would crush any other man. The President now in full flow of Spirits, scattered his repartee in all directions. He took his Seat on the sofa by my side— Said I[, "]Mr President[,] I was in your reception room to day— It was dark— I suppose that clouds & darkness necessarily surround the Secrets of State— There in a corner I saw a man quietly reading[,] who possessed a remarkable physiognomy. I was rivetted [*sic*] to the spot. I stood & stared at him[.] He raised his flashing eyes & caught me in the act. I was compelled to speak— Said I, Are you the President—[?] No[,] replied the Stranger, I am Frederick Douglass. Now[,] Mr P.[resident] are you in favor of miscegenation[?"] [Replied the President: "]That's a democratic mode of producing good Union men, & I dont propose to infringe on the patent.["] We parted from his Excellency, with firmer purpose to sustain the government, at whose head there stands a man who combines in his person all that is valuable in *progress*[,] in conservatism—all that is hopeful in *progress*.

"I Will Manage My Side . . . My Way"

SATURDAY, OCTOBER 15, 1864

¶ *During the Presidential canvass, Lincoln was sharply criticized for his handling of a Democratic delegation from Tennessee. The delegates, claiming to represent the "loyal democrats of Tennessee," met the President to protest against an oath Governor Andrew Johnson required them to take to assure their eligibility to vote in the election. When the Tennesseeans left the White House, they complained bitterly of having been "cavalierly treated" by Mr.*

Lincoln. Later that day, John Lellyett of Nashville, a member of the delegation, wrote an account of the meeting for the press: [1]

I called upon the President to-day and presented and read to him the . . . protest. Having concluded, Mr. Lincoln responded:

"May I inquire how long it took you and the New York politicians to concoct that paper?"

I replied, "It was concocted in Nashville, without communication with any but Tennesseans. We communicated with citizens of Tennessee, outside of Nashville, but not with New-York politicians."

"I will answer," said Mr. Lincoln emphatically, "that *I expect to let the friends of George B. McClellan manage their side of this contest in their own way; and I will manage my side of it in* MY *way.*"

"May we ask an answer in writing," I suggested.

"Not now. Lay those papers down here. I will give no other answer now. I may or may not write something about this hereafter. I understand this. I know you intend to make a point of this. But go ahead, you have my answer."

"Your answer then is that you expect to let General McClellan's friends manage their side of this contest in their own way, and you will manage your side of it in your way?"

"Yes."

I then thanked the President for his courtesy in giving us a hearing at all, and took my leave.

Judge [Charles] Mason of this city [Washington, D. C.], was present at the interview, to whom I refer in regard to the correctness of this report. On stepping outside of the door of the executive mansion I immediately wrote down the President's emphatic response, and submitted it to Judge Mason and another gentleman who happened to be present, and they both pronounced it accurate.

"No Right to Seek Personal Political Favors"

TUESDAY, OCTOBER 18, 1864

¶ *Noah Brooks' October 19th dispatch to the* Sacramento Daily Union *illustrates another facet of Lincoln's attitude toward the Presidential campaign:* [1]

Yesterday a deputation of Hebrews from Chicago, New York, Philadelphia and Baltimore called upon the President to present him with an address, assuring him that their people, as a body, were in favor of his re-election. These men were chiefly priests [rabbis], and assured the President they had heretofore mingled in politics, and that the address presented had been read and adopted in their synagogues throughout the country. The President thanked them for their good wishes and promises, and reminded them that he was only the exponent of the wishes and opinions of a portion of the loyal States, and while he was President he had no right to seek personal political favors at the hands of any, but he believed that the support of the principles of the so-called Union party of the country, whoever might be its nominee, was a more effectual way of putting down this rebellion than the contrary course. The delegation departed, hugely pleased at their reception, and wonderfully surprised at the frank, simple way with which the President disposed of their address.

"Let Me Beg You Not to Try"

SATURDAY, OCTOBER 29, 1864

¶ *Early Saturday morning, October 29th, a deputation "of some ten or eleven persons" came before the President. Almost all the delegates were in the employ of a Baltimore "clothier and merchant tailor," who had been arrested for dealing with the rebels. Previous attempts to have the prisoner released had been fruitless. Now, this delegation was before Lincoln "to again beseech him to interfere in the case." An eyewitness to this encounter was a Washington correspondent of the* Rochester (N. Y.) Express, *whose report of the incident was reprinted in the* Sacramento Daily Union *on December 14, 1864:*

They [the delegates] made a very formidable display, asserting through their speaker, who introduced himself as "an humble tobacconist," but who evidently had had some experience as a speaker . . . that they were all good Union men; that they had even voted for Lincoln, and intended to do so again; consequently, they were entitled to a hearing, and that they were sure of the innocence of their employer. A good deal of eloquence was expended, but the President would not be moved. It was even asserted that this same merchant had given money—some hundreds of dollars—toward carrying on the war. At last the President spoke.

"Gentlemen," said he, "this Government is a big machine, even in times of peace; it is no small thing to keep it in good running order —but now, when added to the usual duties of my position, I have on my hands this great rebellion (which is to be put down), I have no time to waste. I have been visited, already, more than once by parties from Baltimore, urging my interference in this case. You protest that this man is innocent; then let him await his trial, when he can easily prove it."

"But," said the speaker, in behalf of his friend, "but we vote for you."

"Can't help it; it is not so essential that I have votes as that the rebellion be crushed. To what purpose is it that you vote for me; that you pay a small sum of money to soldiers, as a cover up, while you supply the rebels with goods or arms. I tell you, gentlemen, it will not do. Already has the War Department declared to me that it could not, and would not stand by me in this work of subduing the rebels, if every time they catch a rascal I let him loose. Gentlemen, I ain't going to do it."

"Well, but, your Excellency, I am a fighting man. I once paid three hundred dollars for knocking a man down."

The President drew himself back, and with much good nature said: "Let me beg you not to try that on me."

Then the speaker, in behalf of the accused, took another turn.

"Mr. President, even your enemies say you have much goodness of heart. Will you not parole this man, accepting bonds, which we will procure to any amount?"

But the President would not be moved. When appeals were made to his sympathy he said, with great decision:

"I will not listen."

"But, Mr. President, you can do this thing."

"Certainly I can, and I can end this war and let the rebels have their own way, but I'm not going to do it."

"For Aunty Sojourner Truth"
SATURDAY, OCTOBER 29, 1864

¶ *When the Baltimore delegation had left, the President welcomed
a tall, lean, black-skinned woman known as Sojourner Truth. She
had a faculty for attracting attention wherever she went. They used
to say that she nursed George Washington. But that was not true
although she had suckled many a white child. At best she admitted
to being over seventy.*

    *Having been sold three times on an auction block, she had
emerged from slavery to freedom. One night at a prayer meeting in
New York, she arose to declare that she was "Sojourner Truth" and
that she would follow the Lord's bidding to travel throughout the
land to spread the Truth!*

    *Harriet Beecher Stowe described her as embodying all the elements
of an African prophetess or sibyl. And wherever she preached—and
she spoke out boldly—large crowds flocked to listen to her.*

    *Sojourner Truth was an abolitionist leader who was no stranger
to Union army camps, primarily those in Michigan. She would come
to distribute gifts to soldiers and to offer bits of motherly advice.
Then she would move on, earning money for new gifts by lecturing
and singing.[1]*

    *In October 1864, when she was well over eighty, she left her
home in Battle Creek, Michigan, with the unalterable purpose of
seeing Abraham Lincoln before she died. During the interview,
the President proudly showed her a Bible given him by a group of
Maryland Negroes.*

    *After her meeting with President Lincoln, Sojourner Truth—her-
self illiterate—dictated to a friend the following account of her
visit with the Chief Executive:[2]*

It was about eight o'clock, A.M., when I called on the President.
Upon entering his reception-room we found about a dozen persons
in waiting, among them two colored women. I had quite a pleasant
time waiting until he was disengaged, and enjoyed his conversation
with others; he showed as much kindness and consideration to the
colored persons as to the whites,—if there was any difference, more.

One case was that of a colored woman, who was sick and likely to be turned out of her house on account of her inability to pay her rent. The President listened to her with much attention, and spoke to her with kindness and tenderness. He said he had given so much he could give no more, but told her where to go and get the money, and asked Mrs. C——, who accompanied me, to assist her, which she did.

The President was seated at his desk. Mrs. C. said to him: "This is Sojourner Truth, who has come all the way from Michigan to see you." He then arose, gave me his hand, made a bow, and said: "I am pleased to see you."

I said to him: "Mr. President, when you first took your seat I feared you would be torn to pieces, for I likened you unto Daniel, who was thrown into the lions' den; and if the lions did not tear you into pieces, I know that it would be God that had served you; and I said if He spared me I would see you before the four years expired, and He has done so, and now I am here to see you for myself."

He then congratulated me on my having been spared. Then I said: "I appreciate you, for you are the best President who has ever taken the seat." He replied thus: "I expect you have reference to my having emancipated the slaves in my proclamation. But," said he, mentioning the names of several of his predecessors, (and among them emphatically that of Washington,) "they were all just as good, and would have done just as I have done if the time had come. If the people over the river (pointing across the Potomac) had behaved themselves, I could not have done what I have; but they did not, and I was compelled to do these things." I then said: "I thank God that you were the instrument selected by Him and the people to do it."

He then showed me the Bible presented to him by the colored people of Baltimore. . . . After I had looked it over, I said to him: "This is beautiful indeed; the colored people have given this to the Head of the Government, and that Government once sanctioned laws that would not permit its people to learn enough to enable them to read this Book. And for what? Let them answer who can."

I must say, and I am proud to say, that I never was treated by any one with more kindness and cordiality than was shown me by the great and good man, Abraham Lincoln, by the grace of God President of the United States for four years more. He took my little book, and with the same hand that signed the death-warrant of slavery, he wrote as follows:—

"For Aunty Sojourner Truth,
"Oct. 29, 1864.   A. LINCOLN."

As I was taking my leave, he arose and took my hand, and said he would be pleased to have me call again. I felt that I was in the presence of a friend, and I now thank God from the bottom of my heart that I always advocated his cause, and have done it openly and boldly. I shall feel still more in duty bound to do so in time to come. May God assist me.

"In Carpet Slippers"
OCTOBER [?], 1864

¶ *George Borrett, an English barrister visiting America, had been "very anxious to get an introduction" to the President. One night, his desire was gratified. The daughter of George Harrington, Assistant Secreary of the Treasury, decided to take Borrett and his friends out to Soldiers' Home, where the Lincolns were staying.*

It was quite late when the party reached the President's summer residence, and the servant—"a buttonless buttons, apparently the sole domestic on the premises," according to Borrett—suggested that it was "rather late" for an interview with the President and his lady. However, Miss Harrington—"one of those strong-minded young ladies," Borrett thought—insisted upon seeing the Chief Magistrate. "We were ushered into a moderate-sized, neatly furnished drawing room, where we were told the President would see us immediately," Borrett recounted. He wrote home about his evening with the American President: [1]

We had sat there but a few minutes, when there entered through the folding doors the long, lanky, lath-like figure [of the President] . . . with hair ruffled, and eyes very sleepy, and—hear it, ye votaries of court etiquette!—feet enveloped in carpet slippers. We all rose somewhat confused by this abrupt introduction to the presence of the highest in the land, except, of course, the Secretary's daughter, who immediately offered her hand to the President, and in a few apt words explained who she was, and why she was there. Mr. Lincoln advanced to me and my fellow-travellers, shook each of us warmly by the hand, expressed his pleasure at seeing us, and told us to take seats and make ourselves comfortable. We did so, and were at home at once. All my uneasiness and awe vanished in a moment before the homely greeting of the President, and the genial smile which accompanied it; and had they not, a glance at one of the carpet slippers jogging up and down upon the knee of the other leg in the most delightful freedom of attitude, would have reassured me. . . .

The conversation was briskly kept up by the President. It began, naturally enough, with questions about our tour, and the invariable interrogation that every American puts to a stranger as to what he thinks of "our great country;" and then, after a passing allusion to the war, and a remark that we were seeing his country at an un-fortunate time, Mr. Lincoln turned to England, and its political aspect and constitution; and thence he went off, unasked, into a forci-bly drawn sketch of the constitution of the United States, and the ma-terial points of difference between the governments of the two coun-tries. . . . We had heard several [expositions on the American Con-stitution] before this, and began to get rather tired of them; but we were glad, of course, to listen to anything upon the matter from the highest authority in the land, especially as his commentary was very lucid and intelligent. Of course he asked what our trade was; and hearing that it was law, he launched off into some shrewd remarks about the legal systems of the two countries, and then talked of the landed tenures of England, and said we had some "queer things in the legal way" at home, of which he seemed to think "quit rents" as queer as any. And then he told us how, "in the State of Kentucky, where he was raised, they used to be troubled with the same mysteri-ous relics of feudalism, and titles got into such an almighty mess with these pettifoggin' incumbrances turnin' up at every fresh tradin' with the land, and no one knowin' how to get rid of 'em, as this here airth never saw;" and how he managed to relieve the titles, and made his first step to fame in doing so. It was a treat to hear him talk of his early life, with a certain quiet pride in his rise from the bottom of the ladder. . . .

The conversation next turned upon English poetry, the President saying that when we disturbed him he was deep in Pope. He seemed to be a great admirer of Pope, especially of his "Essay on Man;" going so far as to say that he thought it contained all the religious instruction which it was necessary for a man to know. Then he mused for a moment or two, and asked us if we could show him any finer lines than those ending, as he quoted them without hesitation—

> "All nature is but art, unknown to thee;
> All chance, direction, which thou canst not see;
> All discord, harmony not understood;
> All partial evil, universal good:
> And, spite of pride, in erring treason's spite,
> One truth is clear, whatever is, is right."

And here, on getting to the last few words, his instinctive humor broke out, for to an extremely flat remark of mine upon the beauty of the verses he had repeated, he replied with a smile—

"Yes, that's a convenient line, too, the last one. You see, a man may turn it, and say, 'Well, if whatever *is* is right, why, then, whatever *isn't* must be wrong.' "

And then he went off into a broad laugh, and we laughed, too—not so much at the joke, which we thought decidedly poor, as at the way in which he delivered himself of it. The laugh ended, and I rose to go. I had heard the President make a joke—a very mild one, it is true—but I felt that the second great object of my visit to the country (Niagara being my first) had been achieved. . . . The Secretary's daughter, after . . . [a] hint at her regret that we could not have the chance of seeing Mrs. Lincoln—to which the President replied, "I guess we shall not get to see Mrs. Lincoln down here again to-night"—arose and thanked him for his courtesy in according us so pleasant an interview; and the President, in return, assured her and us that the meeting had been equally agreeable to himself; and thanking us cordially for coming to see him, gave us each a hearty grip of the hand—it was much more than a shake—and we withdrew.

Chapter Eleven

"IT MADE MY HEART JUMP"

FOR three years the Armies of the Potomac and Northern Virginia had fought desperate battles "without materially changing the vantage ground of each." To bolster Southern morale, the Confederacy embarked upon a carefully angled propaganda campaign, which Grant analyzed in these terms:

"The Southern press and people, with more shrewdness than was displayed in the North, finding that they had failed to capture Washington and march on to New York, as they had boasted they would do, assumed that they only defended their capital and Southern territory. Hence, Antietam, Gettysburg and all the other battles that had been fought, were by them set down as failures on our part, and victories for them. Their army believed this. It produced a *morale* which could only be overcome by desperate and continuous hard fighting. The battles of the Wilderness, Spotsylvania, North Anna, and Cold Harbor, bloody and terrible as they were on our side, were even more damaging to the enemy, and so crippled him as to make him wary ever after of taking the offensive." [1]

Before Petersburg and Richmond, Grant's strategy was to hammer continuously against the rebels and their resources "until by mere attrition, if no other way," the enemy was pounded into submission. Grant had his orders from Lincoln: "Hold on with bull-dog gripe [*sic*], and chew & choke, as much as possible." [2]

This was not a campaign to be punctuated by spectacular victories to elevate Northern spirits. And yet, this was a time when victories

350

were needed earnestly for Republican success at the polls. Daniel S. Dickinson summed things up in August 1864: "The war has been protracted beyond popular expectation. Men and money have been given freely. The helm has not been held with a firm and steady grasp, and there is a cry of change, which, no matter whether wise or ill-founded, should be both heard and heeded." [3]

Henry J. Raymond, chariman of the Republican National Committee, believed the people feared "that we are not to have peace in any event under this Administration until slavery is abandoned." Lincoln should send a peace commission to Jefferson Davis, the New Yorker proposed. Raymond was certain Davis would reject the olive branch, but reasoned that this rejection would "unite the North as nothing since the firing on Fort Sumter." Lincoln, however, frowned upon this plan; said it would be "utter ruination." [4]

Suddenly the situation changed. Immediately after the Democratic National Convention came news from General Sherman: "Atlanta is ours and fairly won." The North went "wild" with joy. The Union occupation of Atlanta brought the significance of Farragut's Mobile Bay victories into proper focus. Seward announced: "Sherman and Farragut have knocked the bottom out of the Chicago nominations." And politicians echoed: "Atlanta has turned the tide and it is running in his [Lincoln's] favor." On October 19th, following upon the heels of Union military gains in Alabama and Georgia, came Philip Sheridan's defeat of Jubal Early—"with great slaughter"—at Cedar Creek, Virginia, ending any further rebel attempt to invade the North through the Shenandoah Valley.[5]

The Lincoln band wagon began rolling again and his critics and opponents made haste to clamber aboard. The conspiracy to supersede Lincoln had collapsed. The Lincoln men mobilized their resources to vanquish the Democrats; patronage and government contract were bartered for votes. It was as James Gordon Bennett had foreseen it in August:

"Whatever they say now, we venture to predict that Wade and his tail; and Wendell Phillips and his tail; and Weed, Barney, Chase and their tails; and Winter Davis, Raymond, Opdyke and Forney who have no tails; will all make tracks for Old Abe's plantation, and will soon be found crowing and blowing, and vowing and writhing, and swearing and stumping . . . declaring that he and he alone, is the hope of the nation, the bugaboo of Jeff Davis, the first of Conservatives, the best of Abolitionists, the purest of patriots, the most gullible of mankind, the easiest President to manage, and the person especially predestined and foreordained by Providence to carry on the war, free the niggers, and give all the faithful a fair share of the spoils." [6]

On September 21st, Frémont withdrew from the Presidential race. He had done so, he said, "not to aid in the triumph of Mr. Lincoln, but to do my part towards preventing the election of the Democratic candidate." The Pathfinder still maintained that Lincoln's Administration was "politically, militarily, and financially a failure," noting that "its necessary continuance is a cause of regret for the country." [7]

Two days later, Montgomery Blair resigned from the Cabinet at Lincoln's request and was succeeded by former Governor William Dennison of Ohio. There was talk that "the retirement of Mr. Blair from the Cabinet was one of the conditions insisted upon by the Chase party as part of the price to be paid for the return of that faction to the support of Mr. Lincoln." [8] In later years, Zachariah Chandler claimed it was part of a deal by which Frémont's withdrawal from the Presidential race could be assured. At any rate, it helped clear the political air within Republican ranks and Theodore Tilton, editor of the *New York Independent,* told his radical friend Anna E. Dickinson: "I was opposed to Mr. Lincoln's nomination but now it becomes the duty of all Unionists to present a united front." [9]

Lincoln and McClellan, following custom, did not campaign publicly. However, the President did manage to make his political points in his little responses to serenades, especially to the soldiers. That soldier vote was vital to Republican pluralities. Its significance was demonstrated in the fall elections when the Republicans emerged victorious. Whenever he appeared before soldiers, Lincoln remarked, he felt "tempted" to talk to them about the nature of the struggle. And he did. It was "an attempt on the one hand to overwhelm and destroy the national existence, while, on our part, we are striving to maintain the government and institutions of our fathers, to enjoy them ourselves, and transmit them to our children and our children's children forever." He told an Ohio regiment: "To do this the constitutional administration of our government must be sustained, and I beg of you not to allow your minds or your hearts to be diverted from the support of all necessary measures for that purpose, by any miserable picayune arguments addressed to your pockets, or inflammatory appeals made to your passions or your prejudices." [10]

Lincoln was uneasy about the results of the Presidential election. But in October, Republican politicians were confident. Chase wrote Senator John Sherman of Ohio: "There is not, now, the slightest uncertainty about the re-election of Mr. Lincoln. The only question is, by what popular and what electoral majority." [11]

The popular vote cast in 36 states on November 8th was 4,015,902. Lincoln received 2,213,665 and McClellan 1,802,237. In the Electoral College, 212 votes went to Lincoln and 21 to McClellan. The President carried every state in the Union except Delaware, Kentucky and New Jersey. His, too, was an overwhelming "soldier vote." Although a number of ballots arrived too late to be counted, those admitted gave Lincoln 116,887 and McClellan 33,748.[12]

Lincoln did not exult openly over his political opponents. "While I am deeply sensible to the high compliment of a re-election . . . it adds nothing to my satisfaction that any other man may be disappointed or pained by the result," he said to a group of serenaders. "May I ask those who have not differed with me, to join with me, in this same spirit towards those who have?" The election, he believed, had done the country good: "It has demonstrated that a people's government can sustain a national election, in the midst of a great civil war. Until now it has not been known to the world that this was a possibility." [13]

The political campaign ended, the national attention focused upon military developments. On November 16th—two weeks before Schofield thrashed his classmate Confederate General John B. Hood, at Franklin, Tennessee—Sherman, heading an army of 60,000, left Atlanta on his "march to the sea." That 300-mile march "directly through the insurgent region" Lincoln considered the "most remarkable feature in the military operations of the year." [14] On December 10th, after a ravaging march through Georgia, Sherman invested Savannah. Six days later, General George H. Thomas defeated Hood at Nashville.

On Christmas day, "the sleeping works of Washington was aroused at an early hour . . . by the thunders of one hundred guns, fired by order of the War Department." The occasion was Lincoln's receipt of Sherman's message: "I beg to present you as a Christmas gift the city of Savannah." [15]

354 CONVERSATIONS WITH LINCOLN

The rebellion appeared to be hurtling toward the finale. The new year sent the senior Blair to Richmond on peace missions. Blair returned with a letter from Jefferson Davis in which the Confederate leader averred his readiness to send a peace commission to the North or "to receive a commission if the U. S. Gov't. shall choose to send one." [16] This paved the way for the Hampton Roads Conference, in which Lincoln and Seward met with Confederate emissaries. When the rebels insisted upon Northern recognition of Confederate independence, the conference became a fruitless endeavor.

Of historic importance was the passage of the resolution calling for approval of a Thirteenth Amendment to the Constitution, abolishing slavery throughout the land. On April 8, 1864, the proposed amendment had passed the Senate but failed to secure the necessary two-thirds vote in the House. In the new Congressional session, the House again took up the measure. The "voice of the people" had sanctioned the Baltimore platform, which had called for such an amendment. It was, as Lincoln declared, "only a question of *time* as to when the proposed amendment will go to the States for their action." [17] After a good deal of political manipulation, the measure finally passed the House amid great jubilation on January 31st. "The cheering in the hall and densely packed galleries exceeded anything I ever saw before and beggared description," Indiana Congressman George W. Julian wrote in his *Journal*. "Members joined in the shouting and kept it up for some minutes. Some embraced one another, others wept like children. . . . I have felt, ever since the vote, as if I were in a new country." By the time Lincoln was inaugurated on March 4th for his second term, eighteen states had ratified the amendment.[18]

Peace was on the horizon as Lincoln spoke his Inaugural Address. Briefly, he covered the last four years of "this terrible war." But what he focused on was the end of bloodshed:

"With malice toward none; with charity for all; with firmness in the right, as God gives us to see the right, let us strive on to finish the work we are in; to bind up the nation's wounds; to care for him who shall have borne the battle, and for his widow, and his orphan— to do all which may achieve and cherish a just, and a lasting peace, among ourselves, and with all nations." [19]

Rain clouds had obscured the inauguration ceremonies. But just as the President stepped forward to take the oath, the sun "burst forth in splendor." Afterwards, Lincoln said to Noah Brooks: "Did you notice that sunburst? It made my heart jump." [20]

"So Goes the Union, They Say"

TUESDAY, NOVEMBER 8, 1864

¶ *Election day in Washington was dull, gloomy and rainy. The White House was virtually deserted. Stanton was ill with chills and fever; Seward, Usher and Dennison were in their home towns, "voting like honest citizens." Fessenden was "shut up with New York financiers." Left to "run the machine" were Secretary of the Navy Welles and Attorney General Bates. Noah Brooks and John Hay wrote down Lincoln's talk on that fateful November 8th. Brooks begins our narrative:* [1]

About noon I called on President Lincoln, and to my surprise found him entirely alone. . . . Lincoln took no pains to conceal his anxious interest in the result of the election then going on all over the country, and said: "I am just enough of a politician to know that there was not much doubt about the result of the Baltimore convention; but about this thing I am very far from being certain. I wish I were certain." I spent nearly all the afternoon with the President, who apparently found it difficult to put his mind on any of the routine work of his office, and entreated me to stay with him. In the course of the afternoon he told an amusing story about a pet turkey of his boy "Tad." It appears that Jack, the turkey, whose life had been spared the year before at Tad's earnest request, had mingled with the "Bucktail" soldiers from Pennsylvania, quartered in the grounds on the river front of the White House. The soldiers were voting under the direction of a commission sent on from their State, as was the custom in several States of the Union, and Tad, bursting into his father's office, had besought the President to come to the window and see the soldiers who were "voting for Lincoln and Johnson." Noticing the turkey regarding the proceedings with evident interest, Lincoln asked the lad what business the turkey had stalking about the polls in that way. "Does he vote?" "No," was the quick reply of the boy; "he is not of age." The good President dearly loved the boy, and for days thereafter he took pride in relating this anecdote illustrative of Tad's quick-wittedness.

[Hay recorded in his *Diary:*]

I was talking with him to-day. He said "It is a little singular that I who am not a vindictive man, should have always been before the people for election in canvasses marked for their bitterness: always but once: When I came to Congress it was a quiet time: But always besides that the contests in which I have been prominent have been *marked* with great rancor."

At noon [General Benjamin F.] Butler sent a despatch saying, "The quietest city ever seen."

Butler was sent to New York by Stanton [to maintain order during the election]. The President had nothing to do with it. . . .

[Henry W.] Hoffman sent a very cheering despatch giving a rose-coloured estimate of the forenoon's voting in Baltimore. "I shall be glad if that holds," said the President "because I had rather feared that in the increased vote over that on the Constitution [Maryland's vote for an anti-slavery Constitution on October 13th], the increase would rather be against us."

[Brooks picks up our story here. We quote from his "Letter from Washington," written for the *Sacramento Daily Union* three days after the election:]

The first gun came from Indiana, Indianapolis sending word about half-past six in the evening that a gain of fifteen hundred in that city [over Governor Morton's plurality in October] had been made for Lincoln. At seven o'clock, accompanied only by a friend [i.e., Brooks; Hay also accompanied Lincoln], the President went over to the War Department to hear the telegraphic dispatches, as they brought in the returns, but it was nearly nine o'clock before anything definite came in, and then Baltimore sent up her splendid majority of ten thousand plus. The President only smiled good naturedly and said that was a fair beginning. Next Massachusetts sent word that she was good for 75,000 majority (since much increased), and hard upon her came glorious old Pennsylvania's, Forney telegraphing that the State was sure for Lincoln. "As goes Pennsylvania, so goes the Union, they say," remarked Father Abraham, and he looked solemn, as he seemed to see another term of office looming before him. Then there was a lull, and nothing heard from New York, the chosen battle

ground of the Democracy, about which all were so anxious. New
Jersey broke the calm by announcing a gain of one Congressman for
the Union, but with a fair prospect of the State going for McClellan;
then the President had to tell a story about the successful New
Jersey Union Congressman, Dr. [W. A.] Newell, a family friend of
the Lincolns, which was introduced by a dispatch from New York
city, claiming the State by 10,000. "I don't believe that," remarked
the incredulous Chief Magistrate, and when Greeley telegraphed at
midnight that we should have the State by about four thousand,
he thought that more reasonable.

[Hay relates:]

[Major Thomas T.] Eckert came in shaking the rain from his
cloak, with trousers very disreputably muddy. We sternly demanded
an explanation. He had slipped he said & tumbled prone, crossing
the street. He had done it watching a fellow-being ahead and chuck-
ling at his uncertain footing. Which reminded the Tycoon, of course.
The President said "For such an awkward fellow, I am pretty sure-
footed. It used to take a pretty dextrous man to throw me. I remember, the evening of the day in 1858, that decided the contest for the
Senate between Mr. Douglas and myself, was something like this,
dark, rainy & gloomy. I had been reading the returns, and had
ascertained that we had lost the Legislature and started to go home.
The path had been worn hog-backed & was slippery. My foot slipped
from under me, knocking the other one out of the way, but I recovered myself & lit square: and I said to myself, *'It's a slip and not
a fall.'* "

The President sent over the first fruits to Mrs. Lincoln. He said
"She is more anxious than I."

We went into the Secretary's room. Mr. Welles and Fox soon
came in. They were especially happy over the election of [Alexander
H.] Rice [chairman of the Naval Affairs Committee] regarding it as
a great triumph for the Navy Department. Says Fox "There are two
fellows that have been especially malignant to us, and retribution has
come upon them both, [John P.] Hale and Winter Davis." **"You**
have more of that feeling of personal resentment than I," said
Lincoln. "Perhaps I may have too little of it, but I never thought it
paid. A man has not time to spend half his life in quarrels. If any
man ceases to attack me, I never remember the past against him.
It has seemed to me recently that Winter Davis was growing more

sensible to his own true interests and has ceased wasting his time by attacking me. I hope for his own good he has. He has been very malicious against me but has only injured himself by it. His conduct has been very strange to me. I came here, his friend, wishing to continue so. I had heard nothing but good of him; he was the cousin of my intimate friend Judge Davis. But he had scarcely been elected when I began to learn of his attacking me on all possible occasions. It is very much the same with [Congressman John] Hickman [of Pennsylvania]. I was much disappointed that he failed to be my friend. But my greatest disappointment of all has been with [Senator James W.] Grimes [of Iowa]. Before I came here, I certainly expected to rely upon Grimes more than any other one man in the Senate. I like him very much. He is a great strong fellow. He is a valuable friend, a dangerous enemy. He carries too many guns not [to] be respected in any point of view. But he got wrong against me, I do not clearly know how, and has always been cool and almost hostile to me. I am glad he has always been the friend of the Navy and generally of the Administration.". . .

Towards midnight we had supper, provided by Eckert. The President went awkwardly and hospitably to work shovelling out the fried oysters. He was most agreeable and genial all the evening in fact. Fox was abusing the coffee for being so hot—saying quaintly, it kept hot all the way down to the bottom of the cup as a piece of ice staid cold till you finished eating it.

"Before My Own Conscience"

FRIDAY, NOVEMBER 11, 1864

¶ *On November 11th, John Hay told his* Diary:[1]

At the meeting of the Cabinet today, the President took out a paper from his desk and said, "Gentlemen do you remember last summer I asked you all to sign your names to the back of a paper of which I did not show you the inside? This is it. Now, Mr. Hay, see if you can get this open without tearing it?" He had pasted it up in so singular [a] style that it required some cutting to get it open. He then read as follows:

EXECUTIVE MANSION
WASHINGTON Aug. 23, 1864

This morning, as for some days past, it seems exceedingly probable that this Administration will not be re elected. Then it will be my duty to so cooperate with the President elect, as to save the Union between the election and the inauguration; as he will have secured his election on such ground that he cannot possibly save it afterwards.

A LINCOLN

This was indorsed

William H. Seward
W. P. Fessenden
Edwin M Stanton
Gideon Welles
Edwd. Bates
M Blair
J P Usher

August 23, 1864.

The President said "You will remember that this was written at a time (6 days before the Chicago nominating Convention) when as yet we had no adversary, and seemed to have no friends. I then solemnly resolved on the course of action indicated above. I resolved, in case of the election of General McClellan being certain that he would be the candidate, that I would see him and talk matters over with him. I would say, 'General, the election has demonstrated that you are stronger, have more influence with the American people than I. Now let us together, you with your influence and I with all the executive power of the Government, try to save the country. You raise as many troops as you possibly can for this final trial, and I will devote all my energies to assisting and finishing the war.' "

Seward said, "And the General would answer you *'Yes, Yes;'* and the next day when you saw him again & pressed these views upon him, he would say, 'Yes, Yes' & so on forever and would have done nothing at all."

"At least" added Lincoln "I should have done my duty and have stood clear before my own *conscience.*"

"If All the Rest Oppose"
MID-NOVEMBER 1864

¶ *The death of Roger B. Taney on October 12th had touched off a scramble for the Chief Justiceship of the United States. There were numerous candidates: Chase, Montgomery Blair, Bates, Supreme Court Justices David Davis and Noah B. Swayne, among others. Hay said Lincoln, from the beginning, had determined to be "shut pan" about the appointment. Brooks believed "the President never desired to appoint any other man than Chase."* [1] *The pressure was on the President to make his choice. Mary Lincoln complained to Francis P. Blair, Sr.: "Chase and his friends are besieging my Husband for the Chief-Justiceship. I wish you could prevent them." The senior Blair thought he would be acceding to Mary's request if he went to see the President to urge Montgomery for the place. Francis P. wrote Governor John A. Andrew of Massachusetts a "confidential" letter about the interview:* [2]

On "this hint I spoke," went up to the office and told the President that if he would make one of his Ex-Cabinet men a Judge, I thought Montgomery was his man, that he had been tried as a Judge and not found wanting, that his practice in the West had made him conversant with our land law, Spanish law, as well as the common and civil law in which his university studies had grounded him, that his practice in the Supreme Court brought him into the circle of commercial and constitutional questions. That, besides on political issues he sustained him [the President] in every thing, on the proclamation he had been quoted even by Sumner as authority to prove that it put the emancipation of the Slaves beyond the reach of Judicial or legislative power, State or national. This was the vital question for the races and the Government. Then when Chase and every other member of Cabinet declined to make war for Sumter,[3] Montgomery stood by him declaring it betrayal to surrender it without defence; and held his resignation in his pocket to hand him, if overruled. Chase was ready to let . . . the Union go, give half the continent to Slavery, resign a wronged race to eternal bondage, and sacrifice our whole cause to rebellion to promote his ambition to rule in the North.

Lincoln told me he must soon act in the matter but would not, in advance, commit himself. Adverting to his wishes in the matter, he said those of others must be consulted. His idea was forcibly expressed in another good thing. "Although I may be stronger as an authority yet if all the rest oppose, I must give way. Old Hickory who had as much iron in his neck as any body, did so some times. If the strongest horse in the team *would* go ahead, he *cannot, if all the rest hold back."* I replied to these delphic hints, "I dislike[,] Mr. President[,] to trouble you with the importunities of friends to show that they would give me their support. It might not be satisfactory to you either." He said "I would not consider the trouble. It would be satisfactory if I were not called on to direct the course you propose." From the tenor and manner of his remarks I infer that he is well disposed to appoint Montgomery.

"A Very Excellent Judge"

TUESDAY, DECEMBER 6, 1864

¶ *Senator LaFayette S. Foster of Connecticut remembered the day Chase was nominated and confirmed as Chief Justice. In 1878, Foster told Nicolay:* [1]

[B]eing at the White House, and saying to the President[:]
"Mr. President you sent us up a Chief Justice today, whom we confirmed at once. There have been so many contradictory reports and rumors that we had begun to have some doubts and anxieties on the subject.["]
Mr. Lincoln replied:
"Mr. Chase will make a very excellent judge if he devotes himself exclusively to the duties of his office, and dont meddle with politics.
"But if he keeps on with the notion that he is destined to be President of the United States, and which in my judgment he will never be, he will never acquire that fame and influence as a Chief Justice which he would otherwise certainly attain."

"The King's Cure-All for All Evils"

WEDNESDAY, DECEMBER 28[?], 1864

¶ *On January 31, 1865, the House—by a vote of 119 to 56—passed a Constitutional amendment prohibiting involuntary servitude, except for crime, throughout the United States. To Lincoln, the measure was "a very fitting, if not an indispensable adjunct to the winding up of this great difficulty." The Emancipation Proclamation fell short "of what the constitutional amendment will do when finally consummated," he maintained. It would be "the king's cure-all for all evils."* [1]

It was a hard pull to swing the required two-thirds majority in the House and Lincoln personally took a hand in the political maneuverings. He was a hardheaded, practical politician. He had to be in order to perpetuate himself and his party in power. "He handled and moved men remotely as we do pieces upon a chessboard," Leonard Swett remembered. He was "a trimmer, and such a trimmer the world has never seen . . . yet Lincoln never trimmed in principles, it was only in his conduct with men." He used patronage to "feed the hunger" of political factions. And when he set about procuring approval of the Thirteenth Amendment, he resorted "to almost any means" to achieve for "that down-trodden race such a boon." [2]

Lincoln began lobbying for the amendment in December. He called House members to the White House for conferences and apparently made a number of deals. James S. Rollins of Missouri was among those who answered Lincoln's summons. After the war, Rollins wrote: [3]

I was prompt in calling upon him and found him alone in his office. He received me in the most cordial manner, and said in his usual familiar way: "Rollins, I have been wanting to talk to you for sometime about the thirteenth amendment proposed to the Constitution of the United States, which will have to be voted on now, before a great while." I said: "Well, I am here, and ready to talk upon that subject." He said: "You and I were old whigs, both of us followers of that great statesman, Henry Clay, and I tell you I never had an opinion upon the subject of slavery in my life that I did not get from him. I am very anxious that the war should be brought to a close at the earliest possible date, and I don't believe this can be accomplished as long as those fellows down South can rely upon the border states to help them; but if the members from the border states would unite, at least enough of them to pass the thirteenth amendment to the Constitution, they would soon see that they could not expect much help from that quarter, and be willing to give up their opposition and quit their war upon the government; this is my chief hope and main reliance to bring the war to a speedy close, and I have sent for you as an old whig friend to come and see me, that I might make an appeal to you to vote for this amendment. It is going to be very close, a few votes one way or the other will decide it."

To this I responded: "Mr. President, so far as I am concerned you need not have sent for me to ascertain my views on this subject, for although I represent perhaps the strongest slave district in Missouri, and have the misfortune to be one of the largest slaveowners in the county where I reside, I had already determined to vote for the thirteenth amendment." He arose from his chair, and grasping me by the hand, gave it a hearty shake, and said: "I am most delighted to hear that."

He asked me how many more of the Missouri delegates in the House would vote for it. I said I could not tell; the republicans of course would; General [Benjamin] Loan, Mr. [Henry T.] Blow, Mr. [Sempronius H.] Boyd, and Colonel [Joseph W.] McClurg. He said: "Won't General [Thomas L.] Price vote for it? He is a good Union man." I said I could not answer. "Well, what about Governor [Austin A.] King?" I told him I did not know. He then asked about Judges [William A.] Hall and [Elijah H.] Norton. I said they would both vote against it, I thought.

"Well," he said, "are you on good terms with Price and King?" I responded in the affirmative, and that I was on easy terms with the entire delegation. He then asked me if I could not talk with those who might be persuaded to vote for the amendment, and report to him as soon as I could find out what the prospect was. I answered that I would do so with pleasure, and remarked at the same time, that when I was a young man, in 1848, I was the whig competitor of King for Governor of Missouri and as he beat me very badly, I thought now he should pay me back by voting as I desired him on this important question. I promised the President I would talk to this gentleman upon the subject. He said: "I would like you to talk to all the border state men whom you can approach properly, and tell them of my anxiety to have the measure pass; and let me know the prospect of the border state vote," which I promised to do. He again said: "The passage of this amendment will clinch the whole subject; it will bring the war, I have no doubt, rapidly to a close."

"It Was Only a Good Idea"

SUNDAY, JANUARY 15, 1865

¶ *On Sunday, January 15th, death claimed Edward Everett, the celebrated orator and statesman. Lincoln subsequently referred to Everett's passing as "a public loss," but that night, privately, the President voiced a different opinion. Noah Brooks, who was with Lincoln shortly after the news was received at the White House, recalled the incident in 1878:* [1]

[The] conversation naturally fell upon that topic [Everett's death]. Lincoln said, "Now, you are a loyal New Englander—loyal to New England—what great work of Everett's do you remember?" I was forced to say that I could not recall any. The President persisted and wanted to know if I could not recollect any great speech. Not receiving satisfaction, he said, looking around the room in his half-comical fashion, as if afraid of being overheard, "Now, do you know, I think Edward Everett was very much overrated. He hasn't left any enduring monument. But there was one speech in which, addressing a statue of John Adams and picture of Washington, in Faneuil Hall, Boston, he apostrophied them and said, 'Teach us the love of liberty protected by law!' That was very fine, it seems to me. Still, it was only a good idea, introduced by noble language."

Continuing his discussion of Everett, he referred to his celebrated address on Washington, which was delivered through the South, as if in the hope that the rising storm of the rebellion might be quelled by this oratorical oil on the waters. Lincoln recalled a story told of

Everett's manner. It was necessary, in his Washington oration, to relate an anecdote accompanied by the jingle of coin in the lecturer's pocket. This was done at each of the five hundred repetitions of the address, in the same manner, and with unvarying accuracy. When gold and silver disappeared from circulation, Mr. Everett procured and kept for this purpose a few coins with which, and a bunch of keys, the usual effect was produced. "And I am told," added Lincoln, "that whenever Mr. Everett delivered that lecture, he took along those things. They were what, I believe, the theatrical people would call his 'properties.' "

While this talk was going on, the cards of Congressman [Samuel] Hooper [of Massachusetts] and Professor [Louis] Agassiz [the distinguished scientist] were brought in by a servant.

[In his "Personal Recollections of Abraham Lincoln," published in 1865, Brooks reports on the Hooper-Agassiz visit to the White House:²]

The President had never met Agassiz at that time, I believe, and said, "I would like to talk with that man; he is a good man, I do believe; don't you think so?" But one answer could be returned to the query, and soon after the visitors were shown in, the President first whispering, "Now sit still and see what we can pick up that's new." To my surprise, however, no questions were asked about the Old Silurian, the Glacian Theory, or the Great Snow-storm, but, introductions being over, the President said: "I never knew how to properly pronounce your name; won't you give me a little lesson at that, please?" Then he asked if it were of French or Swiss derivation, to which the Professor replied that it was partly of each. That led to a discussion of different languages, the President speaking of several words in different languages which had the same root as similar words in our own tongue; then he illustrated that by one or two anecdotes, one of which he borrowed from Hood's "Up the Rhine." But he soon returned to his gentle cross-examination of Agassiz, and found out how the Professor studied, how he composed, and how he delivered his lectures; how he found different tastes in his audiences in different portions of the country. When afterward asked why he put such questions to his learned visitor he said, "Why, what we got from him isn't printed in the books; the other things are."

At this interview, it may be remarked in passing, the President said that many years ago, when the custom of lecture-going was more common than since, he was induced to try his hand at composing a literary lecture—something which he thought entirely out of his line. The subject, he said, was not defined, but his purpose was to analyze inventions and discoveries—"to get at the bottom of things" —and to show when, where, how, and why such things were invented or discovered; and, so far as possible, to find out where the first mention is made of some of our common things. The Bible, he said, he found to be the richest store-house for such knowledge; and he then gave one or two illustrations, which were new to his hearers.[8]

[In his 1878 narrative, Brooks says:]

Agassiz begged that Lincoln would finish the lecture, sometime. Lincoln replied that he had the manuscript somewhere in his papers, "and," said he, "when I get out of this place, I'll finish it up, perhaps, and get my friend B[rooks] to print it somewhere." When these two visitors had departed, Agassiz and Lincoln shaking hands with great warmth, the latter turned to me with a quizzical smile and said, "Well, I wasn't so badly scared, after all, were you?" He had evidently expected to be very much oppressed by the great man's learning.

"I Will Meet Them Personally"

FRIDAY. FEBRUARY 3, 1865

¶ *Francis P. Blair, Sr., had gone to Richmond on two unofficial peace missions in January. He had talked with Jefferson Davis and Davis was not averse to ironing out a peace for "the two countries." Lincoln, too, wanted peace. But that peace would have to be secured "to the people of our one common country." In general terms, the* Philadelphia Public Ledger *summed up Lincoln's views on the subject: "All we ask is their submission to the laws. When they are ready to do this they cease to be enemies, and it is our duty to act so as to make them our friends."* [1]

On January 29th, Confederate commissioners—Vice-President Alexander H. Stephens, Assistant Secretary of War John A. Campbell, and R. M. T. Hunter, president pro tem *of the Senate—arrived at City Point, Virginia. Lincoln had made it known that he was ready "informally" to receive "any agent . . . or any other influen-*

tial person now resisting the national authority" that Jefferson Davis might send to talk peace.[2] *Stephens, Campbell and Hunter were there for that purpose. They now wished a safe-conduct to Washington to see the President.*

Lincoln dispatched Major Eckert to determine the intentions of the rebel emissaries. After an interview with them, Eckert was dissatisfied with their instructions and refused to permit them to proceed to Washington. However, Grant, who talked with them after Eckert, became "convinced . . . that their intentions are good and their desire sincere to restore peace and union." But the general regretted that "Mr. Lincoln cannot have an interview" with them. When Lincoln heard this, he instructed Grant: "Say to the gentlemen I will meet them personally at Fortress Monroe as soon as I can get there." To Seward went a Presidential request to participate in this meeting.[3]

On February 3rd, a four-hour conference was held in the saloon of the River Queen, *anchored at Hampton Roads near Fortress Monroe. There were no stenographers to record the proceedings. The whole session was in confidence and none of the principals were to be held responsible for anything that was said. Our account of this conference is supplied by Alexander H. Stephens:*[4]

After usual salutations on the part of those who were previously acquainted, and introductions of the others who had never met before, conversation was immediately opened by the revival of reminiscences and associations of former days.

This was commenced by myself addressing Mr. Lincoln, and alluding to some of the incidents of our Congressional acquaintance —especially, to the part we had acted together in effecting the election of General Taylor in 1848. To my remarks he responded in a cheerful and cordial manner, as if the remembrance of those times, and our connection with the incidents referred to, had awakened in him a train of agreeable reflections, extending to others. Mutual inquiries were made after the fate and well-being of several who had been our intimate friends and active associates in a "Congressional Taylor Club," well-known at the time. . . . With this introduction I said in substance: Well, Mr. President, is there no way of putting an end to the present trouble, and bringing about a restoration of the general good feeling and harmony *then* existing between the different States and Sections of the country?

Mr. Seward said: It is understood, gentlemen, that this is to be an informal Conference. There is to be no clerk or secretary—no writing or record of anything that is said. All is to be verbal.

I, speaking for the Commissioners, said that was our understanding of it. To this all assented, whereupon I repeated the question.

Mr. Lincoln in reply said, in substance, that there was but one way that he knew of, and that was, for those who were resisting the laws of the Union to cease that resistance. All the trouble came from an armed resistance against the National Authority.

But, said I, is there no other question that might divert the attention of both Parties, for a time, from the questions involved in their present strife, until the passions on both sides might cool, when they would be in better temper to come to an amicable and proper adjustment of those points of difference out of which the present lamentable collision of arms has arisen? Is there no Continental question, said I, which might thus temporarily engage their attention? We have been induced to believe that there is.

Mr. Lincoln seemed to understand my allusion instantly, and said in substance: I suppose you refer to something that Mr. Blair has said. Now it is proper to state at the beginning, that whatever he said was of his own accord, and without the least authority from me. When he applied for a passport to go to Richmond, with certain ideas which he wished to make known to me, I told him flatly that I did not want to hear them. If he desired to go to Richmond of his own accord, I would give him a passport; but he had no authority to speak for me in any way whatever. When he returned and brought me Mr. Davis's letter, I gave him the one to which you alluded in your application for leave to cross the lines. I was always willing to hear propositions for peace on the conditions of this letter and on no other. The restoration of the Union is a *sine qua non* with me, and hence my instructions that no conference was to be held except upon that basis.

From this I inferred that he simply meant to be understood, in the first place, as disavowing whatever Mr. Blair had said as coming authoritatively from him; and, in the second place, that no arrangement could be made on the line suggested by Mr. Blair, without a previous pledge of assurance being given, that the Union was to be ultimately restored.

After a short silence, I continued: But suppose, Mr. President, a line of policy should be suggested, which, if adopted, would most probably lead to a restoration of the Union without further bloodshed, would it not be highly advisable to act on it, even without the absolute pledge of ultimate restoration being required to be first given? May not such a policy be found to exist in the line indicated by the interrogatory propounded? Is there not now such a Continental question in which all the parties engaged in our present war feel a deep and similar interest? I allude, of course, to Mexico, and what is called the "Monroe Doctrine,"—the principles of which are directly involved in the contest now waging there. From the tone of leading Northern papers and from public speeches of prominent men, as well as from *other* sources, we are under the impression that the Administration at Washington is decidedly opposed to the establishment of an Empire in Mexico by France, and is desirous to prevent it. In other words, they wish to sustain the principles of the Monroe Doctrine, and that, as I understand it, is, that the United States will maintain the right of Self-government to all Peoples on this Continent, against the domination or control of any European power.

Mr. Lincoln and Mr. Seward both concurred in the expression of opinion that such was the feeling of a majority of the people of the North.

Could not both Parties then, said I, in our contest, come to an understanding and agreement to postpone their present strife, by a suspension of hostilities between themselves, until this principle is maintained in behalf of Mexico; and might it not, when successfully sustained there, naturally, and would it not almost inevitably, lead to a peaceful and harmonious solution of their own difficulties? Could any pledge now given, make a permanent restoration or re-organization of the Union more probable, or even so probable, as such a result would?

Mr. Lincoln replied with considerable earnestness, that he could entertain no proposition for ceasing active military operations, which was not based upon a pledge first given, for the ultimate restoration of the Union. He had considered the question of an Armistice fully, and he could not give his consent to any proposition of that sort, on the basis suggested. The settlement of our existing difficulties was a question now of supreme importance, and the only basis on which he would entertain a proposition for a settlement was the recognition and re-establishment of the National Authority throughout the land.

These pointed and emphatic responses seemed to put an end to the Conference on the subject contemplated in our Mission, as we had no authority to give any such pledge, even if we had been inclined to do so, nor was it expected that any such would really be required to be given.

Judge Campbell then inquired in what way the settlement for a restoration of the Union was to be made? Supposing the Confederate States should consent to the general terms as stated by Mr. Lincoln, how would the re-establishment of the National Authority take place? He wished to know something as to the details.

These inquiries were made by him upon the line agreed upon by the Commissioners before, that if we failed in securing an Armistice, we would then endeavor to ascertain on what terms the Administration at Washington would be willing to end the war.

Mr. Seward said, he desired that any answer to Judge Campbell's inquiries might be postponed, until the general ideas advanced by me might be more fully developed, as they had, as he expressed it, "a philosophical basis." All seemed to acquiesce in this suggestion. . . .

Mr. Seward said, that the Northern people were weary of the war. They desired peace and a restoration of harmony, and he believed would be willing to pay as an indemnity for the slaves, what would be required to continue the war, but stated no amount.

After thus going through with all these matters, in a conversation of about four hours, of which I have given . . . only the prominent leading points, and these in substance only, there was a pause, as if all felt that the interview should close. I arose and stated that it seemed our mission would be entirely fruitless, unless we could do something in the matter of the Exchange of Prisoners. This brought up that subject.

Mr. Lincoln expressed himself in favor of doing something on it, and concluded by saying that he would put the whole matter in the hands of General Grant, then at City Point, with whom we could interchange views on our return. Some propositions were then made for immediate special exchanges, which were readily agreed to.

I then said: I wish, Mr. President, you would re-consider the subject of an Armistice on the basis which has been suggested.

Great questions, as well as vast interests, are involved in it. If, upon so doing, you shall change your mind, you can make it known through the Military.

Well, said he, as he was taking my hand for a farewell leave, and with a peculiar manner very characteristic of him: Well, Stephens, I will re-consider it, but I do not think my mind will change, but I will re-consider.

The two parties then took formal and friendly leave of each other, Mr. Lincoln and Mr. Seward withdrawing first from the saloon together.

"I Always Plucked a Thistle . . ."
THURSDAY, FEBRUARY 23[?], 1865

¶ *During their boyhood days, Lincoln and Joshua Speed were intimate friends. That bond of friendship was not broken when Speed left Illinois to settle in Kentucky. During the war, Lincoln often turned to Speed for advice on matters relating to the Blue Grass state. Joshua's brother, James, was appointed Attorney General when Bates resigned at the end of 1864.*

The last time Joshua Speed saw Lincoln was about ten days before the inauguration of 1865. Speed wrote about it in a letter to Herndon on January 12, 1866: [1]

When I entered his office it was quite full and . . . Senators & Members waiting—As soon as I entered the room the President remarked that he desired to see me after he was through giving audiences and that if I had nothing to do I could take the Papers and amuse myself till he was ready—

In the room when I entered I observed two ladies in humble attire —sitting across the fire place from where the President sat—modestly waiting their turn—One after another came & went, (each and all of them went on their own business—Some satisfied, and others grumbling)—The hour had now come to close the door to all visitors—No one was left in the room except myself two women & the President—

With rather a peevish & fretful air he turned to them and said

"Well ladies what can I do for you[?]" They both commenced to speak at once. From what they said he soon learned that one was the wife and the other Mother of two men imprisoned for resisting the draft in Western Pennsylvania—Stop said he—don't say any more—Give me your petition—The old lady responded—Mr. Lincoln—we've got no petition—we couldnt write one, and have no money to pay for writing one—I thought it best to come & see you—Oh said he—Dont say any thing more I understand your cases—He rang his bell & ordered one of the Messengers to tell Genl Dana to bring him the names of all the men in prison for resisting the Draft in Western Pennsylvania—The Genl soon came with the list—He inquired if there was any difference in the charges in degree of guilt—The Genl replied that he knew of none—"Well[,"] said he[, "]these fellows suffered long enough and I have thought so for some time and now that my mind is on it, I believe I will turn out the *flock*—" "So draw up the order General and let me sign it—["] It was done & the General left the room—Turning then to these women he said "now ladies you can go—"

The young woman ran forward & was about to kneel in thankfulness—Get up he said dont kneel to me—Thank God & go—

The old woman came forward with tears in her eyes to say Good bye—Good bye said she Mr Lincoln—I shall never see you again till we meet in Heaven—

She had the Presidents hand in hers—He instantly took her right hand in both of his and following her to the door said I am afraid with all my troubles I shall never get there—But if I do I will find you—That you wish me to go there is the best wish you could make for me—good bye—

We were alone—I said to him—Lincoln with my knowledge of your nervous sensibility it is a wonder that such scenes as this dont kill you—I am said he very unwell—My feet and hands always cold—I suppose I ought to be in bed—

But things of that sort dont hurt me—For to tell you the truth—that scene which you witnessed is the only thing I have done to day which has given me any pleasure—I have in that made two people happy—That old lady was no counterfeit—The Mother spoke out in all the features of her face—It is more than we can often say that in doing right we have made two people happy in one day—

"Speed, die when I may I want it said of me by those who know

me best to say that I always plucked a thistle and planted a flower
when I thought a flower would grow—"
Such is the nature of the interview[.]

"Here Comes My Friend Douglass"
SATURDAY, MARCH 4, 1865

> ¶ *Frederick Douglass was right up front during the inauguration
> ceremonies. From the platform, Lincoln pointed Douglass out to
> the Vice-President Johnson, but, the Negro leader remembered, "Mr.
> Johnson . . . looked quite annoyed that his attention should be
> called in that direction." To Douglass, that look of annoyance meant
> that Johnson was "no friend to my people."*
>
> *That evening, Douglass, after experiencing some difficulty in
> gaining admission to the White House, attended the Presidential re-
> ception. In 1885, he wrote:* [1]

I could not have been more than ten feet from him when Mr.
Lincoln saw me: his countenance lighted up and he said in a voice
which was heard all around "Here comes my friend Douglass." As
I approached him he reached out his hand, gave me a cordial shake
and said: "Douglass, I saw you in the crowd to-day listening to my
inaugural address. There is no man's opinion that I value more than
yours: what do you think of it?" I said: "Mr. Lincoln I cannot stop
here to talk with you, as there are thousands waiting to shake you by
the hand"; but he said again: "What did you think of it?" I said:
"Mr. Lincoln it was a sacred effort," and then I walked off. "I am
glad you liked it," he said. That was the last time I saw him to
speak with him.

"That Troubles Me Most"
SUNDAY, MARCH 12, 1865

> ¶ *Dr. Anson G. Henry went to Washington in February. For almost
> four years, he had been Surveyor General of Washington Territory.*

Now he wanted something better. He desired to be Commissioner of Indian Affairs. As he pressed for his own appointment, he also worked with Mrs. Lincoln to get Nicolay "out as private Secretary [to the President] and Mr. Brooks in his place." Dr. Henry talked to his friend the Chief Magistrate about these matters on March 12th. The next day, he wrote his wife about the discussion: [1]

Mr. Lincoln had never intimated what he would do, in reply to my suggestions, that Mr. Brooks was capable of rendering him infinitely more substantial service than Mr. Nicolay[2] could, and that I presumed Mr. N. would like to go abroad. But to our happy surprise it was officially announced yesterday morning that Mr. Nicolay had been confirmed as Consul to Paris, hence the importance of seeing him before any body else could see him. I am quite sure he will make Mr. Brooks his Secretary. . . .

After Mr. Brooks' matter was laid aside, I said—Mr. Lincoln, you will bear me witness that I have never yet made a claim on you for preferment on personal grounds, and have sought this interview for the purpose that I desire you to decide the application now being pressed upon you by the Pacific Delegation, as if you had never before seen or heard of me; not because I would not be gratified with receiving from you an additional manifestation of confidence. I wish my application to rest entirely upon the claim of our coast for a representation here at Washington in the Government. But while I say this, I think it is not egotism in me to say, that I am capable of serving you faithfully & efficiently, and to the general satisfaction of the country.

Mr. Lincoln replied. The thing that troubles me most is, that I dislike the idea of removing Mr. Dole who has been a faithful and devoted personal & political friend. I took up my hat & said, Well Mr. Lincoln, I will go home & remain where I am, not only, without a murmur, but entirely satisfied that you have done what you believe to be best calculated to promote the welfare and prosperity of the Government.

Mr. Lincoln said rather emphatically, Henry—you must not understand me as having decided the matter—and then said, "The delegation from Minnesota are pressing very strongly for that place for Ex-Senator [Morton S.] Wilkinson, and the Delegation from Illinois headed by [Richard] Yates & Trumbull are pressing their man Judge [William Pitt] Kellogg.["] I replied—yes—our Pacific men are beginning to think that the Old North West are getting the Lyons [*sic*] share of the offices. He replied laughing, "It does look a little that way." After some general conversation, we left very well pleased with the interview.

"It Was the Easiest Thing"

TUESDAY, MARCH 21, 1865

¶ *While visiting Washington, a reporter for Baltimore's* American and Commercial Advertiser *dropped into the White House. The* New York Tribune *had been writing about the President's "debility or failing health." But the Maryland journalist found nothing of the sort. As a matter of "especial public interest," he announced, "the President looked extremely well, seemed in excellent spirits. . . . Indeed, there is good reason to hope that he will not only live many years to witness the future of his restored country, but should the people so decide, . . . administer its Executive functions even beyond his present term of office."*

However, the newsman noted his astonishment at finding "so few waiting in the ante-room for interviews with the President." Lincoln began receiving visitors that day at 10 A.M., *but at 11:30* A.M. *the Cabinet went into session until almost 2* P.M. *"So soon as the Cabinet members had withdrawn, the reception of visitors was resumed, those having members of Congress with them taking precedence" over the others, the reporter observed. He stayed on to write about the "frank, cordial and candid manner" in which the President disposed of petitioners:* [1]

The first case was that of an old gentleman whose sons had been killed in battle, and who had come to Washington in hope of being able to obtain some kind of employment. The President replied that Washington was the worst place in the country for any one to seek to better their condition, and advised him to go home again by the first train. He wished some species of saffron tea could be administered to produce an eruption of those already in Washington and make this migration fever strike out instead of striking in. The supplicant replied that he had not the means to go, and hoped that the President would give him a note to one of the quartermasters, who might probably give him some kind of employment. After thinking a minute, he wrote something on a piece of paper and gave it to him, when the old man's countenance brightened, and with profuse thanks he retired.

A gentleman largely engaged in bringing out cotton, &c., from the Rebel States, inquired of the President whether it was his intention to sustain the recent order issued by General Grant putting a stop to the whole business.—The President replied that in no case would he interfere with the wishes of General Grant. He held him responsible for inflicting the hardest blows possible on the enemy, and as desirable as it was to possess cotton, if he thought that bacon was of more importance to the enemy at this moment than cotton was to us, why we must do without the cotton. Gen. Grant was no lawyer, and consequently used no unnecessary words to amplify his order; but the President understood him to mean that this trade was giving aid and comfort to the enemy, and consequently it must stop. "Under no circumstances," concluded the President, "will I interfere with the orders of General Grant."

The next was an applicant for a small country post office, accompanied by a Democratic member of Congress. On reading his application he responded at once, "you shall have it," and endorsed his approval on the back. The member remarked, "I presume, Mr. President, that it is because I trouble you so little that you so promptly grant my request." The President responded, "That reminds me of my own experience as an old Whig member of Congress. I was always in the opposition, and I had no troubles of this kind at all. It was the easiest thing imaginable to be an opposition member —no running to the Departments and the White House."

Next came an old gentleman who wished to get a man pardoned from the Penitentiary, convicted of stealing two pairs of pantaloons and a pair of shoes belonging to the Government, from a box he was hauling on his dray. A statement of the case from the State's Attorney was presented, which admitted that one witness had testified that he had sold him a pair of shoes. "Yes," said the President, "so much for the shoes, but nothing about the pantaloons. The jury had the whole facts before them, and convicted the man, and I am bound to regard him as guilty. I am sorry for his wife and children, sir, but the man must be punished."

Next was the case of a youth who had been arrested as a deserter in Baltimore, having a pass for one day, the time having expired. He stated that he was on his way to his home to see a sick sister, who had subsequently died; had no intention of deserting, but merely intended to overstay his time on his pass and return to camp. He was now at the Dry Tortugas under a three years' sentence, with a ball and chain on his leg. The President, in view of his recent proclamation to deserters who had not been arrested, promptly pardoned him.

A young widow, the mother of three children, whose husband had been killed in battle, presented an application for the appointment of post-mistress of a small town in Orange county, New York. The President received her very kindly—told her to leave all her papers with him, and that he would examine the matter thoroughly, and would do the best he could for her case. She was advised to return home and trust her case in his hands, as he would attend to it as well in her absence as if she were present. He "could not act on it at once; for, although he was President, she must remember that he was but one horse in the team, and if the others pulled in a different direction it would be a hard matter for him to out-pull them." The lady left much pleased with her interview.

A wounded officer was an applicant for an office, and presented a memorial signed by a large number of citizens of his district. The President replied that he was disposed to favor the application, but that he must wait to hear from the member of Congress from that district. He would be forever in hot water if he did not pay some deference to the wishes of members on these appointments.

An applicant for the discharge of a minor from service, assured him that an officer, whom he named, had said the case was one deserving of Executive interference. The President immediately remarked, "Bring me his opinion to that effect in writing, and I will promptly discharge him. His word will be sufficient for me; I will require no argument on the subject."

A man who wished to escape from the draft on the plea of being in the employ of the Government and being physically disabled, was told that the President could not take action against the army surgeons, and he doubted if there were not a dozen gentlemen in the room who would gladly relieve him of his Government employment. "I don't know why it is that I am troubled with these cases," said the President, "but if I were, by interfering, to make a hole through which a kitten might pass, it would soon be large enough for the old cat to get through also."

Several other applicants for Executive interference in small matters were kindly received and their cases promptly disposed of, all retiring apparently well pleased with their reception, and in most cases gratified with the decision of the President.

A singular case occurred at an early hour in the morning, of a young woman who presented herself to the usher with three children, one almost an infant. She demanded to see the President, and on being told that the Cabinet was in session and that she could not see him, she set the children on the floor in the East Room, declaring that as her husband had been killed in battle she had brought her children to the President and intended to leave them with him. She was ascertained to be a poor deranged creature, whose afflictions had over-balanced her mind, and by direction of Mrs. Lincoln was properly cared for.

"Willing to Share Their Dangers"

SATURDAY, MARCH 25, 1865

¶ *The Southern Confederacy was "played out," a Washington newsman reported on March 22nd. "Sherman and his great captains" were "rolling up a tide of destruction from the south of Richmond, and, wasting North Carolina with flame and sword." They were expected soon "at the gates of Petersburg and Richmond." In north and northwest Virginia, Sheridan was playing havoc, severing Lee's communications, extinguishing "the last sparks of Early, totally ruining the great feeder of Richmond—the James River Canal—consuming millions of dollars worth of supplies, and making a broad track of desolation from the Shenandoah to the Pamunkey." Almost uniting these two Union armies, "Grant, the master mind of the whole, sits grimly and remorselessly, the Giant Despair of Richmond, across the James and holding the army of Lee at Petersburg and the rebel Capital." Grant's anxiety was over the possible escape of the enemy from Richmond before "he could be struck a crushing blow." To prevent this, Grant was taking "every possible precaution."* [1]

On March 20th, the general invited the President to visit City Point "for a day or two." Lincoln, accompanied by his wife and youngest son, Tad, arrived aboard the River Queen *on March 24th. He returned to Washington on April 9th. For more than two weeks, Lincoln was with his troops, saw them in action, conferred with their generals, witnessed the fall of Petersburg and Richmond, and entered the capital of rebeldom, where he again talked peace. The Yanks gave the President a tumultuous welcome wherever he went. L. A. Hendricks of the* New York Herald, *who covered the Lincoln visit, wrote that "when no one could tell what fierce onslaught of battle any moment might bring forth, he was not afraid to show himself" among the soldiers, "and willing to share their dangers here."* [2]

The afternoon of March 25th, after some heavy skirmishing about Petersburg, Lincoln and Grant visited that front. Horace Porter, in his Campaigning with Grant, *continues:* [3]

Upon the return to headquarters at City Point, he [the President] sat for a while by the camp-fire; and as the smoke curled about his head during certain shiftings of the wind, and he brushed it away from time to time by waving his right hand in front of his face, he entertained the general-in-chief and several members of the staff by talking in a most interesting manner about public affairs, and illustrating the subjects mentioned with his incomparable anecdotes. At first his manner was grave and his language much more serious than usual. He spoke of the appalling difficulties encountered by the administration, the losses in the field, the perplexing financial problems, and the foreign complications; but said they had all been overcome by the unswerving patriotism of the people, the devotion of the loyal North, and the superb fighting qualities of the troops. After a while he spoke in a more cheerful vein, and said: "England will live to regret her inimical attitude toward us. After the collapse of the rebellion John Bull will find that he has injured himself much more seriously than us. His action reminds me of a barber in Sangamon County in my State. He had just gone to bed when a stranger came along and said he must be shaved; that he had a four days' beard on his face, and was going to take a girl to a ball, and that beard must come off. Well, the barber got up reluctantly and dressed, and seated the man in a chair with a back so low that every time he bore down on him he came near dislocating his victim's neck. He began by lathering his face, including his nose, eyes, and ears, stropped his razor on his boot, and then made a drive at the man's countenance as if he had practised mowing in a stubble-field. He cut a bold swath across the right cheek, carrying away the beard, a pimple, and two warts. The man in the chair ventured to remark: 'You appear to make everything level as you go.' 'Yes,' said the barber; 'and if this handle don't break, I guess I'll get away with most of what 's there.' The man's cheeks were so hollow that the barber could n't get down into the valleys with the razor, and the ingenious idea occurred to him to stick his finger in the man's mouth and press out the cheeks. Finally he cut clear through the cheek and into his own finger. He pulled the finger out of the man's mouth, snapped the blood off it, glared at him, and cried: 'There, you lantern-jawed cuss, you 've made me cut my finger!' And so England will discover that she has got the South into a pretty bad scrape by trying to administer to her, and in the end she will find that she has only cut her own finger."

After the laugh which followed this story had exhausted itself, General Grant asked: "Mr. President, did you at any time doubt the final success of the cause?" "Never for a moment," was the prompt and emphatic reply, as Mr. Lincoln leaned forward in his camp-chair and enforced his words by a vigorous gesture of his right hand. "Mr. Seward, when he visited me last summer, gave a very interesting account of the complications and embarrassments arising from the Mason and Slidell affair, when those commissioners were captured on board the English vessel *Trent*," remarked General Grant. "Yes," said the President; "Seward studied up all the works ever written on international law, and came to cabinet meetings loaded to the muzzle with the subject. We gave due consideration to the case, but at that critical period of the war it was soon decided to deliver up the prisoners. It was a pretty bitter pill to swallow, but I contented myself with believing that England's triumph in the matter would be short-lived, and that after ending our war successfully we would be so powerful that we could call her to account for all the embarrassments she had inflicted upon us. I felt a great deal like the sick man in Illinois who was told he probably had n't many days longer to live, and he ought to make his peace with any enemies he might have. He said the man he hated worst of all was a fellow named Brown, in the next village, and he guessed he had better begin on him. So Brown was sent for, and when he came the sick man began to say, in a voice as meek as Moses's, that he wanted to die at peace with all his fellow-creatures, and he hoped he and Brown could now shake hands and bury all their enmity. The scene was becoming altogether too pathetic for Brown, who had to get out his handkerchief and wipe the gathering tears from his eyes. It was n't long before he melted, and gave his hand to his neighbor, and they had a regular love-feast of forgiveness. After a parting that would have softened the heart of a grindstone, Brown had about reached the room door when the sick man rose up on his elbow and called out to him: 'But see here, Brown; if I should happen to get well, mind, that old grudge stands.' So I thought that if this nation should happen to get well we might want that old grudge against England to stand." . . .

The President now went aboard his boat to spend the night.

"I Want No One Punished"

TUESDAY, MARCH 28, 1865

¶ *General Sherman, on March 21st, made a junction with Schofield's and Alfred H. Terry's forces—just in from Newbern and Wilmington—at Goldsboro, North Carolina. Four days later, leaving Schofield in command, Sherman hastened to City Point. "My army," Sherman remembered later, "was hard up for food and clothing." He wanted to talk to Grant about this as well as about strategy.*[1]

While at City Point, Sherman and Grant had a conversation with Lincoln about the progress of the war. The next day, accompanied by Admiral David D. Porter, they had another meeting aboard the River Queen.

The March 28th council dealt in part with the kind of surrender terms Sherman should offer Confederate General Joseph E. Johnston, who was penned up in North Carolina by the Union forces. Subsequently, when Johnston surrendered, Sherman was charged with being too liberal. Sherman claimed he was merely following Lincoln's

*instructions. But Lincoln was dead when the controversy broke and
could not defend the general.*

*Both Sherman and Porter left accounts of the conference with
Lincoln. However, the general's report obviously was influenced by
the admiral's version, which has been subject to considerable criticism and doubt. With this caution, we reproduce Porter's story:* [2]

At this meeting Mr. Lincoln and General Sherman were the
speakers, and the former declared his opinions at length before
Sherman answered him. The President feared that Lee—seeing our
lines closing about him, the coast completely blockaded, his troops
almost destitute of clothing and short of provisions—might make
an attempt to break away from the fortified works at Richmond,
make a junction with General Joe Johnston, and escape South or
fight a last bloody battle.

Any one looking at the situation of the armies at that time will
see that such an attempt would not have been possible.

Sherman had eighty thousand fine troops at Goldsboro', only one
hundred and fifty miles from Richmond and one hundred and twenty
miles from Greensborough, which latter place cut the Richmond
and Danville Railroad, the only one by which Lee could escape.

The President's mind was made easy on this score, yet it was
remarkable how many shrewd questions he asked on the subject,
and how difficult some of them were to answer. He stated his views
in regard to what he desired; he felt sure, as did every one at that
council, that the end of the war was near at hand; and, though
some thought a bloody battle was impending, all thought that
Richmond would fall in less than a week.

He wanted the surrender of the Confederate armies, and desired
that the most liberal terms should be granted them. "Let them once
surrender," he said, "and reach their homes, they won't take up
arms again. Let them all go, officers and all. I want submission, and
no more bloodshed. Let them have their horses to plow with, and,
if you like, their guns to shoot crows with. I want no one punished;
treat them liberally all round. We want those people to return to
their allegiance to the Union and submit to the laws. Again I say,
give them the most liberal and honorable terms."

"But, Mr. President," said Sherman, "I can dictate my own terms to General Johnston. All I want is two weeks' time to fit out my men with shoes and clothes, and I will be ready to march upon Johnston and compel him to surrender; he is short of clothing, and in two weeks he would have no provisions at all."

"And," added the President, "two weeks is an age, and the first thing you will know General Johnston will be off South again with those hardy troops of his, and will keep the war going indefinitely. No, General, he must not get away; we must have his surrender at all hazards, so don't be hard on him about terms. Yes, he will get away if he can, and you will never catch him until after miles of travel and many bloody battles."

"Mr. President," said Sherman, "there is no possible way of General Johnston's escaping; he is my property as he is now situated, and I can demand an unconditional surrender; he can't escape."

"What is to prevent him from escaping with all his army by the Southern railroads while you are fitting out your men?" asked Grant.

"Because," answered Sherman, "there are no Southern railroads to speak of; my bummers have broken up the roads in sections all behind us—and they did it well."

"But," said Grant, "can't they relay the rails, the same as you did the other day, from Newbern and Wilmington to Goldsboro'?"

Sherman laughed. "Why, no," he said, "my boys don't do things by halves. When they tore up the rails they put them over hot fires made from the ties, and then twisted them more crooked than a ram's horn. All the blacksmiths in the South could not straighten them out."

"Mr. President," said Sherman, turning to Mr. Lincoln, "the Confederacy has gone up, or will go up. We hold all the line between Wilmington and Goldsboro', where my troops are now fitting out from the transports. My transports can come up the Neuse River as far as Newbern. We could flood the South with troops and provisions without hindrance. We hold the situation, and General Johnston can surrender to me on my own terms."

"All very well," said the President, "but we must have no mistakes, and my way is a sure way. Offer Johnston the same terms that will be offered to Lee; then, if he is defiant, and will not accept them, try your plan. But as long as the Confederate armies lay down their arms, I don't think it matters much how it is done. Only don't let us have any more bloodshed if it can be avoided. General Grant is for giving Lee the most favorable terms."

To this General Grant assented.

"Well, Mr. President," said Sherman, "I will carry out your wishes to the letter, and I am quite satisfied that, as soon as Richmond falls, Joe Johnston will surrender also."

Sherman, at the end of the council, supposed he was acting under instructions, which he carried out, so far as I can understand it, pretty much as the President desired.

The council over, and the President being desirous that General Sherman should return to his command as soon as possible, the latter determined to return that afternoon by sea.

"I Reckon They'll Accept"

TUESDAY, MARCH 28, 1865

¶ *Charles Carleton Coffin of the* Boston Journal, *sitting in the office of General Theodore S. Bowers, Grant's Adjutant General at City Point, spoke with Lincoln there. As Coffin remembered it:* [1]

[The] President . . . saw and recognized me, extended his hand, and said smilingly:

"What news have you?" I never have been able to settle in my own mind the significance of the question, but I think humor prompted it, for in those days correspondents often sent news which was not altogether reliable.

"I have just arrived from Charleston and Savannah," I replied.

"Indeed!" It was a tone indicative of a pleasant surprise. "Well, I am right glad to see you. How do the people like being back in the Union again?" he said, as he sat down in the chair placed for him by General Bowers.

"I think some of them are reconciled to it," I replied, "if we may draw conclusions from the action of one planter, who, while I was there, came down the Savannah River with his whole family—wife, children, negro woman and her children, of whom he was father—

and with his crop of cotton, which he was anxious to sell at the highest price."

The President's eyes sparkled, as they always did when his humor was aroused.

"Oh, yes, I see," he said with a laugh which was peculiarly his own—"I see; patriarchal times once more; Abraham, Sarah, Isaac, Hagar and Ishmael, all in one boat!" He chuckled a moment, and added:

"I reckon they'll accept the situation now that they can sell their cotton."

"Glory Enough for All"

MONDAY, APRIL 3, 1865

¶ *General Sheridan, on April 1st, had bested the rebels at Five Forks. The next day, Lincoln telegraphed his wife—who had returned to Washington by now—that "General Grant . . . has Petersburg completely enveloped from river below to river above. . . ."* [1] *Richmond and Petersburg had been abandoned by Lee. Jefferson Davis and his Cabinet, except War Secretary Breckinridge, had fled the rebel capital. On April 3rd, Union forces entered both cities. That day, Tom Cook of the* New York Herald *filed his report from City Point to his newspaper:* [2]

I have just arrived here from Petersburg, and have had the pleasure of giving the first detailed news from Petersburg to the President, whom I met with Admiral Porter at General Grant's headquarters.

PRESIDENT LINCOLN'S JOKE

When asked where I came from, and replying Petersburg, the President very dryly asked if I saw anybody there I knew. The joke was scarcely perceptible, but still, under the circumstances it will do.

A CONTEST FOR GLORY

Admiral Porter claims Petersburg as his victory. The President asked him how that could be. "Why," said Porter, "my Monitors up the river the other night scared the rebels away. Didn't they tell you so in Petersburg?" to me. I was forced to reply that I hadn't heard exactly that remark. "Well," continued the Admiral, "Mrs. Grant says I can have Petersburg for my victory if I won't claim Richmond, and I think I had better accept the terms, or Grant will have all the honors." The President suggested that there was glory enough for all, and certainly all seem to be full of it, from highest to lowest, as this brief colloquy indicated.

"A Sort of Sneaking Idea"

MONDAY, APRIL 3, 1865

¶ After his chat with Tom Cook, the President, Tad and Admiral Porter boarded a special train and headed for Petersburg, where he met with General Grant. Horace Porter was present and wrote: [1]

He [the President] dismounted in the street, and came in through the front gate with long rapid strides, his face beaming with delight. [Grant had taken over the residence of Thomas Wallace at No. 21 Market Street, where he awaited the President.] He seized General Grant's hand as the general stepped forward to greet him, and stood shaking it for some time, and pouring out his thanks and congratulations with all the fervor of a heart which seemed overflowing with its fullness of joy. I doubt whether Mr. Lincoln ever experienced a happier moment in his life. The scene was singularly affecting, and one never to be forgotten. He said: "Do you know, general, I had a sort of sneaking idea all along that you intended to do something like this; but I thought some time ago that you would so manoeuver as to have Sherman come up and be near enough to coöperate with you." "Yes," replied the general; "I thought at one time that Sherman's army might advance far enough to be in supporting distance of the Eastern armies when the spring campaign against Lee opened; but I had a feeling that it would be better to let Lee's old antagonists give his army the final blow, and finish up the job. If the Western troops were even to put in an appearance against Lee's army, it might give some of our politicians a chance to stir up sectional feeling in claiming everything for the troops from their own section of the country. The Western armies have been very successful in their campaigns, and it is due to the Eastern armies to let them vanquish their old enemy single-handed." "I see, I see," said Mr. Lincoln; "but I never thought of it in that light. In fact, my anxiety has been so great that I did n't care where the help came from, so that the work was perfectly done." "Oh," General Grant continued, "I do not suppose it would have given rise to much of the bickering I mentioned, and perhaps the idea would not have occurred to any one else. I feel sure there would have been no such feeling among the soldiers. Of course I would not have risked the result of the campaign on account of any mere sentiment of this kind. I have always felt confident that our troops here were amply able to handle Lee." Mr. Lincoln then began to talk about the civil complications that would follow the destruction of the Confederate armies in the field, and showed plainly the anxiety he felt regarding the great problems in statecraft which would soon be thrust upon him. He intimated very plainly, in a conversation that lasted nearly half an hour, that thoughts of leniency to the conquered were uppermost in his heart.

Meanwhile his son Tad, for whom he always showed a deep affection, was becoming a little uneasy, and gave certain appealing looks, to which General [George H.] Sharpe [assistant provost marshal general], who seemed to understand the mute expressions of small boys, responded by producing some sandwiches, which he offered him, saying: "Here, young man, I guess you must be hungry." Tad seized them as a drowning man would seize a life-preserver, and cried out: "Yes, I am; that's what's the matter with me." This greatly amused the President and the general-in-chief, who had a hearty laugh at Tad's expense.

A gentleman whom we supposed was the proprietor of the house asked the general to go into the parlor; but he declined politely, saying, "Thank you, but I am smoking."

The general hoped that before he parted with Mr. Lincoln he would hear that Richmond was in our possession; but after waiting about an hour and a half, he said he must ride on to the front and join [General Edward O. C.] Ord's column, and took leave of the President, who shook his hand cordially, and with great warmth of feeling wished him God-speed and every success.

"Spirit of Sincere Liberality"
WEDNESDAY, APRIL 5, 1865

¶ *Unheralded and without pomp or parade, Lincoln entered Richmond the afternoon of April 4th. Coffin, the Boston Journal man, wrote in an on-the-spot description of the event: "He walked through the streets as if he were only a private citizen, and not the head of a mighty nation. He came not as a conqueror, not with bitterness in his heart, but with kindness. He came as a friend, to alleviate sorrow and suffering—to rebuild what had been destroyed." Leading his son Tad, the President made his way to Union Army Headquarters in what used to be Jeff Davis' White House, "amid a surging mass of men, women and children, black, white and yellow, shouting, dancing, swinging their caps, cheering in wild enthusiasm."*

There were cries of "Thank you, dear Jesus, for this!" "Bless de Lord!" "Glory, glory, glory!" "God bless you, Massa Linkum!" And there was a white woman in "a large and elegant building," who "turned away her head as if it was a disgusting sight."

Lincoln walked silently, acknowledging the salutes of officers, soldiers and citizens. At the Davis mansion, he was greeted by General Godfrey Weitzel to the cheers of the "excited multitude, two thirds of whom were colored." The President then received Yankee officers in the reception room. Afterward, he had a brief interview with Judge Campbell in the drawing room. Lincoln and Campbell agreed to meet the next day to discuss peace.[1]

On April 5th, Campbell, accompanied by Gustavus A. Myers, Richmond attorney and member of the rebel Congress, came aboard the gunboat Malvern *for their meeting with the President. In a memorandum—probably written that day or very soon after—Myers tells of this conference:*[2]

Our interview with the President commenced by his stating that he understood we came in no official capacity and that we were unauthorized to act on any matter that might be the subject of our conversation, which we of course confirmed. He then told us that he had written a paper which he would read to us, accompanied by a verbal running commentary of his own when he considered explanation was necessary. He then read to us the paper which he afterwards handed to Judge Campbell, and which is in the possession of that Gentleman. The President required that the authority of the U. S. should be recognized and established in all parts of the Country, and declared that he could not retract from anything he had heretofore announced as his opinion in his public message to Congress, and said that independently of his own opinion about the question of property in Slaves, he could not without a violation of good faith change any of his sentiments in that behalf. In reference to confiscation of property, the Prest said that *that* was in his power, and he should be disposed to exercise that power in the spirit of sincere liberality. He stated that it had not gone to any great extent, and that, except in the cases of the rights of third persons intervening [?] by purchase, a question he must of course leave to the Courts to decide, he did not think there would [be] any [?] insurmountable obstacle in adjusting the matter. He professed himself really desirous to see an end of the struggle, and said he hoped in the Providence of God that there never would be another. He also said that he was thinking over a plan by which the Virginia Legislature might be brought to hold their meeting in the Capitol of Richmond,—for the purpose of seeing whether they desired to take any action on behalf of the States in view of the existing state of affairs, and informed Genl W[e]itzel [who was present at this meeting] that he would write to him from City Point on that subject in a day or two. The outline of his plan being, that safe conduct should be given to the members to come hither, and that after a reasonable time were allowed them to deliberate, should they arrive at no conclusion, they would have safe conduct afforded them to leave Richmond. We then spoke of the oath of allegiance being required. I informed the President that the conciliatory course pursued by the Federal forces since their arrival in Richmond, had had a powerful effect in allaying apprehension and producing kindly feelings on the part of the Citizens, and expressed the opinion that the adoption of any other course on the part of the Federal authorities would be productive of irritation and conducive to no good result. The President remarked that he had never attached much importance to the oath of allegiance being required, but that Genl W[e]itzel was present and that it depended on his view. "Then," said Genl W. "Mr. President, I never did administer it in Louisiana, except in some few instances in which it appeared proper, but never generally, and certainly do not feel disposed to do it here."

Other conversation occurred, in which the President declared his disposition to be lenient towards all persons, however prominent, who had taken part in the struggle, and certainly no exhibition was made by him of any feeling of vindictiveness or of exultation.

Judge Campbell handed to the President a paper, a copy of which he retained, containing proposed articles for a military convention to be held by Genls Grant and Lee, having an armistice for its basis, for a time [truce] to be agreed upon between those Officers during which negotiations might be opened and conducted. The President after hearing it read, requested that he might take it which was done accordingly, and our interview ended.

Throughout, it was conducted with entire civility and good humor.

"It Is Our Lawful Prize"
THURSDAY, APRIL 13, 1865

¶ *The afternoon Lincoln returned to Washington—April 9th—"look-ing much better for his extended absence from the capital," Robert E. Lee surrendered to Ulysses S. Grant at Appomattox Courthouse. Grant had given Lee's men a general amnesty, permitted them to retain their horses and side arms. The war—to all intents and pur-poses—was ended. Two days later, Lincoln spoke to a rejoicing crowd at the White House: "I have always thought 'Dixie' one of the best tunes I have ever heard. Our adversaries over the way at-tempted to appropriate it, but I insisted . . . that we fairly captured it. . . . I presented the question to the Attorney General, and he gave it as his legal opinion that it is our lawful prize." When he had ended his remarks, the band struck up the tune.*[1]

On April 12th, Lincoln telegraphed General Weitzel that Judge Campbell "assumes" that "I have called the insurgent Legislature of Virginia together, as the rightful Legislature of the State, to settle all differences with the United States. I have done no such thing. I spoke of them not as a Legislature, but as 'the gentlemen who have acted as the Legislature of Virginia in support of the rebellion.' " However, now that Grant had captured the Virginian army, Lincoln's discussion with Campbell on this point was "no longer applicable." [2]

Gideon Welles talked with Lincoln about this on April 13th, and later recorded in his Diary:[3]

The President asked me what views I took of Weitzel's calling the Virginia legislature together. Said Stanton and others were dissatisfied. Told him I doubted the policy of convening a Rebel legislature. It was a recognition of them, and once convened, they would, with their hostile feelings be inclined perhaps to conspire against us. He said he had no fear of that. They were too badly beaten—too much exhausted. His idea was, that the members of the legislature, being the prominent and influential men of their respective counties, had better come together and undo their own work. He felt assured they would do this, and the movement he believed a good one. Civil government must be reestablished, he said, as soon as possible,—there must be courts, and law, and order, or society would be broken up—the disbanded armies would turn into robber bands and guerrillas—which we must strive to prevent. These were the reasons why he wished them to come together and turn themselves and their neighbors into good union men. But as we all took a different view he had perhaps made a mistake, and was ready to correct it if he had.

I remarked, in the course of conversation, that if the so called legislature came together, they would be likely to propose terms which might seem reasonable, but which we could not accept,— that I had not great faith in negotiating with large bodies of men —each would encourage the other in asking and doing what no one of them would do alone—that he could make an arrangement with any one—the worst of them—than with all—that he might be embarrassed by recognizing and treating with them, when we were now in condition to prescribe what should be done.

"Take a Message for Me"

FRIDAY, APRIL 14, 1865

¶ *The President was breakfasting with his son Captain Robert T. Lincoln, when word came that Speaker Schuyler "Smiler" Colfax—*

about to embark upon a "continental tour"—had arrived at the
White House. Colfax described this visit in a speech in Virginia City,
Nevada, on June 26, 1865, reprinted on August 7th in the Washing-
ton Daily Morning Chronicle:

I went . . . to see our President, whom I believed I had a right
to call friend as well as President, and whom I loved as I never loved
man before, to ask him whether public duties would allow my long
absence from home; whether there was any danger or prospect of
an extra session of Congress being called during the summer.
. . . After conversing familiarly for some time on matters of public
interest, he suddenly turned to me and asked if I was not going
to the Pacific. I told him I was going if there was no danger of an
extra session of Congress this summer. He assured me there was
none; and then rising, and with much more than his usual emphasis,
he made what seemed to be a speech which he had thought over,
in regard to the miners and their interests, and he impressed it
upon me that I should communicate it to them. After his death I
thought that I would write it down, as it was fresh in my recollection,
instead of trusting his communication to my memory for delivery
some months afterward. I think I wrote it down in nearly his own
words:
"Mr. Colfax, I want you to take a message from me to the miners
whom you visit. I have," said he, "very large ideas of the mineral
wealth of our nation. I believe it practically inexhaustible. It
abounds all over the western country from the Rocky Mountains
to the Pacific, and its development has scarcely commenced. During
the war, when we were adding a couple of millions of dollars every
day to our national debt, I did not care about encouraging the increase in the volumes of our precious metals. We had the country to
save first. But now that the rebellion is overthrown and we know
pretty nearly the amount of our national debt, the more silver and
gold we mine makes the payment of that debt so much the easier.
Now," said he, speaking with much emphasis, "I am going to encourage them in every possible way. We shall have hundreds of
thousands of disabled soldiers, and many have feared that their
return home in such great numbers might paralyze industry by
furnishing suddenly a greater supply of labor than there will be

demand for. I am going to try to attract them to the hidden wealth of our mountain ranges, where there is room enough for all. Immigration, which even the war has not stopped, will land upon our shores hundreds of thousands more per year from over-crowded Europe. I intend to point them to the gold and silver that waits for them in the West. Tell the miners for me, that I shall promote their interests to the utmost of my ability, because their prosperity is the prosperity of the nation, and," said he, his eyes kindling with enthusiasm, "we shall prove in a very few years, that we are indeed the treasury of the world." . . .

I told him I was happy to be his messenger, and to bear such a message as this. He asked me to come again in the evening, as he was going to the theatre on that night and desired me to accompany him. I told him . . . that as I had engagements for the whole evening, and intended to leave the city the next morning to return home, it would be impossible for me to accompany him.

"This Strange Dream Again"

FRIDAY, APRIL 14, 1865

¶ *It was Good Friday and victory had made the country "drunk with joy." At noon that day, the Union flag was hoisted over the ruins of Fort Sumter; it was the same flag that had been lowered by the Federals when they surrendered the stronghold to the Palmettos four years earlier.[1]*

In Washington, Lincoln held a Cabinet meeting. Writing about it "two days after it occurred," Welles relates:[2]

Genl Grant was present at the meeting of the Cabinet today, and remained during the session. The subject was the relations of the rebels—the communications—the trade etc. Stanton proposed that intercourse should be reopened by *his* issuing an order—that the Treasury would give permits to all, who wished them, to trade, excluding contraband, and he [Stanton] would order the vessels to be received into any port. I suggested that it would be better that the President should issue a proclamation enjoining the course to be pursued by the several Departments.

[Hugh] McCulloch [who had replaced Fessenden as Secretary of the Treasury] expressed a willingness to be relieved of the Treasury agents. Genl Grant expressed himself very decidedly against them, thought them demoralizing etc. The President said we, *i.e.* the Secys of Treasury War and Navy had given the subject more attention than he had and he would be satisfied with any conclusion we would unite upon. I proposed opening the whole coast to any one who wished to trade, and who had a regular clearance and manifest, and was entitled to a coast license. Stanton thought it should not extend beyond the military lines. Genl Grant thought they might embrace all this side of the Mississippi.

Secretary Stanton requested the Cabinet to hear some remarks which he desired to make, and to listen to a proposition or ordinance which he had prepared with much care and after a great deal of reflection for reconstruction in the rebel states. The plan or ordinance embraced two distinct heads. One for asserting the Federal authority in Virginia,—the other for re establishing a State government there. The first struck me favorable with some slight emendations—the second seemed to me objectionable in several essentials, and especially as in conflict with the principles of self government which I deem essential. There was little said on the subject, for the understanding was that we should each be furnished with a copy for criticism and suggestion, and in the mean time we were requested by the President to deliberate and carefully consider the proposition. He remarked that this was the great question now before us, and we must soon begin to act. Was glad Congress was not in session.

I objected that Virginia occupied a different position from that of any other State in rebellion. That while regular State governments were to be established in other States, whose secession governments were nullities and would not be recognized, Virginia had a skeleton organization which she had maintained through the war, which we had recognized and still recognized—that we to day acknowledged [Francis H.] Pierpont as the legitimate Governor of Virginia. He had been elected by only a few border counties it was true,—had never been able to enforce his authority over but a small portion of the territory or population, nevertheless we had recognized & sustained him.

The President said the point was well taken.

Gov Dennison said he thought we should experience little difficulty from Pierpont. Stanton said none whatever.

I remarked that the act was not to be controverted, that we had treated with the existing government and could not ignore our own acts. The President and a portion of the Cabinet had, in establishing the new State of West Virginia recognized the validity of the government of Virginia which had given its assent to that division. Without that consent no division could have taken place. I had differed with others in that matter, but consistency and the validity of our own act required us to acknowledge the existing government. It was proper we should enforce the Federal authority and it was proper we should aid Gov Pierpont, whose government was established. In North Carolina a government was to be organized and the State re established in her proper relations to the Union.

Inquiry was made as to army news on the first meeting of the Cabinet, and especially if any information had been rec[eive]d from Sherman. None of the members had heard any thing and Stanton who makes it a point to be late, and who has the telegraph in his Department had not arrived. Grant who was present said he was hourly expecting word. The President remarked it would, he had no doubt come soon, and come favorable, for he had last night the usual dream which he had preceding nearly every great and important event of the War. Generally the news had been favorable which succeeded this dream, and the dream itself was always the same. I inquired what this remarkable dream could be. He said it related to the water—that he seemed to be in some singular, indescribable vessel, and that he was moving with great rapidity. That he had this dream preceding Sumter, Bull Run, Antietam, Gettysburg, Stone River, Vicksburg, Wilmington etc. . . .

Genl Grant interrupted to say Stone River was no victory,—that a few such fights would have ruined us. The President looked at Grant curiously and inquiringly—said they might differ on that point,—at all events his dream preceded it. . . .

["]I had,["] the President remarked, ["]this strange dream again last night, and we shall, judging from the past, have great news very soon. I think it must be from Sherman. My thoughts are in that direction as are most of yours.["] [3] [Johnston surrendered to Sherman on April 26th.]

[Many years later, Hugh McCulloch remembered that at this Cabinet session:⁴]

The question, "What shall be done to the Confederate leaders" was referred to, but not discussed . . . Mr. Lincoln merely remarked in his humorous manner, "I am a good deal like the Irishman who had joined a temperance society, but thought that he might take a drink now and then if he drank unbeknown to himself. A good many people think that all the big Confederates ought to be arrested and tried as traitors. Perhaps they ought to be; but I should be right glad if they would get out of the country unbeknown to me."

"You Almost Startle Me"

FRIDAY, APRIL 14, 1865

¶ *In the afternoon, Abraham and Mary Lincoln went for a ride. On November 15, 1865, Mary wrote Francis B. Carpenter about it:* ¹

The Friday I never saw him so supremely cheerful—his manner was even playful. At three o'clock, in the afternoon, he drove out with me in the open carriage. In starting, I asked him, if any one, should accompany us. He immediately replied—"No, I prefer to ride by ourselves to day." During the drive he was so gay, that I said to him laughingly, "Dear Husband, you almost startle me, by your great cheerfulness;" he replied "and well I may feel so, Mary, I consider *this day*, the war has come to a close."—and then added, "We must *both*, be more cheerful in the future—between the war & the loss of our darling Willie—we have both, been very miserable." Every word then uttered, is deeply engraven, on my poor broken heart.

[That night, the President and his wife went to the theatre.]

Annotations

(*Manuscript diaries of Salmon P. Chase, John Hay, and Gideon Welles have been used in the preparation of this volume. Their published diaries also have been cited as a convenience to the reader.*)

PREFACE

1. Robert B. Warden, *Account of the Private Life and Public Services of Salmon Portland Chase* (Cincinnati, 1874), 40.
2. *Ibid.*, 56.

Chapter One—"MISCELLANEOUS AND INCONGRUOUS ELEMENTS"

1. *De Bow's Review,* XXXII (1862), 8.
2. William H. Russell, *The Civil War in America* (Boston, 1861), 44.
3. James G. Blaine, *Twenty Years of Congress: From Lincoln to Garfield* (Norwich, Conn., 1884-1886), I, 160.
4. *Ibid.*, 161.
5. George Lunt, *The Origins of the Late War* (New York, 1866), 353.
6. MS. in New York Historical Society; quoted in Allan Nevins, *The Emergence of Lincoln* (New York, 1950), II, 260.

"PENNSYLVANIA BOWS TO ILLINOIS"

1. *New York Tribune,* May 25, 1860. For another version by Charles Carleton Coffin, correspondent of the *Boston Journal,* see Allen Thorndike Rice (ed.), *Reminiscences of Abraham Lincoln by Distinguished Men of His Time* (New York, 1886), 172-175 (hereinafter cited as *Rice's Reminiscences*). See also Carl Schurz, *The Reminiscences of Carl Schurz* (New York, 1907-1908), II, 187-188.
2. For Lincoln's letter accepting the nomination, see Lincoln to George

398 *CONVERSATIONS WITH LINCOLN*

Ashmun, May 23, 1860, in Roy P. Basler, *et al.* (eds.), *The Collected Works of Abraham Lincoln* (New Brunswick, N. J., 1953), IV, 52 (hereinafter cited as *Collected Works*).
3. Incorrectly spelled "Blakie" in source.

"HE LIKED TO SEE HIS FRIENDS"

1. *New York Herald,* Oct. 20, 1860.
2. *Utica* (N. Y.) *Morning Herald,* June 27, 1860, reprinted in *Sacramento Daily Union,* Aug. 15, 1860.

"IF THEY HEAR NOT MOSES . . ."

1. Horace Greeley, *The American Conflict: A History of The Great Rebellion in the United States of America, 1860-'65* . . . (Hartford, Conn., 1864-1866), I, 326-327.
2. Lincoln to William S. Speer, Oct. 23, 1860, in *Collected Works,* IV, 130.
3. John G. Nicolay and John Hay, *Abraham Lincoln: A History* (New York, 1890), III, 279-282 (hereinafter cited as *Abraham Lincoln*). See also original memorandum by Nicolay, dated Springfield, Ill., Nov. 5, 1860, in John G. Nicolay MSS., Library of Congress.

Chapter Two—"FORTUNATE FOR THE PEACE"

1. Edward Stanwood, *A History of the Presidency from 1788 to 1897* (Boston, 1916), 297.
2. Theodore C. Pease and James G. Randall (eds.), *The Diary of Orville Hickman Browning, 1850-1881* (Springfield, Ill., 1925-1933), I, 415 (hereinafter cited as *Browning Diary*).
3. Lincoln to William H. Seward, Dec. 8, 1860, in *Collected Works,* IV, 148-149.
4. Passage for Lyman Trumbull's speech, Nov. 20, 1860, in *ibid.,* 141-142.
5. Edward McPherson, *The Political History of the United States of America, During the Great Rebellion* . . . (Washington, D. C., 1865), 50 (hereinafter cited as *Political History*).

"MY DECLARATIONS HAVE BEEN MADE"

1. *New York Evening Post,* Nov. 14, 1860, reprinted in *New York Tribune,* Nov. 20, 1860, and in *Illinois State Journal,* Nov. 24, 1860.

"A RELATIVE OF MRS. L."

1. Nicolay memorandum, Nov. 16, 1860, in Nicolay MSS.
2. For discussion on identity of Lincoln's relative, see David L. Smiley, "Abraham Lincoln Deals with Cassius M. Clay: Portrait of a Patient Politician," in *Lincoln Herald* (Winter, 1953), 18, 29.

"MR LINCOLN DID NOT BELIEVE . . ."

1. Donn Piatt, *Memories of the Men Who Saved the Union* (New York, 1887), 33-34.

"I ACCEPTED HIS INVITATION"

1. *Reminiscences of Carl Schurz*, II, 175.
2. Howard K. Beale (ed.), *The Diary of Edward Bates, 1859-1866* (Washington, D. C., 1933), 164 (hereinafter cited as *Bates Diary*).
3. Quoted in O. J. Hollister, *Life of Schuyler Colfax* (New York, 1886), 200.
4. Burton J. Hendrick, *Lincoln's War Cabinet* (Boston, 1946), 46.
5. Nicolay memorandum, Dec. 15, 1860, in Nicolay MSS.
6. *Bates Diary*, 157.
7. Nicolay memorandum, *supra*.
8. *Bates Diary*, 164-167.
9. Brackets here and in two preceding paragraphs are in source.
10. Appears as "wd." in source.
11. Name in bracket inserted by editor.
12. Appears as "N Carolina" in source. Other brackets in this paragraph are as in the printed *Diary*.

"THE 'BLACK REPUBLICAN' LION"

1. *New York Herald*, Nov. 22, 1860.
2. *The New York Times*, Dec. 27, 1860.
3. For another report of this incident, see dispatch of Dec. 19, 1860, in Henry Villard, *Lincoln on the Eve of '61: A Journalist's Story*, edited by Harold G. and Oswald Garrison Villard (New York, 1941), 41-43.

"NEVER A BOSS CABINET-MAKER"

1. Thurlow Weed to William H. Seward, May 20, 1860, in Thurlow Weed MSS., University of Rochester.
2. R. Campbell to Salmon P. Chase, Apr. 8, 1861, in Salmon P. Chase MSS., Library of Congress.
3. Horace White, *Life of Lyman Trumbull* (Boston, 1913), 140.
4. *New York Herald*, June 28, 1858.
5. Gideon Welles (postwar recollection), 16, MS., in Illinois State Historical Library.
6. Lincoln to Lyman Trumbull, Dec. 21, 1860, in *Collected Works*, IV, 158. Contemporary newspapers reported Weed was in Springfield only one day. See William E. Baringer, *A House Dividing* (Springfield, Ill., 1945), 117n.
7. Thurlow Weed, *Autobiography of Thurlow Weed* (Boston, 1883), 605-611. Years later, Leonard Swett recalled the interview lasted "several days." See Thurlow Weed Barnes, *Memoir of Thurlow Weed* (Boston, 1884), 293; Swett to Editor, in *Chicago Tribune*, July 15, 1878.
8. *Autobiography of Thurlow Weed*, 605-614. See also Swett in Barnes, *Memoir of Thurlow Weed*, 293-295.
9. Lincoln to W. H. Seward, Dec. 8, 1860, in *Collected Works*, IV, 148-149.
10. Lincoln to Trumbull, Dec. 21, 1860, in *ibid.*, 158. For the resolution, see *ibid.*, 156-157.
11. James Ford Rhodes, *History of the United States from the Compromise of 1850* (New York, 1893-1906), III, 150-177.

"GOOD GROUND TO LIVE AND TO DIE BY"

1. Nicolay memorandum, Dec. 22, 1860, in Nicolay MSS.

"THE REAL QUESTION AT ISSUE"

1. Duff Green to James Buchanan, Dec. 28, 1860, in James Buchanan MSS., Historical Society of Pennsylvania. For another version of this meeting by Duff Green, see *New York Herald,* Jan. 8, 1861.
2. Lincoln to Trumbull, Dec. 28, 1860, in *Collected Works,* IV, 163. See also Lincoln to Duff Green, Dec. 28, 1860, in *ibid.,* 162-163.
3. Duff Green to Jefferson Davis, May 26, 1862 [?], in Nicolay and Hay, *Abraham Lincoln,* III, 286. All efforts to locate the original letter have failed.

"CAMERON CANNOT BE TRUSTED"

1. *The Diary of a Public Man and a Page of Political Correspondence: Stanton to Buchanan,* with a foreword by Carl Sandburg and prefatory notes by F. Lauriston Bullard (New Brunswick, N. J., 1946), 74.
2. See Lincoln's memorandum on charges against Simon Cameron, Dec. 31, 1860, in *Collected Works,* IV, 165.
3. Quoted in Hendricks, *Lincoln's War Cabinet,* 51.
4. Henry C. Carey to Lincoln, Jan. 7, 1861, copy in Henry C. Carey MSS., Historical Society of Pennsylvania.
5. White, *Life of Lyman Trumbull,* 146-147.
6. W. H. Herndon to Lyman Trumbull, Jan. 27, 1861, in Lyman Trumbull MSS., Library of Congress.
7. Thomas J. McCormack (ed.), *Memoirs of Gustave Koerner, 1809-1896* (Cedar Rapids, Iowa, 1909), II, 114.

"THE CONDITIONS OF THE PEONS"

1. Communication, Ocampo, to Matias Romero, Vera Cruz, Dec. 22, 1860, Reservada, Numero 17, Archivo de Relationes Esteriores, Mexico, D. F., copy in Library of Congress. See also Ernest G. Hildner, Jr., "The Mexican Envoy Visits Lincoln," in *Abraham Lincoln Quarterly* (Sept., 1950), 184-189.
2. Communication, Matias Romero to Minister of Foreign Relations, Chicago, Jan. 23, 1861, Reservada, Numero 2, Archivo de Relationes Esteriores, Mexico, D. F., copy in Library of Congress.
3. *Ibid.* See also Lincoln to Romero, Jan. 21, 1861, in *Collected Works,* IV, 177-178; J. Fred Rippy, *The United States and Mexico* (New York, 1926), Chaps. 13 and 14; Ralph Roeder, *Juarez and His Mexico* (New York, 1947), I, 366-370, and *passim.*

"NO GOOD RESULTS WOULD FOLLOW"

1. *Browning Diary,* I, 453.

"NO CHANGE IN THE FIRM"

1. William H. Herndon to Caroline H. Dall, Dec. 30, 1866, quoted in David Donald, *Lincoln's Herndon* (New York, 1948), 18-19.
2. W. H. Herndon and Jesse W. Weik, *Herndon's Lincoln: The True Story of a Great Life* . . . (Chicago, Ill., 1889), III, 483-485. For Lincoln's offer to appoint Herndon to a government post, see *ibid.*, 484n.
3. Jesse W. Weik, *The Real Lincoln* (Boston, 1922), 301.

"ONE TERM MIGHT SATISFY"

1. Villard, *Lincoln on the Eve of '61*, 67.
2. *Illinois State Journal*, Feb. 12, 1861.
3. Lincoln's Farewell Address, Feb. 11, 1861, in *ibid.*
4. *Domestic Medicine, or Poor Man's Friend in Sickness* (Madisonville, Tenn., 1836).

"HOSTILITY . . . TO GEN. CAMERON"

1. James Millikin to Simon Cameron, Feb. 22, 1861, in Harry E. Pratt (ed.), *Concerning Mr. Lincoln in Which Abraham Lincoln is Pictured as He Appeared to Letter Writers of His Time* (Springfield, Ill., 1944), 57-59.
2. Titian J. Coffey to Simon Cameron, Feb. 22, 1861, in *ibid.*, 60-61.

"MR. LINCOLN . . . HAD NO FEARS"

1. Norma B. Cuthbert (ed.), *Lincoln and the Baltimore Plot 1861: From Pinkerton Records and Related Papers* (San Marino, Calif., 1949), 66-67.
2. *Ibid.*, 67.
3. *Ibid.*, 77-79. For other conversations relating to the Baltimore plot, see Frederick W. Seward, *Reminiscences of a War-Time Statesman* (New York, 1916), 134-138; Cuthbert, *Lincoln and the Baltimore Plot*, 82-84, 88, 109-113, 114-123.

"PLAIN AS A TURNPIKE ROAD"

1. *Washington Evening Star*, Feb. 25, 1861.
2. Mary Boykin Chesnut, *A Diary from Dixie*, edited by Ben Ames Williams (Boston, 1949), 19.
3. *New York Herald*, Feb. 25, 1861.
4. *Ibid.* See also report of Rudolph Schleiden to Government of Bremen, Feb. 26, 1861, quoted in Ralph H. Lutz, "Rudolph Schleiden and the Visit to Richmond, April 25, 1861," in *Annual Report of American Historical Association* (1915), 210.
5. *New York Tribune*, Feb. 25, 1861.
6. L. E. Chittenden, *Recollections of President Lincoln and His Administration* (New York, 1891), 71-78. See also *New York Tribune*, Feb. 25, 1861.

"IF . . . WASHINGTON OCCUPIED THE SEAT"

1. *Liverpool Mercury*, Oct. 9, 1862, reprinted in D. R. Barbee and M. L. Bonham, Jr. (eds.), "Fort Sumter Again," in *Mississippi Valley Historical*

Review (June, 1941), 63-73. While the newspapers refer to Rives as "Reeves," and to General Doniphan as "Donovon," the correct spellings of the names are used for our purposes.
2. *Ibid.* See also C. S. Morehead to John J. Crittenden, Feb. 23, 1862, in John J. Crittenden MSS., Library of Congress.
3. Spelled "Sumpter" in original.

Chapter Three—"THINK CALMLY AND WELL"

1. W. H. Seward letter, Jan. 23, 1861, in Frederick W. Seward, *Seward at Washington as Senator and Secretary of State* (New York, 1891), I, 497.
2. Dwight L. Dumond (ed.), *Southern Editorials on Secession* (New York, 1931), 300.
3. Chittenden, *Recollections of President Lincoln and His Administration*, 38.
4. Ben: Perley Poore, *Reminiscences of Sixty Years in the National Metropolis* (Philadelphia, 1886), II, 69.
5. Lincoln's Inaugural Address, Mar. 4, 1861, in *Collected Works*, IV, 262-271.
6. Quoted in Benjamin P. Thomas, *Abraham Lincoln* (New York, 1952), 248.
7. *Ibid.*
8. *Charleston Mercury*, Mar. 5, 1861.
9. *Chicago Tribune*, Mar. 5, 1861.
10. *New York Tribune*, Mar. 5, 1861.
11. *Baltimore Sun*, quoted in *New York Tribune*, Mar. 7, 1861.
12. *St. Louis Republican*, quoted in *The New York Times*, Mar. 6, 1861.
13. B. B. Munford, *Virginia's Attitude Toward Slavery and Secession* (New York, 1909), 266.
14. John A. Gilmer to Stephen A. Douglas, Mar. 8, 1861, in Stephen A. Douglas MSS., University of Chicago.
15. Nicolay and Hay, *Abraham Lincoln*, III, 374.
16. David C. Mearns (ed.), *The Lincoln Papers* (Garden City, N. Y., 1948), 476-478; *Collected Works*, IV, 279n.
17. Seward's "Some Thoughts for the President's Consideration," Apr. 1, 1861, in *ibid.*, 317n-318.
18. Lincoln to Seward, Apr. 1, 1861, in *ibid.*, 316-317.
19. Lincoln's Message to Congress, July 4, 1861, in *ibid.*, 424-425.
20. *New York Tribune*, May 2, 1861.
21. Lincoln's Proclamation, Apr. 15, 1861, in *Collected Works*, IV, 331-332.
22. Nicolay and Hay, *Abraham Lincoln*, III, 443.
23. *Chicago Tribune*, Mar. 14, 1861.

"SOME MAN . . . WHO COULD GET ON A HORSE"

1. Nicolay and Hay, *Abraham Lincoln*, III, 385.
2. *Ibid.*, 394.

3. *Ibid.,* 395.
4. *Ibid.,* 430.
5. *Official Records of the Union and Confederate Navies in the War of The Rebellion* (Washington, D. C., 1894-1922), ser. I, vol. IV, 227.
6. Montgomery C. Meigs, "General M. C. Meigs on the Conduct of the Civil War," in *American Historical Review* (January, 1921), 299.
7. *Ibid.,* 299-300.

"WHAT HAVE I DONE WRONG?"

1. Narrative of Gideon Welles, MS. in vol. I, *Diary of Gideon Welles,* in Library of Congress. See also Howard K. Beale (ed.), *The Diary of Gideon Welles* (New York, 1960), I, 16 (hereinafter cited as *Beale ed.*).
2. Narrative of Gideon Welles; *Beale ed.,* I, 16-19, 20-21.
3. In his article, "Fort Sumter," in *The Galaxy* (Nov., 1870), 624, Welles says the letter was in Montgomery C. Meigs' handwriting and that Porter wrote the postscript.

"MR. PRESIDENT, IF I HAD CONTROL"

1. Nicolay and Hay, *Abraham Lincoln,* III, 422.
2. *Ibid.,* 423.
3. *Report of the Joint Committee on Reconstruction,* 39th Congress, 1st session (1866), Report No. 30, vol. II, part 2, 102-106. See also John B. Baldwin, *Interview Between President Lincoln and Col. John B. Baldwin, April 4, 1861* (Staunton, Va., 1866), 28pp.; Allan B. Magruder, "A Piece of Secret History: President Lincoln and the Virginia Convention of 1861," in *Atlantic Monthly* (April, 1875), 438-440.
4. Spelled "Sumpter" in original.
5. George Plumer Smith to John Hay, July 9, 1863, in Robert Todd Lincoln Collection of Lincoln Papers (hereinafter cited as RTL), Library of Congress; Hay to Smith, July 10, 1863, in *ibid.* For John Minor Botts' and other testimony conflicting with Baldwin's on this point, see *Report of the Joint Committee on Reconstruction, supra.,* 69-70, 114-120. See also J. M. Botts to Nicolay, July 2, 1866, in Nicolay MSS., and Jacob M. Howard to W. H. Herndon, Nov. 18, 1866, in Herndon-Weik MSS., Library of Congress. For discussion of this controversy, see Thomas, *Abraham Lincoln,* 540; Richard N. Current, *The Lincoln Nobody Knows* (New York, 1958), 120-121; W. L. Hall, "Lincoln's Interview with John B. Baldwin," in *South Atlantic Quarterly,* XIII (1914), 260-269; Nicolay and Hay, *Abraham Lincoln,* III, 423-428; James G. Randall, *Lincoln the Liberal Statesman* (New York, 1947), 97-98, 226 note 4; *idem., Lincoln the President: Springfield to Gettysburg* (New York, 1946), I, 325-327.

"THE POWHATAN MUST BE RESTORED"

1. Nicolay and Hay, *Abraham Lincoln,* III, 4.
2. Welles MS. Narrative in Welles MSS.; *Beale ed.,* I, 24-25.
3. Nicolay and Hay, *supra.,* 440.

"MR. PRESIDENT, I . . . CONCUR"

1. *Official Records of the Union and Confederate Armies in the War of the Rebellion* (Washington, D. C., 1880-1901), ser. I, vol. I, 291 (hereinafter cited as *O.R.*).
2. Nicolay and Hay, *Abraham Lincoln,* IV, 46.
3. *O.R.,* ser. I, vol. I, 301.
4. *Ibid.,* 14.
5. A. R. Chisholm MS., quoted in Randall, *Lincoln the President,* I, 341.

"TROOPS . . . THROUGH BALTIMORE"

1. Ben: Perley Poore, *Reminiscences,* II, 74.
2. *Ibid.*
3. Henry J. Raymond, *History of the Administration of Abraham Lincoln . . .* (New York, 1864), 125.
4. *Ibid.,* 125-126.
5. Lincoln to Thomas H. Hicks and George W. Brown, Apr. 20, 1861, in *Collected Works,* IV, 341.
6. Raymond, *History of the Administration of Abraham Lincoln,* 127-128. See also Frank Moore, *The Rebellion Record . . .* (New York, 1861-1871), I (Docs.), 123-124. Mayor Brown's report of his conversation with Lincoln was also published in *The South,* Apr. 22, 1861.

"ABOUT THE LAW OF NATIONS"

1. Lincoln's Proclamation of Blockade, Apr. 19, 1861, in *Collected Works,* IV, 338-339.
2. *New York Herald,* July 8, 1867.
3. *Ibid.*
4. Lincoln's Proclamation of Blockade, Apr. 27, 1861, in *Collected Works,* IV, 346-347.

"TO LOSE KENTUCKY . . ."

1. Lincoln to O. H. Browning, Sept. 22, 1861, in Browning MSS., Illinois State Historical Library.
2. Garrett Davis's letter, Apr. 28, 1861, in Frankfort, Ky., *Commonwealth,* May 3, 1861, reprinted in *Congressional Globe,* 37th Congress, 2nd session, *Appendix,* 81.
3. *Ibid.,* 82-83.

Chapter Four—"THE HEATHER IS ON FIRE"

1. Horace Binney to Sir J. T. Coleridge, Philadelphia, May 27, 1861, in Charles Chauncey Binney, *The Life of Horace Binney* (Philadelphia, 1903), 330.
2. George Ticknor to Sir Edmund Head, Boston, Apr. 21, 1861, in Anna Ticknor and George S. Hillard (eds.), *Life, Letters, and Journals of George Ticknor* (Boston, 1876), II, 434.

3. John D. Billings, quoted in Otto Eisenschiml and Ralph Newman (eds.), *The Civil War: The American Iliad* . . . (New York, 1956), I, 32.

4. Jane Stuart Woolsey to a friend in Paris, May 10, 1861, in Georgeanna Woolsey Bacon and Eliza Woolsey Howland (eds.), *Letters of a Family During the War for the Union, 1861-1865* (Privately printed, 1899), I, 68.

5. *Detroit Free Press*, Apr. 10, 1861.

6. Ticknor to Head, Apr. 21, 1861, in Ticknor and Hillard, *Life, Letters, and Journals of George Ticknor*, II, 433.

7. Clarence C. Buel and Robert U. Johnson (eds.), *Battles and Leaders of the Civil War* (New York, 1887-1888), I, 7n.

8. *Detroit Free Press*, Apr. 19, 1861.

9. Theodore F. Upson, *With Sherman to the Sea* . . . , edited by Oscar O. Winther (Baton Rouge, La., 1943), 19.

10. Thomas, *Abraham Lincoln*, 258-259.

11. *Ibid.*, 259.

12. Edward Everett to J. J. Crittenden, Apr. 18, 1861, in Crittenden MSS.

13. War Department, Adjutant General's Office, *General Orders*, 1861, No. 54.

14. Edward Dicey, *Six Months in the Federal States* (London and Cambridge, 1863), II, 9.

15. Quoted in Bruce Catton, *This Hallowed Ground* (New York, 1956), 22.

16. *Military Essays and Recollections: Papers Read before the Commandary of the State of Illinois, Military Order of the Loyal Legion of the United States* (Chicago, 1899), III, 402; *Diary of an Ohio Volunteer*, by a Musician, Co. H, 19th Regiment (Cleveland, 1861), 15.

17. *Richmond Examiner*, Apr. 23, 1861.

18. Lincoln's Call, May 3, 1861, in *Collected Works*, IV, 353-354.

19. Lincoln's Suspension of *Habeas Corpus* in Florida, May 16, 1861, in *ibid.*, 364-365.

20. Lincoln's Message to Congress, July 4, 1861, in *ibid.*, 421-441.

21. *U. S. Statutes at Large*, XII, 326.

22. McPherson, *Political History*, 115; J. G. Randall, *The Civil War and Reconstruction* (Boston, 1937), 367.

23. *Congressional Globe*, 37th Congress, 1st session, 222-223, 265; *ibid.*, 37th Congress, 2nd session, 15.

24. Moore, *Rebellion Record*, II (Docs.), 376.

25. Memoranda of Military Policy Suggested by the Bull Run Defeat, July 23 and 27, 1861, in *Collected Works*, IV, 457-458; George B. McClellan, *McClellan's Own Story* (New York, 1887), 66, 82.

26. Lincoln's Message to Congress, July 4, 1861, in *Collected Works*, IV, 426.

"THAT HAS TO COME DOWN"

1. *Washington Evening Star*, May 24, 1861.

2. *New York Herald*, May 25, 1861.

3. *Ibid.*

4. *Ibid.*

5. _Ibid._ See also _ibid._, Feb. 20, 1861; Nicolay, _The Outbreak of Rebellion_ (New York, 1881), 111.

6. Lincoln to Ephraim D. and Phoebe Ellsworth, May 25, 1861, in _Collected Works_, IV, 385-386.

7. _New York Herald_, May 25, 1861.

8. The word "take" in the source obviously is a typographical error.

9. Nicolay, _The Outbreak of Rebellion_, 114.

"MIXED UP WITH OFFICE-SEEKERS"

1. Edward Bates to Barton Bates, Mar. 22, 1861, in Edward Bates MSS., Missouri Historical Society; Nathaniel Hawthorne, "Chiefly About War Matters," in _Atlantic Monthly_ (July, 1862), 43-61; Lincoln to Ninian W. Edwards, June 19, 1861, in _Collected Works_, IV, 412.

2. Robert L. Wilson to W. H. Herndon, Feb. 10, 1866, in Herndon-Weik MSS.; _Collected Works_, IV, 452.

"THE GREATEST COWARD"

1. Alfred Roman, _Military Operations of General Beauregard in the War Between the States 1861-65_ (New York, 1864), I, 121-122.

2. William H. Russell, _My Diary North and South_ (Boston, 1863), 373; Moore, _Rebellion Record_, II (Docs.), 385.

3. _O.R._, ser. I, vol. II, 316; W. H. Russell letter to London _Times_, in Moore, _Rebellion Record_, II (Docs.), 52; Russell, _My Diary_, 467.

4. Moore, _Rebellion Record_, II (Docs.), 284; Russell letter to London _Times_, in _ibid._, 64.

5. W. A. Richardson's remarks (July 24, 1861), in _Congressional Globe_, 37th Congress, 1st session, 388. For further discussion of this conversation, see remarks of Elihu B. Washburne (Aug. 1, 1861), in _ibid._, 387, and those of Thaddeus Stevens and Frank Blair (Feb. 17, 1862), in _ibid._, 37th Congress, 2nd session, 852.

"NO CURSE COULD BE GREATER"

1. M. A. DeWolfe Howe (ed.), _Home Letters of General Sherman_ (New York, 1909), 209; W. T. Sherman, _Personal Memoirs of General W. T. Sherman_ (New York, 1875), I, 216.

2. Russell, _My Diary_, 474; Sherman, _Personal Memoirs_, I, 217-219. In his _Memoirs_, Sherman states Lincoln's visit to Fort Corcoran was made "about July 26th." However, in a letter to his wife, dated July 24, 1861 (see _Home Letters_, 203), Sherman wrote: "Yesterday the President and Mr. Seward visited me . . ." Russell (_My Diary_, 474) corroborates the fact that Lincoln and Seward visited Fort Corcoran on July 23rd, and refers to Sherman's threat to shoot one of his officers for insubordination (_ibid._, 474-475). See also _New York Herald_, July 24, 1861.

"THAT . . . IS . . . EMANCIPATION"

1. McPherson, _Political History_, 195.

2. _Congressional Globe_, 37th Congress, 1st session 262 and 413.

3. Speech by Robert Mallory (June 15, 1864), in *ibid.*, 38th Congress, 1st session, 2981-2982.

"QUITE A FEMALE POLITICIAN"

1. *O.R.*, ser. I, vol. III, 540-549; Gustave Koerner to Lyman Trumbull, Nov. 12, 1861, in Trumbull MSS.
2. *O.R.*, ser. I, vol. III, 466-467.
3. Lincoln to John C. Frémont, "Private and Confidential," Sept. 2, 1861, in *Collected Works*, IV, 506-507.
4. *Ibid.*, 515; Undated Memorandum by Mrs. Jessie Benton Frémont, and Unpublished Memoir of Mrs. Frémont, both in Bancroft Library, University of California.

" 'THE LITTLE CORPORAL' OF UNFOUGHT FIELDS"

1. *McClellan's Own Story*, 229; Russell, *My Diary*, 521.
2. *Ibid.*, 479-480; *McClellan's Own Story*, 85.
3. Russell, *My Diary*, 499, 519-520, and 535.
4. *McClellan's Own Story*, 86, 167, 169-170.
5. John Hay MS. Diary (Oct. 10, 1861), in John Hay MSS., Brown University; see also Tyler Dennett (ed.), *Lincoln and the Civil War in the Diaries and Letters of John Hay* (New York, 1939), 26-27 (hereinafter cited as *Dennett ed.*).

"I HAVE A NOTION . . ."

1. Joshua R. Giddings to George W. Julian, Jan. 28, 1862, in Giddings-Julian MSS., Library of Congress; Senator Graham N. Fitch of Indiana, in *Congressional Globe*, 36th Congress, 1st session, 2403; Noah Brooks, *Washington in Lincoln's Time* (New York, 1896), 211.
2. *Report of the Joint Committee on the Conduct of the War*, II (1863), 13 (hereinafter cited as *CCW*); Russell, *My Diary*, 561.
3. John Hay MS. Diary (Oct. 26, 1861); *Dennett ed.*, 31-32.

"IF OLD SCOTT HAD LEGS . . ."

1. Russell, *My Diary*, 432.
2. *Bates Diary*, 199.
3. Russell, *My Diary*, 525.
4. John Hay MS. Diary (undated entry covering Nov. 1, 1861); *Dennett ed.*, 32.

Chapter Five—*"THE FAT'S IN THE FIRE"*

1. *Bates Diary*, 205; Worthington C. Ford (ed.), *A Cycle of Adams Letters, 1861-1865* (Boston, 1920), I, 88; *ibid.*, 75.
2. *Ibid.*, 88; John Bigelow, *Retrospections of an Active Life* (New York, 1909), I, 399-400.
3. Benson J. Lossing, *Pictorial History of the Civil War* (Philadelphia, 1866-1869), II, 156-157.

4. John Bigelow to Charles Sumner, Jan. 20, 1862, in Charles Sumner MSS., Harvard University Library.
5. Russell, *My Diary*, 98.
6. Lord John Russell to Lord Lyons, Apr. 20, 1861, in Lord John Russell MSS., G.D. 22/96, in Public Records Office, London, England; E. D. Adams, *Great Britain and the American Civil War* (London, 1925), I, 64-65.
7. Russell, *My Diary*, 40; Adams, *Great Britain and the American Civil War*, I, 67.
8. Seward to C. F. Adams, June 8, 1861, in *Senate Document No. 1*, 37th Congress, 2nd session, 101; Lincoln's Revision of Seward's Communication to C. F. Adams, May 21, 1861, in *Collected Works*, IV, 376-380.
9. Ford, *A Cycle of Adams Letters*, I, 16-17.
10. *Ibid.*, 11.
11. *Ibid.*, 14.
12. Gerrit Smith to Owen Lovejoy, July 12, 1861, MS. in New York Historical Society; quoted in Allan Nevins, *The War for the Union* (New York, 1959), I, 334; Gen. J. R. Hawley to Gideon Welles, New Haven, Sept. 17, 1861, in Welles MSS., Illinois State Historical Library; Charles Sumner to Miss Booth, Mar. 7, 1864, in C. M. Segal Collection of Sumner MSS.
13. *St. Cloud Democrat*, Jan. 16, 1862.
14. Report of Secretary of War, in *Congressional Globe*, 37th Congress, 2nd session, *Appendix*, 16; *Congressional Globe*, 37th Congress, 2nd session, 59; Lincoln to H. W. Halleck, Jan. 7, 1862, in *Collected Works*, V, 92.

"THE POLICY OF PAYING"

1. *Browning Diary*, I, 512.

"SEWARD . . . CAUSED US UNEASINESS"

1. See Julius W. Pratt, *A History of the United States Foreign Policy* (New York, 1955), 307.
2. Typewritten copy, MG 27, I, D 8, vol. 2, p. 672, in A. T. Galt MSS., Public Archives of Canada.
3. Original, MG 27, I, D 8, vol. 7, pp. 2652A-2652E, in *ibid.*
4. Galt spelled this name "Ashman."

"A MONSTROUS EXTRAVAGANCE"

1. John A. Briggs to John Sherman, New York, Feb. 20, 1861, in John Sherman MSS., Library of Congress; Elizabeth Todd Grimsley, "Six Months in the White House," in *Journal of the Illinois State Historical Society* (Oct., 1926), 47.
2. Mary Lincoln to B. B. French, July 26, 1862, MS., in Illinois State Historical Library.
3. Milton Hay to his Wife, Springfield, Ill., Apr. 6, 1862, in Stuart-Hay MSS., Illinois State Historical Library; Hay to Nicolay, Apr. 9, 1862, in *Dennett ed.*, 41.

4. B. B. French to Pamela French, Dec. 24, 1861, in B. B. French MSS., Library of Congress.
5. *Ibid.*

"HE WOULD LIKE TO BORROW IT"

1. *Congressional Globe,* 37th Congress, 2nd session, 190.
2. *Bates Diary,* 220; *Browning Diary,* I, 523.
3. William Swinton, *Campaigns of the Army of the Potomac* (New York, 1866), 80-82.
4. Lincoln to H. J. Raymond, Oct. 7, 1864, in *Collected Works,* VIII, 39-40.

"WHISPERING . . . RECOMMENCED"

1. Swinton, *Campaigns of the Army of the Potomac,* 82-83.
2. *McClellan's Own Story,* 156.
3. McDowell memorandum in Swinton, *Campaigns of the Army of the Potomac,* 84-85; *McClellan's Own Story,* 156-158; "General M. C. Meigs on the Conduct of the Civil War," in *American Historical Review* (Jan., 1921), 292-293.
4. Spelled "Tadd" in source.
5. Lincoln's General Order No. 1, Jan. 27, 1862, in *Collected Works,* V, 111-112; Lincoln's Special War Order No. 1, Jan. 31, 1862, in *ibid.,* 115.

"A FRANK CONFESSION"

1. Phillips Russell, *Emerson: The Wisest American* (New York, 1929), 264; Edward Waldo Emerson and Waldo Emerson Forbes (eds.), *Journals of Ralph Waldo Emerson* (Boston, 1913), IX, 325.
2. *Ibid.,* 386-388.

"THE GALLANT . . . ILLS. TROOPS"

1. *Battles and Leaders of the Civil War,* I, 427; Ulysses S. Grant, *Personal Memoirs of U. S. Grant* (New York, 1885), I, 311-312.
2. Nicolay memorandum, Feb. 17, 1862, in Nicolay MSS.

"IT IS A D—D FIZZLE"

1. Nicolay memoranda, Feb. 18 and Feb. 20, 1862, in Nicolay MSS.
2. Swinton, *Campaigns of the Army of the Potomac,* 88; Nicolay and Hay, *Abraham Lincoln,* V, 168.
3. Nicolay memorandum, Feb. 27, 1862, in Nicolay MSS.

"A VERY UGLY MATTER"

1. Nicolay and Hay, *Abraham Lincoln,* V, 169.
2. *McClellan's Own Story,* 195-197.

"DAY-STAR OF A NEW . . . DAWN"

1. *New York Tribune,* Mar. 7, 1862.
2. Lincoln's Message to Congress, Mar. 6, 1862, in *Collected Works,* V, 144-146.

3. *New York Herald,* Mar. 8, 1862; *New York Tribune,* Mar. 7, 1862.
4. Nicolay memorandum, Mar. 9, 1862, in Nicolay MSS.
5. Lincoln to H. J. Raymond, Mar. 9, 1862, in *Collected Works,* V, 152-153.

"THE SENSIBILITIES OF THE SLAVE STATES"

1. John A. Logan, *The Great Conspiracy: Its Origin and History* (New York, 1886), 385-389.

"YESTERDAY . . . HE SHED TEARS"

1. Lincoln's War Order No. 3, Mar. 11, 1862, in *Collected Works,* V, 155. See also *Dennett ed.,* 37.
2. *McClellan's Own Story,* 220.
3. *Browning Diary,* I, 537-538.

"IN . . . STRICTEST CONFIDENCE"

1. *New York Herald,* Apr. 8, 1862.
2. *Ibid.,* Apr. 6, 1862.
3. *Ibid.,* Apr. 5, 1862.
4. Lincoln to Horace Greeley, Mar. 24, 1862, in *Collected Works,* V, 169.
5. *Browning Diary,* I, 541.
6. This Act liberated 3,026 Negroes out of a District slave population—by the 1860 census—of 3,185. The cost: $934,873.10, borne by the Federal Government. See Alfred G. Harris, "Lincoln and the Question of Slavery in the District of Columbia," in *Lincoln Herald* (Spring, 1952), 12-21. While Lincoln withheld his "unwilling consent" for two days (*New York Herald,* Apr. 17, 1862), Sumner quipped that by holding back the bill, the President was "making himself . . . for the time being, the largest slaveholder in the country." (Sumner to John A. Andrew, Apr. 22, 1862, in John A. Andrew MSS., Massachusetts Historical Society.) For Lincoln's Message to Congress on this bill, see *Collected Works,* V, 192.

"THE NEXT MOST TROUBLESOME SUBJECT"

1. *New York Herald,* Apr. 17 and 18, 1862.
2. *Ibid.,* June 21, 1862.

"NOBODY WAS HURT"

1. See Lincoln's Remarks in Jersey City, N. J., June 24, 1862, and General Scott's Statement, in *Collected Works,* V, 284 and note.
2. *New York Herald,* June 26, 1862.

"THE BLOW MUST FALL"

1. Gideon Welles, "The History of Emancipation," in *The Galaxy* (Dec., 1872), 842-843.

Chapter Six—*"THE GASES OF PUBLIC EXASPERATION"*

1. Allan Nevins and Milton Halsey Thomas (eds.), *The Diary of George Templeton Strong 1835-1875* (New York, 1952), III, 239, 237 and 244 (hereinafter cited as *Strong Diary*).

2. *Detroit Free Press,* July 3, 1862; *New York Herald,* July 8 and 9, 1862; *McClellan's Own Story,* 346.

3. For Lincoln's notes on his interviews with the generals at Harrison's Landing, see *Collected Works,* V, 309-312; *O.R.,* ser. I, vol. XII, pt. 2, 5.

4. F. B. Carpenter, *Six Months at the White House with Abraham Lincoln* (New York, 1866), 20-21 (hereinafter cited as *Six Months*).

5. Lincoln's Proclamation revoking General Hunter's Order, May 19, 1862, in *Collected Works,* V, 222-223; Lincoln's Appeal to the Border State Representatives, in *ibid.,* 317-319.

6. Noah Brooks (Castine), "Letter from Washington," Feb. 4, 1863, in *Sacramento Daily Union,* Mar. 3, 1863.

7. Report of Wendell Phillips' speech in *New York Herald,* Aug. 8, 1862.

8. William L. Garrison to Oliver Johnson (copy), Sept. 9, 1862, in William L. Garrison MSS., Boston Public Library; Don C. Seitz, *Lincoln the Politician* . . . (New York, 1931), 332; S. G. Arnold to S. P. Chase, Sept. 12, 1862, in Chase MSS., Library of Congress; J. G. Randall, *Lincoln and the South* (Baton Rouge, La., 1946), 84.

9. Joshua F. Speed to Joseph Holt, Washington, D. C., Dec. 8, 1861, in Joseph Holt MSS., Library of Congress; *New York Herald,* May 11 and June 17, 1862; David Davis to Joseph Holt, Bloomington, Ill., Mar. 27, 1862, in Holt MSS.

10. Brooks (Castine), in *Sacramento Daily Union,* Mar. 3, 1863.

11. Lincoln to Henry W. Hoffman, Oct. 10, 1864, in *Collected Works,* VIII, 41; Lincoln to Joshua F. Speed, Aug. 24, 1855, in *ibid.,* II, 320-323; Lincoln's Peoria, Ill., Speech, Oct. 16, 1855, in *ibid.,* 255.

12. Lincoln's Peoria Speech, in *ibid.*

13. *Ibid.*

14. Lincoln's Charleston, Ill., Speech, Sept. 18, 1858, in *ibid.,* III, 145-146.

15. Protest of Lincoln *et al.,* Mar. 3, 1837, in *ibid.,* I, 74-75; Lincoln to N. P. Banks, Aug. 5, 1863, in *ibid.,* VI, 364-365.

16. Lincoln used this phrase in his address to the Young Men's Lyceum, Springfield, Ill., Jan. 27, 1838, in *ibid.,* I, 115. See also Lincoln to August Belmont, July 31, 1862, in *ibid.,* V, 350-351.

17. Lincoln to Albert G. Hodges, Apr. 4, 1864, in *ibid.,* VII, 281-283; Lincoln to James C. Conkling, Aug. 26, 1863, in *ibid.,* VI, 406-410.

18. Robert Dale Owen to S. P. Chase, Nov. 10, 1862, in *Sacramento Daily Union,* Dec. 22, 1862.

19. Carpenter, *Six Months,* 22.

20. *Ibid.*

"THE . . . HANDS TO ETHIOPIA"

1. Lincoln's Message to Congress, July 17, 1862, in *Collected Works,* V, 328-331.

2. Carpenter, *Six Months,* 21-22; Salmon P. Chase MS. Diary (July 22, 1862), in Library of Congress, printed in David Donald (ed.), *Inside Lincoln's Cabinet: The Civil War Diaries of Salmon Portland Chase* (New York, 1954), 97-100 (hereinafter cited as *Donald ed.*). See also E. M. Stanton's

fragmentary memorandum on the July 22, 1862, Cabinet meeting in Nicolay and Hay, *Abraham Lincoln,* VI, 128.

3. MS. in RTL.

"TWO COLORED REGIMENTS"

1. *New York Herald,* Aug. 6, 1862; Chase MS. Diary (Aug. 3, 1862); Donald ed., 104-110.
2. *New York Herald,* Aug. 5, 1862.

"WHAT THE EXECUTIVE HAD TO SAY"

1. Lincoln's Message to Congress, Dec. 3, 1861, in *Collected Works,* V, 48; U. S. *Statutes at Large,* XII, 378; *ibid.,* 582.
2. See also *Cincinnati Daily Gazette,* Aug. 20, 1862; Benjamin Quarles, *The Negro in the Civil War* (Boston, 1953), Chap. VII.
3. Edward M. Thomas to Lincoln, Aug. 16, 1862, in *Collected Works,* V, 370n-371.

"DISTRESSED . . . EXCEEDINGLY"

1. *O.R.,* ser. I, vol. XII, pt. 2, 63; McClellan to H. W. Halleck, Aug. 31, 1862, in Moore, *Rebellion Record,* XII (Docs.), 616.
2. *Battles and Leaders of the Civil War,* II, 541-542.
3. Chase MS. Diary (Sept. 2, 1862); *Donald ed.,* 118-120. See also *Beale ed.,* I, 104-106; *McClellan's Own Story,* 534-535.

"I CAN NEVER FEEL CONFIDENT"

1. Welles MS. Diary (Sept. 8, 1862); *Beale ed.,* I, 115-118.

"THE POPE'S BULL AGAINST THE COMET"

1. *New York Tribune,* Aug. 25, 1862.
2. *The New York Times,* Aug. 25, 1862.
3. *Strong Diary,* III, 256; *The New York Times,* Sept. 13, 1862.
4. *New York Herald,* Sept. 26, 1862; *Chicago Tribune,* Sept. 23, 1862; *National Intelligencer,* Sept. 26, 1862. Original MS. in Chicago Historical Society.

"DESIRE TO DO YOU JUSTICE"

1. *McClellan's Own Story,* 613; Lincoln's Response to Serenade, Sept. 24, 1862, in *New York Tribune,* Sept. 25, 1862; Lincoln to McClellan, Oct. 13, 1862, in *O.R.,* ser. I, vol. XIX, pt. 1, 13.
2. See James D. Horan and Howard Swiggett, *The Pinkerton Story* (New York, 1951), 111-114.
3. Quoted in *ibid.,* 115-119.

"PROMISE . . . TO MY MAKER"

1. Chase MS. Diary (Sept. 22, 1862); *Donald ed.,* 149-153; Welles MS. Diary (Sept. 22, 1862), *Beale ed.,* I, 142-145.

2. Artemus Ward (Charles Farrar Browne), *Artemus Ward: His Book* (New York, 1862), 24-25.

"WOULD YOU . . . SHAKE HANDS WITH ME . . . ?"

1. *New York Herald,* Oct. 3, 1862; *McClellan's Own Story,* 627; Baltimore correspondence reprinted in *Sacramento Daily Union,* Nov. 29, 1862.

Chapter Seven—*"LIKE A CHINAMAN BEATING HIS SWORDS"*

1. E. M. Stanton's report to Lincoln, in *Congressional Globe,* 37th Congress, 3rd session, *Appendix,* 29-30.
2. Report of H. W. Halleck, in Moore, *Rebellion Record,* VI (Docs.), 220-221.
3. Lincoln to McClellan, Oct. 13, 1862, in *O.R.,* ser. I, vol. XIX, pt. 1, 13; Nicolay to Hay, Oct. 26, 1862, in Nicolay MSS.; Nicolay to Therena Bates, Oct. 26, 1862, in *ibid.*
4. William E. Smith, *The Francis Preston Blair Family in Politics* (New York, 1933), I, 144-145.
5. Elijah H. Norton's remarks (Jan. 9, 1863), in *Congressional Globe,* 37th Congress, 3rd session, 261; A. E. Burnside to H. W. Halleck, Dec. 19, 1862, in Moore, *Rebellion Record,* VI (Docs.), 79.
6. Ford, *A Cycle of Adams Letters,* I, 240-241.
7. Francis Fessenden, *Life and Public Services of William Pitt Fessenden . . .* (Boston, 1907), I, 265-266.
8. John D. Baldwin to Charles Sumner, Worcester, Mass., Dec. 30, 1862, in Sumner MSS., Harvard University Library; *Browning Diary,* I, 596-597.
9. Fessenden, *Life and Public Services of W. P. Fessenden,* I, 266; *CCW,* II, pt. 1 (1863), 38; Lincoln to A. E. Burnside, Dec. 30, 1862, in *Collected Works,* VI, 22.
10. Dispatch of Feb. 2, 1863, in *Sacramento Daily Union,* Feb. 28, 1863.
11. *Boston Transcript,* reprinted in *ibid.,* Oct. 16, 1862.
12. Paris correspondence, in *New York Herald,* Oct. 26, 1862; London *Star,* Oct. 6, 1862; London *Times,* Oct. 7, 1862.
13. Lincoln's Proclamation Suspending the Writ of *Habeas Corpus,* in *Collected Works,* V, 436-437.
14. Garrett Davis' remarks (Dec. 15, 1862), in *Congressional Globe,* 37th Congress, 3rd session, 89; Burt Van Buren's remarks (Feb. 18, 1863), in *ibid.,* 1076; John W. Menzies' remarks (Dec. 11, 1862), in *ibid.,* 81.
15. Hendrick B. Wright's remarks (Jan. 14, 1863), in *ibid.,* 319.
16. S. S. Cox's remarks (Dec. 15, 1862), in *ibid.,* 94.
17. Washington dispatch, Nov. 23, 1862, in *Sacramento Daily Union,* Dec. 12, 1862.
18. *Lexington Observer & Reporter,* June 16, 1864, quoted in William H. Townsend, *Lincoln and the Bluegrass* (Lexington, 1955), 321.

"TELL ME FRANKLY . . ."

1. Kelley, in *Rice's Reminiscences,* 271-272.

2. *Ibid.*, 271-279; see also Kelley, *Lincoln and Stanton* . . . (New York, 1885), 72-76.

"WHAT DO THESE MEN WANT?"

1. *New York Herald*, Dec. 21, 1862.
2. Edward L. Pierce, *Memoir and Letters of Charles Sumner* (London, 1878-1893), IV, 111; HM 21996, Sumner to W. W. Story, Dec. 16, 1866, in Sumner MSS., Henry E. Huntington Library; Joseph Medill to Schuyler Colfax, quoted in Hollister, *Life of Schuyler Colfax*, 200; G. F. Williams to Sumner, Boston, Dec. 18, 1862, in Sumner MSS., Harvard University Library.
3. *Browning Diary*, I, 598.
4. *Ibid.*, 596-599; Fessenden, *Life and Public Services of W. P. Fessenden*, I, 233, 236-238.
5. *Ibid.*, 251-252; *Bates Diary*, 269.
6. *Browning Dairy*, I, 599-601. For reports of special Cabinet meeting, see Beale ed., I, 194-196; *Bates Diary*, 268-270. See also *Browning Diary*, I, 598-599.

"TO TENDER . . . THEIR FRIENDLY COUNSEL"

1. Fessenden, *Life and Public Services of W. P. Fessenden*, I, 239-240.
2. *Ibid.*, 240-243.
3. Misspelled "Mitchell" in original.
4. Seward to C. F. Adams, July 5, 1862, quoted in *Congressional Globe*, 37th Congress, 3rd session, 97.
5. Welles MS. Diary (Dec. 19, 1862). See also Beale ed., I, 194-196; *Bates Diary*, 268-270.

LINCOLN'S FEAR: "A GENERAL SMASH-UP"

1. Fessenden, *Life and Public Services of W. P. Fessenden*, I, 243-246.

"THIS . . . CUTS THE GORDIAN [K]NOT"

1. Welles MS. Diary (Dec. 20, 1862); Beale ed., I, 199-200.
2. Welles MS. Diary (Dec. 20, 1862); Beale ed., I, 201-202.

"THE PRESIDENT . . . EXPRESSED MISGIVINGS"

1. Lincoln to A. E. Burnside, Dec. 30, 1862, in *Collected Works*, VI, 22; Burnside testimony, in *CCW*, II, pt. 1 (1863), 717.
2. *Ibid.*, 717-718.

"MY WHOLE SOUL IS IN IT"

1. John Forney's speech as reported in the *Rochester* (N. Y.) *Express* is quoted in Carpenter, *Six Months*, 269-270. See also Seward, *Reminiscences of a War-Time Statesman and Diplomat*, 226-227.

"STRONGER WITH THE COUNTRY"

1. Lincoln to Burnside, Jan. 8, 1863, in *Collected Works*, VI, 46-48; *O.R.*, ser. I, vol. XXI, 998-999.

2. Henry J. Raymond, "Extracts from the Journal of Henry J. Raymond," edited by his son, in *Scribner's Monthly* (Mar., 1880), 704-705. See also Burnside testimony, in *CCW*, II, pt. 1 (1863), 718-720.

"NO REASON . . . TO RESIGN"

1. *CCW*, II, pt. 1 (1863), 720-721.
2. *O.R.*, ser. I, vol. XXI, 998-999 and 1008-1009.

"HE HAD TO MAKE WAY FOR JOSHUA"

1. [Moncure D. Conway], "President Lincoln, by an American Abolitionist," in *Fraser's Magazine* (Jan., 1865), 11-13. Frémont's name is spelled without the accent in the source. The report of Conway in the Senate Chamber is in the *New York Herald*, Jan. 26, 1863.
2. Incorrectly spelled "Stanley" in source.
3. Gov. Stanly's resignation in February was reported in *New York Herald*, Feb. 16, 1863.
4. Frémont's name is spelled without the accent in source.

"HE DID NOT KNOW WHAT BETTER TO DO"

1. Lincoln to Joseph Hooker, Jan. 26, 1863, in *Collected Works*, VI, 78-79. See also *Beale ed.*, I, 229-230.
2. *Browning Diary*, I, 619-620.
3. McClellan.

"AS WATER BUBBLING"

1. Pp. 612-614.

"EVILS OF BEING SO FAR APART"

1. Agnes Macdonnel letter, Feb., 1864 [1863], in Agnes Macdonnel, "America Then and Now: Recollections of Lincoln," in *The Contemporary Review* (May, 1917), 566-568.

"THE TAIL OF THE ARMY"

1. *His Talk with Lincoln: Being a Letter Written by James M. Stradling*, with a preface by Lord Charnwood and an introduction by Leigh Mitchell Hodges (New York, 1922), 12-31.

"BECAUSE THEY CULTIVATE THE EARTH"

1. *Washington Daily Morning Chronicle*, Mar. 28, 1863.
2. Brackets in source.

"FULL LENGTH 'LANDSCAPE'"

1. Quoted in Carl Haverlin, "Lincoln at Brady's Gallery," in *Journal of the Illinois State Historical Society* (Spring, 1955), 54-57.

"WHAT WILL THE COUNTRY SAY!"

1. Brooks, *Washington in Lincoln's Time*, 56; Moore, *Rebellion Record*, VI (Docs.), 593; *The New York Times*, May 6, 1863; James R. Gilmore,

Personal Recollections of Abraham Lincoln and the Civil War (Boston, 1898), 103.
2. Rhodes, *History of the United States,* IV, 264; *New York Herald,* May 7, 1863.
3. Pp. 57-58.

"WHOSE WIFE WILL I TAKE?"

1. Quarles, *The Negro in the Civil War,* 199.
2. Lincoln to Andrew Johnson, Mar. 26, 1863, in *Collected Works,* VI, 149-150. See also Lincoln to Sumner, June 1, 1863, in *ibid.,* 242-243.
3. *Sacramento Daily Union,* July 4, 1863, and *New York Herald,* June 12, 1863. In the sources, Frémont's name is spelled without the accent. See also *New York Tribune,* June 1, 1863; and *New York Sun,* June 12, 1863.
4. Lincoln used this story in March, 1863, in a similar connection regarding Frémont. See George W. Julian, in *Rice's Reminiscences, 55.*
5. See, for example, Lincoln to Johnson, Mar. 26, 1863, *supra.*
6. See letter by Thaddeus Stevens, Lancaster, Pa., June 9, 1863, in Thaddeus Stevens MSS., Library of Congress.

"A VERY LONG GRACE FOR A THIN PLATE OF SOUP"

1. Adams S. Hill to S. H. Gay, Oct. 13, 1862, in S. H. Gay MSS., Butler Library, Columbia University. See also J. M. Winchell, "Three Interviews with President Lincoln," in *The Galaxy* (July, 1873), 34-35.
2. A. S. Hill to Gay, Apr. 14, 1863, in Gay MSS.
3. Brooks, "Personal Reminiscences of Lincoln," in *Scribner's Monthly* (Mar., 1878), 674; *idem., Washington in Lincoln's Time,* 36-38.

"HOOKER HAD TAKEN UMBRAGE"

1. Bruce Catton, *Mr. Lincoln's Army* (Garden City, N. Y., 1951), 117; Welles MS. Diary (June 28, 1863); *Beale ed.,* I, 347-350.

Chapter Eight—"ANYTHING BUT A BED OF ROSES"

1. W. H. Seward to John Bigelow, Mar. 3, 1863, in John Bigelow, *Retrospections of an Active Life,* I, 606.
2. Brooks, "Personal Reminiscences of Lincoln," in *Scribner's Monthly* (Mar., 1878), 676; Nicolay memorandum of conversation with Lot M. Morrill, Sept. 20, 1878, in Nicolay MSS.
3. Ward H. Lamon, *Recollections of Abraham Lincoln, 1847-1865,* edited by Dorothy Lamon Teillard (Chicago, 1895), 182-183.
4. J. G. Randall, *Lincoln the President: Midstream* (New York, 1952), 215-217; Moore, *Rebellion Record, VII* (Diary), 15.
5. Lincoln to Erastus Corning and others, June 12[?], 1863, in *Collected Works,* VI, 260-269.
6. *New York Evening Post,* June 23, 1863; George W. Smalley, *Anglo-American Memories* (New York and London, 1911), 155; Lincoln to Alexander

K. McClure, June 30, 1863, in *Collected Works*, VI, 311; Brooks (Castine), "Letter from Washington," July 4, 1863, in *Sacramento Daily Union*, July 28, 1863.

7. *O.R., ser.* I, vol. XXVII, pt. 1, 92; Welles MS. Diary (July 24, 1863); *Beale ed.*, I, 381; *New York Herald*, Sept. 9, 1863.
8. *Dennett ed.*, 76 and 91.
9. Chauncey M. Depew, in *Rice's Reminiscences*, 428-429; Brooks, "Personal Recollections of Abraham Lincoln," in *Harper's Monthly* (July, 1865), 226-227.
10. *Ibid.*, 225.
11. Seward quoted in Henry W. Bellows to his Wife, Apr. 23, 1863, in Henry W. Bellows MSS., Massachusetts Historical Society; Brooks, *Washington in Lincoln's Time*, 50.
12. Schuyler Colfax, *Life and Principles of Abraham Lincoln* (Philadelphia, 1865), 11; Brooks, "Personal Reminiscences of Lincoln," in *Scribner's Monthly* (Mar., 1878), 675; John A. Dahlgren, quoted in Robert V. Bruce, *Lincoln and the Tools of War* (Indianapolis, 1956), 21; Anna L. Boyden, *Echoes from Hospital and White House . . .* (Boston, 1884), 85.
13. Unidentified clipping in "Miscellaneous Lincoln Material," in Nicolay MSS.
14. Boyden, *Echoes from Hospital and White House*, 82.
15. David Davis to Leonard Swett, Nov. 26, 1862, in Pratt, *Concerning Mr. Lincoln*, 95; Hay MS. Diary (Dec. 31, 1863); *Dennett ed.*, 146.
16. David R. Locke, in *Rice's Reminiscences*, 448.
17. John W. Forney, *Anecdotes of Public Men* (New York, 1873-1881), I, 38.
18. Brooks, "Personal Reminiscences of Lincoln," in *Scribner's Monthly* (Feb., 1878), 564.
19. *Idem.*, "Personal Recollections of Abraham Lincoln," in *Harper's Monthly* (July, 1865), 228; *idem.*, "Personal Reminiscences of Lincoln," in *Scribner's Monthly* (Mar., 1878), 679-680.
20. W. H. Herndon to Jesse W. Weik, Nov. 17, 1885, in Herndon-Weik MSS.; *New York Herald*, July 22, 1863.

"HERE GOES FOR TWO YEARS MORE"

1. George G. Meade's *General Orders No. 68*, July 4, 1863, in *O.R.*, ser. I, vol. XXVII, pt. 3, 559; Lincoln to H. W. Halleck, July 6, 1863, in *ibid.*, 567; Hay MS. Diary (July 14, 1863); *Dennett ed.*, 67.
2. *New York Herald*, July 18, 1863.
3. Hay MS. Diary (July 14, 1863); *Dennett ed.*, 67; Brooks, *Washington in Lincoln's Time*, 94.
4. Welles MS. Diary (July 14, 1863); *Beale ed.*, I, 369-371.
5. Welles MS. Diary (June 16, 1863); *Beale ed.*, I, 331.

"THE FIRST GREAT MAN"

1. *New York Herald*, Aug. 19, 1863.
2. *Douglass' Monthly* (May, 1861), 451; Frederick Douglass, *The Life and Times of Frederick Douglass Written by Himself . . .* (Hartford, 1882), 374.

3. *Ibid.*, 394.
4. See also, *ibid.*, 385-388; *idem.*, in *Rice's Reminiscences*, 185-189.

"MORE ANGRY THAN I EVER SAW HIM"

1. Charles Sumner to Francis Lieber, Jan. 17, 1863, in Pierce, *Memoir and Letters of Charles Sumner*, IV, 114; Joseph Hooker's testimony in *CCW*, I (1865), 112.
2. Lincoln's Opinion of the Draft, Sept. 14[?], 1863, in *Collected Works*, VI, 444.
3. See, for example, *New York Sun*, June 12, 1863.
4. Report on reaction to the draft, in *O.R.*, ser. III, vol. III, 513.
5. *Bates Diary*, 306.
6. Chase MS. Diary (Sept. 14, 1863); *Donald ed.*, 192-194. See also Welles MS. Diary (Sept. 14, 1863); *Beale ed.*, I, 431-435; *Bates Diary*, 306-307.

"OUR MILITARY HOROSCOPE IS . . . CLOUDED"

1. Brooks (Castine), "Letter from Washington," Sept. 23, 1863, in *Sacramento Daily Union*, Oct. 17, 1863.
2. Welles MS. Diary (Sept. 21, 1863); *Beale ed.*, I, 439-440.

"BEWARE OF BEING ASSAILED BY ONE"

1. *New York Herald*, Oct. 4, 1863; Lincoln to John M. Schofield, May 27, 1863, in *Collected Works*, VI, 234.
2. Hay MS. Diary (Sept. 29, 1863); *Dennett ed.*, 95; Lincoln to Schofield, May 27, 1863, *supra*.
3. J. G. Nicolay, *A Short Life of Abraham Lincoln* (New York, 1902), 434.
4. *New York Tribune*, reprinted in *Sacramento Daily Union*, Oct. 28, 1863; *New York Herald*, Sept. 27 and Oct. 1, 1863; *Sacramento Daily Union*, Oct. 3, 1863.
5. Nicolay and Hay, *Abraham Lincoln*, VIII, 212-220. See also Hay MS. Diary (Sept. 29, 1863); *Dennett ed.*, 95-96. For Lincoln's written reply to Charles D. Drake and others of the Missouri-Kansas delegation, Oct. 5, 1863, see *Collected Works*, VI, 499-504.
6. Hay MS. Diary (Oct. 28, 1863); *Dennett ed.*, 108.

Chapter Nine—"A LEADER TO SPEAK THE BOLD WORD"

1. Moore, *Rebellion Record*, VII (Docs.), 438.
2. *New York Herald*, Oct. 12, 1863; *New York Tribune*, Oct. 3, 1863.
3. Moore, *Rebellion Record*, VII (Docs.), 438-439.
4. Welles MS. Diary (Oct. 13, 1863); *Beale ed.*, I, 469-470.
5. Lincoln to James C. Conkling and others, Aug. 26, 1863, in *Collected Works*, VI, 406-410.
6. James C. Conkling to Lincoln, Sept. 4, 1863, in RTL; Hay to Nicolay, Sept. 11, 1863, in *Dennett ed.*, 91.
7. London *Times*, Sept. 17, 1863, in *New York Herald*, Oct. 4, 1863.
8. London *Star*, in *Sacramento Daily Union*, Oct. 28, 1863.

9. George H. Porter, *Ohio Politics During the Civil War Period* (Columbia University Studies, XL, no. 2) (New York, 1911), 183; *Appleton's American Annual Cyclopaedia and Register of Important Events of 1863*, 740; Alexander K. McClure, *Lincoln and Men of War-Times* (Philadelphia, 1892), 261; Lincoln to Zachariah Chandler, Nov. 20, 1863, in *Collected Works*, VII, 24.

10. Brooks (Castine), "Letter from Washington," Oct. 14, 1863, in *Sacramento Daily Union*, Nov. 7, 1863; J. K. Moorhead to Lincoln, Oct. 15, 1863, in *Collected Works*, VI, 512n; E. B. Washburne to Lincoln, Oct. 12, 1863, in *ibid.*, 540n-541; Lincoln to Washburne, "Private and Confidential," Oct. 26, 1863, in *ibid.*, 540.

11. *New York Tribune*, Nov. 27, 1863; John Sherman to General Sherman, Nov. 14, 1863, quoted in Rhodes, *History of the United States*, IV, 423; Nicolay and Hay, *Abraham Lincoln*, VIII, 190; *The New York Times*, Nov. 21, 1863.

12. Lincoln's Gettysburg Address, Nov. 19, 1863, in *Collected Works*, VII, 22-23.

13. *Ohio State Journal*, Nov. 23, 1863.

14. *Chicago Times*, quoted in Thomas, *Abraham Lincoln*, 403; *Springfield (Mass.) Republican*, Nov. 20, 1863, quoted in Richard Hooker, *The Story of an Independent Newspaper* (New York, 1924), 95-96; *Harper's Weekly*, Dec. 5, 1863; Lamon, *Recollections of Abraham Lincoln*, 173.

15. Hay to Nicolay, Nov. 26, 1863, in *Dennett ed.*, 128; H. W. Halleck's Report of Operations in 1863, in Moore, *Rebellion Record*, VIII (Docs.), 188.

16. *New York Tribune*, Dec. 16, 1863.

17. Lincoln's Annual Message to Congress, Dec. 8, 1863, in *Collected Works*, VII, 36-53; Proclamation of Amnesty and Reconstruction, Dec. 8, 1863, in *ibid.*, 53-56.

18. Hay MS. Diary (Dec. 9, 1863); *Dennett ed.*, 131-132.

"PURSUIT OF THE PRESIDENCY"

1. Brooks (Castine), "Letter from Washington," Oct. 6, 1863, in *Sacramento Daily Union*, Oct. 31, 1863.

2. *New York Tribune*, Sept. 26, 1863; *Bates Diary*, 310; Hay MS. Diary (Oct. 4 and 14, 1863); *Dennett ed.*, 98-99.

3. Hay MS. Diary (Oct. 18, 1863); *Dennett ed.*, 100-101.

4. Frémont spelled without accent in source.

5. Lincoln to Hamilton R. Gamble, Oct. 19, 1863, in *Collected Works*, VI, 526-527.

"CONTROVERSY BETWEEN THE TWO SETS"

1. Brooks (Castine), "Letter from Washington," Oct. 6, 1863, in *Sacramento Daily Union*, Oct. 31, 1863.

2. Quoted in Ralph Korngold, *Thaddeus Stevens: A Being Darkly Wise and Rudely Great* (New York, 1955), 216-217.

3. Thaddeus Stevens to Charles Sumner, Oct. 9, 1863, in Sumner MSS.,

Harvard University Library; Washington dispatch, Oct. 5, 1863, in *Sacramento Daily Union*, Oct. 27, 1863.
4. Hay MS. Diary (Nov. 1, 1863); *Dennett ed.*, 112-113.
5. Lincoln wrote instead to Montgomery Blair on Nov. 2, 1863. See *Collected Works*, VI, 554-555.

"IT SECURES US TENNESSEE"

1. *Cincinnati Daily Gazette*, Dec. 2, 1863.
2. Nicolay, *A Short Life of Abraham Lincoln*, 391.
3. Nicolay memorandum, Dec. 7, 1863, in Nicolay MSS.

"STAY WITH HER AS LONG AS YOU CAN"

1. *Browning Diary*, I, 651; Katherine Helm, *The True Story of Mary, Wife of Lincoln* (New York, 1928), 220-221, 224.
2. *Ibid.*, 221-222, 224.
3. *Ibid.*, 225-228.

"FULLY APPREHENSIVE OF THE SCHEMES"

1. *New York Herald*, Feb. 24, 1864; Brooks (Castine), "Letter from Washington," Oct. 6, 1863, in *Sacramento Daily Union*, Oct. 31, 1863.
2. *New York Tribune*, Dec. 24, 1863; Hay MS. Diary (Oct. 25, 1863); *Dennett ed.*, 107; *New York Herald*, Oct. 3, 1863.
3. J. W. Stokes to Isaac Newton, Philadelphia, Feb. 10, 1864, in RTL; *Harper's Weekly*, Jan. 2, 1864.
4. *Bates Diary*, 333-334.
5. Spelled "agst" in source.
6. Material within 〈　〉 indicates that it is bracketed in Bates' MS. Diary.
7. Editor inserted "[Lieutenant] Gov[erno]r. [Willard P.]." Source states merely "Govr. Hall."
8. Editor inserted "[William A.]." Source states merely "Judge Hall." All brackets other than indicated in annotations are in source.

"IF IT IS ALL THE SAME TO YOU"

1. Lincoln to Quincy A. Gillmore, Jan. 13, 1864, in *Collected Works*, VII, 126; *New York Herald*, Apr. 18, 1864.
2. Carpenter, *Six Months*, 48-52. In source Shakespeare is spelled "Shakspeare."
3. This sentence is in double quotation marks in the source.
4. Printed "Hamlet" in source.

"THIS IS GENERAL GRANT, IS IT?"

1. *The New York Times*, quoted in *Sacramento Daily Union*, Feb. 5, 1864; Brooks (Castine), "Letter from Washington," Mar. 8, 1864, in *ibid.*, Apr. 9, 1864; A. D. Richardson, *A Personal History of Ulysses S. Grant* (Hartford, 1868), 373-374.
2. Nicolay memorandum, Mar. 8, 1864, in Nicolay MSS.
3. *Ibid.*

4. Lincoln's address to Grant, Mar. 9, 1864, in *Collected Works*, VII, 234; Lincoln's order assigning Grant to command of U. S. Armies, Mar. 10, 1864, in *ibid.*, 236; General Orders No. 98, assigning Halleck as Chief of Staff of the Army, Mar. 12, 1864, in *ibid.*, 239-240.

"I HAVE A CLEAR CONSCIENCE"

1. George Thompson to John A. Andrew, Apr. 6, 1864, in *Proceedings of the Massachusetts Historical Society*, LXIII (1930), 81-82; *New York Herald*, Apr. 7, 1864.
2. Carpenter, *Six Months*, 75-79.

"BEEHIVE . . . KICKED OVER"

1. *New York Herald*, Feb. 22 and 24, 1864.
2. Richard Parsons to Chase, Mar. 2, 1864, in Chase MSS.; Chase to Lincoln, Feb. 22, 1864, in *Collected Works*, VII, 200n-201.
3. Chase to A. G. Riddle, Mar. 7, 1864, in Warden, *Account of the Private Life and Public Services of Salmon Portland Chase*, 576. See also Chase's letter of withdrawal to James C. Hall, Mar. 5, 1864, in *Sacramento Daily Union*, Apr. 4, 1864.
4. *Congressional Globe*, 38th Congress, 1st session, 1832.
5. Albert G. Riddle, *Recollections of War Times . . . 1860-1865* (New York, 1895), 270-277.
6. Frémont spelled without accent in source.
7. See Lincoln to Stanton, Apr. 23, 1864, in *Collected Works*, VII, 312.

"PITY TO SPOIL SO GOOD A STORY"

1. Carpenter, *Six Months*, 81.
2. *Ibid.*, 82-84.
3. Brackets in source.

Chapter Ten—"IT IS NOT BEST TO SWAP HORSES"

1. Dr. Oliver Wendell Holmes to John Lothrop Motley, Oct. 10, 1865, in George William Curtis (ed.), *The Correspondence of John Lothrop Motley* (New York, 1889), II, 210 (hereinafter cited as *Motley Correspondence*); Richardson, *A Personal History of Ulysses S. Grant*, 391; Horace Porter, *Campaigning with Grant* (New York, 1897), 98.
2. Holmes to Motley, Oct. 10, 1865, in *Motley Correspondence*, II, 211; Charles A. Page dispatch, May 5, 1864, in *New York Tribune*, May 9, 1864; *The New York Times*, quoted in *Sacramento Daily Union*, June 8, 1864.
3. Grant, *Personal Memoirs*, II, 276; *O.R.*, ser. I, vol. XXXVI, pt. 1, 188.
4. Colfax, *Life and Principles of Abraham Lincoln*, 11-12; *Boston Journal*, May 2, 1865; Isaac N. Arnold, *The Life of Abraham Lincoln* (Chicago, 1885), 375; *O.R.*, ser. I, vol. XXXVI, pt. 1, 22.
5. Brooks (Castine), "Letter from Washington," May 19, 1864, in *Sacramento Daily Union*, June 16, 1864.

6. S. S. Cox to Manton Marble, June 20, 1864, in Manton Marble MSS., Library of Congress; A. Brisbane to Horace Greeley, Buffalo, N. Y., Aug. 2, 1864, in Horace Greeley MSS., New York Public Library.

7. Report of speech by Henry Winter Davis, in *New York Herald*, Feb. 26, 1864; Mark Howard to Gideon Welles, Hartford, Conn., May 30, 1864, in Welles MSS.; John A. Hiestand to Thaddeus Stevens, Lancaster, Pa., May 29, 1864, in Stevens MSS.

8. A. Homer Byington to S. H. Gay, Mar. 5, 1864, in Gay MSS.; W. H. Kent to Gay, Feb. 25, 1864, in *ibid.;* J. D. Defrees to R. W. Thompson, Washington, D. C., Feb. 2, 1864, MS. in Lincoln National Life Foundation; Miss Sarah B. Howell to Lincoln, June 6, 1864, in RTL.

9. *New York Herald*, June 2, 1864.

10. *Ibid.* Frémont's name is spelled without the accent in the source. For Frémont's letter of acceptance, June 4, 1864, see McPherson, *Political History*, 413-414.

11. *New York Herald*, Apr. 17, 1864. Frémont spelled without the accent in the source.

12. Brooks, "Two War-Time Conventions," in *Century Magazine* (Mar., 1895), 723.

13. *New York Herald*, Dec. 16, 1863; *ibid.*, Feb. 19, 1864; Richardson, *A Personal History of Ulysses S. Grant*, 407 and 434.

14. *New York Herald*, June 4 and 6, 1864; Hay MS. Diary (June 6, 1864); Dennett ed., 186; Arnold, *The Life of Abraham Lincoln*, 358; Nicolay to Hay, Baltimore, June 5, 1864, in Nicolay MSS.

15. *Bates Diary*, 374-375.

16. *New York Herald*, June 9, 1864. For Republican platform, see McPherson, *Political History*, 406-407.

17. Brooks, "Personal Reminiscences of Lincoln," in *Scribner's Monthly* (Mar., 1878), 676; *New York Tribune*, June 10, 1864.

18. Brooks, "Personal Reminiscences of Lincoln," in *Scribner's Monthly* (Mar., 1878), 676-677; *New York Herald*, Aug. 2, 1864.

19. Brooks, "Personal Reminiscences of Lincoln," in *Scribner's Monthly* (Mar., 1878), 679; *George H. Pendleton, The Copperhead Candidate for Vice-President* (Washington, D. C., 1864), 1; Whitelaw Reid, Cincinnati, Sept. 5, 1864, in *New York Sun*, June 30, 1889.

20. See McClellan's letter accepting the Democratic nomination, Sept. 8, 1864, in McPherson, *Political History*, 421.

21. *The New York Times*, Sept. 24, 1864; *New York Tribune*, Sept. 22, 1864; *Chicago Tribune*, Aug. 31, 1864; *Cincinnati Daily Gazette*, Aug. 30, 1864.

"HE WAS . . . NON-COMMITTAL"

1. Brooks, *Washington in Lincoln's Time*, 151-152.

"WHAT! AM I RENOMINATED?"

1. Brooks, *Washington in Lincoln's Time*, 152, 160.

2. Brackets in source. All other brackets are editor's.

3. See *New York Herald*, June 11, 1864.

"THEY HAD TOUCHED HIS CLOTHES"

1. Welles MS. Diary (June 20, 1864); *Beale ed.,* II, 54-55; Brooks (Castine), "Letter from Washington," June 22, 1864, in *Sacramento Daily Union,* July 18, 1864.
2. Porter, *Campaigning with Grant,* 216-220.

"BETTER LET IT ALONE THIS TIME"

1. Brooks, *Washington in Lincoln's Time,* 125; *Boston Courier,* Mar. 10, 1864, reprinted in *New York Herald,* Mar. 11, 1864.
2. Lincoln to Chase (2 letters—one marked "Private"), June 28, 1864, in *Collected Works,* VII, 412-414; Lincoln to Chase, June 30, 1864, in *ibid.,* 419.
3. MS. transcription of shorthand account dictated by John Brough, July 12, 1864, in vol. 20, William Henry Smith MSS., Ohio Historical Society.
4. Brackets in original transcription.
5. Brackets in original transcription.
6. Brackets in original transcription.

"HE KNOWS THE ROPES"

1. Hay MS. Diary (July 1, 1864); *Dennett ed.,* 201-203.

"I DOUBT THE AUTHORITY"

1. Brooks (Castine), "Letter from Washington," July 5, 1864, in *Sacramento Daily Union,* July 27, 1864; *New York Herald,* July 10, 1864.
2. Hay MS. Diary (July 4, 1864); *Dennett ed.,* 204-206.
3. See *Collected Works,* VII, 433-434; *New York Tribune,* Aug. 5, 1864; Amasa J. Parker to Samuel J. Tilden, Albany, N. Y., July 7, 1864, in Samuel J. Tilden MSS., New York Public Library.

"THE PEOPLE WITH THE GOVERNING POWER"

1. *London Free Press,* reprinted in *Sacramento Daily Union,* Aug. 23, 1864.
2. See *Collected Works,* VII, 448-449.

"AM I TO BE THE MERE PUPPET OF POWER . . . ?"

1. Nicolay to Therena Bates, Aug. 21, 1864, in Nicolay MSS.; Henry Wilson to Lincoln, Sept. 5, 1864, in Nicolay and Hay, *Abraham Lincoln,* IX, 339.
2. "The Interview Between Thad Stevens & Mr. Lincoln as Related by Col. R. M. Hoe [to J. G. Nicolay]," in Nicolay MSS.

"I VOTE FOR MASSA LINCOLN"

1. Charles D. Robinson to Lincoln, Aug. 7, 1864, in RTL. Regarding the Niagara Peace Conference, see Lincoln's memorandum, "To Whom It May Concern," July 18, 1864, in *Collected Works,* VII, 451.
2. Diary of Joseph T. Mills, MS., in Wisconsin Historical Society. Mills wrote another version of this interview for the *Grant County* (Wis.) *Herald* (clipping in RTL), which was reprinted in other newspapers, i.e., *New*

York Tribune, Sept. 10, 1864, and *Harper's Weekly,* Sept. 17, 1864. Mills' published version of this interview also was used as a broadside in the 1864 Presidential campaign (copy in Illinois State Historical Library). See also Lincoln to C. D. Robinson (draft of letter), Aug. 17, 1864, in *Collected Works,* VII, 499-500.

3. Incorrectly spelled "Douglass" in source.
4. Incorrectly spelled "Douglass" in source.

"I WILL MANAGE MY SIDE . . . MY WAY"

1. *New York World,* Oct. 18, 1864; *New York Herald,* Oct. 17, 1864; Mc-Pherson, *Political History,* 438-441. For Lincoln's written reply to the delegation, the protest and documents relating to it, see *Collected Works,* VII, 58-72.

"NO RIGHT TO SEEK PERSONAL POLITICAL FAVORS"

1. Brooks (Castine), "Letter from Washington," Oct. 19, 1864, in *Sacramento Daily Union,* Nov. 24, 1864.

"FOR AUNTY SOJOURNER TRUTH"

1. For biographical material on Sojourner Truth, see Carl Sandburg, *Abraham Lincoln: The War Years* (New York, 1939), III, 402-403; Quarles, *The Negro in the Civil War,* 228, 252.
2. This interview was reproduced in Carpenter, *Six Months,* 201-203.

"IN CARPET SLIPPERS"

1. George Borrett, *Letters from Canada and the United States* (London, 1865), 249-256.

Chapter Eleven—"IT MADE MY HEART JUMP"

1. Report of Lieutenant General Grant, July 22, 1865, in Moore, *Rebellion Record,* XI (Docs.), 333.
2. *Ibid.,* 326. See also Lincoln to Grant, Aug. 17, 1864, in *Collected Works,* VII, 499.
3. Daniel S. Dickinson letter, Aug. 26, 1864, in *New York Sun,* June 30, 1889.
4. H. J. Raymond to Lincoln, Aug. 22, 1864, in Nicolay and Hay, *Abraham Lincoln,* IX, 218; Nicolay to Hay, Aug. 24, 1864, in Nicolay MSS.
5. *O.R.,* ser. I, vol. XXXVIII, pt. 5, 777; Benjamin F. Butler to his wife, Sept. 5, 1864, in Benjamin F. Butler, *Private and Official Correspondence of Benjamin F. Butler During the Period of the Civil War,* edited by Jessie A. Marshall (Norwich, Mass., 1917), V, 125; W. H. Seward's speech, Sept. 14, 1864, in *Appleton's American Annual Cyclopaedia and Register of Important Events of 1864,* 794; Charles B. Sedgwick to John Murray Forbes, Sept. 5, 1864, in John Murray Forbes, *Letters and Recollections of John Murray Forbes,* edited by Sarah F. Hughes (Boston, 1899), II, 101. Report of Lieutenant General Grant, July 22, 1865, in Moore, *Rebellion Record,* XI (Docs.), 338.

6. *New York Herald,* Aug. 24, 1864.
7. McPherson, *Political History,* 426.
8. *New York Herald,* Sept. 25, 1864.
9. Theodore Tilton to Anna E. Dickinson, Sept. 30, 1864, in Anna E. Dickinson MSS., Library of Congress.
10. Lincoln's Response to Serenade, Aug. 31, 1864, in *Baltimore Sun,* Sept. 2, 1864.
11. S. P. Chase to John Sherman, Oct. 2, 1864, in John Sherman, *John Sherman's Recollections of Forty Years in the House* . . . (Chicago, 1895), I, 341.
12. McPherson, *Political History,* 623.
13. Colfax, *Life and Principles of Abraham Lincoln,* 13; Lincoln's Response to Serenade, Nov. 10, 1864, in *Collected Works,* VIII, 101.
14. Lincoln's Annual Message to Congress, Dec. 6, 1864, in *ibid.,* 148.
15. *New York Herald,* Dec. 27, 1864; William T. Sherman to Lincoln, Dec. 22, 1864, in RTL. See also *Collected Works,* VIII, 182n.
16. Jefferson Davis to Francis P. Blair, Sr., Jan. 12, 1865, in *ibid.,* 275.
17. Lincoln's Annual Message to Congress, Dec. 6, 1864, in *ibid.,* 149.
18. Grace Julian Clarke (ed.), "George W. Julian's Journal," in *Indiana Magazine of History* (Dec., 1915), 90; Arnold, *The Life of Abraham Lincoln,* 368.
19. Lincoln's Second Inaugural, Mar. 4, 1865, in *Collected Works,* VIII, 333.
20. Brooks, "Personal Reminiscences of Lincoln," in *Scribner's Monthly* (Mar., 1878), 678.

"SO GOES THE UNION, THEY SAY"

1. Brooks, *Washington in Lincoln's Time,* 216-217; *idem.* (Castine), "Letter from Washington," Nov. 11, 1864, in *Sacramento Daily Union,* Dec. 10, 1864; Hay MS. Diary (Nov. 8, 1864); *Dennett ed.,* 232-236; Brooks, "Personal Reminiscences of Lincoln," in *Scribner's Monthly* (Mar., 1878), 677. See also Charles A. Dana, *Recollections of the Civil War* . . . (New York, 1898), 261-262.

"BEFORE MY OWN CONSCIENCE"

1. Hay MS. Diary (Nov. 11, 1864); *Dennett ed.,* 237-238.

"IF ALL THE REST OPPOSE"

1. Hay MS. Diary (Oct. 13, 1864); *Dennett ed.,* 231; Brooks (Castine), "Letter from Washington," Dec. 9, 1864, in *Sacramento Daily Union,* Jan. 11, 1865.
2. Francis P. Blair, Sr., to John A. Andrew, Silver Spring, Md., Nov. 19, 1864, in *Proceedings of the Massachusetts Historical Society* (Jan., 1930), 88-89.
3. Spelled "Sumpter" in source. Other minor errors in spelling have been corrected.

"A VERY EXCELLENT JUDGE"

1. Record of Nicolay conversation with ex-Senator LaFayette S. Foster, Oct. 23, 1878, in Nicolay MSS.

"THE KING'S CURE-ALL FOR ALL EVILS"

1. *Cincinnati Daily Gazette,* Feb. 2, 1865.
2. Leonard Swett to W. H. Herndon, Chicago, Ill., Jan. 17, 1866, in Herndon-Weik MSS.; John B. Alley, in *Rice's Reminiscences,* 586.
3. Quoted in Arnold, *The Life of Abraham Lincoln,* 358-359.

"IT WAS ONLY A GOOD IDEA"

1. Brooks, "Personal Reminiscences of Lincoln," in *Scribner's Monthly* (Mar., 1878), 678.
2. *Harper's Monthly* (July, 1865), 223-224.
3. For Lincoln's lectures on "Discoveries and Inventions," see *Collected Works,* II, 437-442, and III, 356-363.

"I WILL MEET THEM PERSONALLY"

1. Jefferson Davis to F. P. Blair, Sr., Jan. 12, 1865, in *Collected Works,* VIII, 275; Lincoln to F. P. Blair, Sr., Jan. 18, 1865, in *ibid.,* 221; *Philadelphia Public Ledger,* Jan. 11, 1865.
2. Lincoln to F. P. Blair, Sr., Jan. 18, 1865, in *Collected Works,* VIII, 221.
3. Grant to Edwin M. Stanton, Feb. 1, 1865, in *ibid.,* 282; Lincoln to Grant, Feb. 2, 1865, and Lincoln to Seward, Feb. 2, 1865, in *ibid.*
4. Alexander H. Stephens, *A Constitutional View of the Late War Between the States* (Philadelphia, 1868-1870), II, 598-619. For other accounts of the Hampton Roads Peace Conference, see John A. Campbell, *Reminiscences and Documents Relating to the Civil War During the Year 1865* (Baltimore, 1887), 11-17; Seward to C. F. Adams, Feb. 7, 1865, in *Collected Works,* VIII, 286n-287.

"I ALWAYS PLUCKED A THISTLE . . ."

1. Herndon-Weik MSS.

"HERE COMES MY FRIEND DOUGLASS"

1. "Abraham Lincoln: Frederick Douglass's Reminiscences," in *New York Tribune,* July 5, 1885.

"THAT TROUBLES ME MOST"

1. Anson G. Henry to his Wife, Mar. 13, 1865, MS. in Illinois State Historical Library.
2. Misspelled "Nickolay" in original.

"IT WAS THE EASIEST THING"

1. *American and Commercial Advertiser,* Mar. 23, 1865.

"WILLING TO SHARE THEIR DANGERS"

1. Brooks (Castine), "Letter from Washington," Mar. 22, 1865, in *Sacramento Daily Union,* Apr. 19, 1865; Porter, *Campaigning with Grant,* 402.

2. *Ibid.; New York Herald,* Mar. 28, 1865.
3. Pp. 406-409.

"I WANT NO ONE PUNISHED"

1. Arnold, *The Life of Abraham Lincoln,* 421.
2. David D. Porter, *Incidents and Anecdotes of the Civil War* (New York, 1885), 313-315. See also Sherman's later account in Arnold, *The Life of Abraham Lincoln,* 420-423; Sherman, *Personal Memoirs,* II, 322-331.

"I RECKON THEY'LL ACCEPT"

1. C. C. Coffin, in *Rice's Reminiscences,* 176-177.

"GLORY ENOUGH FOR ALL"

1. Lincoln to his Wife, City Point, Va., Apr. 2, 1865, in *O.R.,* ser. I, vol. XLVI, pt. 3, 447-448.
2. *New York Herald,* Apr. 5, 1865.

"A SORT OF SNEAKING IDEA"

1. Porter, *Campaigning with Grant,* 450-452.

"SPIRIT OF SINCERE LIBERALITY"

1. C. C. Coffin correspondence to *Boston Journal,* reprinted in *Littell's Living Age* (Apr. 22, 1865), 137-138.
2. C. G. Chamberlayne, "Abraham Lincoln in Richmond," in *The Virginia Magazine of History and Biography* (Oct., 1933), 320-322. See also J. A. Campbell, *Recollections of the Evacuation of Richmond, April 2d., 1865* (Baltimore, 1880), 9-25.

"IT IS OUR LAWFUL PRIZE"

1. *New York Herald,* Apr. 10, 1865; Lincoln's Response to Serenade, Apr. 10, 1865, in *National Intelligencer,* Apr. 11, 1865.
2. Lincoln to Godfrey Weitzel, Apr. 12, 1865, in *Collected Works,* VIII, 405-407.
3. Welles MS. Diary (Apr. 13, 1865); *Beale ed.,* II, 279-280.

"THIS STRANGE DREAM AGAIN"

1. Montgomery C. Meigs MS. Diary (Apr. 14, 1865), in Montgomery C. Meigs MSS., Library of Congress.
2. Welles MS. Diary (Apr. 14, 1865); *Beale ed.,* II, 280-283. For another version of this Cabinet meeting, see F. W. Seward, *Reminiscences of a War-Time Statesman and Diplomat,* 254-257.
3. The preceding two paragraphs were added in pencil by Welles at a later date.
4. Hugh McCulloch, *Men and Measures of Half a Century* (New York, 1889), 408.

"YOU ALMOST STARTLE ME"

1. Mary Lincoln to F. B. Carpenter, Nov. 15, 1865, quoted in Honoré Willsie Morrow, "Lincoln's Last Day," in *Hearst's International-Cosmopolitan* (Feb., 1930).

Selected Bibliography

MANUSCRIPT COLLECTIONS

John A. Andrew MSS., Massachusetts Historical Society, Boston.
Archivo de Relaciónes Exteriores, Mexico, D. F., MSS., Library of Congress, Washington, D. C.
Edward Bates MSS., Missouri Historical Society, St. Louis.
Henry W. Bellows MSS., Massachusetts Historical Society.
Orville H. Browning MSS., Illinois State Historical Library, Springfield, Ill.
James Buchanan MSS., Historical Society of Pennsylvania, Philadelphia.
Henry C. Carey MSS., Historical Society of Pennsylvania.
Salmon P. Chase MSS., Historical Society of Pennsylvania.
Salmon P. Chase MSS., Library of Congress.
John J. Crittenden MSS., Library of Congress.
Anna E. Dickinson MSS., Library of Congress.
Stephen A. Douglas MSS., University of Chicago.
John C. Frémont MSS., Bancroft Library, University of California, Berkeley.
Benjamin B. French MSS., Library of Congress.
Alexander T. Galt MSS., Public Archives of Canada, Ottawa, Ont.
William Lloyd Garrison MSS., Boston Public Library.
S. H. Gay MSS., Butler Library, Columbia University, New York City.
Giddings-Julian MSS., Library of Congress.
Horace Greeley MSS., New York Public Library.
John Hay MSS., Brown University, Providence, R. I.
Herndon-Weik MSS., Library of Congress.
Joseph Holt MSS., Library of Congress.
Robert Todd Lincoln Collection of Lincoln MSS., Library of Congress.
Manton Marble MSS., Library of Congress.
Montgomery C. Meigs MSS., Library of Congress.
Joseph T. Mills MSS., State Historical Society of Wisconsin, Madison.
John G. Nicolay MSS., Library of Congress.

Lord John Russell MSS., Public Records Office, London, England.
John Sherman MSS., Library of Congress.
William Henry Smith MSS., Ohio Historical Society, Columbus.
Thaddeus Stevens MSS., Library of Congress.
Stuart-Hay MSS., Illinois State Historical Library.
Charles Sumner MSS., Henry E. Huntington Library, San Marino, Calif.
Charles Sumner MSS., Widener Library, Harvard University, Cambridge, Mass.
Charles Sumner MSS., owned by Charles M. Segal, Brooklyn, N. Y.
Samuel J. Tilden MSS., New York Public Library.
R. W. Thompson MSS., Lincoln National Life Foundation, Fort Wayne, Ind.
Lyman Trumbull MSS., Library of Congress.
Thurlow Weed MSS., University of Rochester.
Gideon Welles MSS., Illinois State Historical Library.
Gideon Welles MSS., Library of Congress.

NEWSPAPERS

American and Commercial Advertiser (Baltimore)
Baltimore Sun
·Boston Journal
Charleston Mercury (South Carolina)
Chicago Tribune
Cincinnati Daily Gazette
Detroit Free Press
Illinois State Journal (Springfield, Ill.)
National Intelligencer (Washington, D. C.)
New York Herald
New York Sun
The New York Times
New York Tribune
New York World
Ohio State Journal (Columbus, O.)
Philadelphia Public Ledger
Richmond Examiner
Sacramento Daily Union
St. Cloud Democrat (Minn.)
The South (Baltimore)
Washington Daily Morning Chronicle
Washington Evening Star

BOOKS, PAMPHLETS AND ARTICLES

Adams, Ephraim D., *Great Britain and the American Civil War* (London: Longmans, Green & Co., 1925), 2 vols.
[*Appleton's*] *American Annual Cyclopaedia and Register of Important Events of the Years 1861-1865* (New York: D. Appleton & Co., 1864-1870), 5 vols.
Arnold, Isaac N., *The Life of Abraham Lincoln* (Chicago: Jansen, McClurg & Co., 1885).

Bacon, Georgeanna Woolsey, and Eliza Woolsey Howland (eds.), *Letters of a Family During the War for the Union 1861-1865* (New Haven, Conn.: Privately Printed, 1899), 2 vols.

Baldwin, John B., *Interview Between President Lincoln and Col. John B. Baldwin, April 4, 1861* (Staunton, Va.: "Spectator" job office, 1866), 28 pp.

Bancroft, Frederic, *The Life of William H. Seward* (New York: Harper & Brothers, 1900), 2 vols.

Barbee, D. R., and M. L. Bonham, Jr. (eds.), "Fort Sumter Again," in *Mississippi Valley Historical Review* (June, 1941), 63-73.

Baringer, William E., *A House Dividing: Lincoln as President-Elect* (Springfield, Ill.: Abraham Lincoln Association, 1945).

Barnes, Thurlow Weed, *Memoir of Thurlow Weed* (Boston: Houghton, Mifflin Co., 1884).

Basler, Roy P., *et al.* (eds.), *The Collected Works of Abraham Lincoln* (Springfield, Ill.: Abraham Lincoln Association, 1953), 8 vols.

Beale, Howard K. (ed.), *The Diary of Edward Bates* (Washington, D. C.: Annual Report of the American Historical Association for 1930, vol. IV, 1933).

—— (ed.), *The Diary of Gideon Welles* (New York: W. W. Norton & Co., 1960), 3 vols.

Bigelow, John, *Retrospections of an Active Life* (New York: Baker & Taylor Co., 1909), 3 vols.

Binney, Charles Chauncey, *The Life of Horace Binney* (Philadelphia: J. B. Lippincott Co., 1903).

Blaine, James G., *Twenty Years of Congress from Lincoln to Garfield* (Norwich, Conn.: Henry Bill Publishing Co., 1894), 2 vols.

Borrett, George, *Letters from Canada and the United States* (London: Privately Printed, 1865).

Boyden, Anna L., *Echoes from Hospital and White House: A Record of Mrs. Rebecca R. Pomroy's Experiences in War Times* (Boston: D. Lothrop & Co., 1884).

Brooks, Noah, "Personal Recollections of Abraham Lincoln," in *Harper's Monthly* (July, 1865), 222-230.

—— "Personal Reminiscences of Lincoln," in *Scribner's Monthly* (Feb., 1878), 561-569, and (Mar., 1878), 673-681.

—— "Two War-Time Conventions," in *Century Magazine* (Mar., 1895), 723-736.

—— *Washington in Lincoln's Time* (New York: Century Co., 1896).

Bruce, Robert V., *Lincoln and the Tools of War* (Indianapolis: Bobbs-Merrill Co., 1956).

Buel, Clarence C., and Robert U. Johnson (eds.), *Battles and Leaders of the Civil War* (New York: Century Co., 1887-1888), 4 vols.

Butler, Benjamin F., *Private and Official Correspondence of Benjamin F. Butler During the Period of the Civil War,* edited by Jessie A. Marshall (Norwich, Mass.: Plimpton Press, 1917), 5 vols.

Campbell, John A., *Recollections of the Evacuation of Richmond, April 2d, 1865* (Baltimore: J. Murphy & Co., 1880), 27 pp.

———— *Reminiscences and Documents Relating to the Civil War During the Year 1865* (Baltimore: J. Murphy & Co., 1887), 68 pp.

Carpenter, Francis B., *Six Months at the White House with Abraham Lincoln* (New York: Hurd and Houghton, 1866).

Catton, Bruce, *Mr. Lincoln's Army* (Garden City, N. Y.: Doubleday & Co., 1951).

———— *This Hallowed Ground* (Garden City, N. Y.: Doubleday & Co., 1956).

Chamberlayne, C. G., "Abraham Lincoln in Richmond," in *The Virginia Magazine of History and Biography* (Oct., 1933), 318-322.

Chesnut, Mary Boykin, *A Diary from Dixie,* edited by Ben Ames Williams (Boston: Houghton, Mifflin Co., 1949).

Chittenden, Lucius E., *Recollections of President Lincoln and His Administration* (New York: Harper & Brothers, 1891).

Coffin, Charles Carleton, *Four Years of Fighting* . . . (Boston: Ticknor & Fields, 1866).

Colfax, Schuyler, *Life and Principles of Abraham Lincoln* (Philadelphia: J. B. Rodgers, 1865).

[Conway, Moncure D.] "President Lincoln, by an American Abolitionist," in *Fraser's Magazine* (Jan., 1865), 1-21.

Cornish, Dudley Taylor, *The Sable Arm: Negro Troops in the Union Army, 1861-1865* (New York: Longmans, Green & Co., 1956).

Crawford, Samuel W., *The Genesis of the Civil War* . . . (New York: Charles L. Webster & Co., 1887).

Current, Richard N., *The Lincoln Nobody Knows* (New York: McGraw-Hill Book Co., 1958).

Curtis, George William (ed.), *The Correspondence of John Lothrop Motley* (New York: Harper & Brothers, 1889), 2 vols.

Cuthbert, Norma B. (ed.), *Lincoln and the Baltimore Plot, 1861: From Pinkerton Records and Related Papers* (San Marino, Calif.: Henry E. Huntington Library, 1949).

Dana, Charles A., *Recollections of the Civil War: With the Leaders at Washington and in the Field in the Sixties* (New York: D. Appleton & Co., 1898).

Dennett, Tyler (ed.), *Lincoln and the Civil War in the Diaries and Letters of John Hay* (New York: Dodd, Mead & Co., 1939).

Diary of a Public Man: An Intimate View of the National Administration, Dec. 28, 1860 to March 15, 1861 (New Brunswick, N. J.: Rutgers University Press, 1946).

Dicey, Edward, *Six Months in the Federal States* (London: Macmillan Co., 1863), 2 vols.

Donald, David, *Lincoln's Herndon* (New York: Alfred A. Knopf, 1948).

———— (ed.), *Inside Lincoln's Cabinet: The Civil War Diaries of Salmon Portland Chase* (New York: Longmans, Green & Co., 1954).

———— *Lincoln Reconsidered* (New York: Alfred A. Knopf, 1956).

Douglass, Frederick, *The Life and Times of Frederick Douglass, Written by Himself* . . . (Hartford, Conn.: Park Publishing Co., 1882).

Dumond, Dwight L. (ed.), *Southern Editorials on Secession* (New York: Century Co., 1931).

Eisenschiml, Otto, and Ralph Newman (eds.), *The Civil War: The American Iliad* . . . (New York: Grosset & Dunlap, Inc., 1956), 2 vols.

Emerson, Edward Waldo, and Waldo Emerson Forbes (eds.), *The Journals of Ralph Waldo Emerson* (Boston: Houghton, Mifflin Co., 1913), IX.

Fessenden, Francis, *Life and Public Services of William Pitt Fessenden* . . . (Boston: Houghton, Mifflin Co., 1907), 2 vols.

Forbes, John Murray, *Letters and Recollections of John Murray Forbes,* edited by Sarah F. Hughes (Boston: Houghton, Mifflin Co., 1899), 2 vols.

Ford, Worthington C. (ed.), *A Cycle of Adams Letters, 1861-1865* (Boston: Houghton, Mifflin Co., 1920), 2 vols.

Forney, John W., *Anecdotes of Public Men* (New York: Harper & Brothers, 1873-1881), 2 vols.

Gilmore, James R., *Personal Recollections of Abraham Lincoln and the Civil War* (Boston: L. C. Page & Co., 1898).

Grant, Ulysses S., *Personal Memoirs of U. S. Grant* (New York: Charles L. Webster & Co., 1885), 2 vols.

Greeley, Horace, *The American Conflict* . . . (Hartford, Conn.: O. D. Case & Co., 1864-1866), 2 vols.

Grimsley, Elizabeth Todd, "Six Months in the White House," in *Journal of the Illinois State Historical Society* (Oct., 1926), 43-73.

Gurowski, Adam, *Diary* . . . (Boston: Lee & Shepard, 1862-1866), 3 vols.

Hall, W. L., "Lincoln's Interview with John B. Baldwin," in *South Atlantic Quarterly,* XIII (1914), 260-269.

Harris, Alfred G., "Lincoln and the Question of Slavery in the District of Columbia," in *Lincoln Herald* (Spring, 1952), 12-21.

Haverlin, Carl, "Lincoln at Brady's Gallery," in *Journal of the Illinois State Historical Society* (Spring, 1955), 52-58.

Hawthorne, Nathaniel, "Chiefly About War Matters," in *Atlantic Monthly* (July, 1862), 43-61.

Helm, Katherine, *The True Story of Mary, Wife of Lincoln* . . . (New York: Harper & Brothers, 1928).

Hendrick, Burton J., *Lincoln's War Cabinet* (Boston: Little, Brown & Co., 1946).

Herndon, William H., and Jesse W. Weik, *Herndon's Lincoln: The True Story of a Great Life* . . . (Chicago, Ill.: Belford, Clarke & Co., 1889), 3 vols.

Hildner, Ernest G., Jr., "The Mexican Envoy Visits Lincoln," in *Abraham Lincoln Quarterly* (Sept., 1950), 184-189.

Hollister, O. J., *Life of Schuyler Colfax* (New York: Funk & Wagnalls, 1886).

Hooker, Richard, *The Story of an Independent Newspaper* (New York: Macmillan Co., 1924).

Horan, James D., and Howard Swiggett, *The Pinkerton Story* (New York: G. P. Putnam's Sons, 1951).

Howe, M. A. De Wolfe (ed.), *Home Letters of General Sherman* (New York: Charles Scribner's Sons, 1909).

[Julian, George W.] "George W. Julian's Journal," edited by Grace Julian Clarke, in *Indiana Magazine of History* (Dec., 1915), 324-337.

Kelley, William D., *Lincoln and Stanton* . . . (New York: G. P. Putnam's Sons, 1885).

Koerner, Gustave, *Memoirs of Gustave Koerner, 1809-1896*, edited by Thomas J. McCormack (Cedar Rapids, Iowa: Torch Press, 1909), 2 vols.

Korngold, Ralph, *Thaddeus Stevens: A Being Darkly Wise and Rudely Great* (New York: Harcourt, Brace & Co., 1955).

Lamon, Ward H., *Recollections of Abraham Lincoln, 1847-1865,* edited by Dorothy Lamon Teillard (Chicago: A. C. McClurg & Co., 1895).

Logan, John A., *The Great Conspiracy* . . . (New York: A. R. Hart & Co., 1886).

Lossing, Benson J., *Pictorial History of the Civil War* (Philadelphia: G. W. Childs, 1866-1869), 3 vols.

Lunt, George, *The Origins of the Late War* (New York: D. Appleton & Co., 1866).

Lutz, Ralph H., "Rudolph Schleiden and the Visit to Richmond, April 25, 1861," in *Annual Report of the American Historical Association* (1915), 209-216.

McClellan, George B., *McClellan's Own Story* . . . (New York: Charles L. Webster & Co., 1887).

McClure, Alexander K., *Lincoln and Men of War-Times* (Philadelphia: Times Publishing Co., 1892).

McCulloch, Hugh, *Men and Measures of Half a Century* . . . (New York: Charles Scribner's Sons, 1889).

Mcpherson, Edward, *The Political History of the United States of America During the Great Rebellion* . . . (Washington, D. C.: Philip & Solomons, 1865).

Macdonnel, Agnes, "America Then and Now: Recollections of Lincoln," in *The Contemporary Review* (May, 1917), 562-569.

Magruder, Allen B., "A Piece of Secret History: President Lincoln and the Virginia Convention of 1861," in *Atlantic Monthly* (Apr., 1875), 438-445.

Mearns, David C. (ed.), *The Lincoln Papers* (Garden City, N. Y.: Doubleday & Co., 1948), 2 vols.

Meigs, Montgomery C., "General M. C. Meigs on the Conduct of the Civil War," in *American Historical Review* (Jan., 1921), 285-303.

Military Essays and Recollections: Papers Read before the Commandary of the State of Illinois, Military Order of the Loyal Legion of the United States (Chicago: The Dial Press, 1899), III.

Moore, Frank (ed.), *The Rebellion Record* . . . (New York: G. P. Putnam's Sons, 1861-1869; D. Van Nostrand, 1864-1871), 12 vols.

Morrow, Honoré Willsie, "Lincoln's Last Day," in *Hearst's International-Cosmopolitan* (Feb., 1930).

Munford, B. B., *Virginia's Attitude Toward Slavery and Secession* (New York: Longmans, Green & Co., 1909).

Nevins, Allan, *The Emergence of Lincoln* (New York: Charles Scribner's Sons, 1950), 2 vols.

——— *The War for the Union* (New York: Charles Scribner's Sons, 1959), I.

——— and Milton Halsey Thomas (eds.), *The Diary of George Templeton Strong 1835-1875* (New York: Macmillan Co., 1952), 4 vols.

Nicolay, John G., *The Outbreak of Rebellion* (New York: Charles Scribner's Sons, 1881).

———— *A Short Life of Abraham Lincoln* (New York: Century Co., 1902).

———— and John Hay, *Abraham Lincoln: A History* (New York: Century Co., 1890), 10 vols.

Official Records of the Union and Confederate Armies . . . (Washington, D. C., 1880-1901), 128 vols.

Official Records of the Union and Confederate Navies . . . (Washington, D. C., 1894-1922), 26 vols.

Pease, Theodore C., and James G. Randall (eds.), *The Diary of Orville Hickman Browning,* Illinois State Historical Library Collections, vols. XX, XXII (Springfield, Ill.: Illinois State Historical Library, 1925-1933), 2 vols.

Piatt, Donn, *Memories of the Men Who Saved the Union* (New York: Belford, Clarke & Co., 1887).

Pierce, Edward L., *Memoir and Letters of Charles Sumner* (London: Sampson, Low, Marston, Searle & Rivington, 1878-1893), 4 vols.

Poore, Ben: Perley, *Reminiscences of Sixty Years in the National Metropolis* (Philadelphia: Hubbard Brothers, 1886), 2 vols.

Porter, David D., *Incidents and Anecdotes of the Civil War* (New York: D. Appleton & Co., 1885).

Porter, George H., *Ohio Politics During the Civil War* (New York: Columbia University Press, 1911).

Porter, Horace, *Campaigning with Grant* (New York: Century Co., 1897).

Pratt, Harry E. (ed.), *Concerning Mr. Lincoln* . . . (Springfield, Ill.: Abraham Lincoln Association, 1944).

Quarles, Benjamin, *The Negro in the Civil War* (Boston: Little, Brown & Co., 1953).

Randall, James G., *The Civil War and Reconstruction* (Boston: D. C. Heath & Co., 1937).

———— *Lincoln the President: Springfield to Gettysburg* (New York: Dodd, Mead & Co., 1946), 2 vols.

———— *Lincoln and the South* (Baton Rouge, La.: Louisiana State University Press, 1946).

———— *Lincoln the Liberal Statesman* (New York: Dodd, Mead & Co., 1947).

———— *Lincoln the President: Midstream* (New York: Dodd, Mead & Co., 1952).

Raymond, Henry J., "Extracts from the Journal of Henry J. Raymond," edited by his son, in *Scribner's Monthly* (Mar., 1880), 703-710.

———— *History of the Administration of Abraham Lincoln* . . . (New York: Derby & Miller, 1864).

———— *The Life and Public Services of Abraham Lincoln* . . . (New York: Derby & Miller, 1865).

Report of the Joint Committee on Reconstruction, 39th Congress, 1st session (1866), *Report No. 30,* vol. II, part 2.

Reports of the Joint Committee on the Conduct of the War (Washington, D. C., 1863-1866), 8 vols.

Rhodes, James Ford, *History of the United States from the Compromise of 1850* . . . (New York: Macmillan Co., 1893-1916), 7 vols.

Rice, Allen Thorndike (ed.), *Reminiscences of Abraham Lincoln by Distinguished Men of His Time* (New York: North American Review Publishing Co., 1886).

Richardson, Albert D., *A Personal History of Ulysses S. Grant* (Hartford, Conn.: American Publishing Co., 1868).

Riddle, Albert G., *Recollections of War Times* . . . (New York: G. P. Putnam's Sons, 1895).

Rippy, J. Fred, *The United States and Mexico* (New York: Alfred A. Knopf, 1926).

Roeder, Ralph, *Juarez and His Mexico* (New York: Viking Press, 1947), 2 vols.

Roman, Alfred, *Military Operations of General Beauregard in the War Between the States 1861-65* . . . (New York: Harper & Brothers, 1884), 2 vols.

Russell, Phillips, *Emerson: The Wisest American* (New York: Brentano's Inc., 1929).

Russell, William H., *The Civil War in America* (Boston: Gardner A. Fuller, 1861).

—— *My Diary North and South* (Boston: T. O. H. P. Burnham, 1863).

Sandburg, Carl, *Abraham Lincoln: The War Years* (New York: Harcourt, Brace & Co., 1939), 4 vols.

Schurz, Carl, *The Reminiscences of Carl Schurz* (New York: McClure Co., 1908), 3 vols.

Seitz, Don C., *Lincoln the Politician* . . . (New York: Coward-McCann, Inc., 1931).

Seward, Frederick W., *Seward at Washington as Senator and Secretary of State* (New York: Derby & Miller, 1891).

—— *Reminiscences of a War-Time Statesman, 1830-1915* (New York: G. P. Putnam's Sons, 1916).

Sherman, John, *John Sherman's Recollections of Forty Years in the House, Senate and Cabinet: An Autobiography* (Chicago: Werner Co., 1895), 2 vols.

Sherman, William T., *Personal Memoirs of General W. T. Sherman* (New York: D. Appleton & Co., 1875), 2 vols.

Smalley, George W., *Anglo-American Memories* (New York: G. P. Putnam's Sons, 1911).

Smiley, David L., "Abraham Lincoln Deals with Cassius M. Clay: Portrait of a Patient Politician," in *Lincoln Herald* (Winter, 1953), 15-23.

Smith, William E., *The Francis Preston Blair Family in Politics* (New York: Macmillan Co., 1933), 2 vols.

Stanwood, Edward, *A History of the Presidency from 1788 to 1897* (Boston: Houghton, Mifflin Co., 1916), 2 vols.

Stephens, Alexander H., *A Constitutional View of the Late War Between the States* . . . (Philadelphia: National Publishing Co., 1868-1870), 2 vols.

[Stradling, James M.] *His Talk with Lincoln: Being a Letter Written by James M. Stradling* (Boston: Houghton, Mifflin Co., 1922).

Swinton, William, *Campaigns of the Army of the Potomac* (New York: Charles Scribner's Sons, 1866).

Thomas, Benjamin P., *Abraham Lincoln: A Biography* (New York: Alfred A. Knopf, 1952).

Ticknor, Anna, and George S. Hillard (eds.), *Life, Letters, and Journals of George Ticknor* (Boston: Osgood, 1876), 2 vols.

Townsend, William H., *Lincoln and the Bluegrass* (Lexington, Ky.: University of Kentucky Press, 1955).

Upson, Theodore F., *With Sherman to the Sea . . .*, edited by Oscar O. Winther (Baton Rouge, La.: Louisiana State University Press, 1943).

Villard, Henry, *Lincoln on the Eve of '61: A Journalist's Story*, edited by Harold G. and Oswald G. Villard (New York: Alfred A. Knopf, 1941).

Warden, Robert B., *Account of the Private Life and Public Services of Salmon Portland Chase* (Cincinnati: Wilstach, Baldwin & Co., 1874).

Weed, Thurlow, *Autobiography of Thurlow Weed* (Boston: Houghton, Mifflin Co., 1883).

Weik, Jesse W., *The Real Lincoln: A Portrait* (Boston: Houghton, Mifflin Co., 1922).

Welles, Gideon, "The History of Emancipation," in *The Galaxy* (Dec., 1872), 838-851.

—— *Lincoln and Seward . . .* (New York: Sheldon & Co., 1874).

White, Horace, *Life of Lyman Trumbull* (Boston: Houghton, Mifflin Co., 1913).

Williams, T. Harry, *Lincoln and the Radicals* (Madison, Wis.: University of Wisconsin Press, 1941).

Wilson, Joseph T., *The Black Phalanx: A History of the Negro Soldier of the United States . . .* (Hartford, Conn.: American Publishing Co., 1888).

Winchell, J. M., "Three Interviews with President Lincoln," in *The Galaxy* (July, 1873), 33-41.

Index